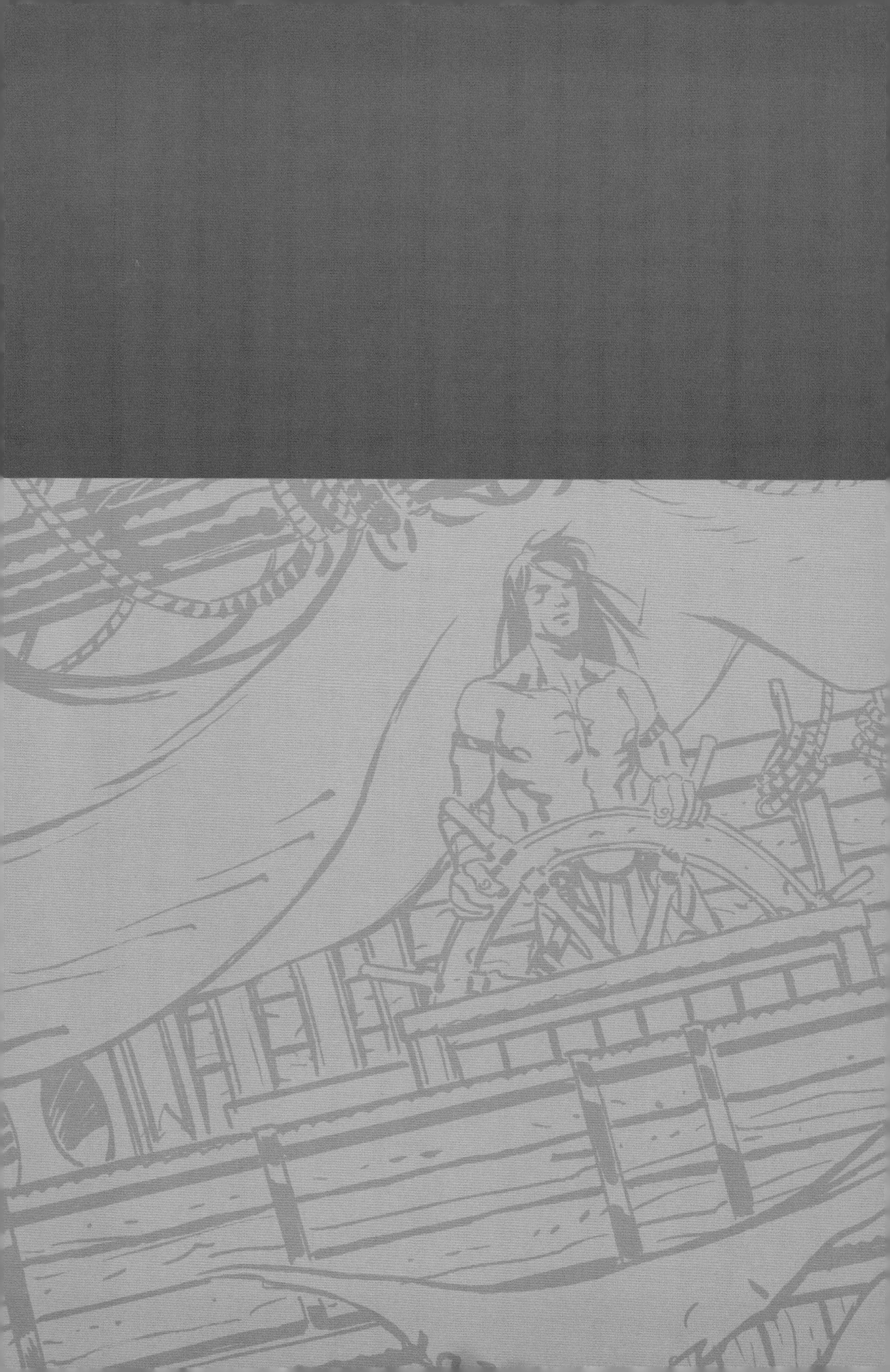

CONAN®

THE SONG OF BÊLIT

Writer BRIAN WOOD

Art by PAUL AZACETA (chapters 19–21)
RICCARDO BURCHIELLI (chapters 22–24)
LEANDRO FERNÁNDEZ (chapter 25)

Colors by DAVE STEWART

Letters by
RICHARD STARKINGS
and COMICRAFT'S JIMMY BETANCOURT

Cover and Chapter-Break Artist
MASSIMO CARNEVALE

Creator of Conan
ROBERT E. HOWARD

DARK HORSE BOOKS

Publisher MIKE RICHARDSON Designer KAT LARSON Digital Production CHRISTIANNE GOUDREAU Assistant Editors ROXY POLK, IAN TUCKER, and AARON WALKER
Editor DAVE MARSHALL

Special thanks to JOAKIM ZETTERBERG at CONAN PROPERTIES.

This volume collects issues #19–#25 of the Dark Horse Comics monthly *Conan the Barbarian* series.

Published by Dark Horse Books
A division of Dark Horse Comics, Inc.
10956 SE Main Street
Milwaukie, OR 97222

DarkHorse.com

International Licensing: (503) 905-2377
To find a comics shop in your area, call the Comic Shop Locator Service toll-free at 1-888-266-4226

First softcover edition: February 2015
ISBN 978-1-61655-524-5

10 9 8 7 6 5 4 3 2 1

Printed in China

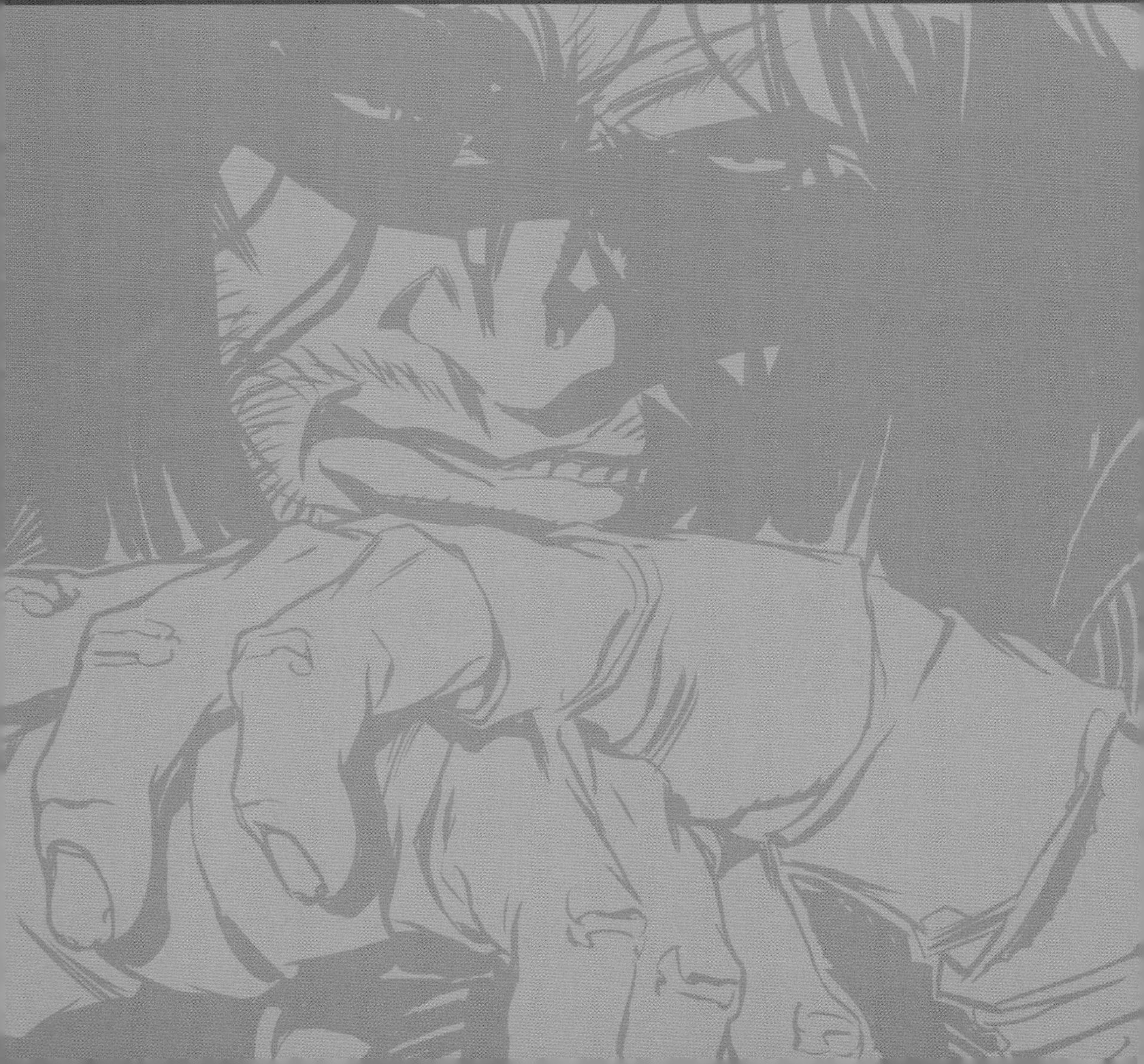

CHAPTER ONE

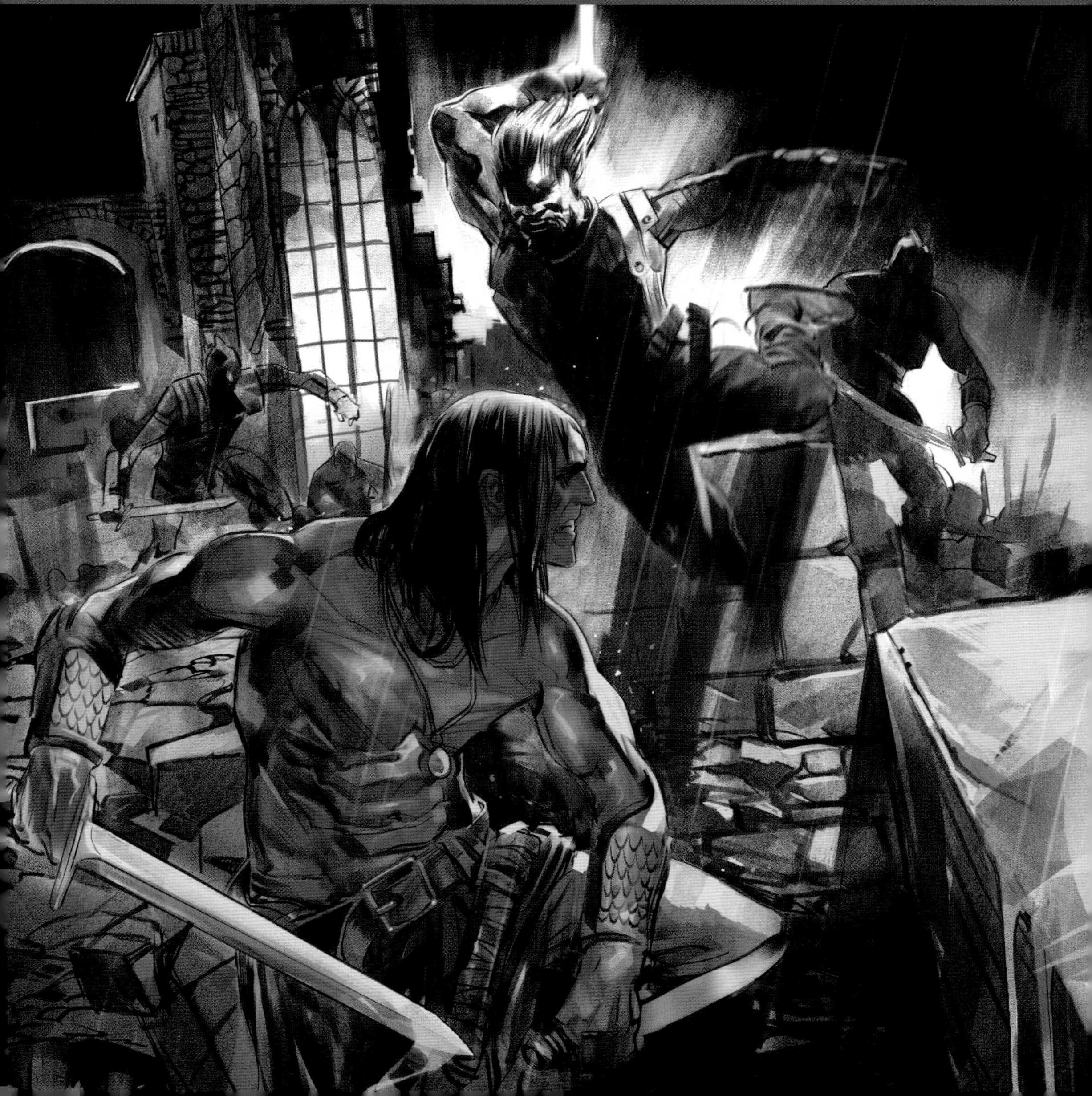

"A man stuffing his guts back inside his belly
isn't thinking about lying, I've found."

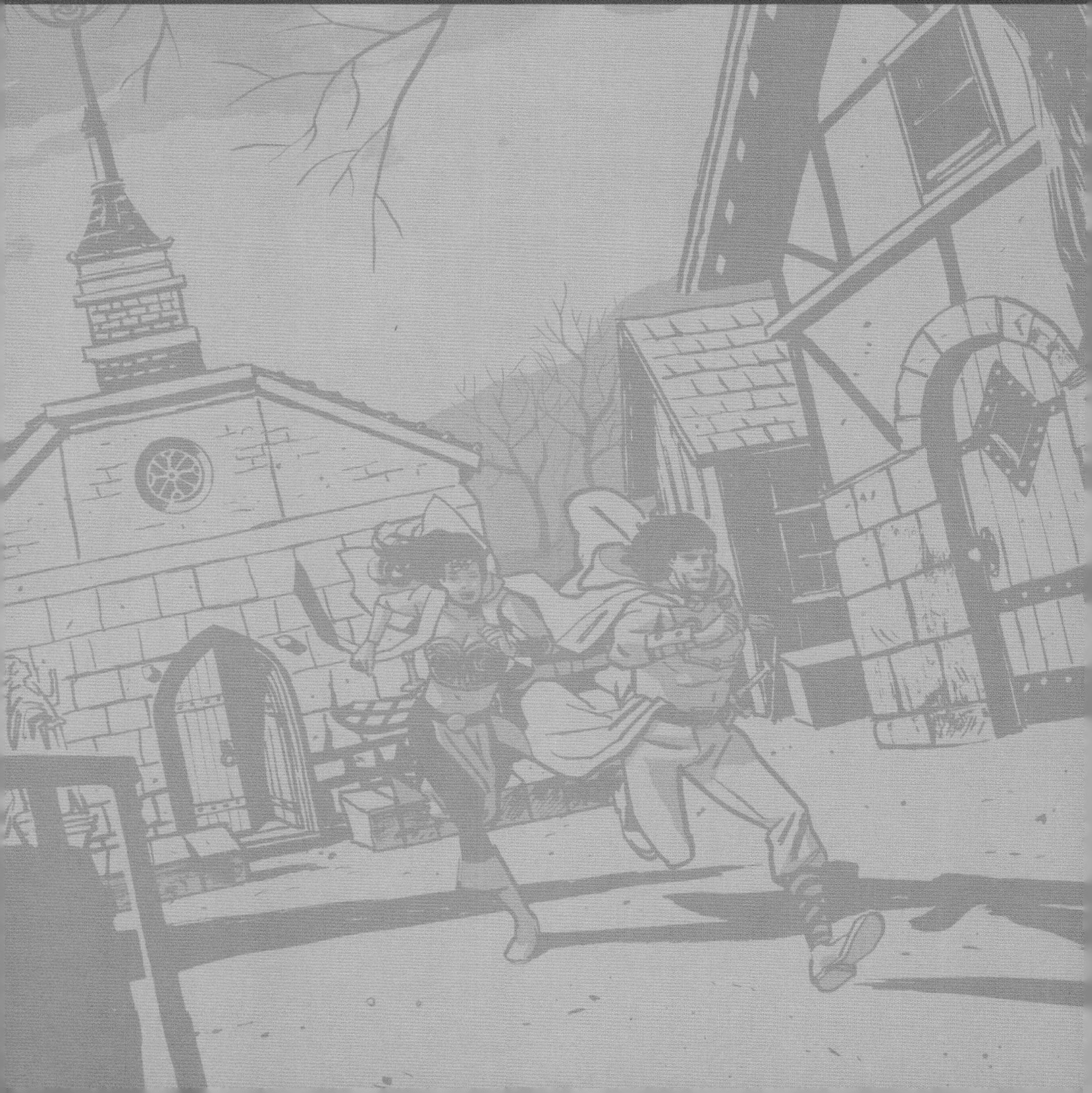

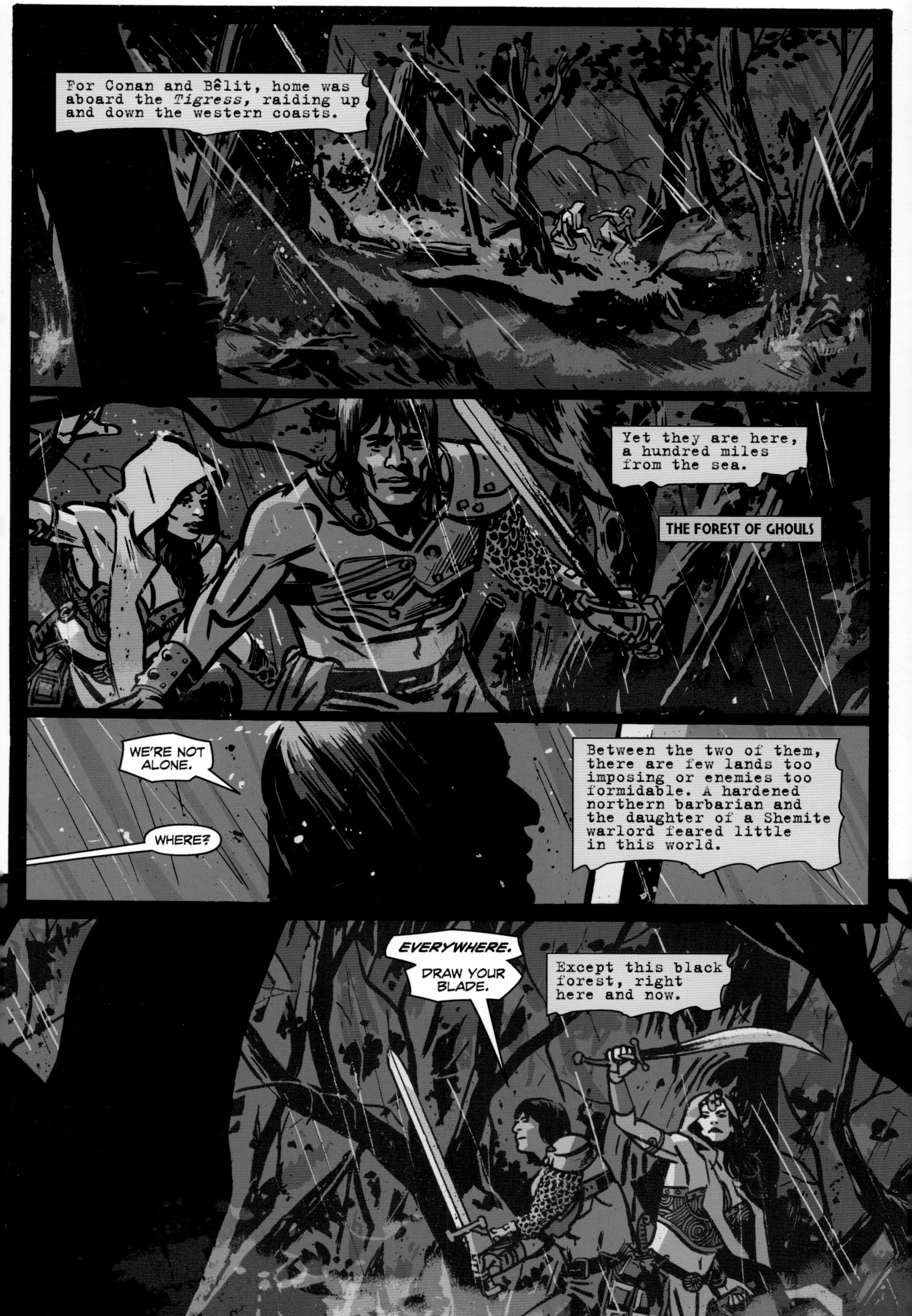

For Conan and Bêlit, home was aboard the *Tigress,* raiding up and down the western coasts.
Yet they are here, a hundred miles from the sea.
THE FOREST OF GHOULS
WE'RE NOT ALONE.
WHERE?
Between the two of them, there are few lands too imposing or enemies too formidable. A hardened northern barbarian and the daughter of a Shemite warlord feared little in this world.
EVERYWHERE.
DRAW YOUR BLADE.
Except this black forest, right here and now.

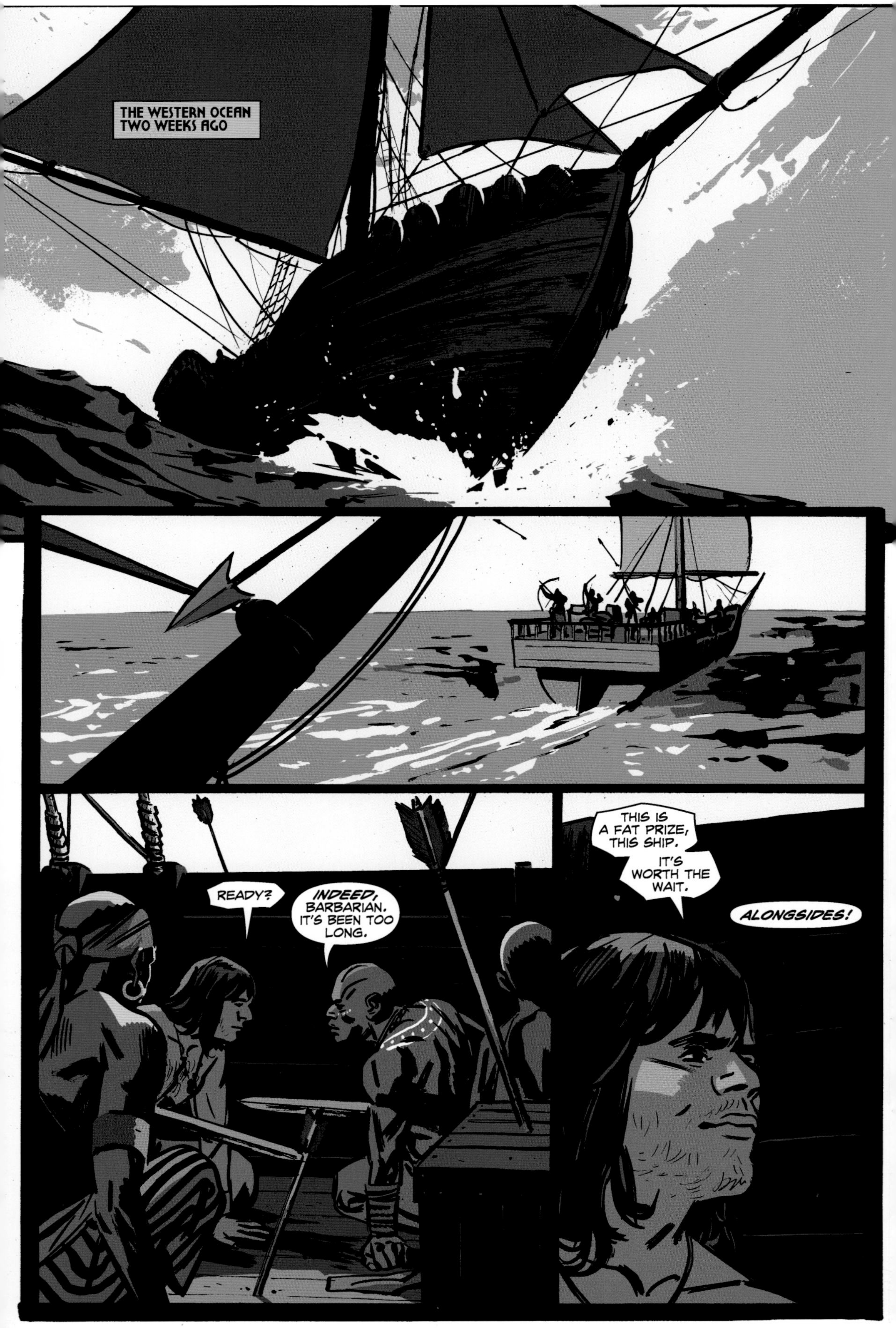
THE WESTERN OCEAN
TWO WEEKS AGO
READY?
INDEED, BARBARIAN. IT'S BEEN TOO LONG.
THIS IS A FAT PRIZE, THIS SHIP.
IT'S WORTH THE WAIT.
ALONGSIDES!

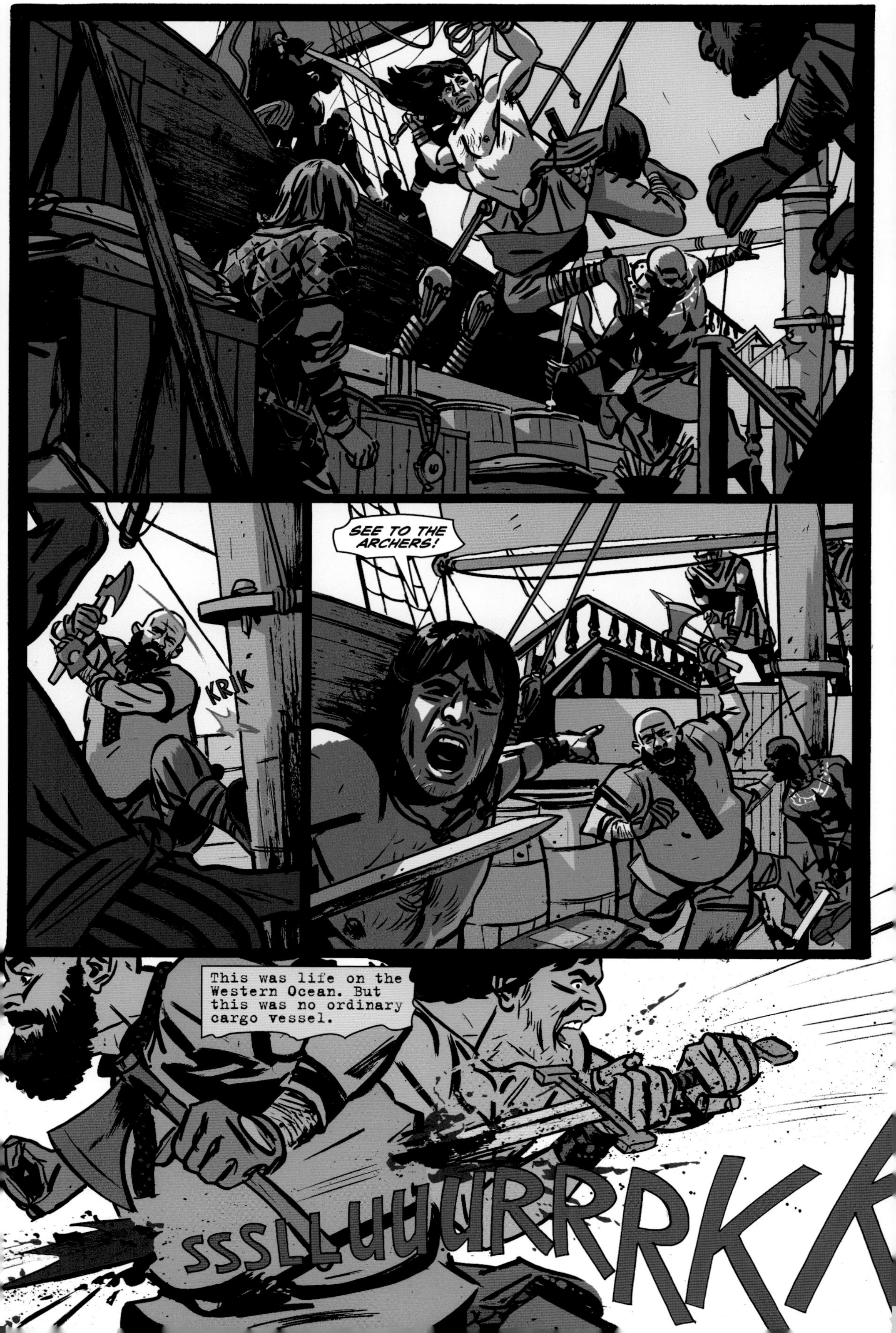
KRIK
SEE TO THE ARCHERS!
This was life on the Western Ocean. But this was no ordinary cargo vessel.
SSSLLUUURRRRKK

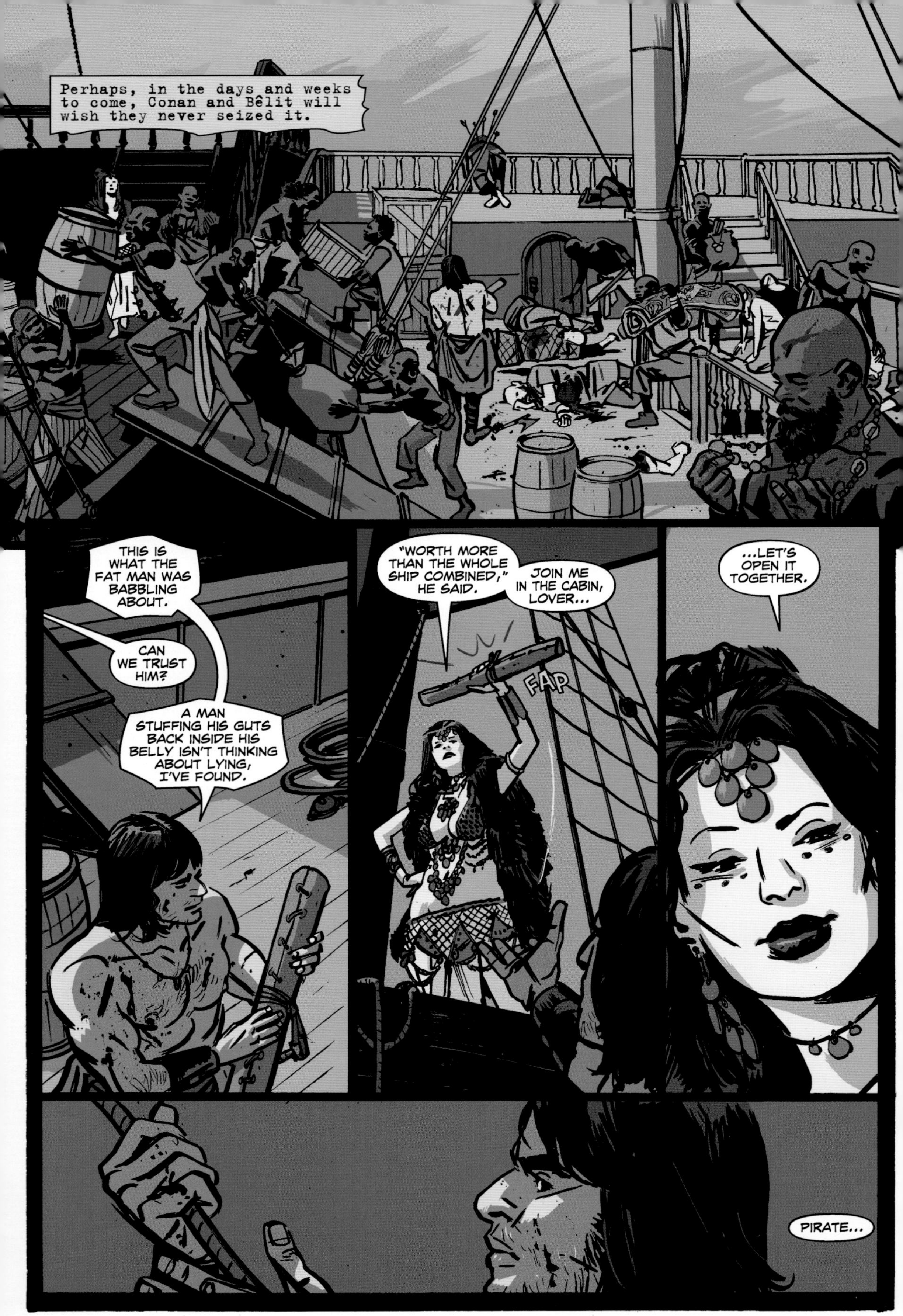
Perhaps, in the days and weeks to come, Conan and Bêlit will wish they never seized it.
THIS IS WHAT THE FAT MAN WAS BABBLING ABOUT.
CAN WE TRUST HIM?
A MAN STUFFING HIS GUTS BACK INSIDE HIS BELLY ISN'T THINKING ABOUT LYING, I'VE FOUND.
"WORTH MORE THAN THE WHOLE SHIP COMBINED," HE SAID.
JOIN ME IN THE CABIN, LOVER...
FAP
...LET'S OPEN IT TOGETHER.
PIRATE...

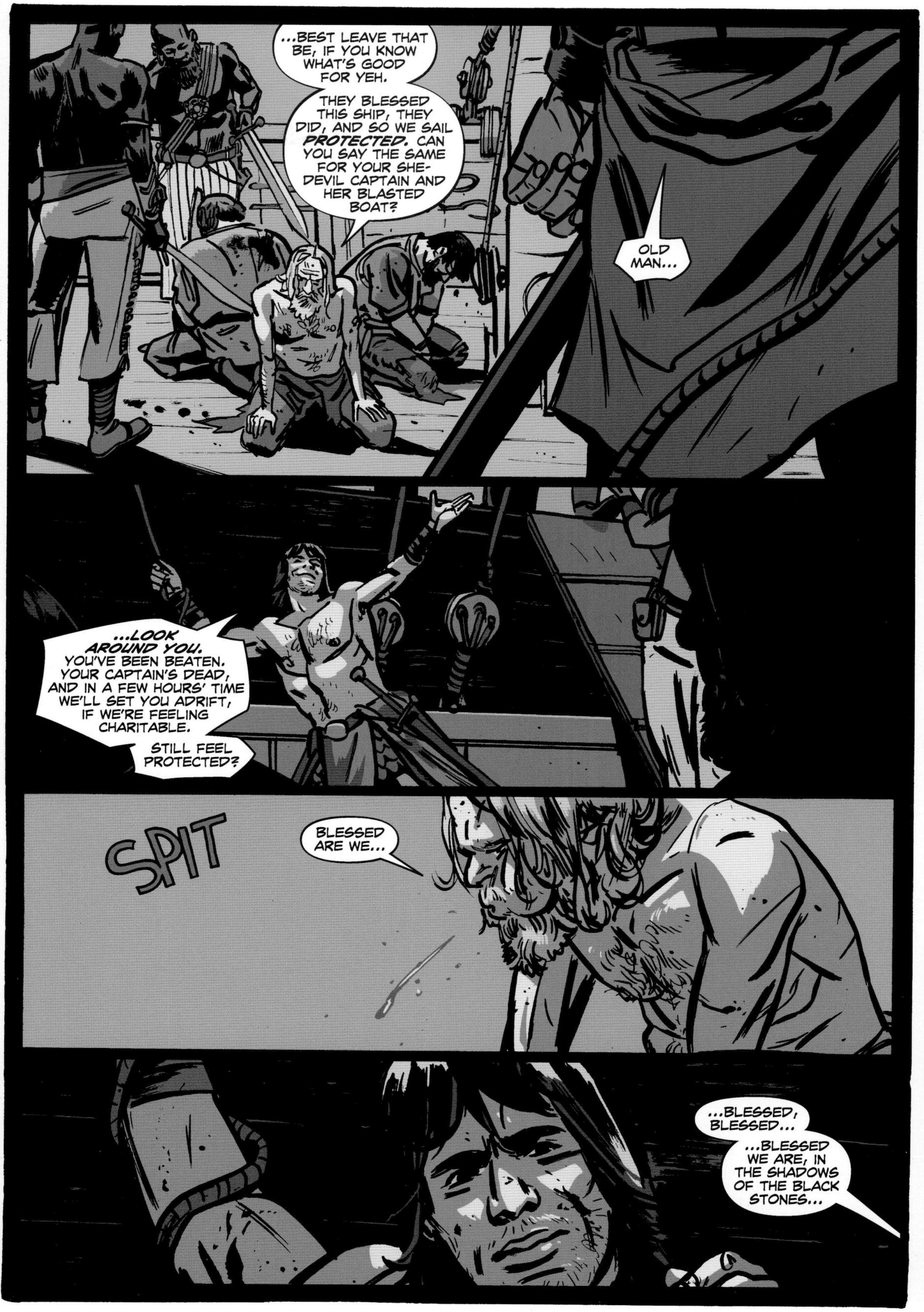
...BEST LEAVE THAT BE, IF YOU KNOW WHAT'S GOOD FOR YEH.
THEY BLESSED THIS SHIP, THEY DID, AND SO WE SAIL PROTECTED. CAN YOU SAY THE SAME FOR YOUR SHE-DEVIL CAPTAIN AND HER BLASTED BOAT?
OLD MAN...
...LOOK AROUND YOU. YOU'VE BEEN BEATEN. YOUR CAPTAIN'S DEAD, AND IN A FEW HOURS' TIME WE'LL SET YOU ADRIFT, IF WE'RE FEELING CHARITABLE.
STILL FEEL PROTECTED?
SPIT
BLESSED ARE WE...
...BLESSED, BLESSED...
...BLESSED WE ARE, IN THE SHADOWS OF THE BLACK STONES...

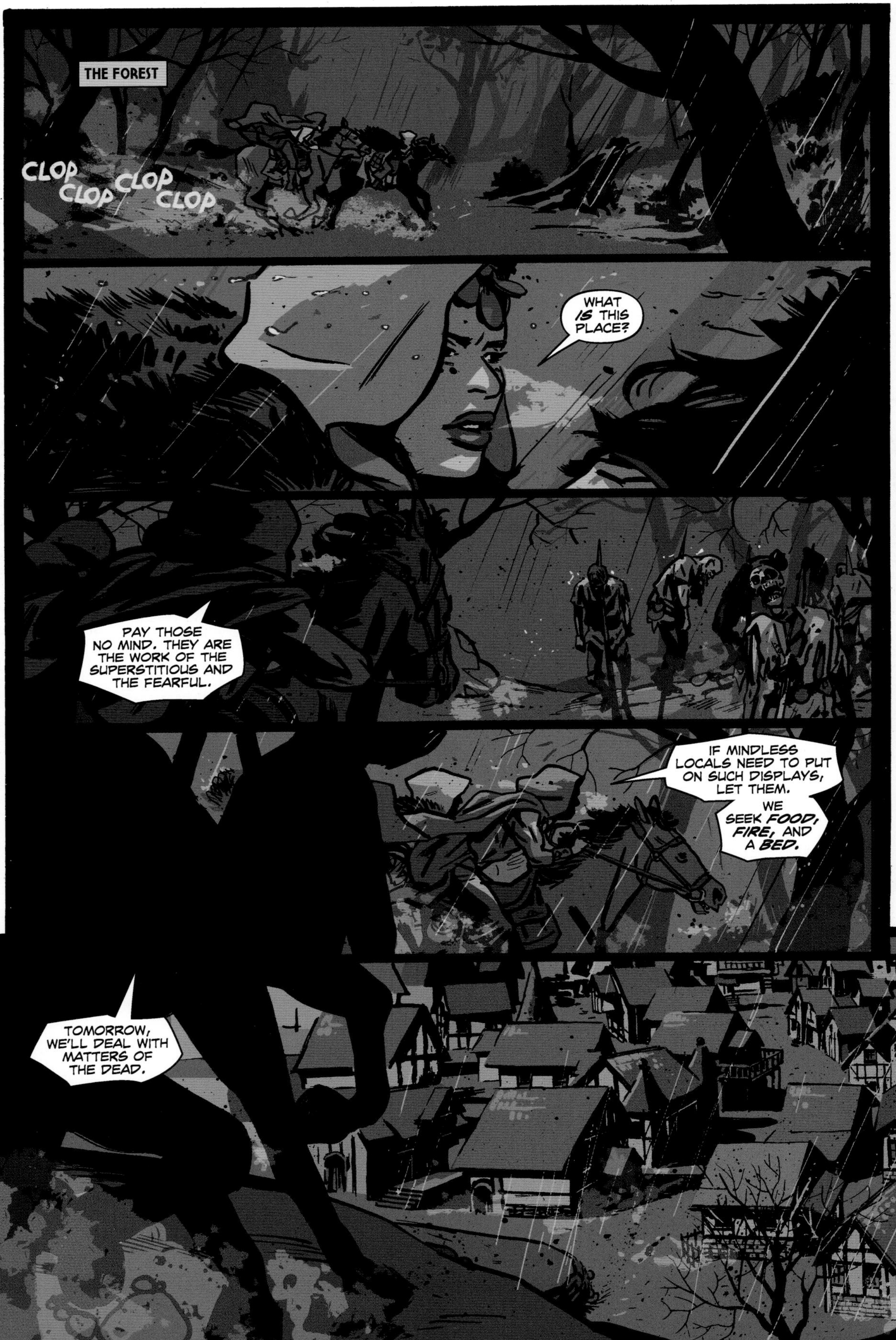
THE FOREST
CLOP CLOP CLOP CLOP
WHAT IS THIS PLACE?
PAY THOSE NO MIND. THEY ARE THE WORK OF THE SUPERSTITIOUS AND THE FEARFUL.
IF MINDLESS LOCALS NEED TO PUT ON SUCH DISPLAYS, LET THEM.
WE SEEK FOOD, FIRE, AND A BED.
TOMORROW, WE'LL DEAL WITH MATTERS OF THE DEAD.

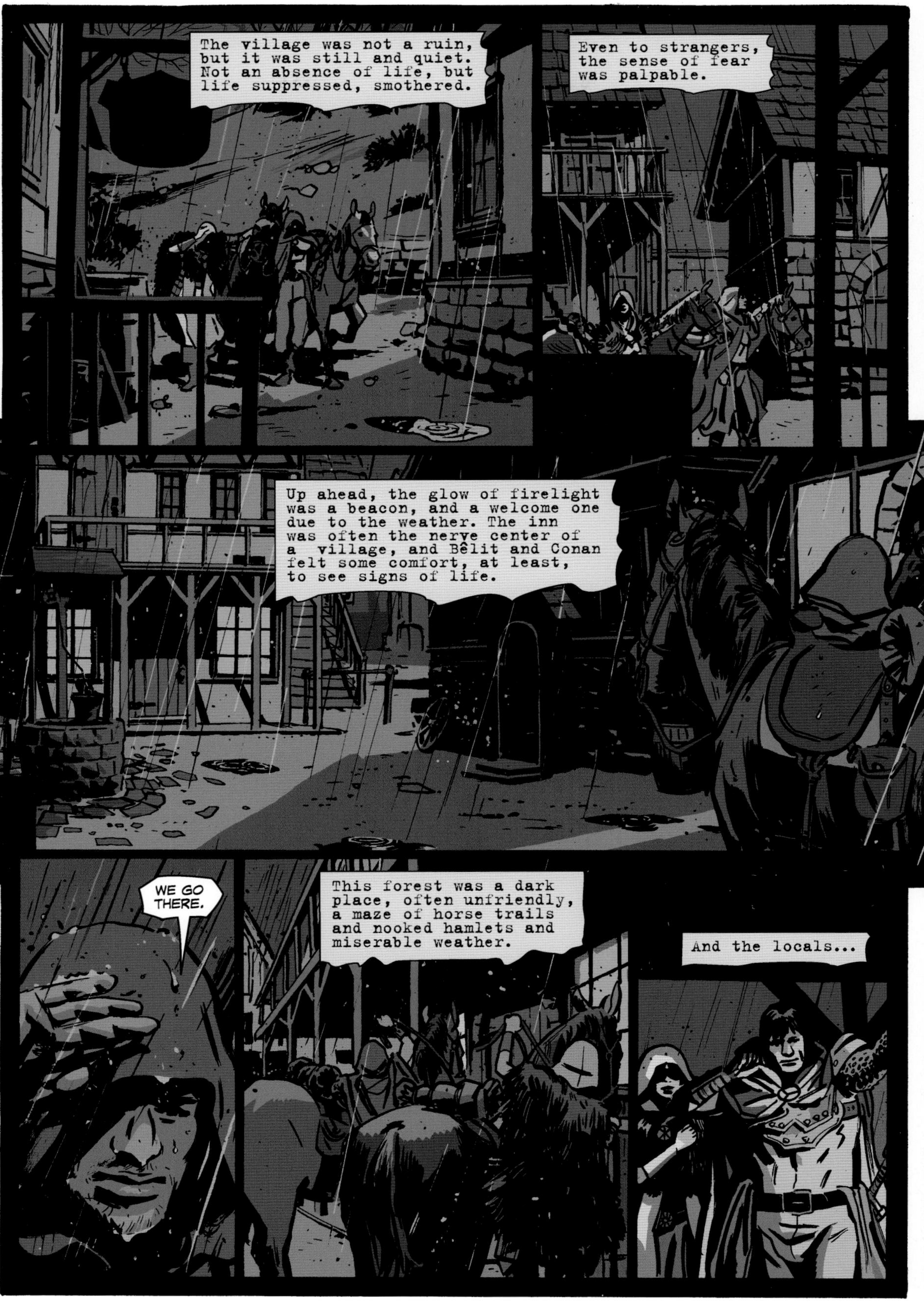
The village was not a ruin, but it was still and quiet. Not an absence of life, but life suppressed, smothered.
Even to strangers, the sense of fear was palpable.
Up ahead, the glow of firelight was a beacon, and a welcome one due to the weather. The inn was often the nerve center of a village, and Bêlit and Conan felt some comfort, at least, to see signs of life.
WE GO THERE.
This forest was a dark place, often unfriendly, a maze of horse trails and nooked hamlets and miserable weather.
And the locals...

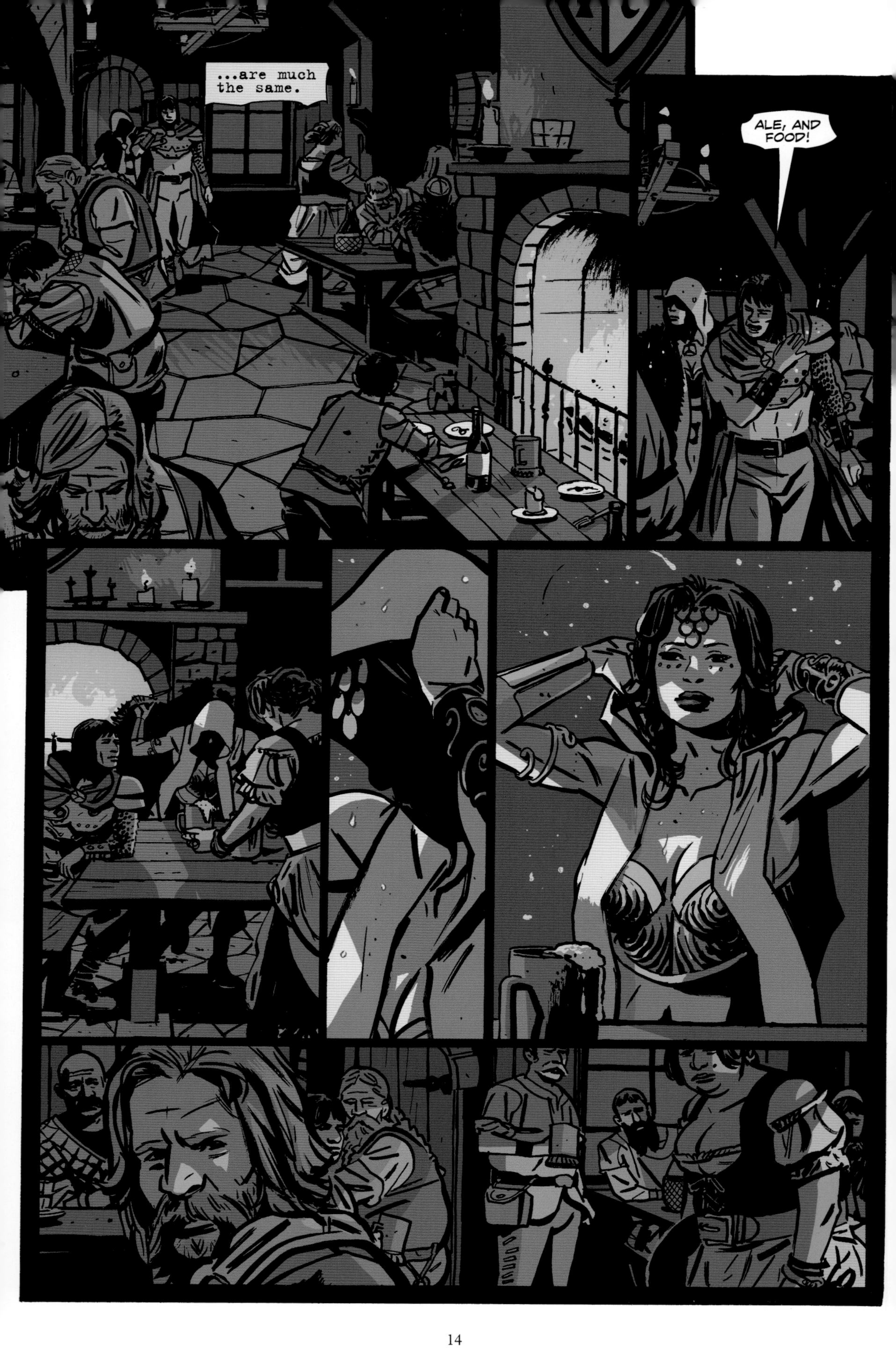
...are much the same.
ALE, AND FOOD!

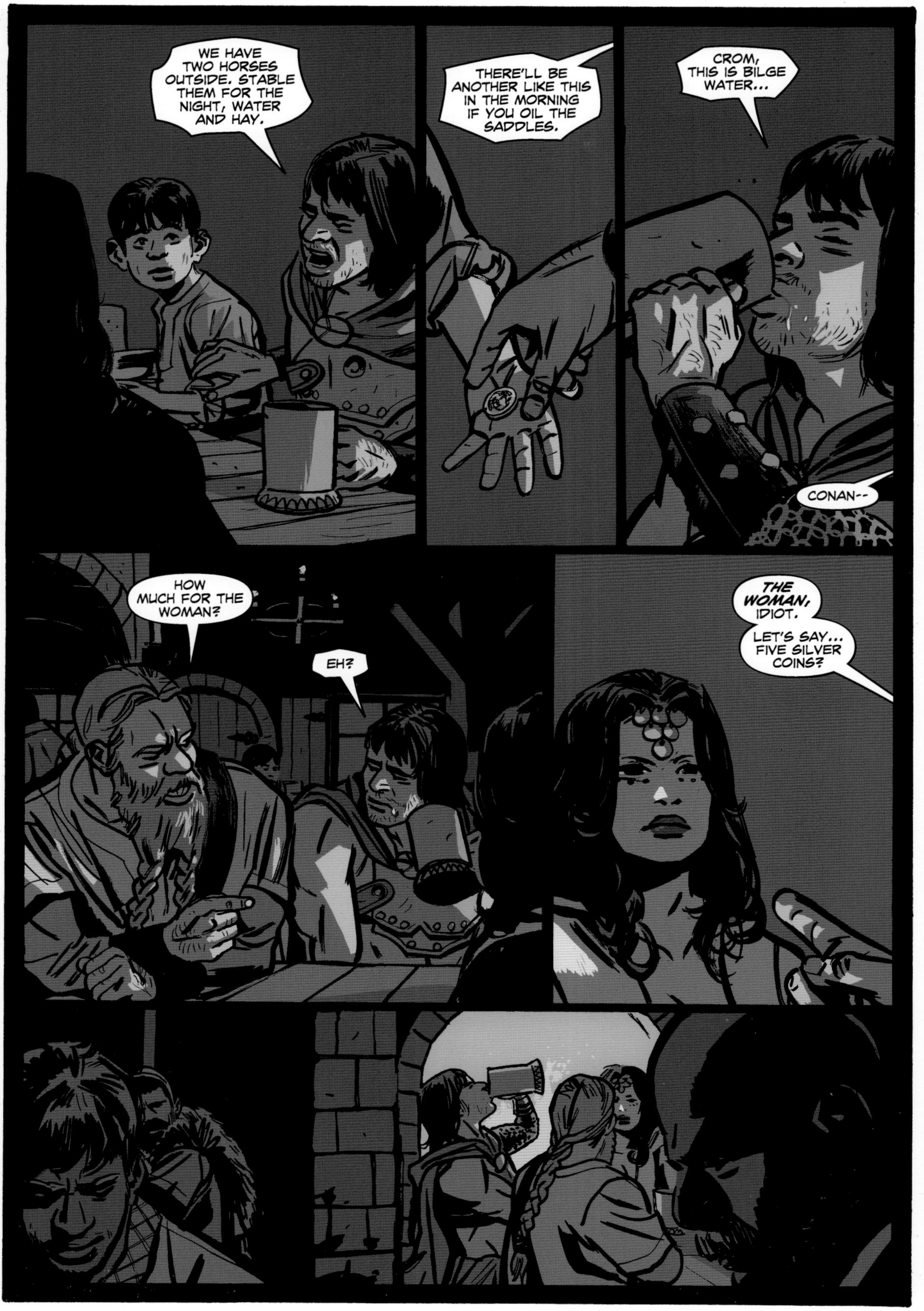
WE HAVE TWO HORSES OUTSIDE. STABLE THEM FOR THE NIGHT, WATER AND HAY.
THERE'LL BE ANOTHER LIKE THIS IN THE MORNING IF YOU OIL THE SADDLES.
CROM, THIS IS BILGE WATER...
CONAN--
HOW MUCH FOR THE WOMAN?
EH?
THE WOMAN, IDIOT.
LET'S SAY... FIVE SILVER COINS?

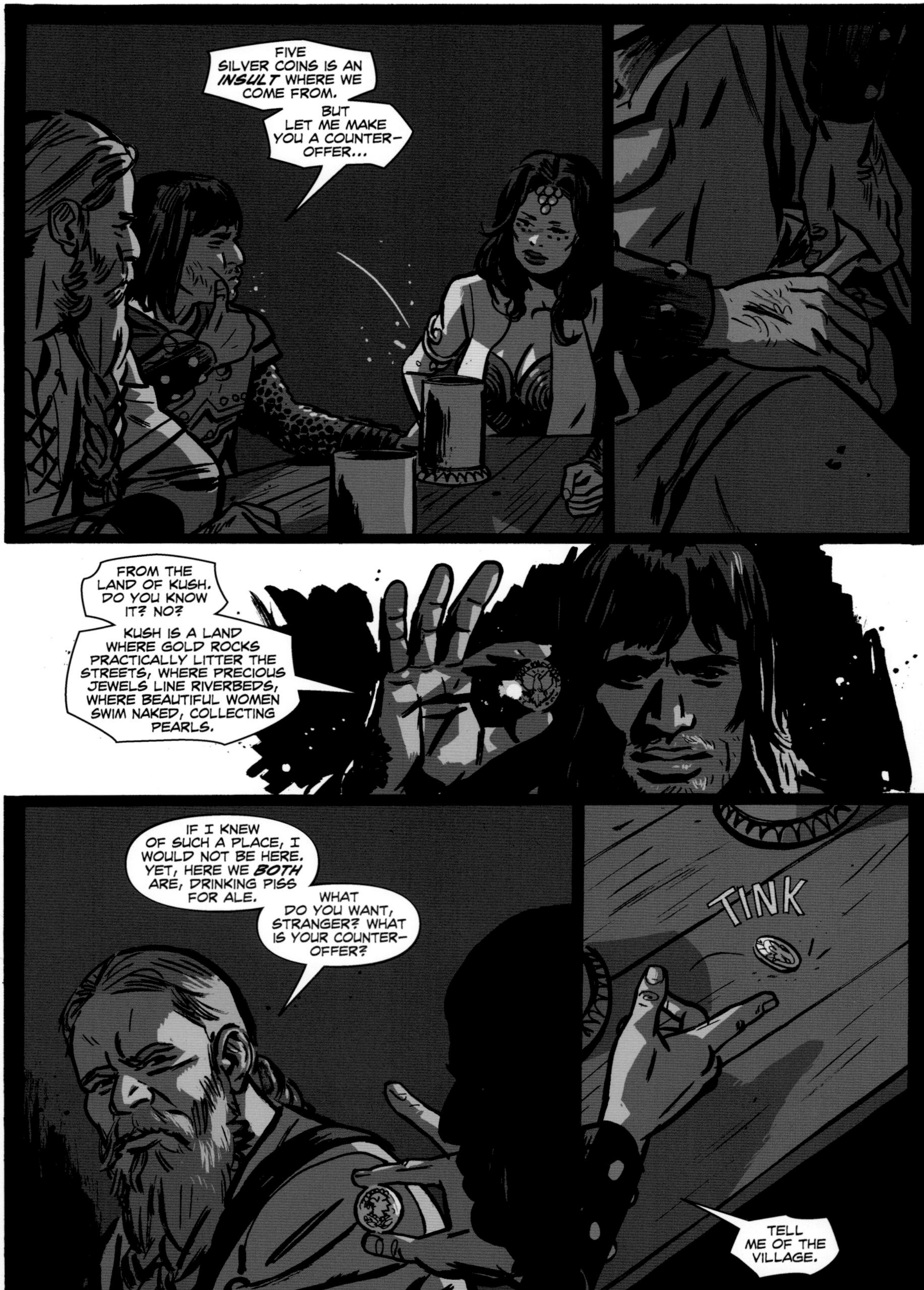
FIVE SILVER COINS IS AN INSULT WHERE WE COME FROM.
BUT LET ME MAKE YOU A COUNTER-OFFER...
FROM THE LAND OF KUSH. DO YOU KNOW IT? NO?
KUSH IS A LAND WHERE GOLD ROCKS PRACTICALLY LITTER THE STREETS, WHERE PRECIOUS JEWELS LINE RIVERBEDS, WHERE BEAUTIFUL WOMEN SWIM NAKED, COLLECTING PEARLS.
IF I KNEW OF SUCH A PLACE, I WOULD NOT BE HERE. YET, HERE WE BOTH ARE, DRINKING PISS FOR ALE.
WHAT DO YOU WANT, STRANGER? WHAT IS YOUR COUNTER-OFFER?
TINK
TELL ME OF THE VILLAGE.

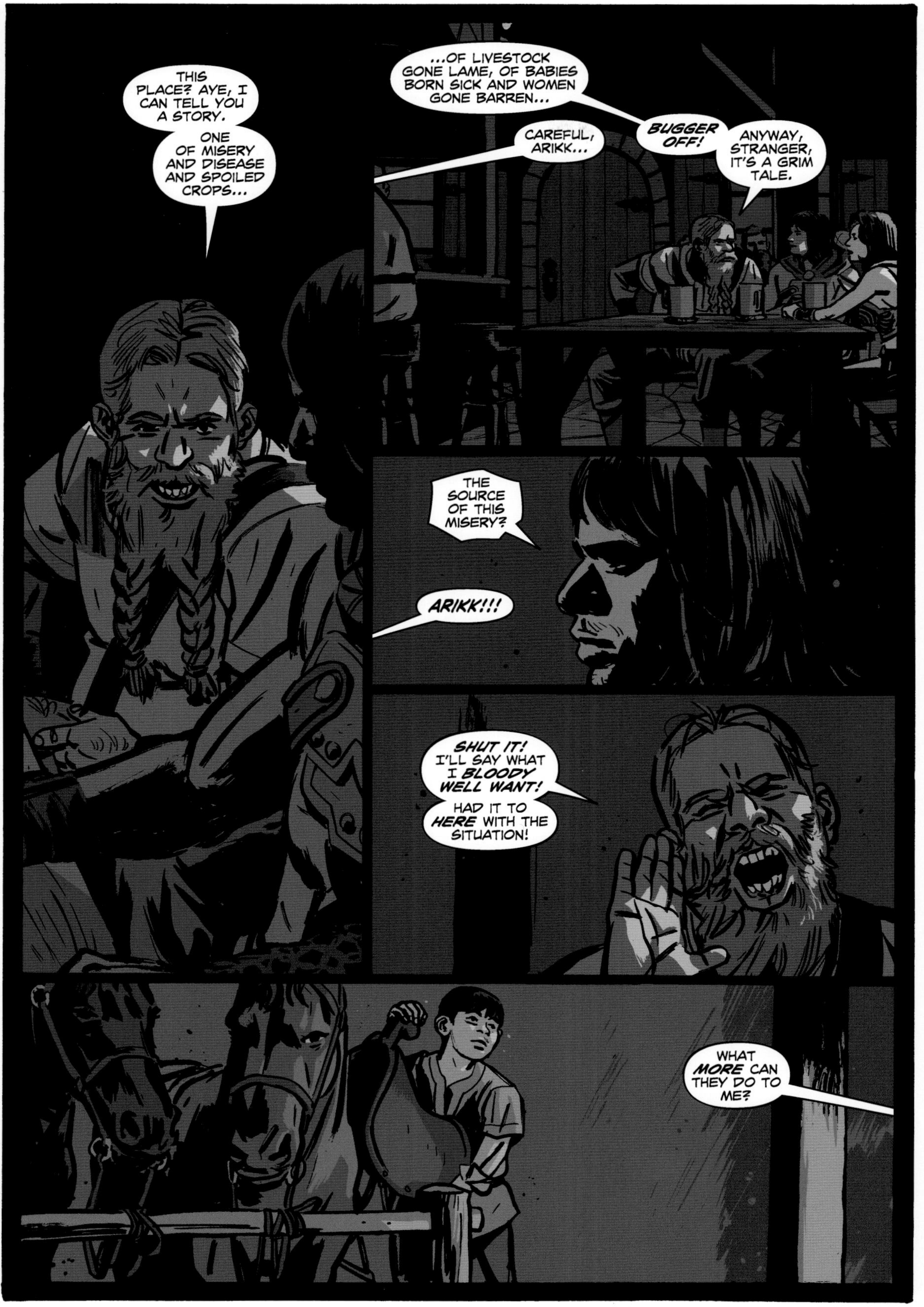
THIS PLACE? AYE, I CAN TELL YOU A STORY.
ONE OF MISERY AND DISEASE AND SPOILED CROPS...
...OF LIVESTOCK GONE LAME, OF BABIES BORN SICK AND WOMEN GONE BARREN...
CAREFUL, ARIKK...
BUGGER OFF!
ANYWAY, STRANGER, IT'S A GRIM TALE.
THE SOURCE OF THIS MISERY?
ARIKK!!!
SHUT IT! I'LL SAY WHAT I BLOODY WELL WANT!
HAD IT TO HERE WITH THE SITUATION!
WHAT MORE CAN THEY DO TO ME?

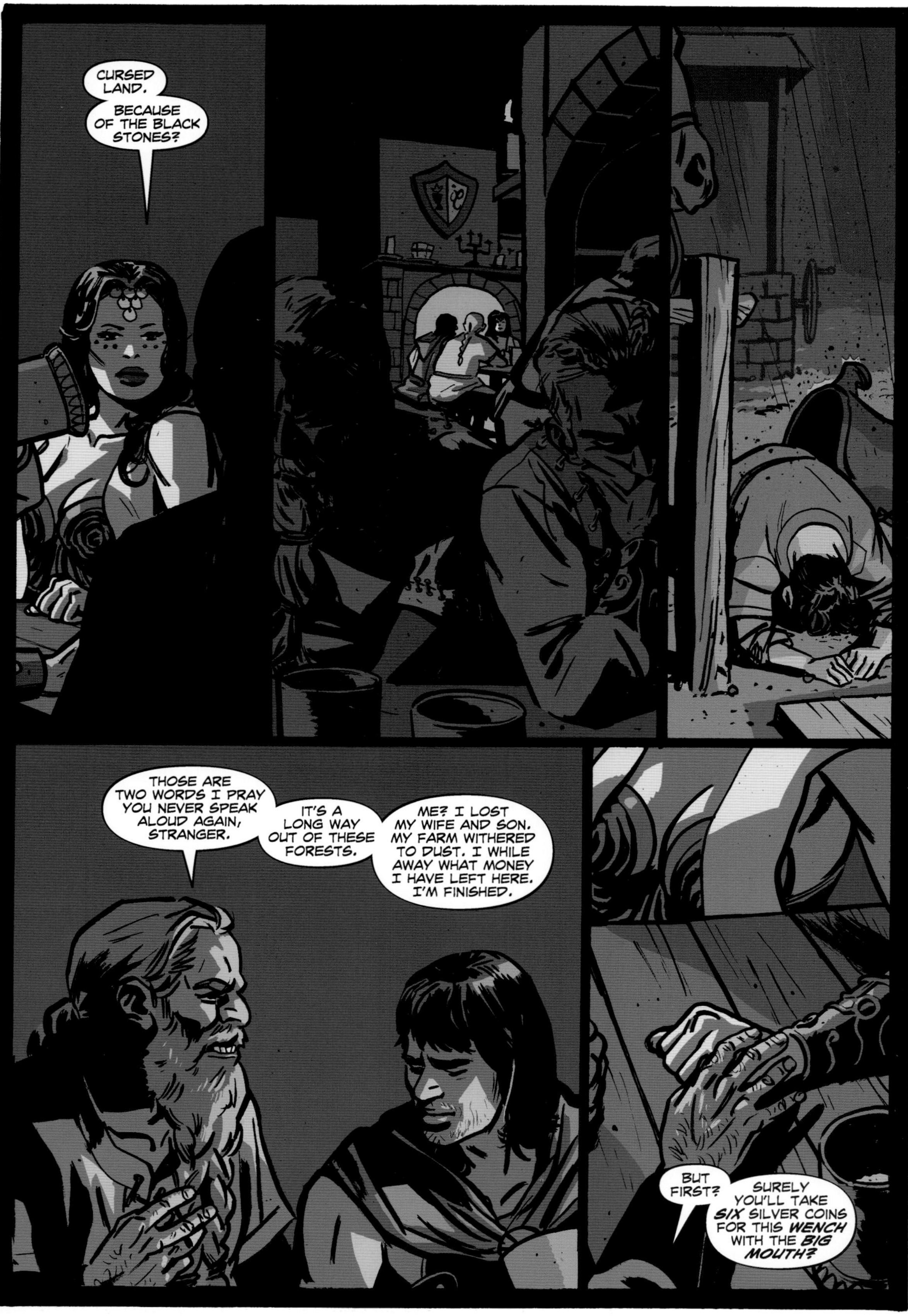
CURSED LAND.
BECAUSE OF THE BLACK STONES?
THOSE ARE TWO WORDS I PRAY YOU NEVER SPEAK ALOUD AGAIN, STRANGER.
IT'S A LONG WAY OUT OF THESE FORESTS.
ME? I LOST MY WIFE AND SON. MY FARM WITHERED TO DUST. I WHILE AWAY WHAT MONEY I HAVE LEFT HERE. I'M FINISHED.
BUT FIRST?
SURELY YOU'LL TAKE SIX SILVER COINS FOR THIS WENCH WITH THE BIG MOUTH?

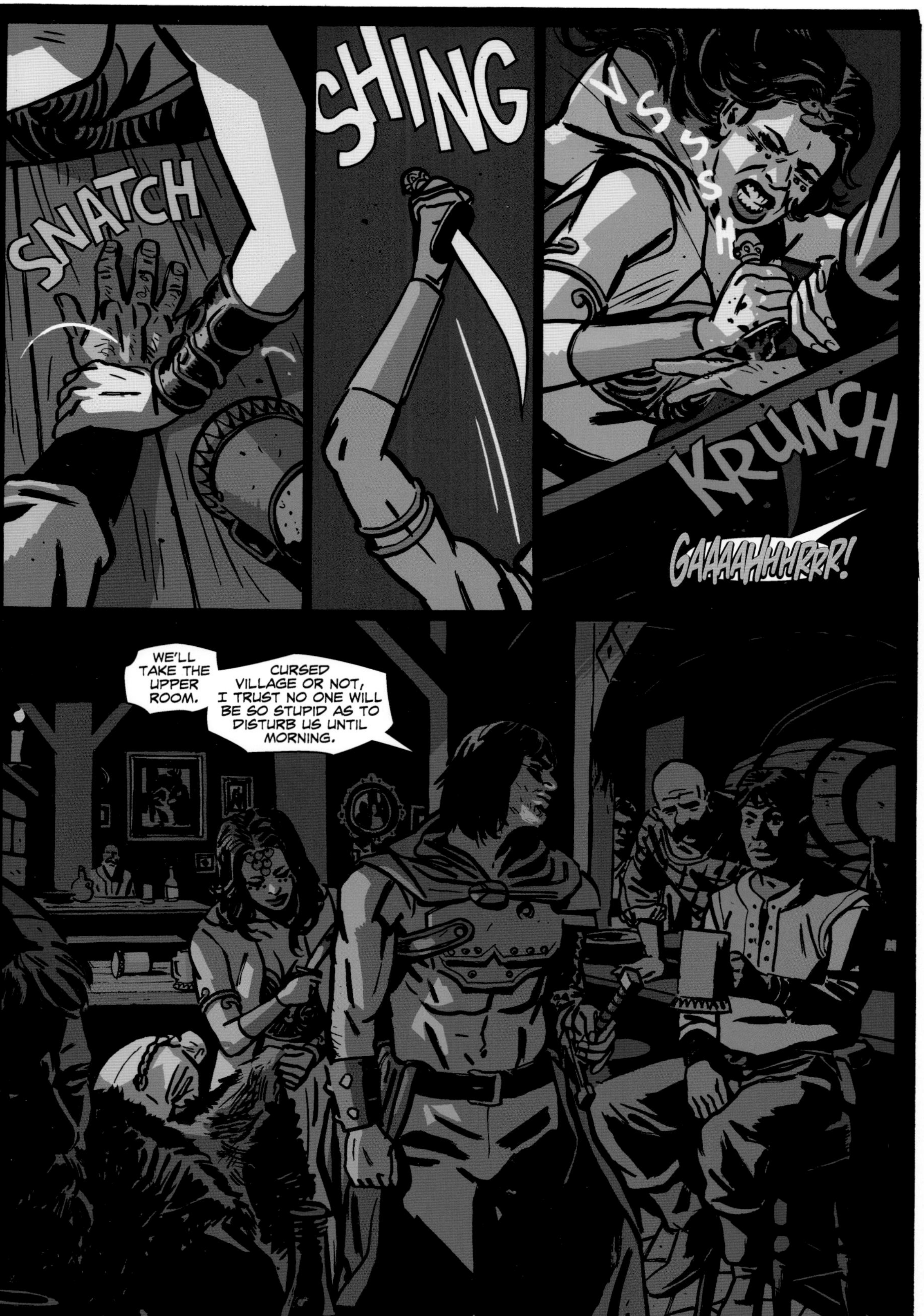
SNATCH
SHING
VSSSSH
KRUNCH
GAAAAHHHRRR!
WE'LL TAKE THE UPPER ROOM.
CURSED VILLAGE OR NOT, I TRUST NO ONE WILL BE SO STUPID AS TO DISTURB US UNTIL MORNING.

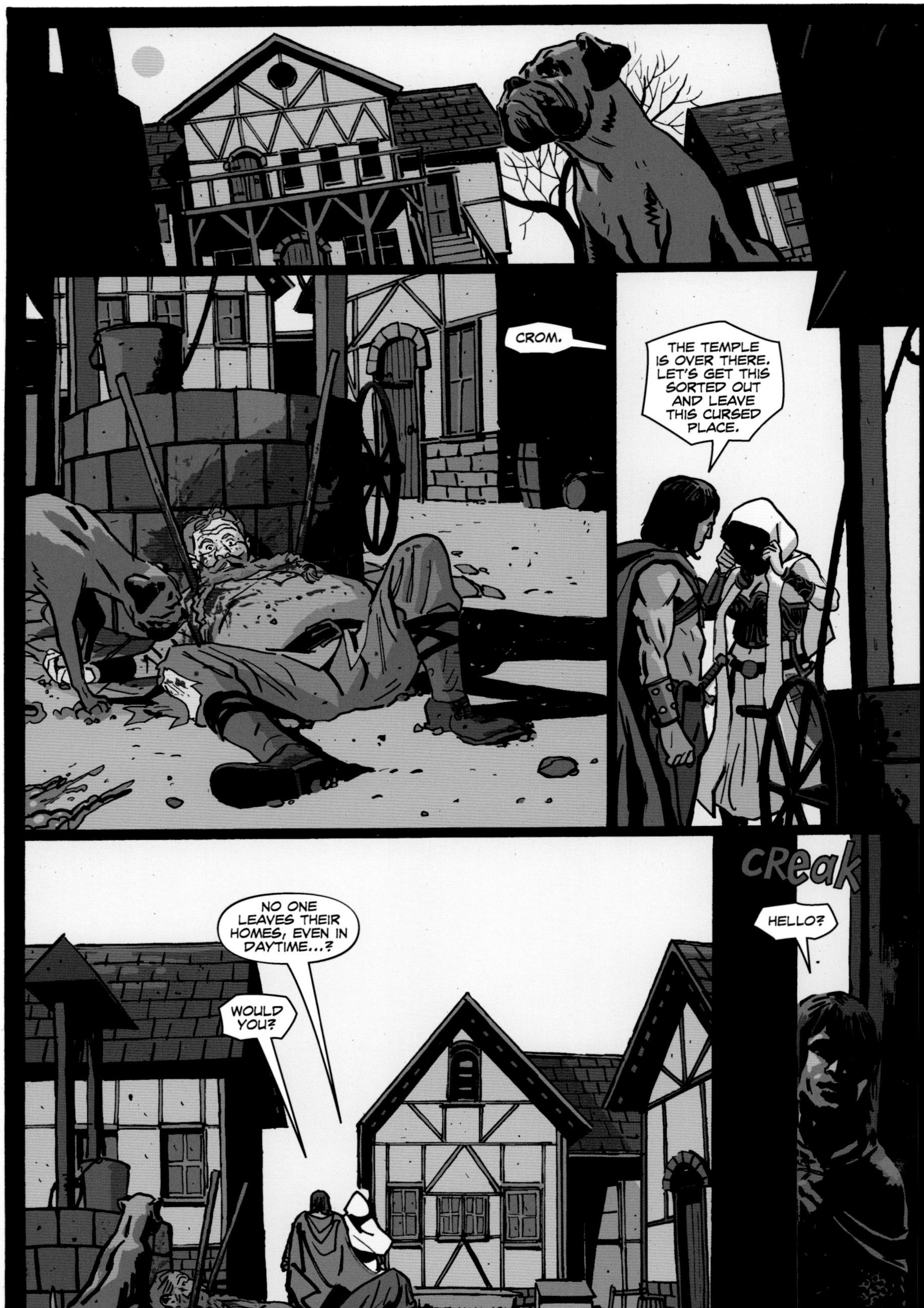
CROM.
THE TEMPLE IS OVER THERE. LET'S GET THIS SORTED OUT AND LEAVE THIS CURSED PLACE.
NO ONE LEAVES THEIR HOMES, EVEN IN DAYTIME...?
WOULD YOU?
CREak
HELLO?

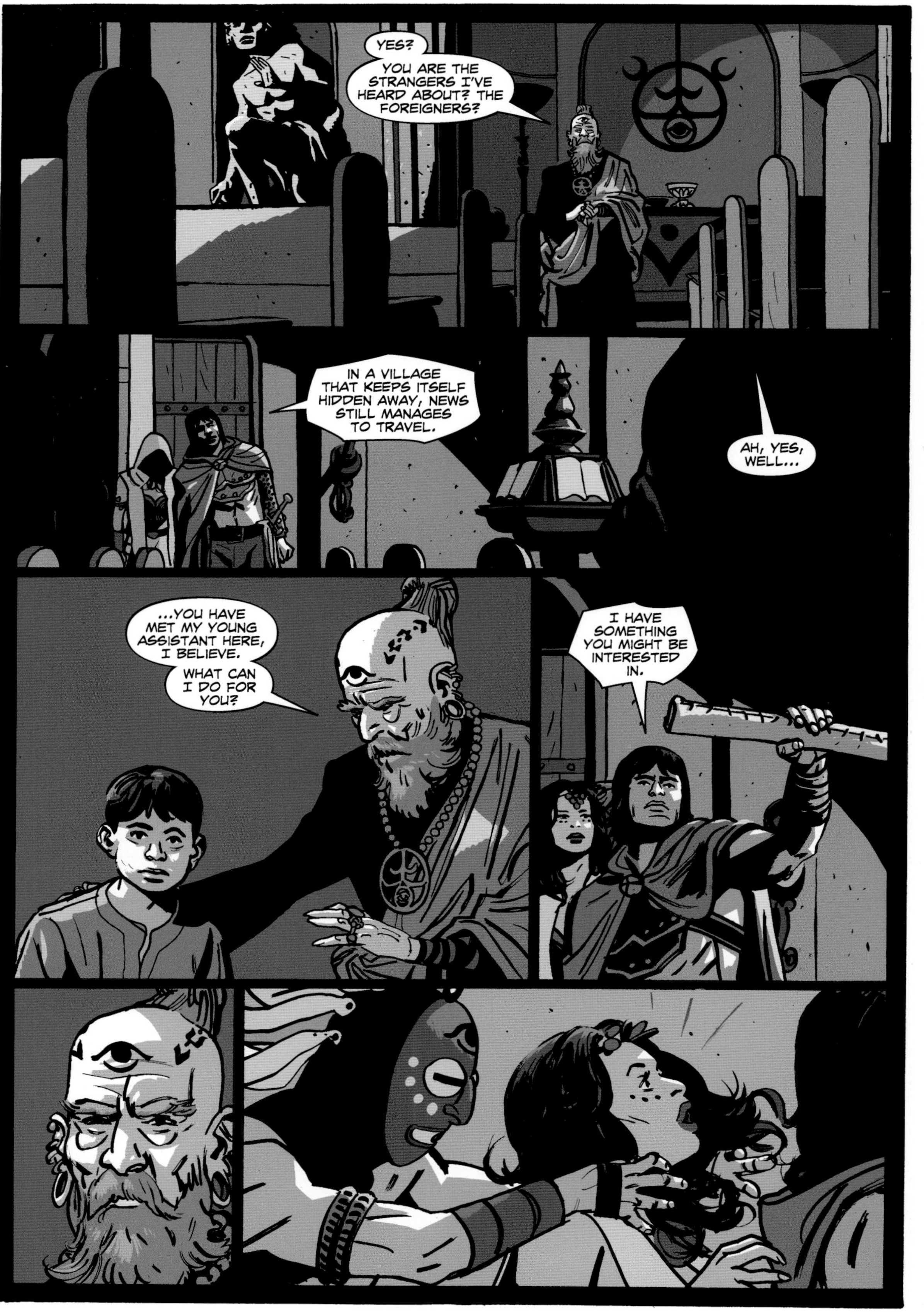
YES?
YOU ARE THE STRANGERS I'VE HEARD ABOUT? THE FOREIGNERS?
IN A VILLAGE THAT KEEPS ITSELF HIDDEN AWAY, NEWS STILL MANAGES TO TRAVEL.
AH, YES, WELL...
...YOU HAVE MET MY YOUNG ASSISTANT HERE, I BELIEVE.
WHAT CAN I DO FOR YOU?
I HAVE SOMETHING YOU MIGHT BE INTERESTED IN.

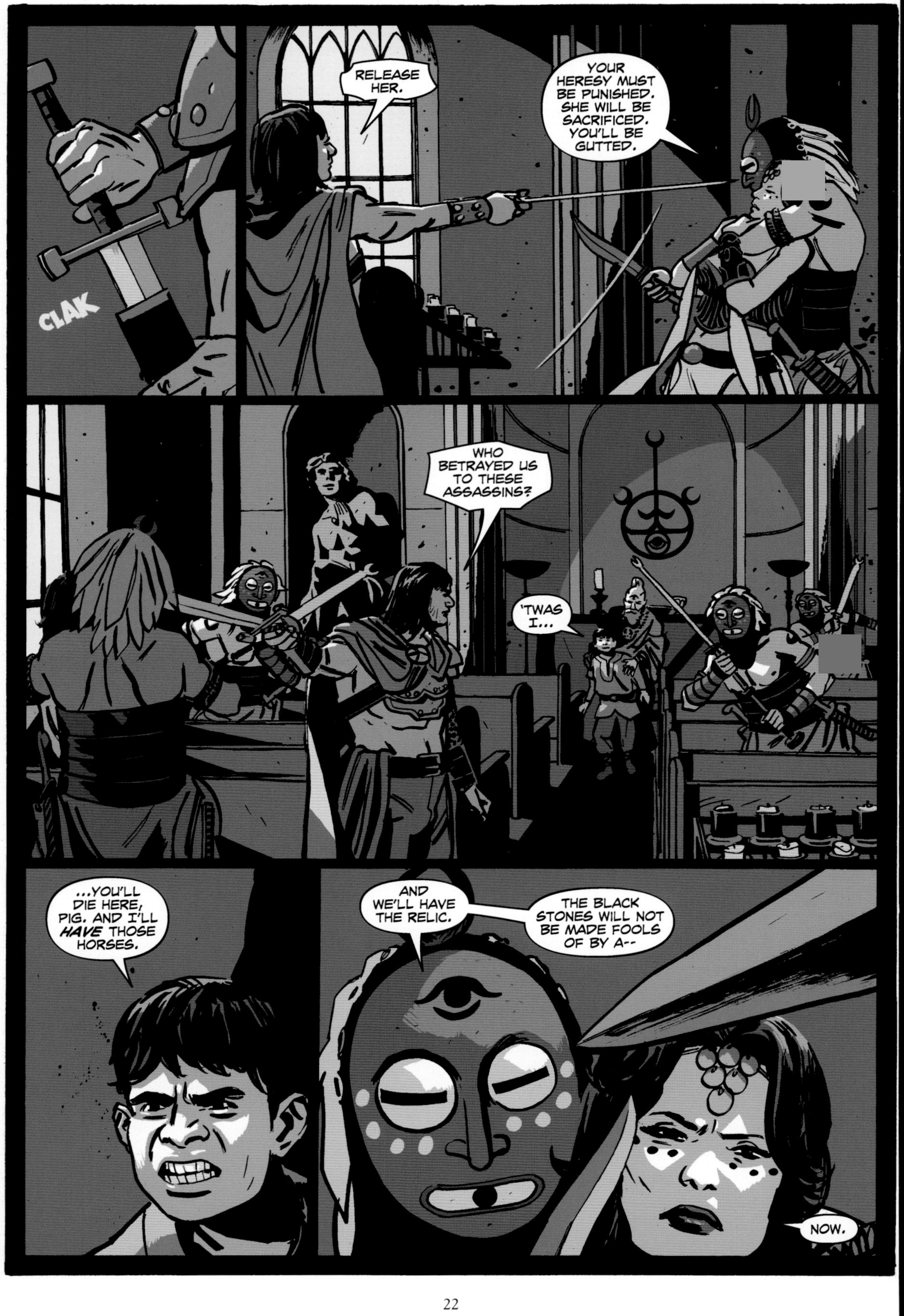
CLAK
RELEASE HER.
YOUR HERESY MUST BE PUNISHED. SHE WILL BE SACRIFICED. YOU'LL BE GUTTED.
WHO BETRAYED US TO THESE ASSASSINS?
'TWAS I...
...YOU'LL DIE HERE, PIG. AND I'LL *HAVE* THOSE HORSES.
AND WE'LL HAVE THE RELIC.
THE BLACK STONES WILL NOT BE MADE FOOLS OF BY A--
NOW.

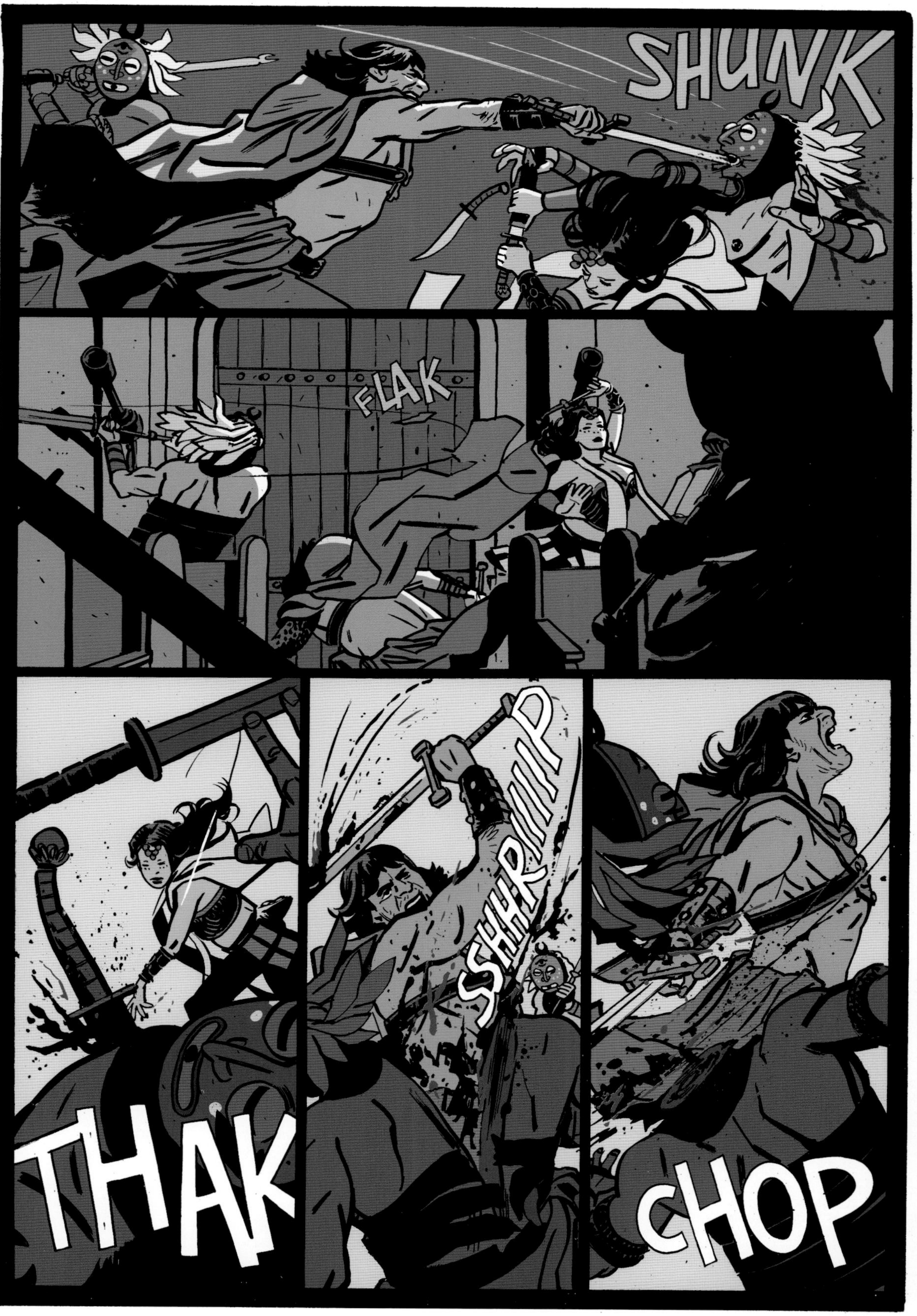
SHUNK
FLAK
THAK
SHHRIIIIP
CHOP

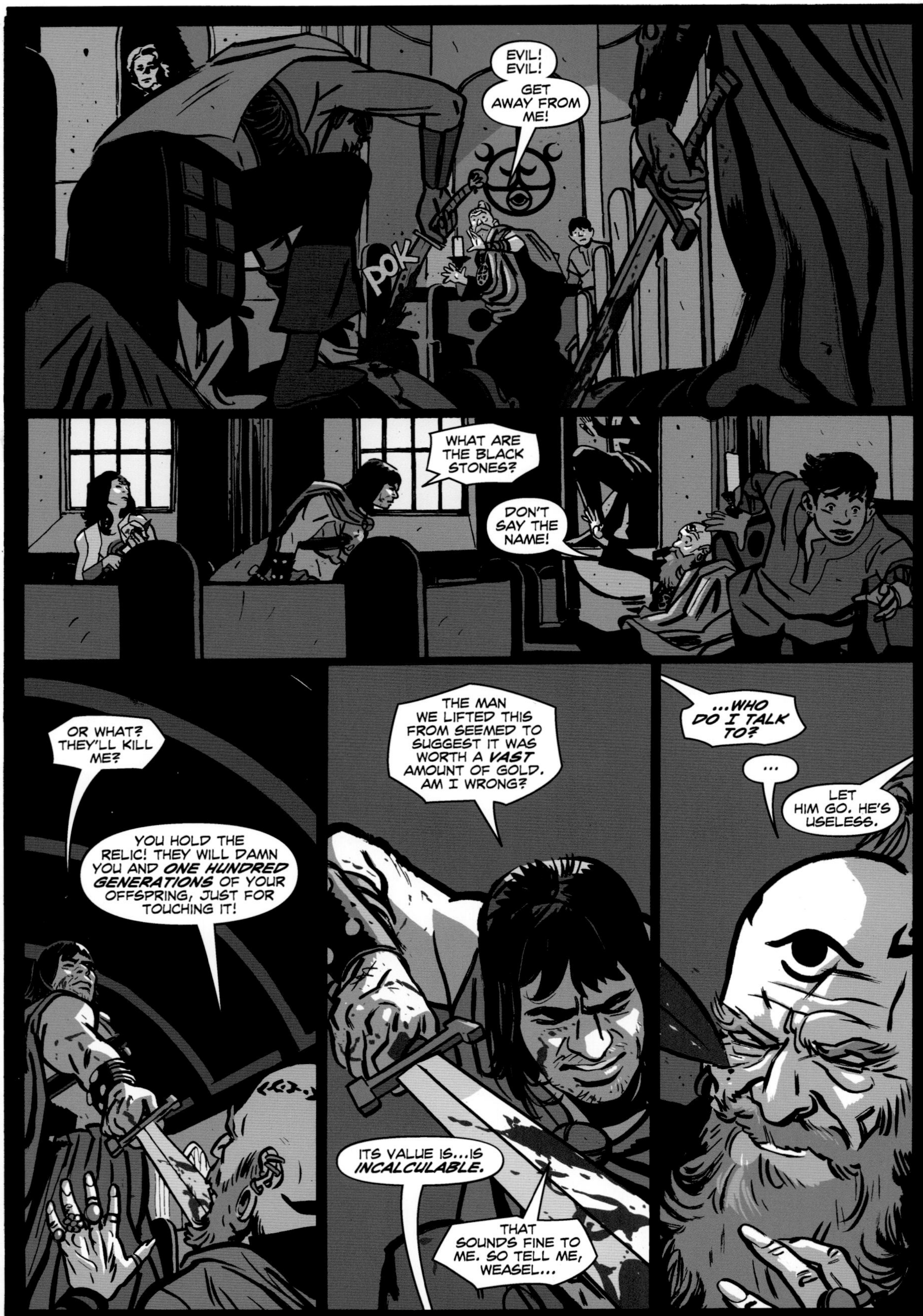
EVIL! EVIL!
GET AWAY FROM ME!
POK
WHAT ARE THE BLACK STONES?
DON'T SAY THE NAME!
OR WHAT? THEY'LL KILL ME?
YOU HOLD THE RELIC! THEY WILL DAMN YOU AND ONE HUNDRED GENERATIONS OF YOUR OFFSPRING, JUST FOR TOUCHING IT!
THE MAN WE LIFTED THIS FROM SEEMED TO SUGGEST IT WAS WORTH A VAST AMOUNT OF GOLD. AM I WRONG?
ITS VALUE IS...IS INCALCULABLE.
THAT SOUNDS FINE TO ME. SO TELL ME, WEASEL...
...WHO DO I TALK TO?
...
LET HIM GO. HE'S USELESS.

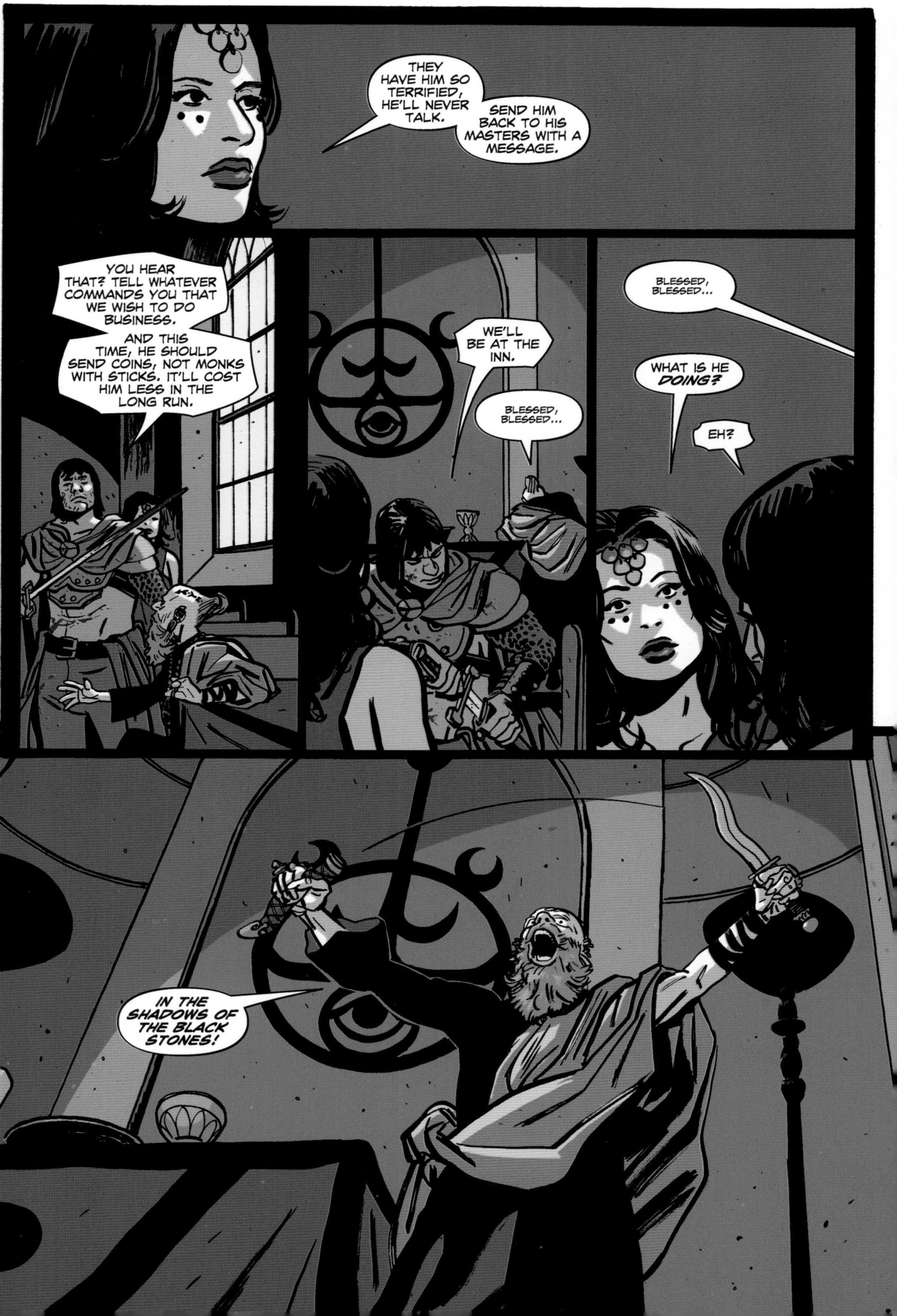
THEY HAVE HIM SO TERRIFIED, HE'LL NEVER TALK.
SEND HIM BACK TO HIS MASTERS WITH A MESSAGE.
YOU HEAR THAT? TELL WHATEVER COMMANDS YOU THAT WE WISH TO DO BUSINESS.
AND THIS TIME, HE SHOULD SEND COINS, NOT MONKS WITH STICKS. IT'LL COST HIM LESS IN THE LONG RUN.
WE'LL BE AT THE INN.
BLESSED, BLESSED...
BLESSED, BLESSED...
WHAT IS HE *DOING?*
EH?
IN THE SHADOWS OF THE BLACK STONES!

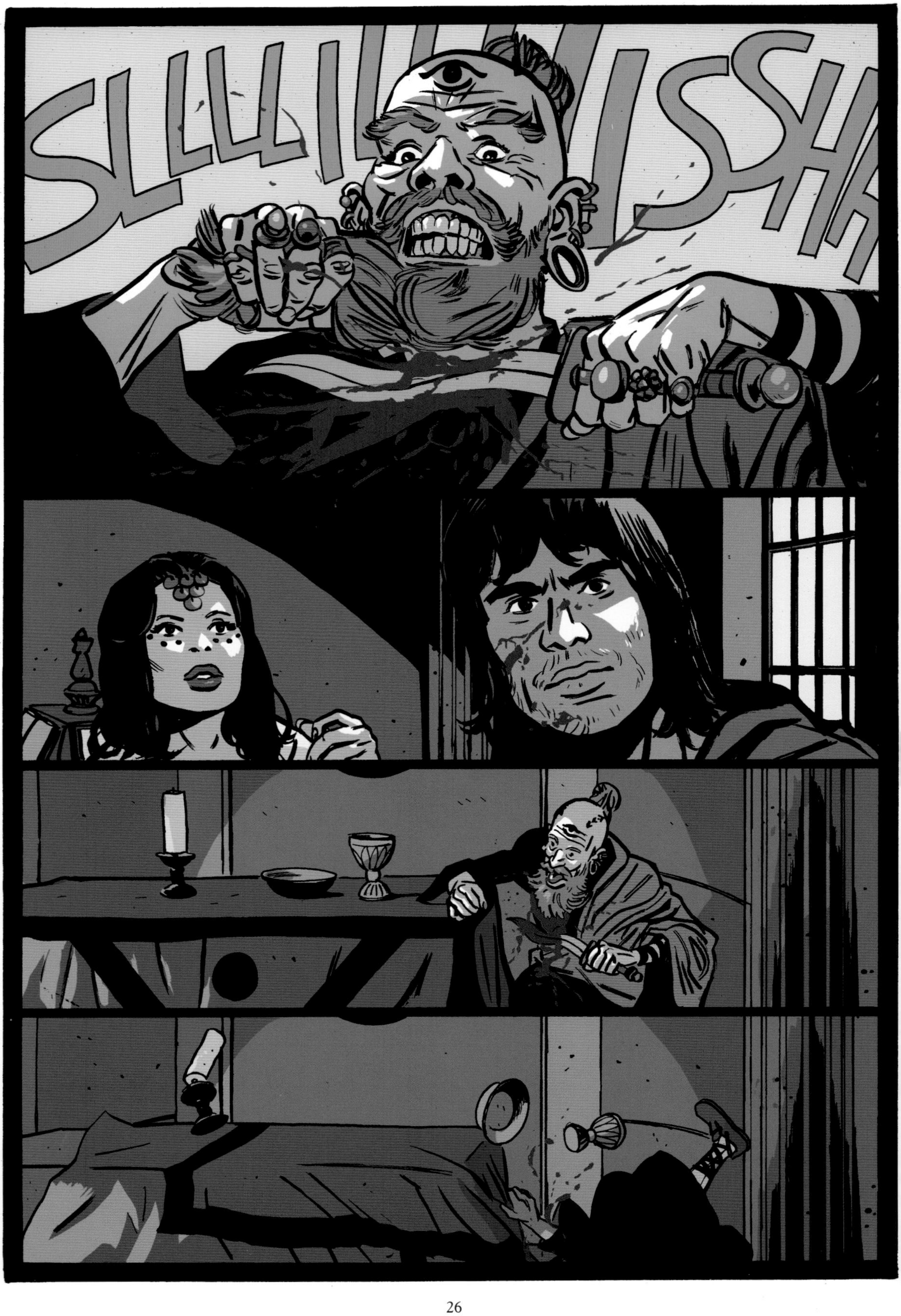
SLLLIIIIIISSH

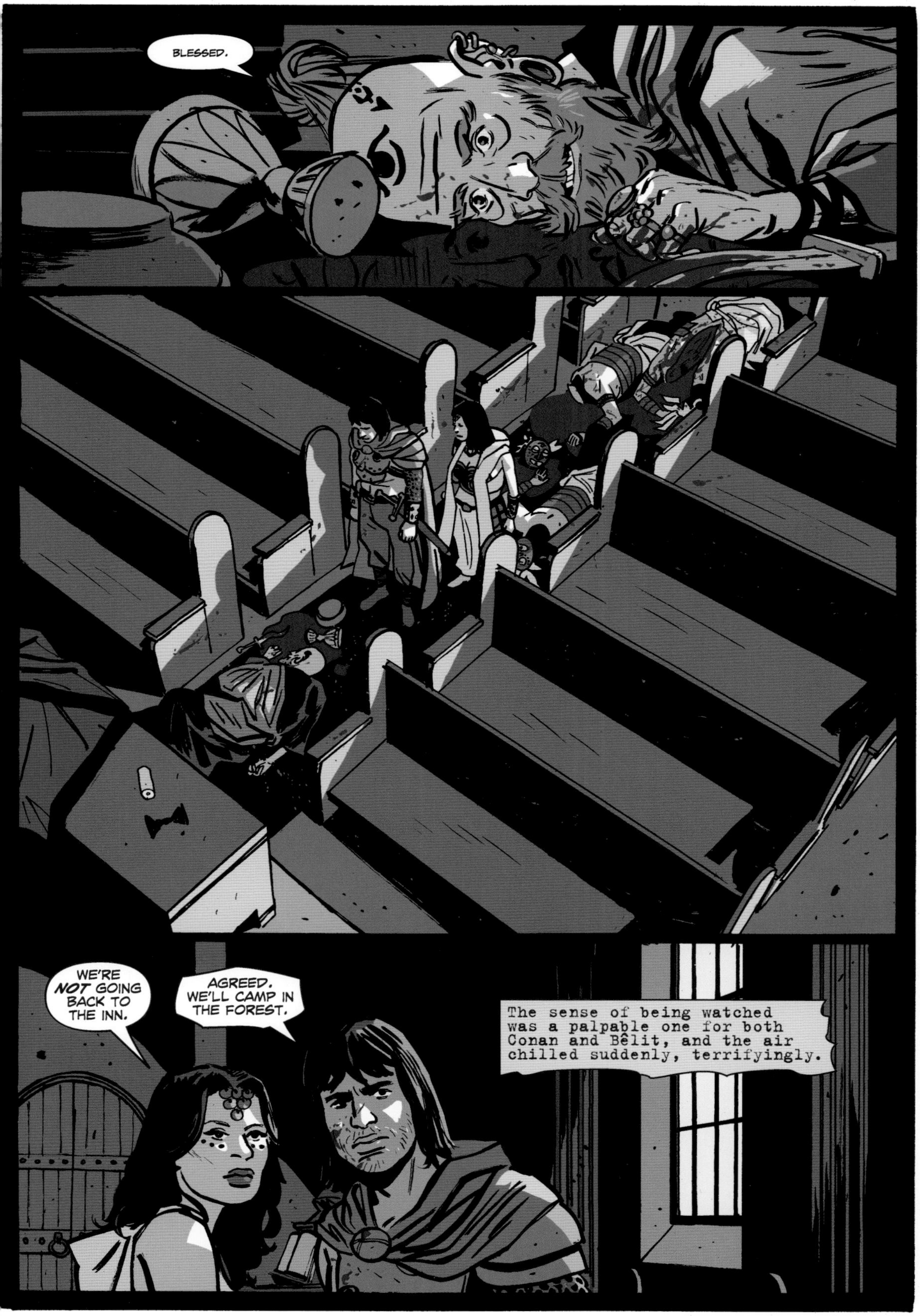
BLESSED.
WE'RE NOT GOING BACK TO THE INN.
AGREED. WE'LL CAMP IN THE FOREST.
The sense of being watched was a palpable one for both Conan and Bêlit, and the air chilled suddenly, terrifyingly.

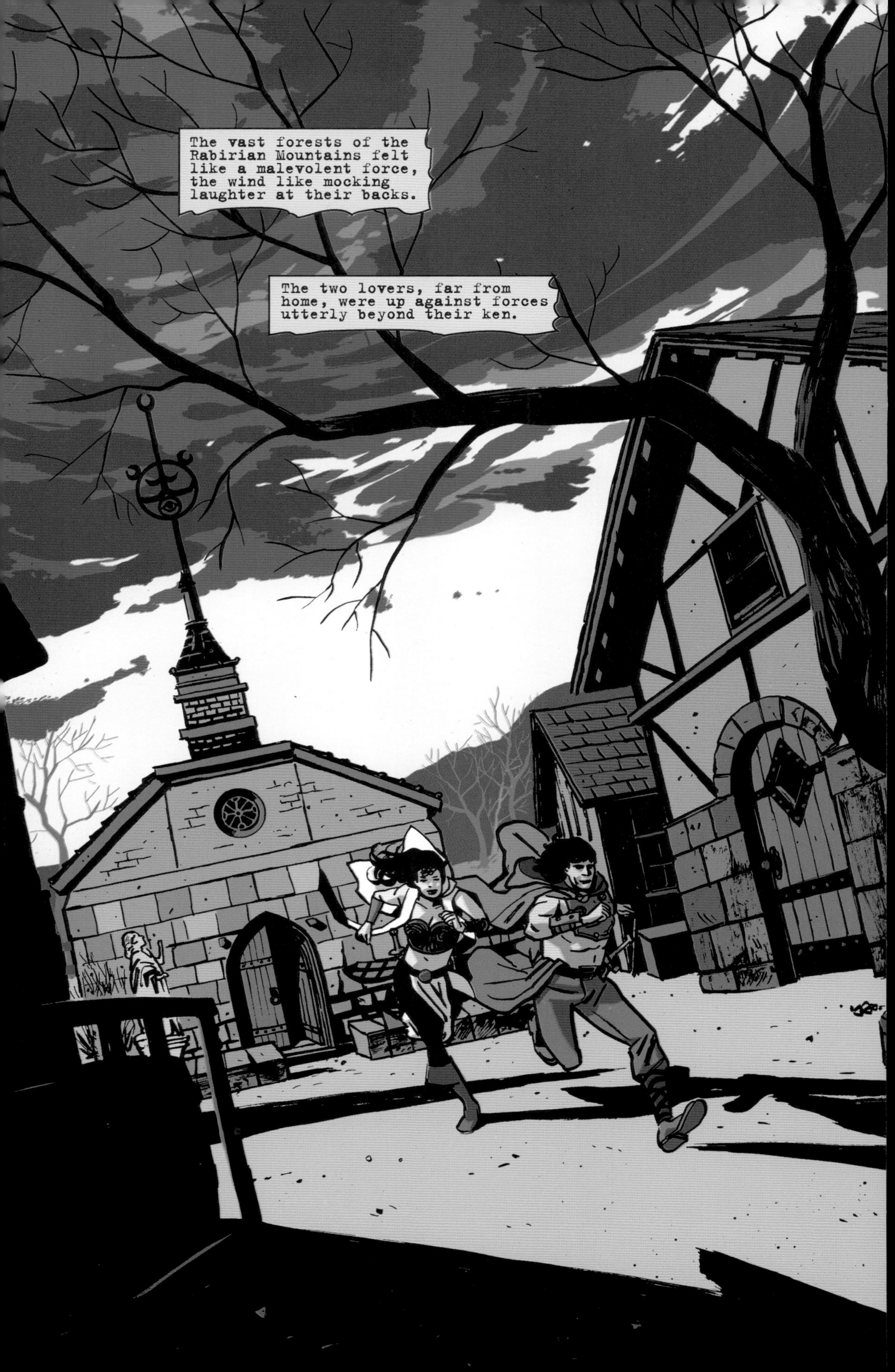
The vast forests of the Rabirian Mountains felt like a malevolent force, the wind like mocking laughter at their backs.
The two lovers, far from home, were up against forces utterly beyond their ken.

CHAPTER TWO

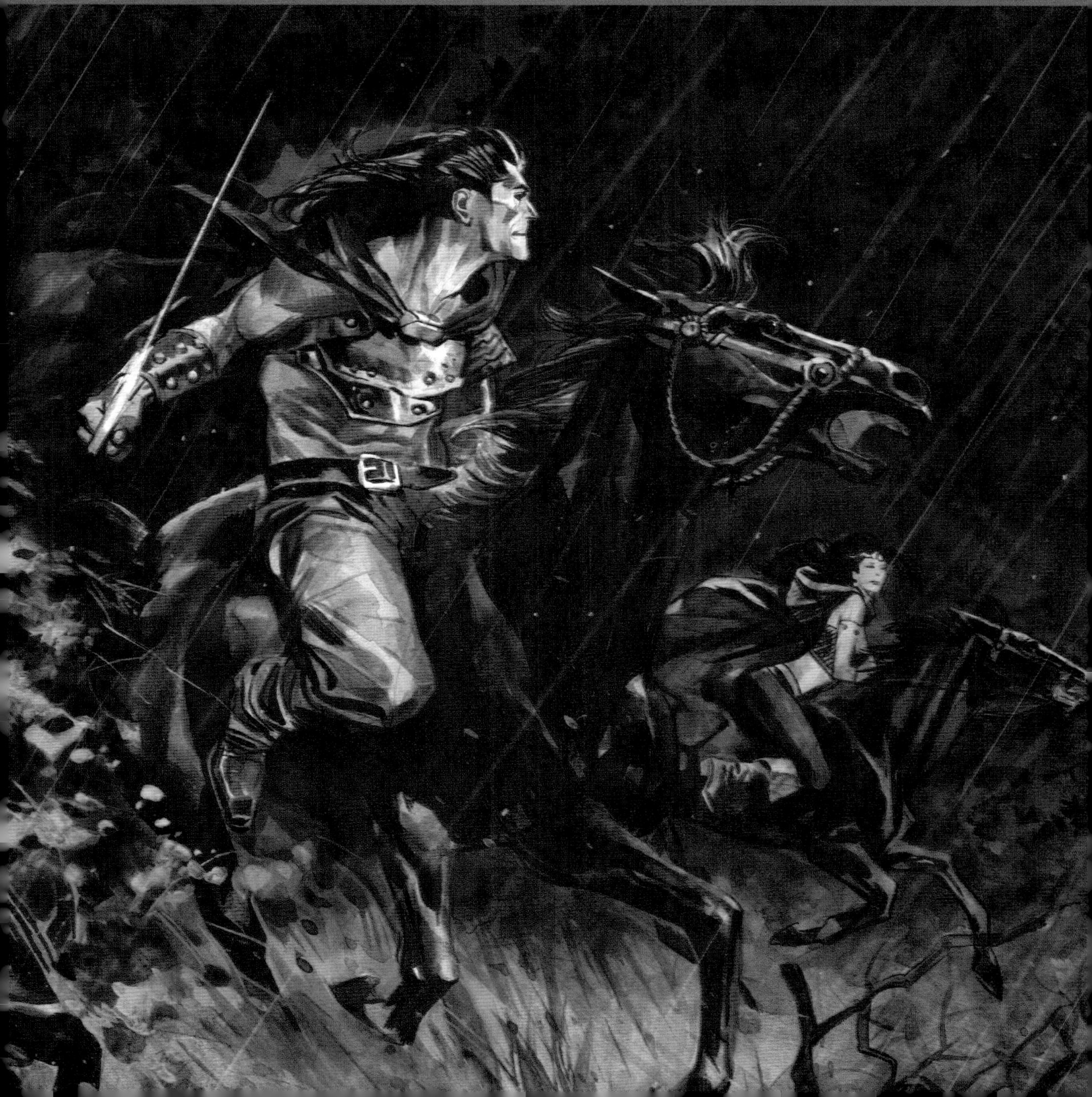

"I will look these madmen in the eye and get our payment. Do you think this is the first *petty warlord* I've had to face down?"

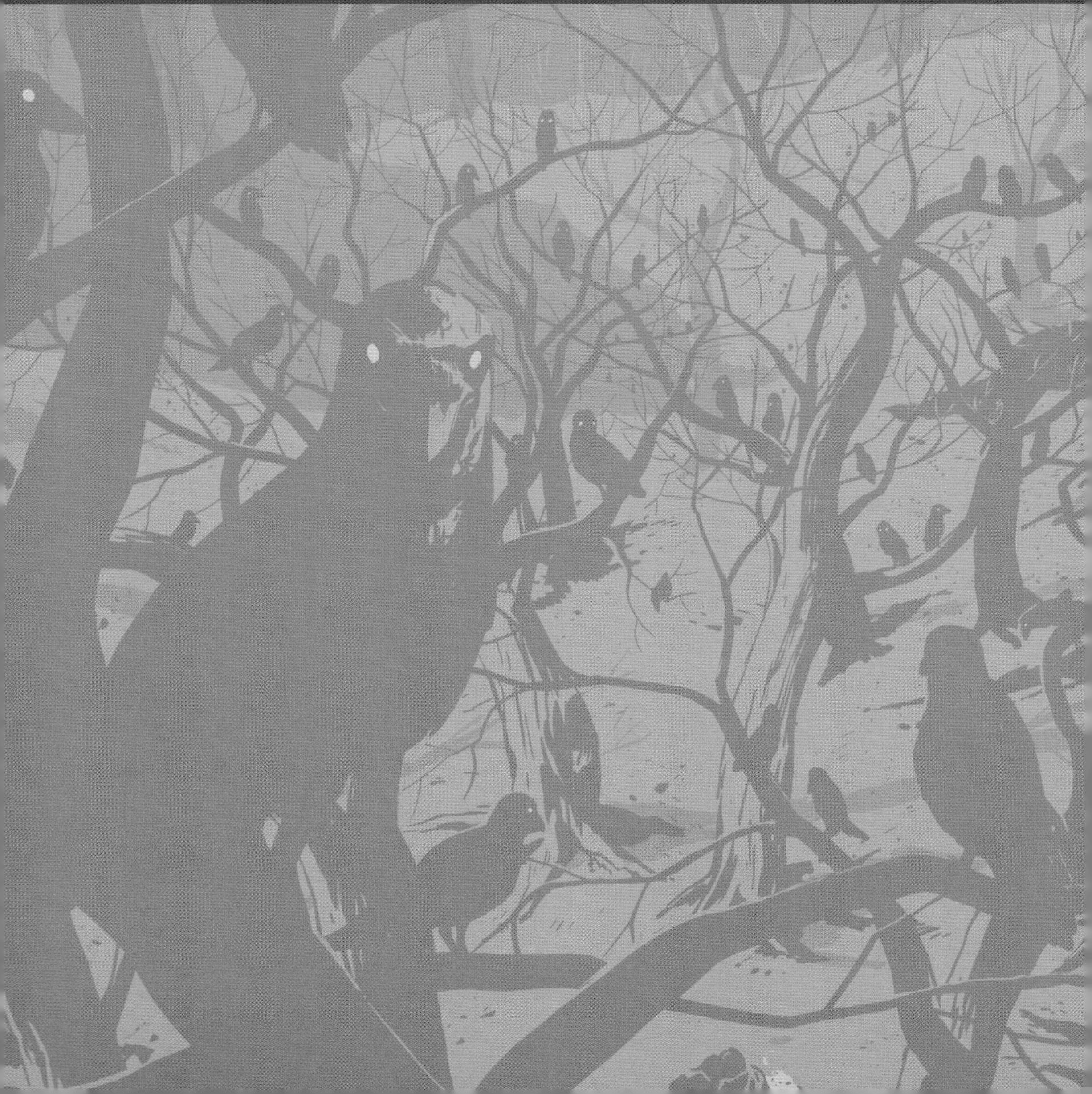

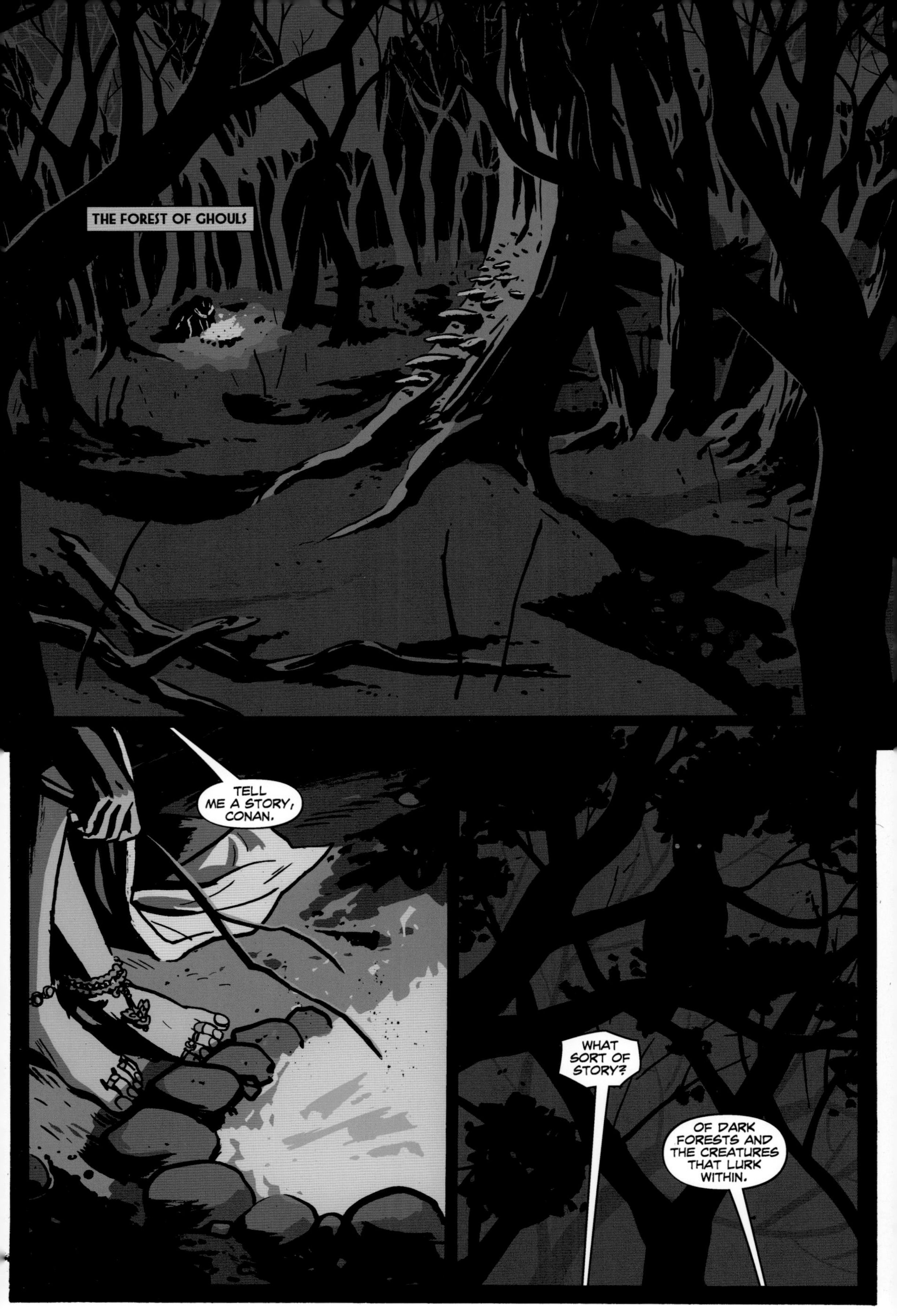
THE FOREST OF GHOULS
TELL ME A STORY, CONAN.
WHAT SORT OF STORY?
OF DARK FORESTS AND THE CREATURES THAT LURK WITHIN.

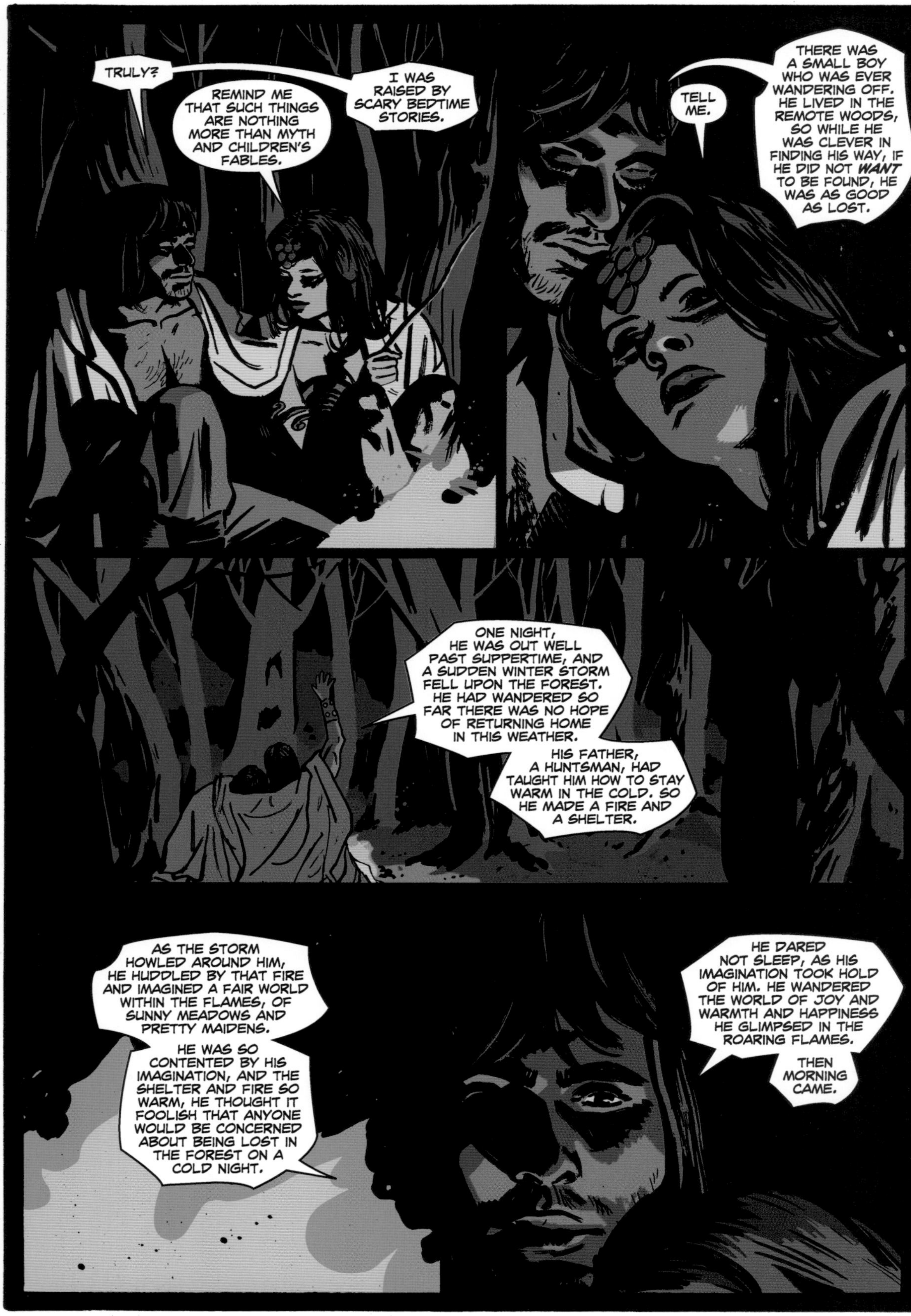

TRULY?
REMIND ME THAT SUCH THINGS ARE NOTHING MORE THAN MYTH AND CHILDREN'S FABLES.
I WAS RAISED BY SCARY BEDTIME STORIES.
TELL ME.
THERE WAS A SMALL BOY WHO WAS EVER WANDERING OFF. HE LIVED IN THE REMOTE WOODS, SO WHILE HE WAS CLEVER IN FINDING HIS WAY, IF HE DID NOT *WANT* TO BE FOUND, HE WAS AS GOOD AS LOST.
ONE NIGHT, HE WAS OUT WELL PAST SUPPERTIME, AND A SUDDEN WINTER STORM FELL UPON THE FOREST. HE HAD WANDERED SO FAR THERE WAS NO HOPE OF RETURNING HOME IN THIS WEATHER.
HIS FATHER, A HUNTSMAN, HAD TAUGHT HIM HOW TO STAY WARM IN THE COLD. SO HE MADE A FIRE AND A SHELTER.
AS THE STORM HOWLED AROUND HIM, HE HUDDLED BY THAT FIRE AND IMAGINED A FAIR WORLD WITHIN THE FLAMES, OF SUNNY MEADOWS AND PRETTY MAIDENS.
HE WAS SO CONTENTED BY HIS IMAGINATION, AND THE SHELTER AND FIRE SO WARM, HE THOUGHT IT FOOLISH THAT ANYONE WOULD BE CONCERNED ABOUT BEING LOST IN THE FOREST ON A COLD NIGHT.
HE DARED NOT SLEEP, AS HIS IMAGINATION TOOK HOLD OF HIM. HE WANDERED THE WORLD OF JOY AND WARMTH AND HAPPINESS HE GLIMPSED IN THE ROARING FLAMES.
THEN MORNING CAME.

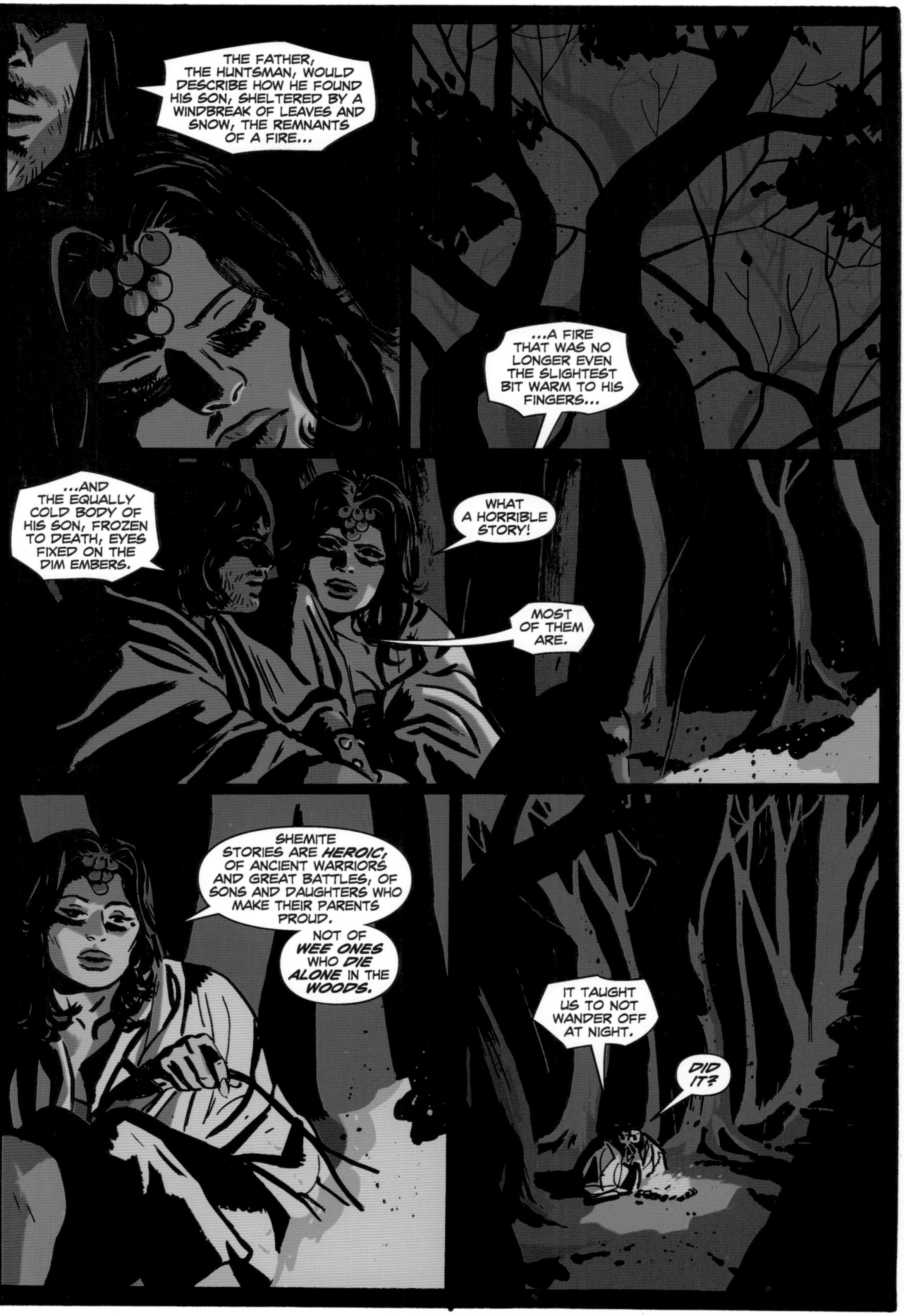
THE FATHER, THE HUNTSMAN, WOULD DESCRIBE HOW HE FOUND HIS SON, SHELTERED BY A WINDBREAK OF LEAVES AND SNOW, THE REMNANTS OF A FIRE...
...A FIRE THAT WAS NO LONGER EVEN THE SLIGHTEST BIT WARM TO HIS FINGERS...
...AND THE EQUALLY COLD BODY OF HIS SON, FROZEN TO DEATH, EYES FIXED ON THE DIM EMBERS.
WHAT A HORRIBLE STORY!
MOST OF THEM ARE.
SHEMITE STORIES ARE *HEROIC*, OF ANCIENT WARRIORS AND GREAT BATTLES, OF SONS AND DAUGHTERS WHO MAKE THEIR PARENTS PROUD.
NOT OF *WEE ONES* WHO *DIE ALONE* IN THE *WOODS*.
IT TAUGHT US TO NOT WANDER OFF AT NIGHT.
DID IT?

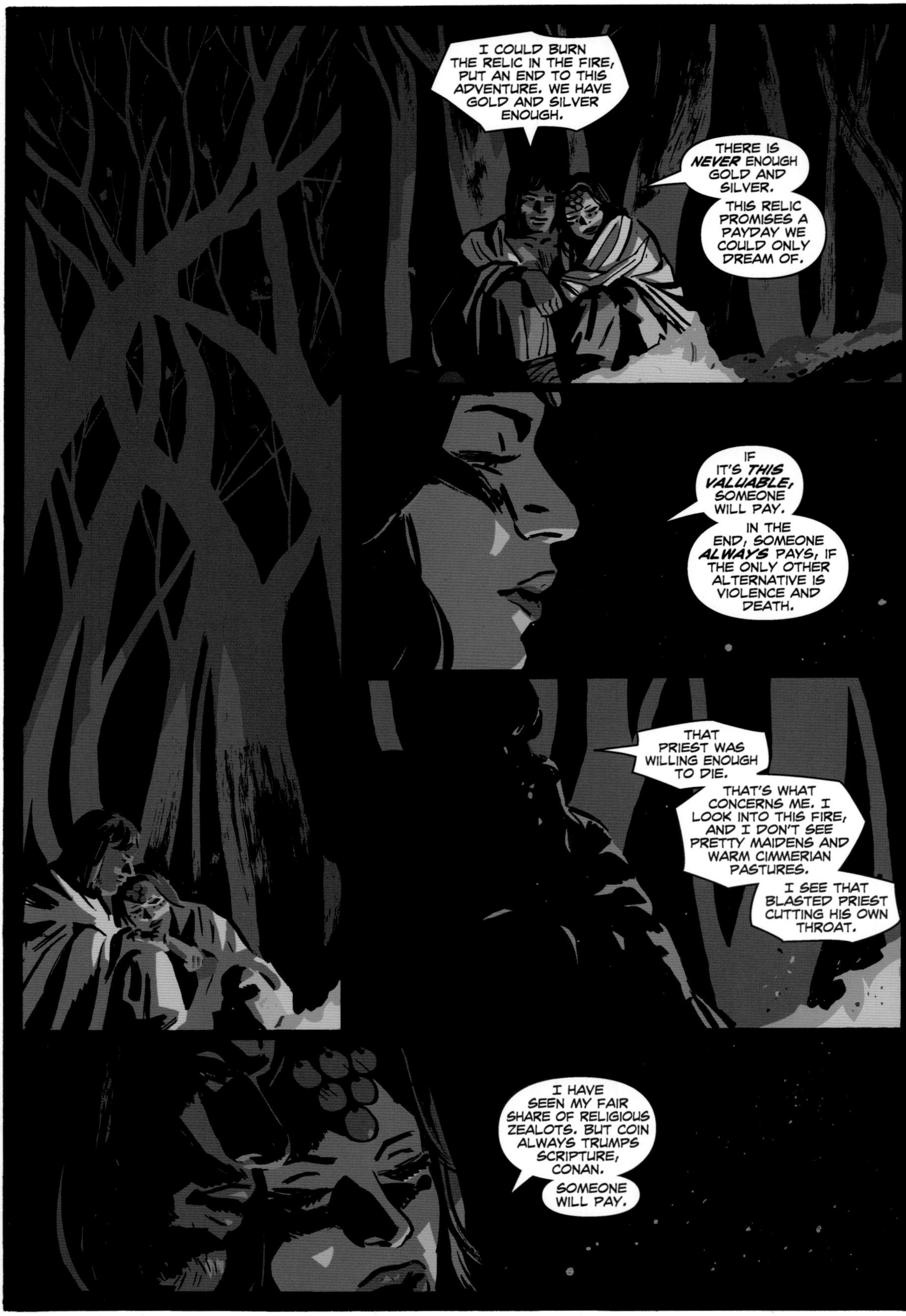
I COULD BURN THE RELIC IN THE FIRE, PUT AN END TO THIS ADVENTURE. WE HAVE GOLD AND SILVER ENOUGH.
THERE IS NEVER ENOUGH GOLD AND SILVER.
THIS RELIC PROMISES A PAYDAY WE COULD ONLY DREAM OF.
IF IT'S THIS VALUABLE, SOMEONE WILL PAY.
IN THE END, SOMEONE ALWAYS PAYS, IF THE ONLY OTHER ALTERNATIVE IS VIOLENCE AND DEATH.
THAT PRIEST WAS WILLING ENOUGH TO DIE.
THAT'S WHAT CONCERNS ME. I LOOK INTO THIS FIRE, AND I DON'T SEE PRETTY MAIDENS AND WARM CIMMERIAN PASTURES.
I SEE THAT BLASTED PRIEST CUTTING HIS OWN THROAT.
I HAVE SEEN MY FAIR SHARE OF RELIGIOUS ZEALOTS. BUT COIN ALWAYS TRUMPS SCRIPTURE, CONAN.
SOMEONE WILL PAY.

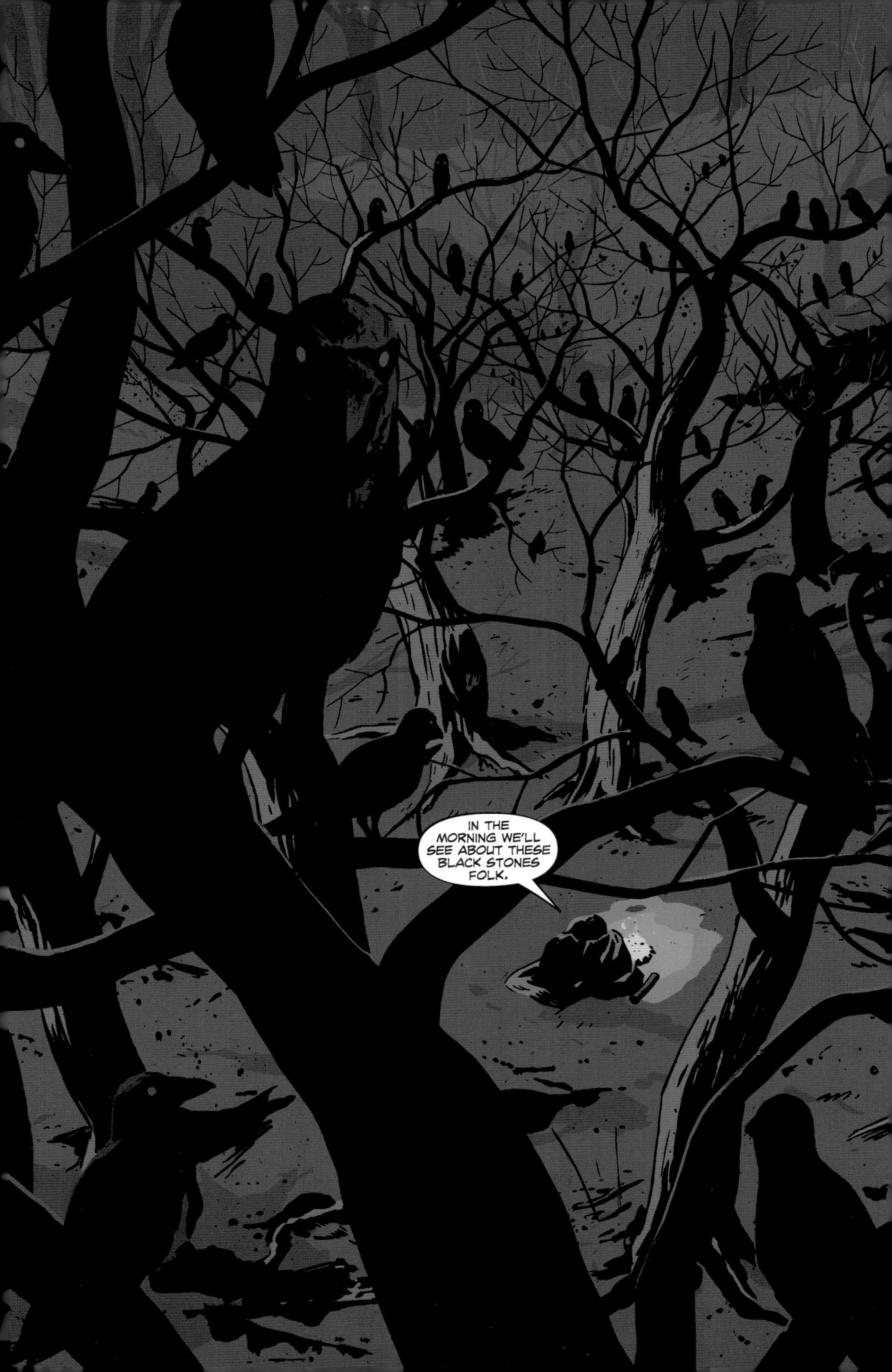
IN THE MORNING WE'LL SEE ABOUT THESE BLACK STONES FOLK.

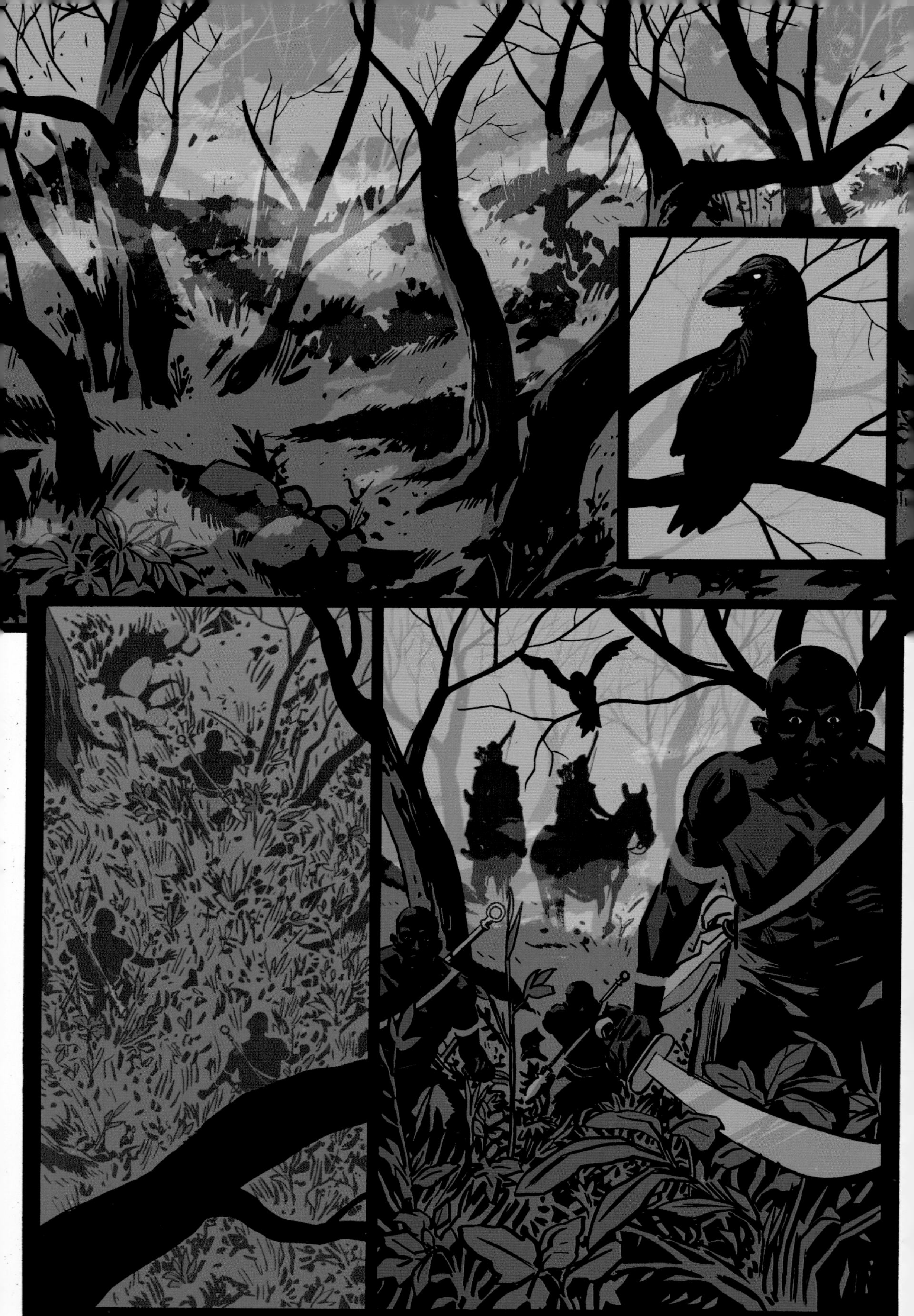

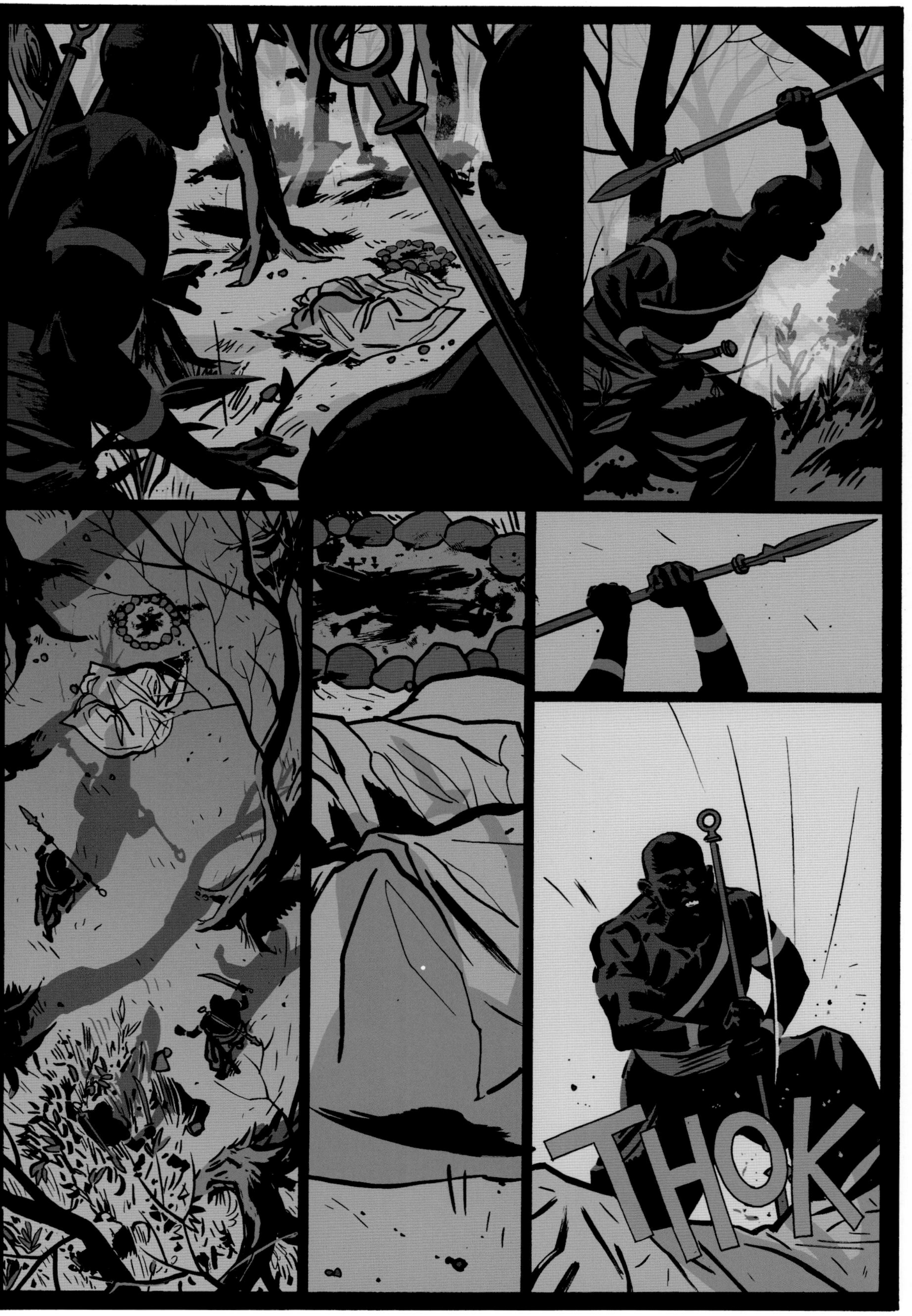
THOK

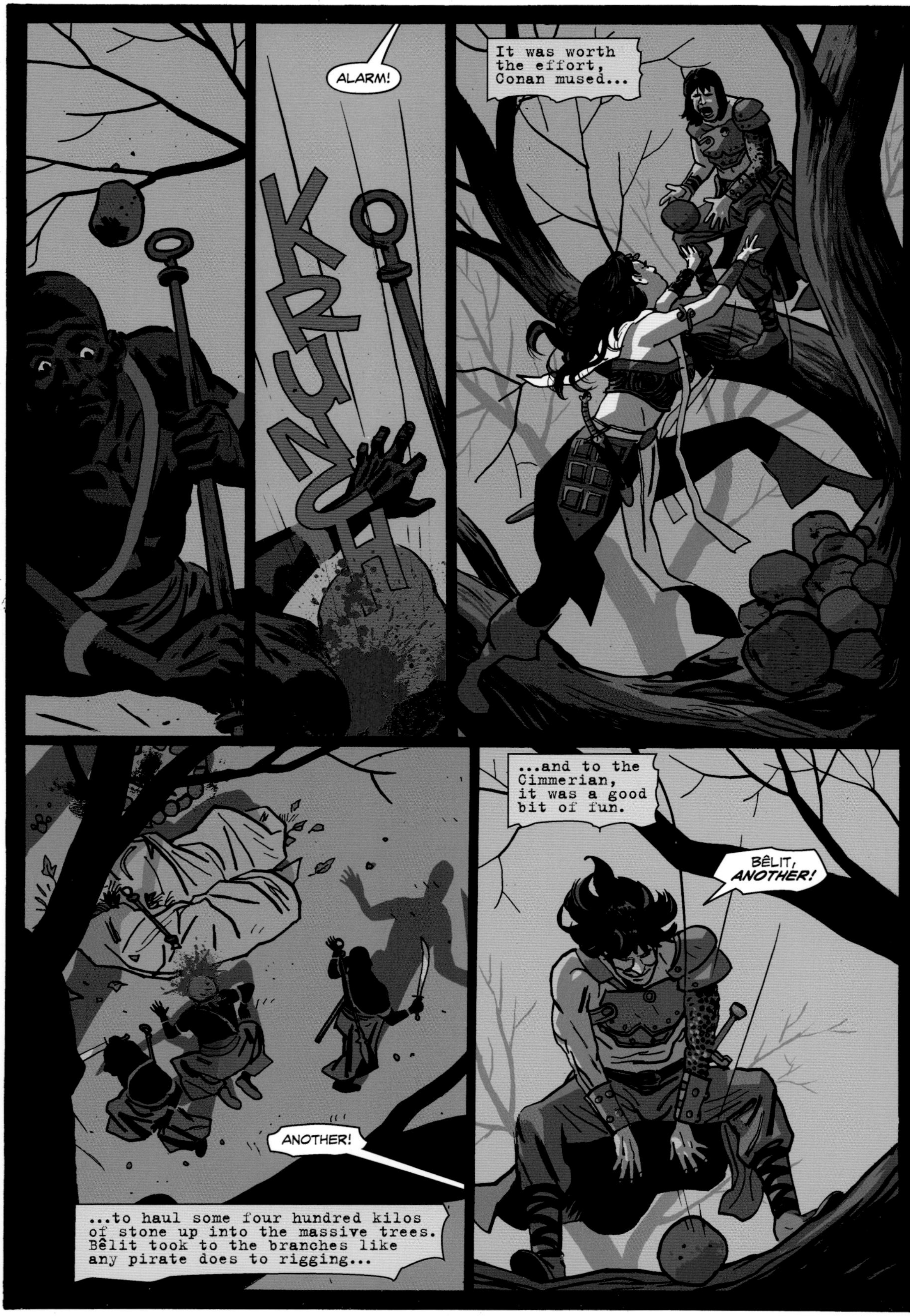
ALARM!
KRUNCH
It was worth the effort, Conan mused...
...to haul some four hundred kilos of stone up into the massive trees. Bêlit took to the branches like any pirate does to rigging...
ANOTHER!
...and to the Cimmerian, it was a good bit of fun.
BÊLIT, ANOTHER!

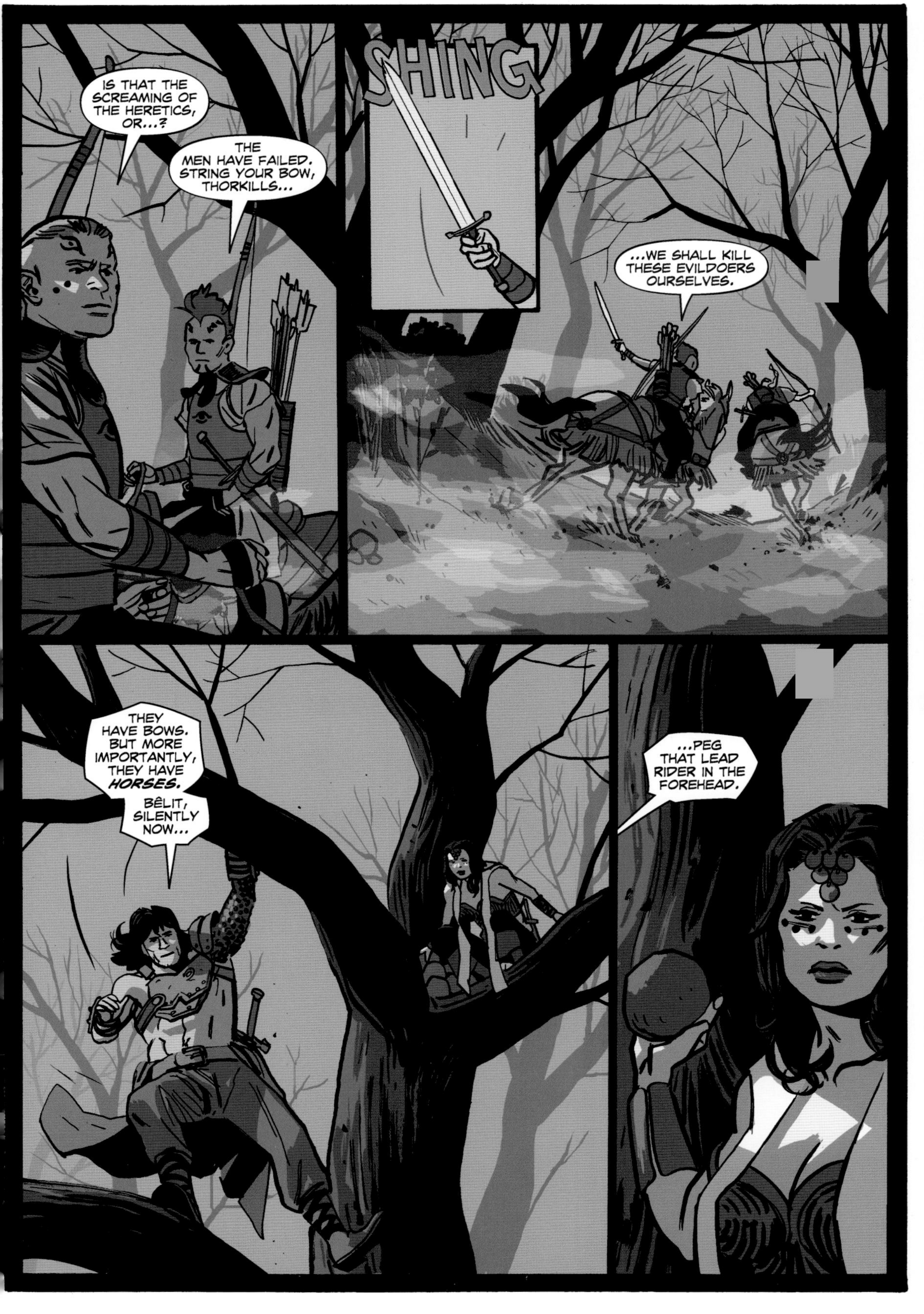
IS THAT THE SCREAMING OF THE HERETICS, OR...?
THE MEN HAVE FAILED. STRING YOUR BOW, THORKILLS...
SHING
...WE SHALL KILL THESE EVILDOERS OURSELVES.
THEY HAVE BOWS. BUT MORE IMPORTANTLY, THEY HAVE HORSES.
BÊLIT, SILENTLY NOW...
...PEG THAT LEAD RIDER IN THE FOREHEAD.

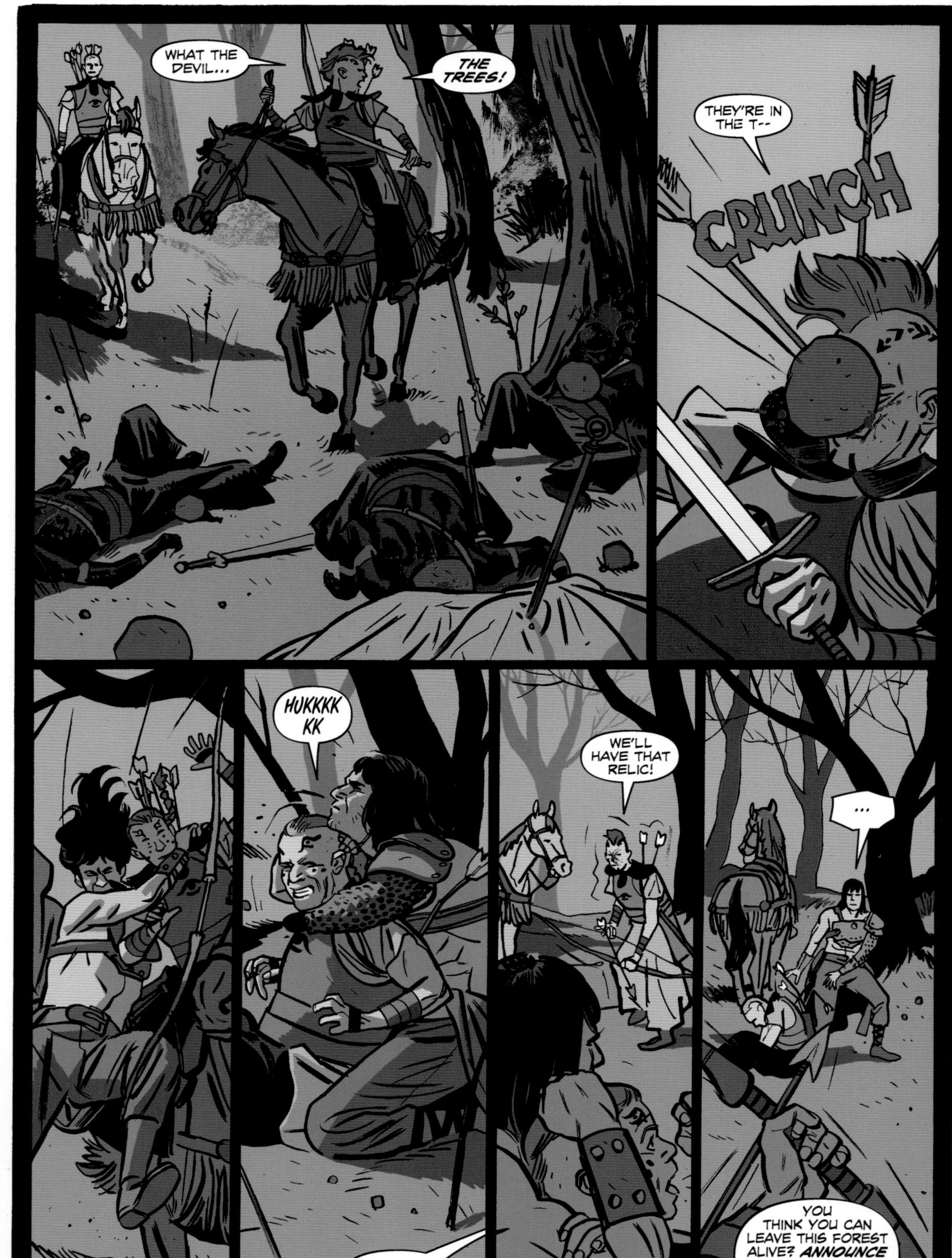

WHAT THE DEVIL...
THE TREES!
THEY'RE IN THE T--
CRUNCH
HUKKKK KK
HEATHEN, SOUL BLACK AS PITCH!
WE'LL HAVE THAT RELIC!
...
YOU THINK YOU CAN LEAVE THIS FOREST ALIVE? ANNOUNCE YOURSELVES, AND FACE THE JUDGMENT...

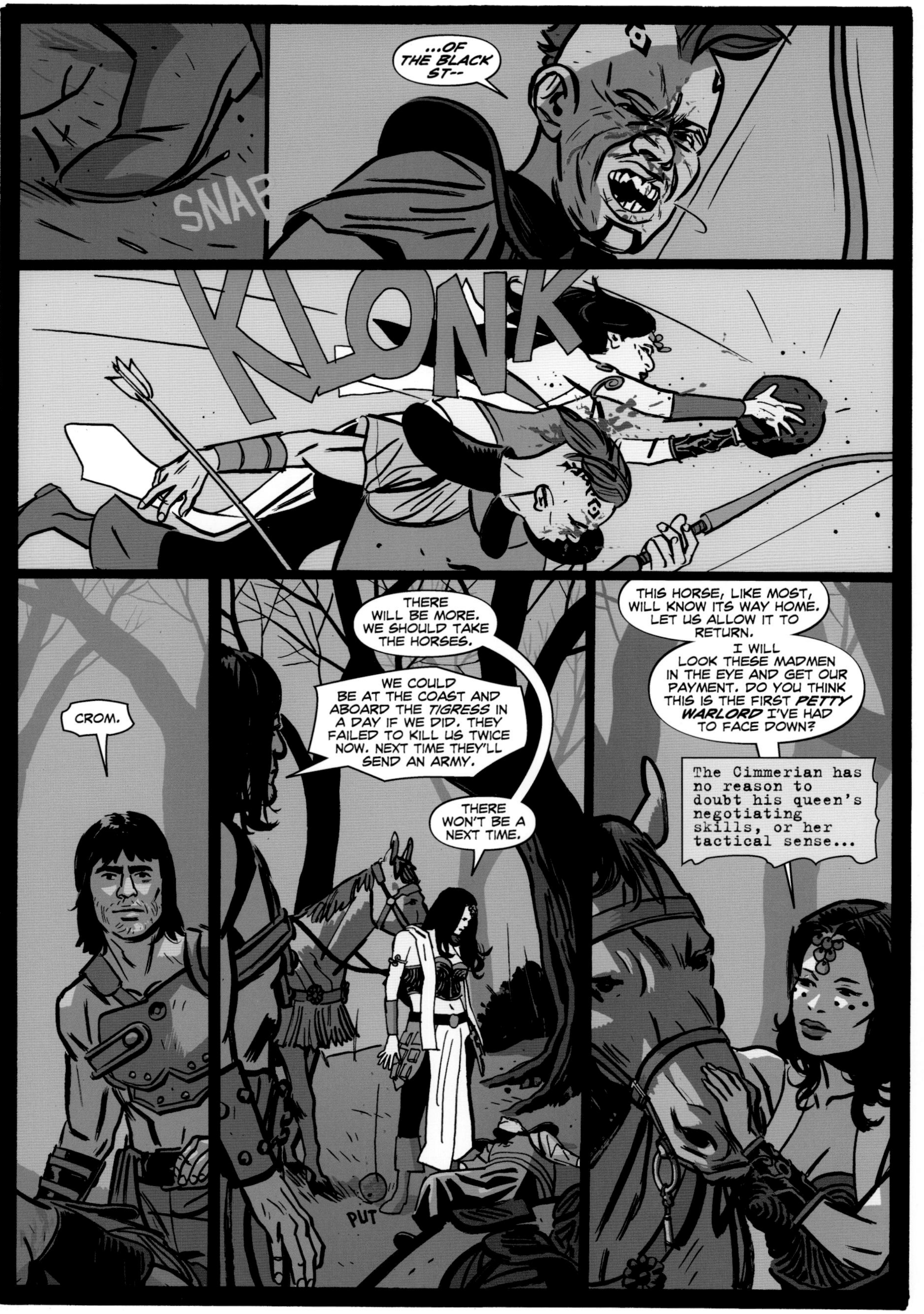

...OF THE BLACK ST--
SNAP
KLONK
CROM.
THERE WILL BE MORE. WE SHOULD TAKE THE HORSES.
WE COULD BE AT THE COAST AND ABOARD THE *TIGRESS* IN A DAY IF WE DID. THEY FAILED TO KILL US TWICE NOW. NEXT TIME THEY'LL SEND AN ARMY.
THERE WON'T BE A NEXT TIME.
PUT
THIS HORSE, LIKE MOST, WILL KNOW ITS WAY HOME. LET US ALLOW IT TO RETURN.
I WILL LOOK THESE MADMEN IN THE EYE AND GET OUR PAYMENT. DO YOU THINK THIS IS THE FIRST ***PETTY WARLORD*** I'VE HAD TO FACE DOWN?
The Cimmerian has no reason to doubt his queen's negotiating skills, or her tactical sense...

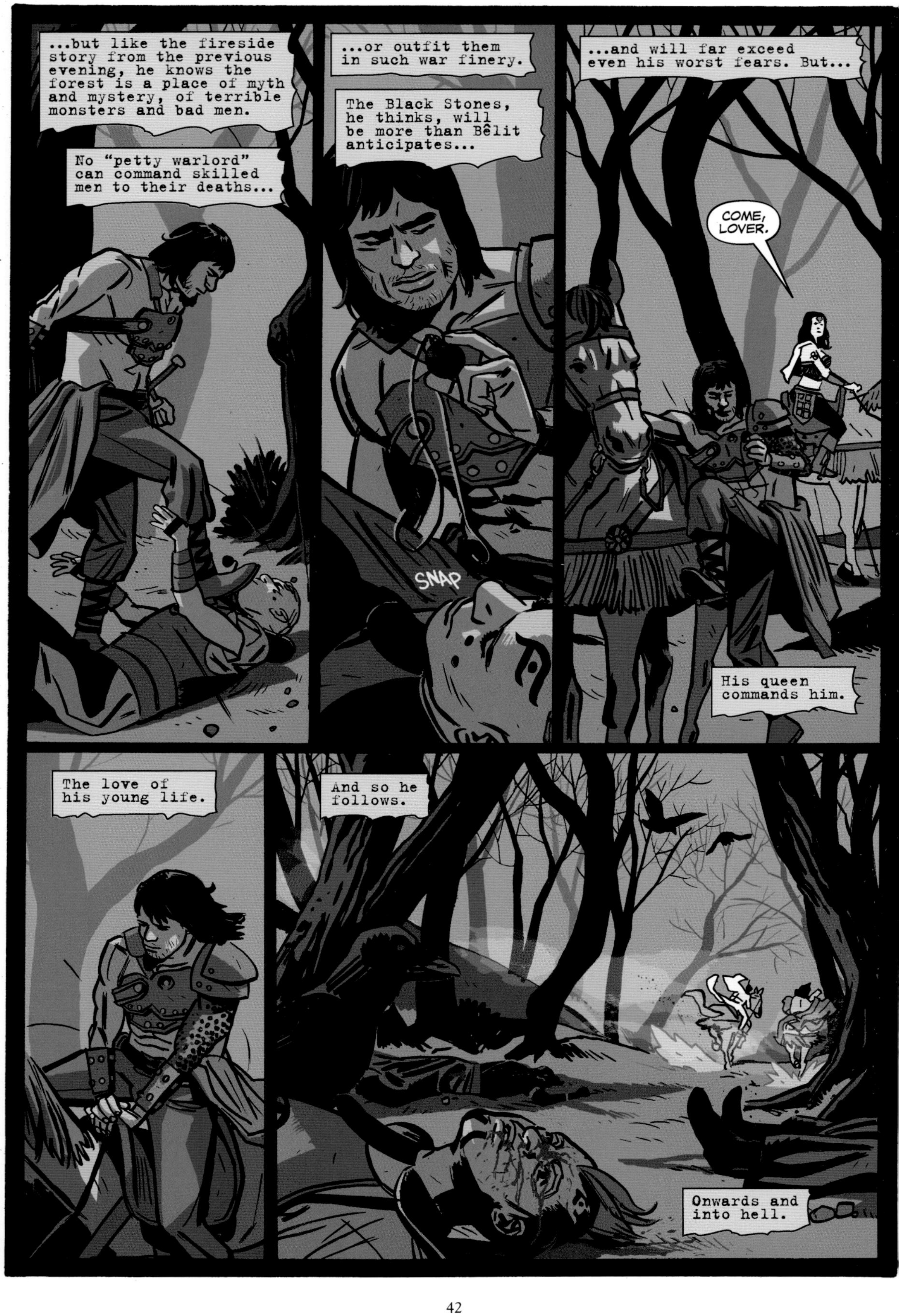
...but like the fireside story from the previous evening, he knows the forest is a place of myth and mystery, of terrible monsters and bad men.
No "petty warlord" can command skilled men to their deaths...
...or outfit them in such war finery.
The Black Stones, he thinks, will be more than Bêlit anticipates...
SNAP
...and will far exceed even his worst fears. But...
COME, LOVER.
His queen commands him.
The love of his young life.
And so he follows.
Onwards and into hell.

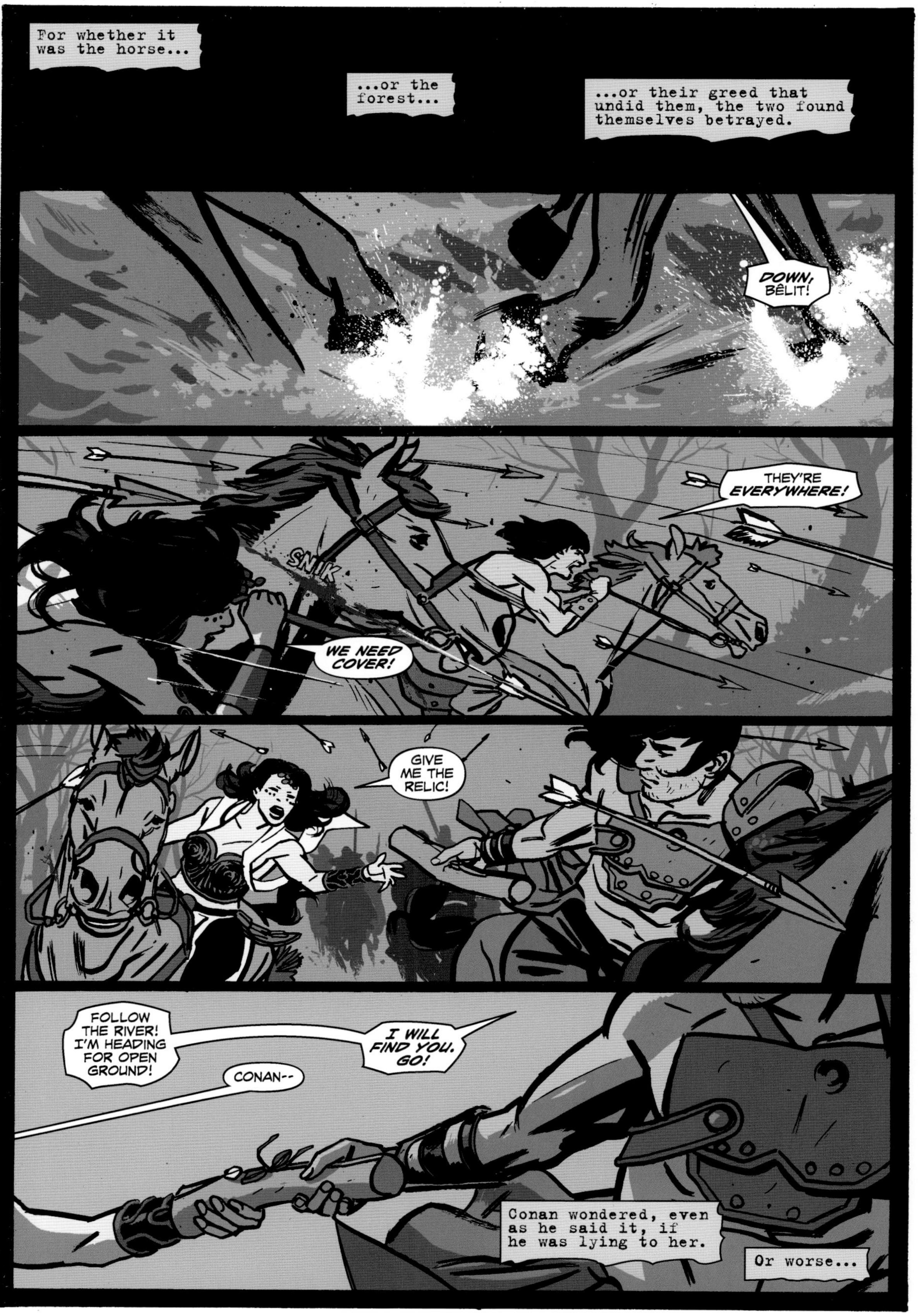
For whether it was the horse...
...or the forest...
...or their greed that undid them, the two found themselves betrayed.
DOWN, BÊLIT!
THEY'RE EVERYWHERE!
SNIK
WE NEED COVER!
GIVE ME THE RELIC!
FOLLOW THE RIVER! I'M HEADING FOR OPEN GROUND!
I WILL FIND YOU. GO!
CONAN--
Conan wondered, even as he said it, if he was lying to her.
Or worse...

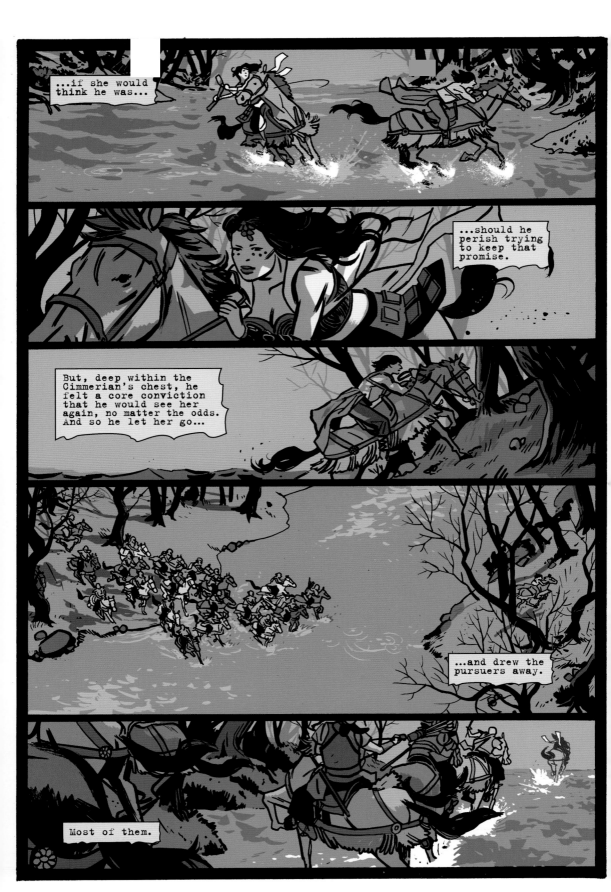

...if she would think he was...

...should he perish trying to keep that promise.

But, deep within the Cimmerian's chest, he felt a core conviction that he would see her again, no matter the odds. And so he let her go...

...and drew the pursuers away.

Most of them.

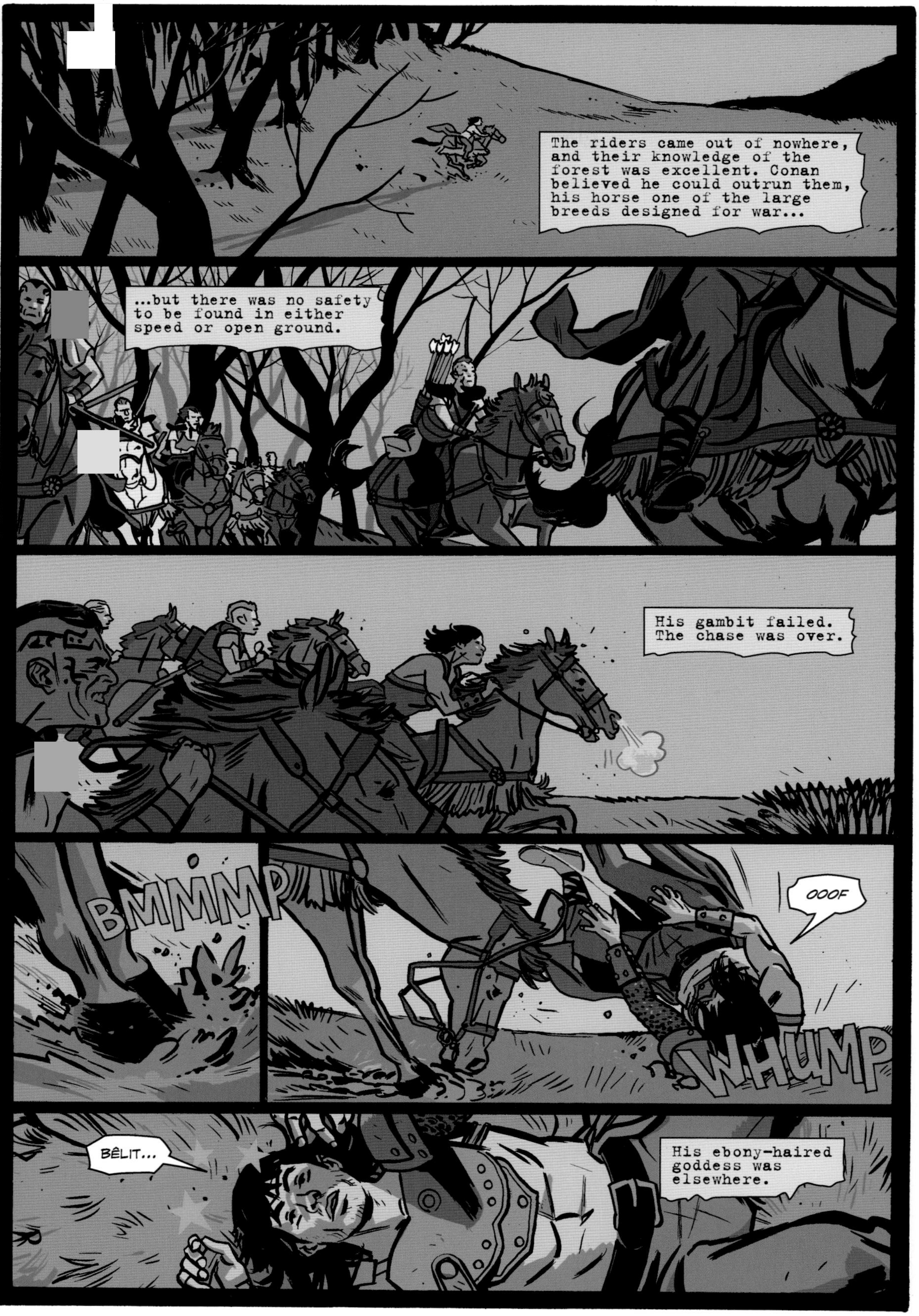

The riders came out of nowhere, and their knowledge of the forest was excellent. Conan believed he could outrun them, his horse one of the large breeds designed for war...
...but there was no safety to be found in either speed or open ground.
His gambit failed. The chase was over.
BMMMP
OOOF
WHUMP
BÊLIT...
His ebony-haired goddess was elsewhere.

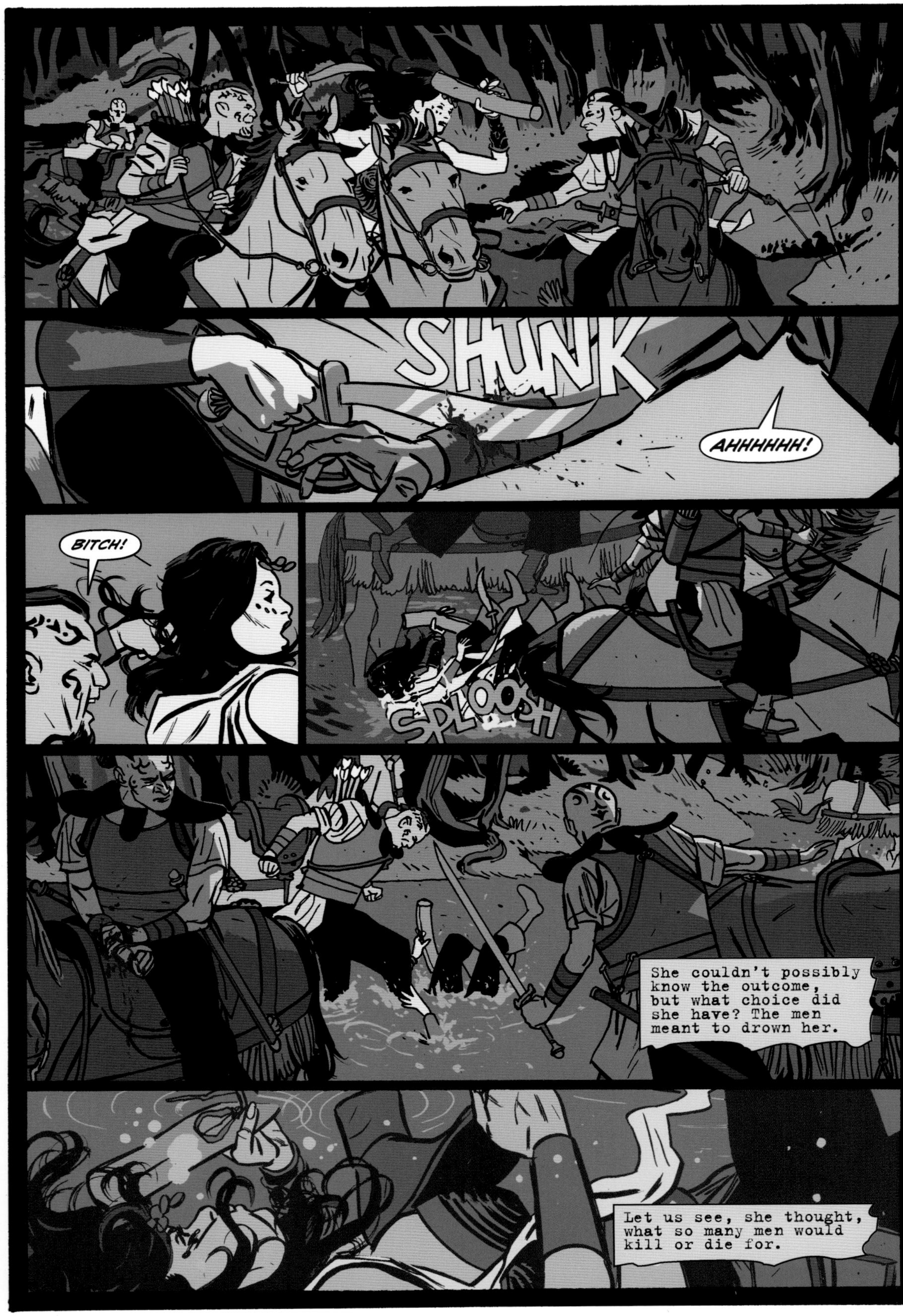
SHUNK
AHHHHHH!
BITCH!
SPLOOSH
She couldn't possibly know the outcome, but what choice did she have? The men meant to drown her.
Let us see, she thought, what so many men would kill or die for.

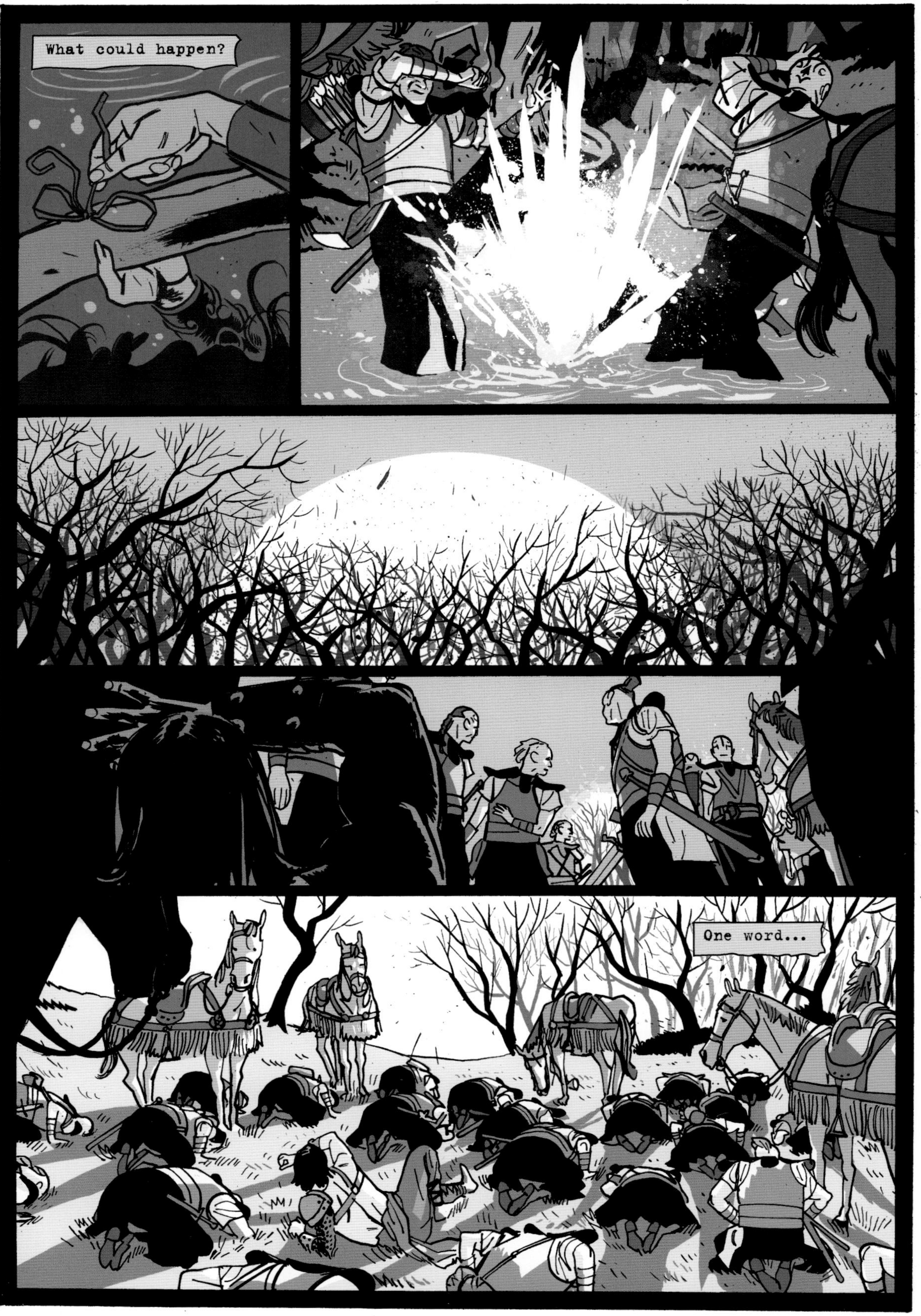
What could happen?
One word...

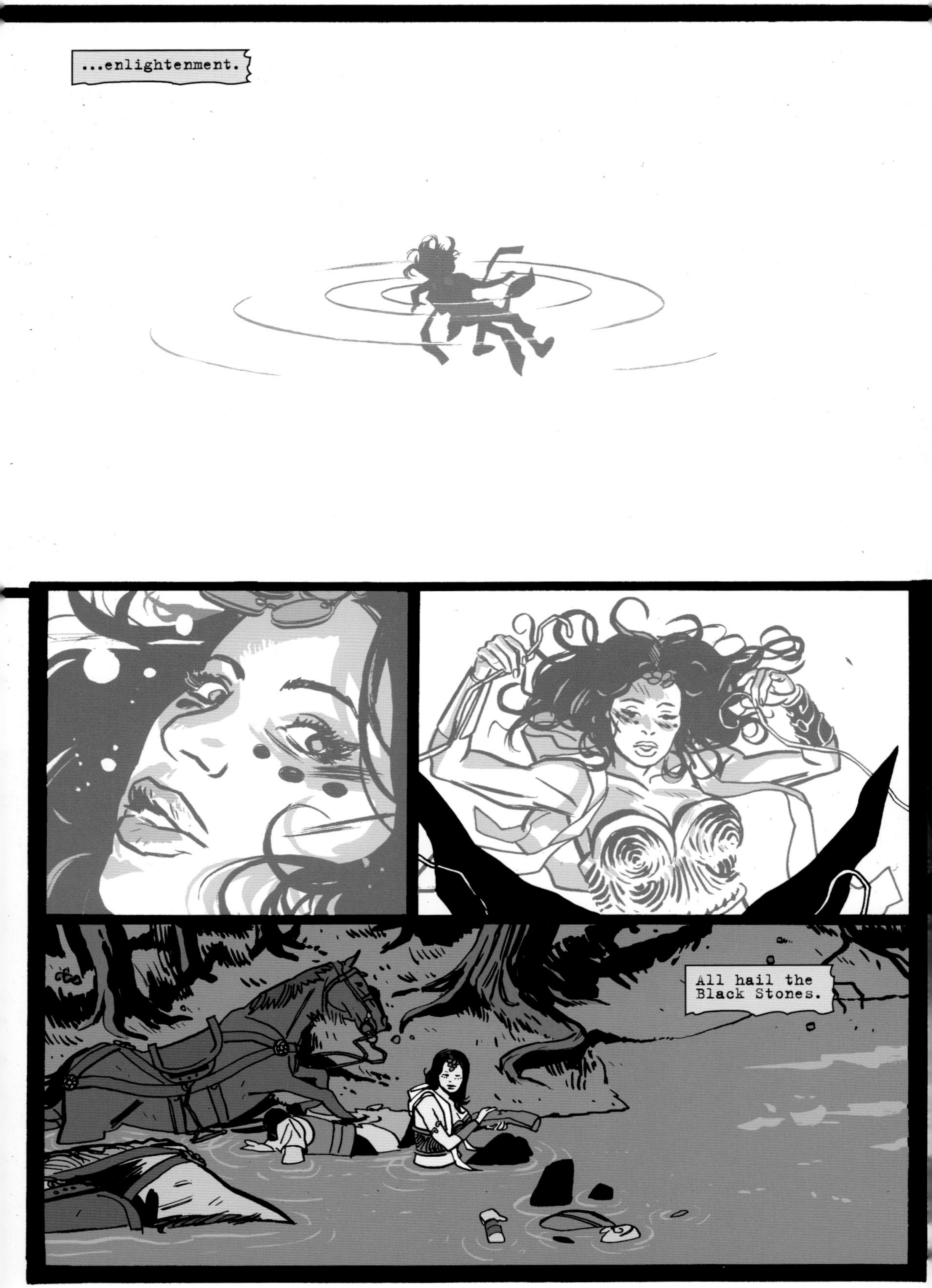
...enlightenment.
All hail the Black Stones.

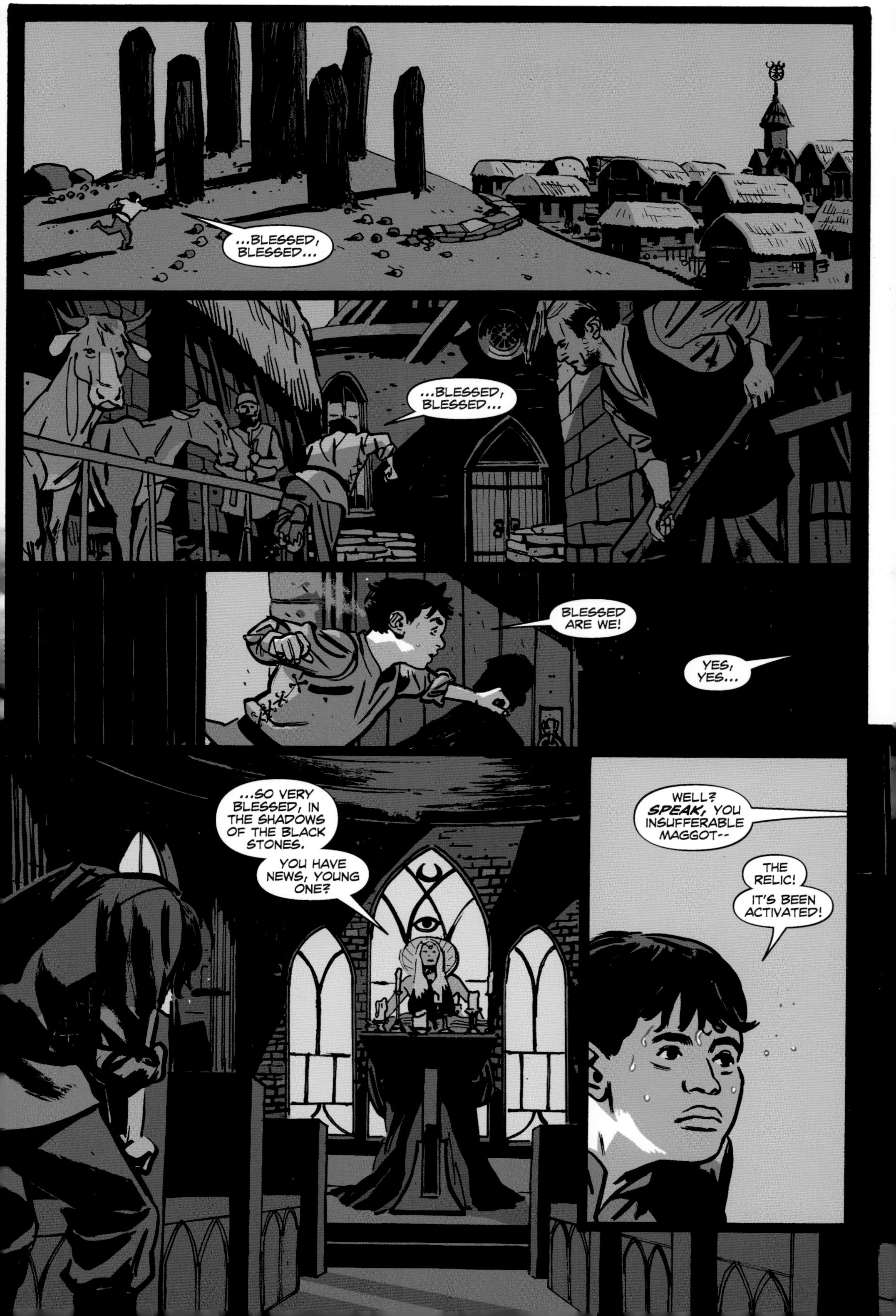

...BLESSED, BLESSED...
...BLESSED, BLESSED...
BLESSED ARE WE!
YES, YES...
...SO VERY BLESSED, IN THE SHADOWS OF THE BLACK STONES.
YOU HAVE NEWS, YOUNG ONE?
WELL? SPEAK, YOU INSUFFERABLE MAGGOT--
THE RELIC!
IT'S BEEN ACTIVATED!

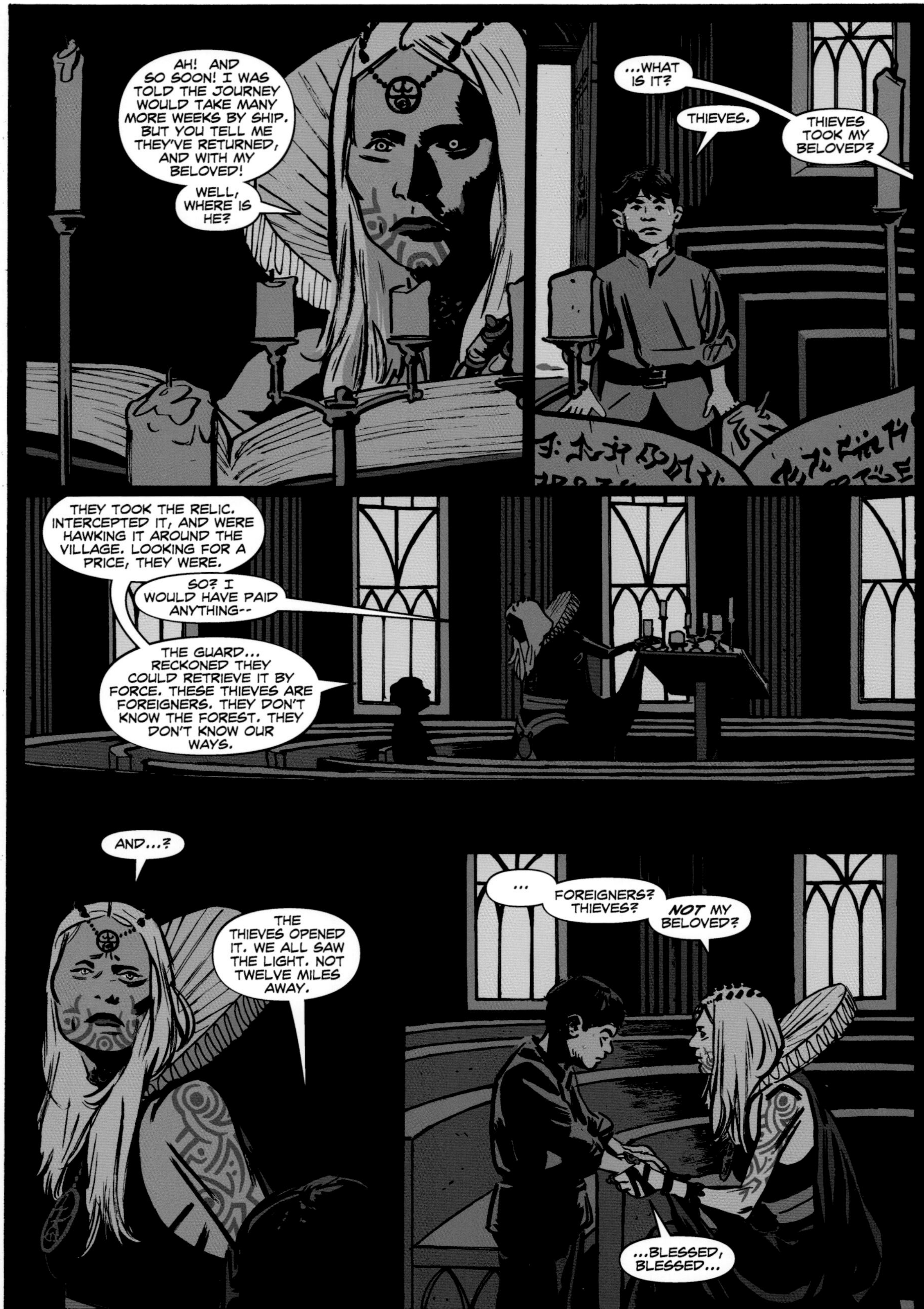
AH! AND SO SOON! I WAS TOLD THE JOURNEY WOULD TAKE MANY MORE WEEKS BY SHIP. BUT YOU TELL ME THEY'VE RETURNED, AND WITH MY BELOVED!
WELL, WHERE IS HE?
...WHAT IS IT?
THIEVES.
THIEVES TOOK MY BELOVED?
THEY TOOK THE RELIC. INTERCEPTED IT, AND WERE HAWKING IT AROUND THE VILLAGE. LOOKING FOR A PRICE, THEY WERE.
SO? I WOULD HAVE PAID ANYTHING--
THE GUARD... RECKONED THEY COULD RETRIEVE IT BY FORCE. THESE THIEVES ARE FOREIGNERS. THEY DON'T KNOW THE FOREST. THEY DON'T KNOW OUR WAYS.
AND...?
THE THIEVES OPENED IT. WE ALL SAW THE LIGHT. NOT TWELVE MILES AWAY.
...
FOREIGNERS? THIEVES?
NOT MY BELOVED?
...BLESSED, BLESSED...

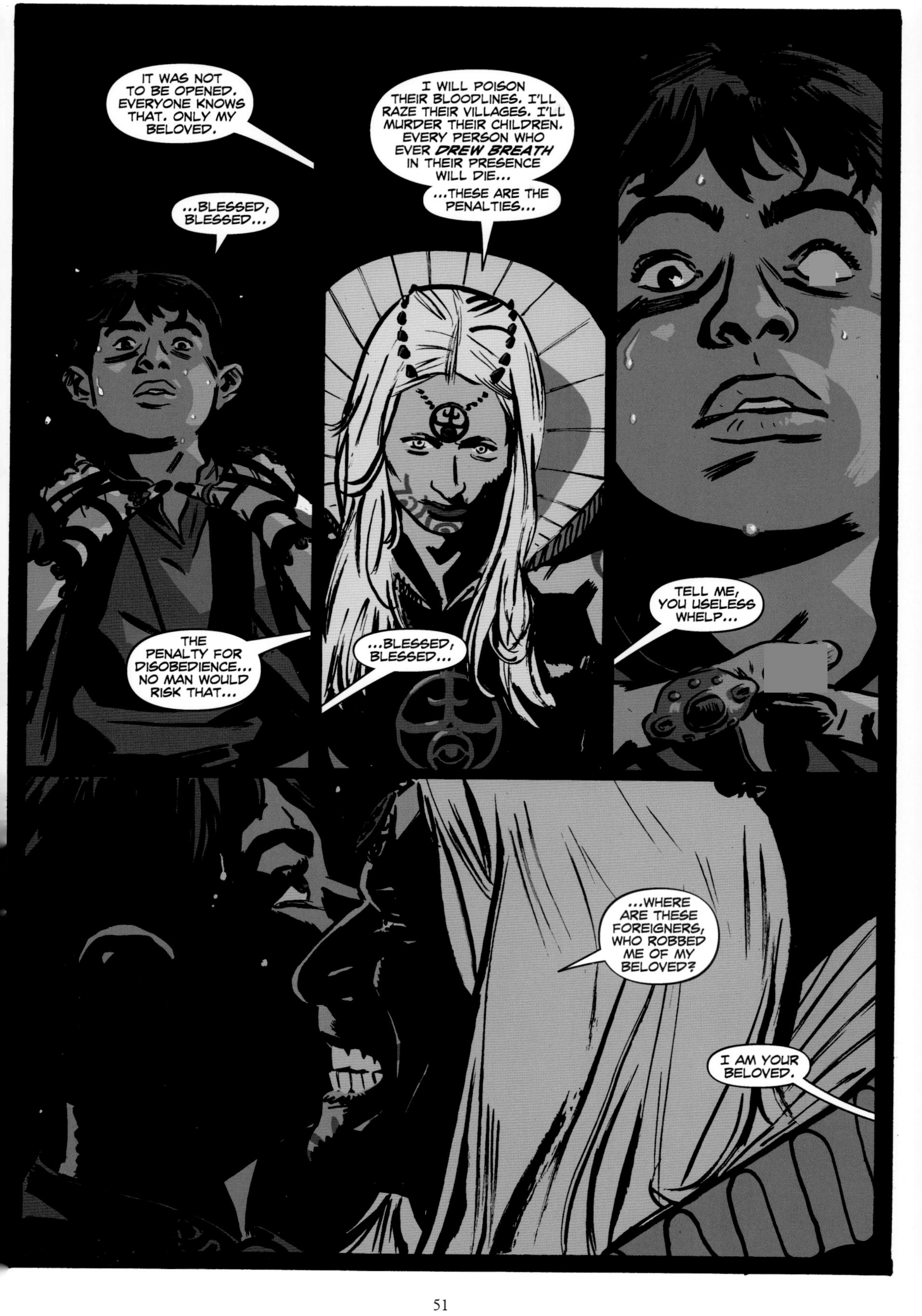
IT WAS NOT TO BE OPENED. EVERYONE KNOWS THAT. ONLY MY BELOVED.
...BLESSED, BLESSED...
I WILL POISON THEIR BLOODLINES. I'LL RAZE THEIR VILLAGES. I'LL MURDER THEIR CHILDREN. EVERY PERSON WHO EVER DREW BREATH IN THEIR PRESENCE WILL DIE...
...THESE ARE THE PENALTIES...
THE PENALTY FOR DISOBEDIENCE... NO MAN WOULD RISK THAT...
...BLESSED, BLESSED...
TELL ME, YOU USELESS WHELP...
...WHERE ARE THESE FOREIGNERS, WHO ROBBED ME OF MY BELOVED?
I AM YOUR BELOVED.

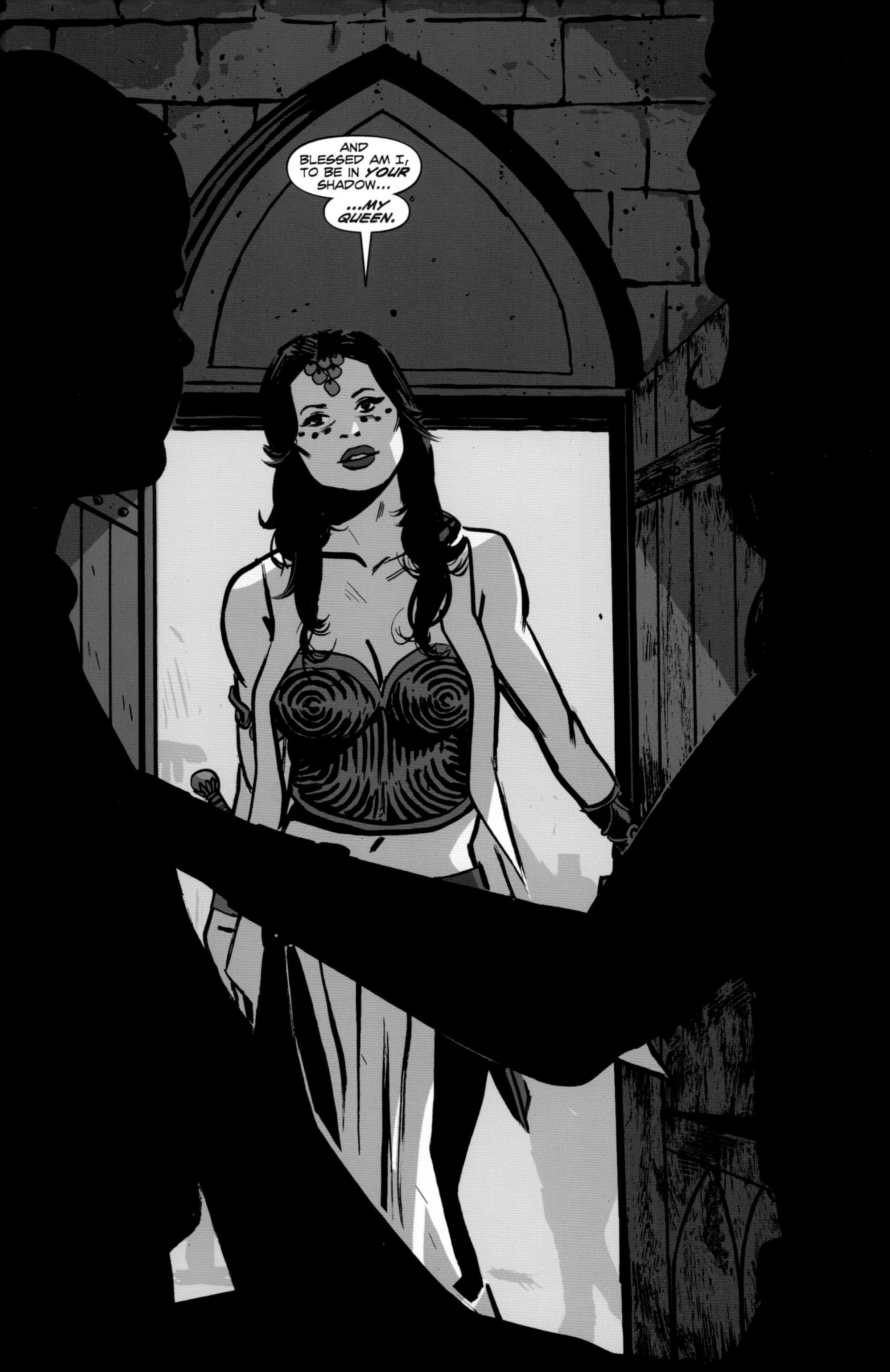
AND BLESSED AM I, TO BE IN YOUR SHADOW...
...MY QUEEN.

CHAPTER THREE

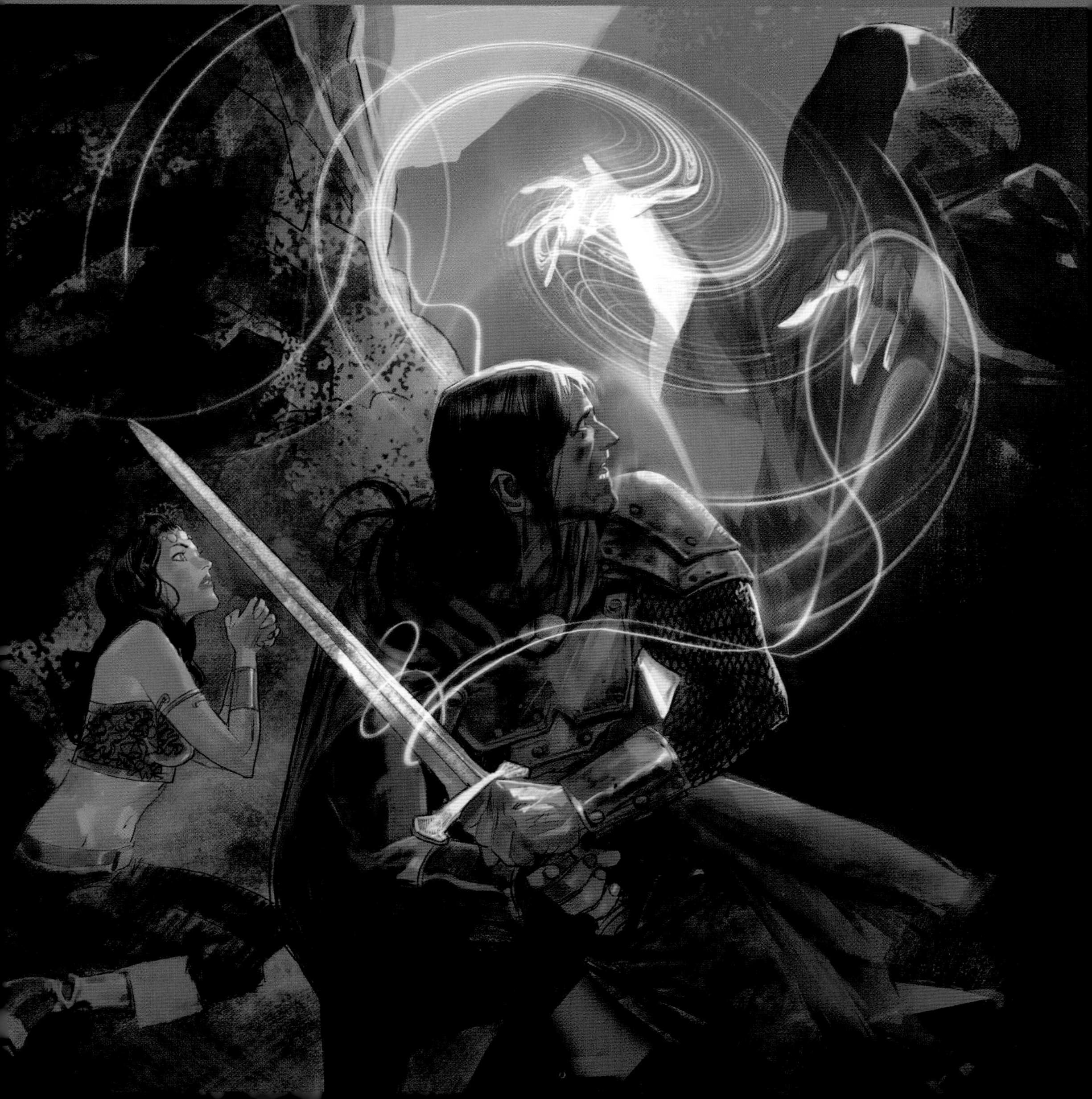

"If you are correct, boy, the stones may strike me down dead, for there is none other for me in this life but my beloved."

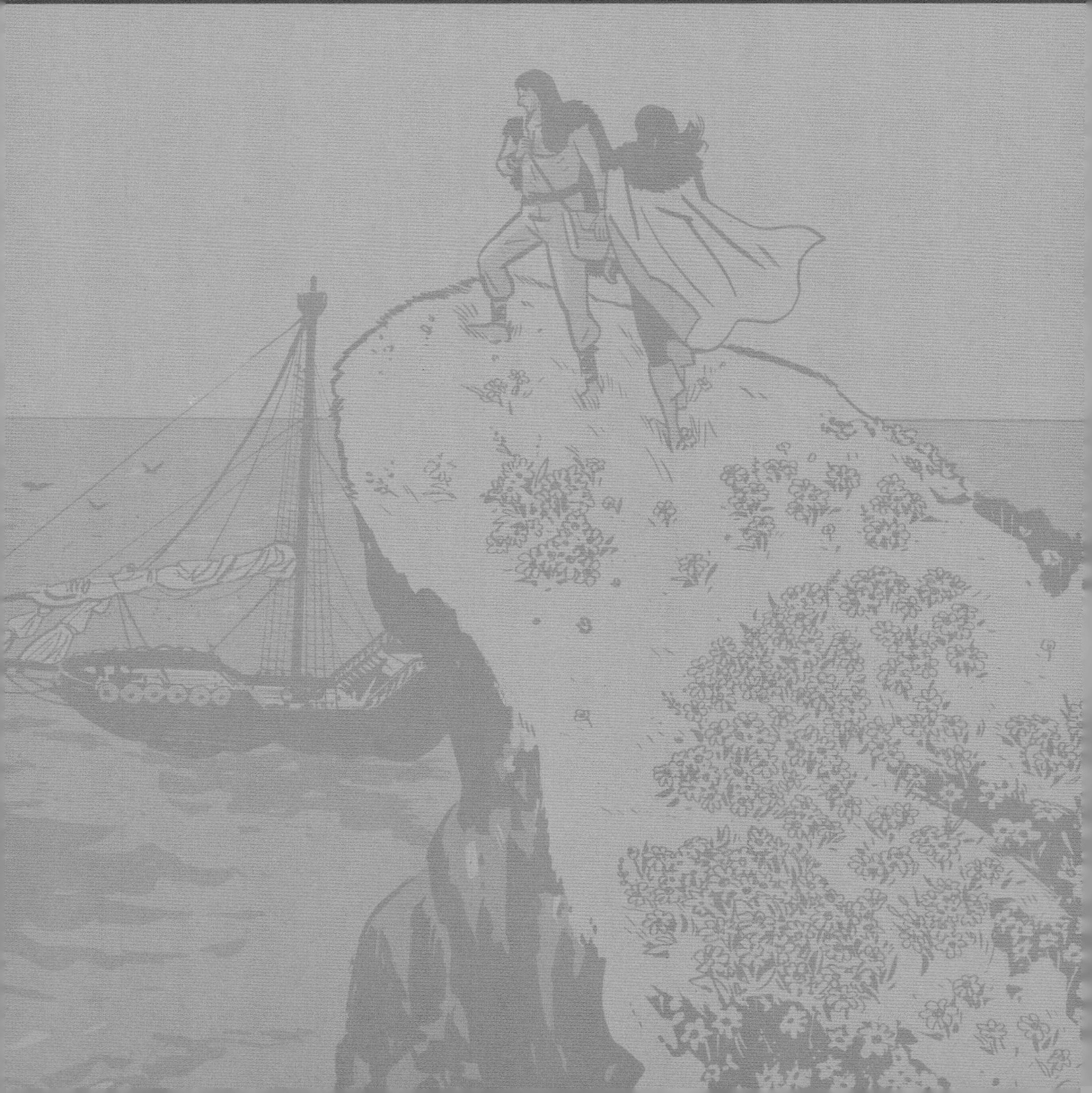

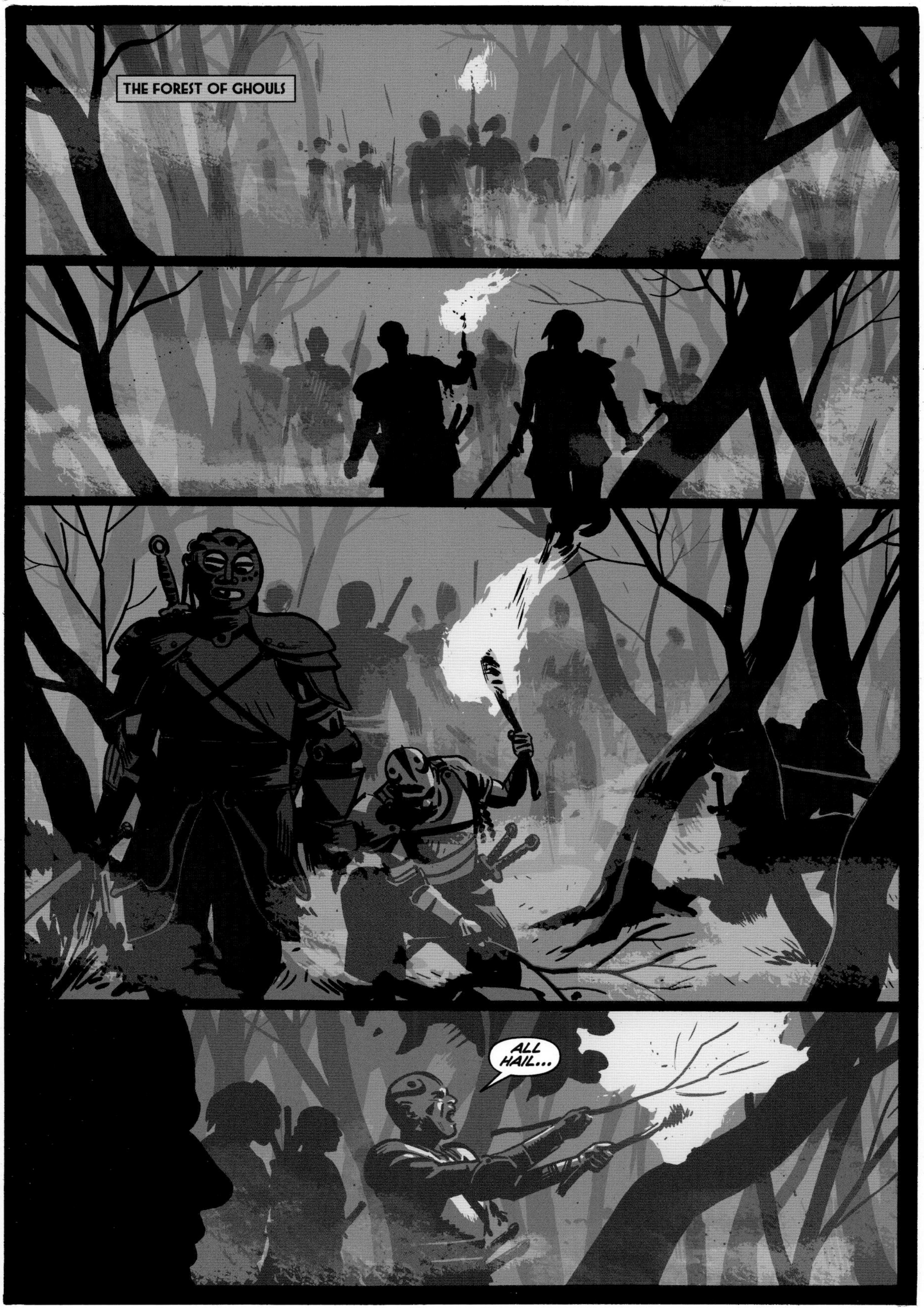
THE FOREST OF GHOULS
ALL HAIL...

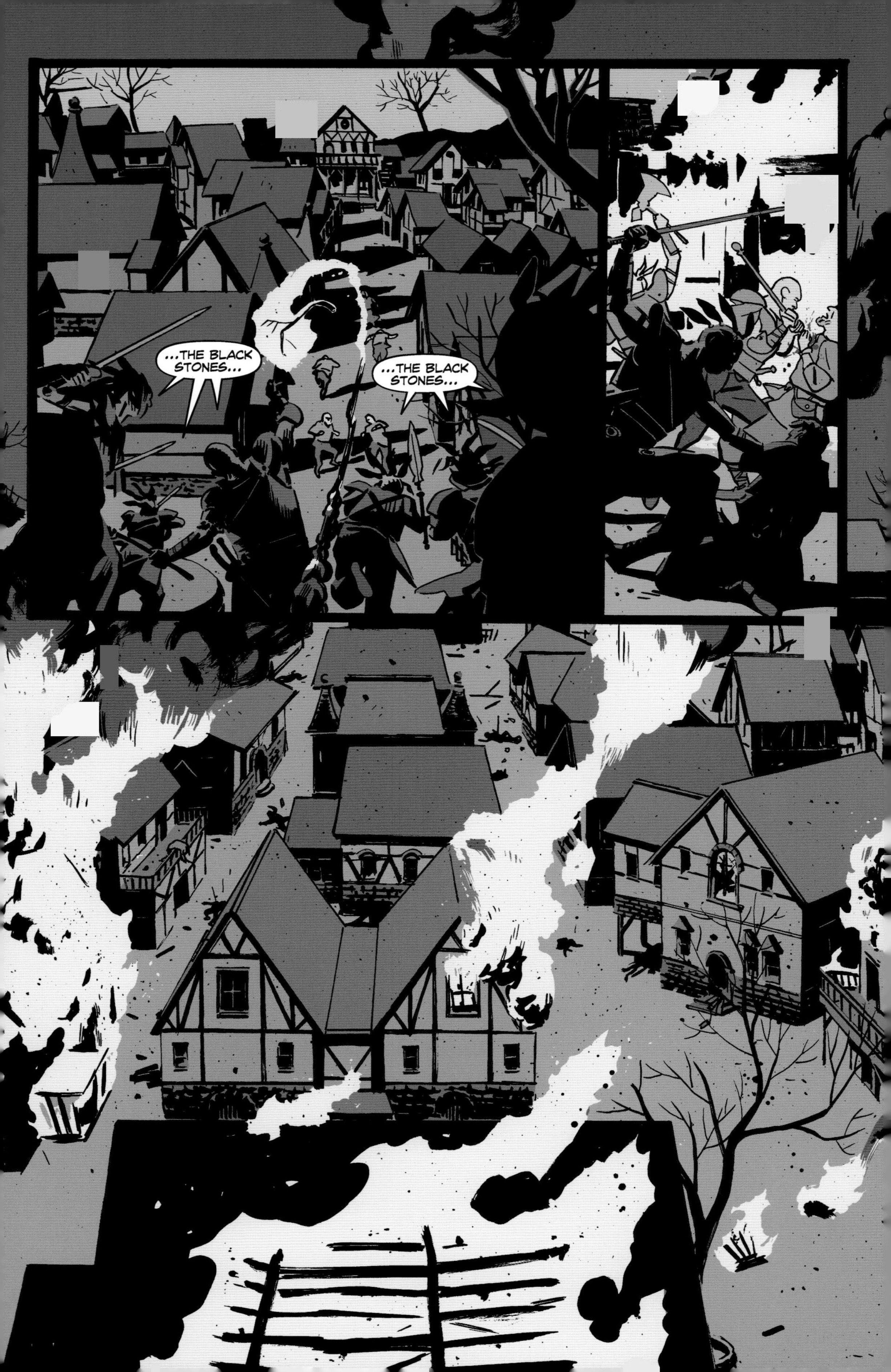
...THE BLACK STONES...
...THE BLACK STONES...

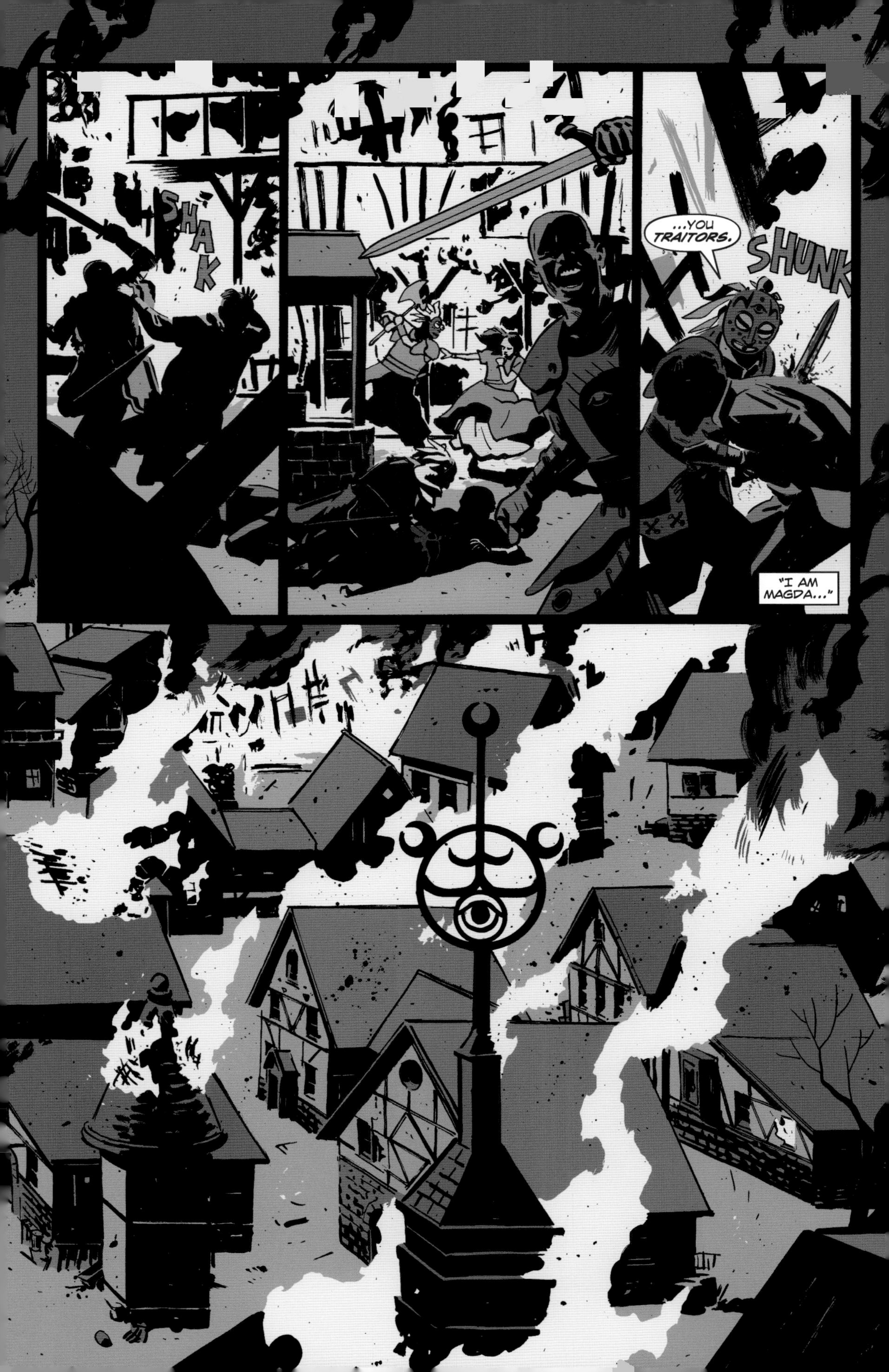
SHAK
...YOU TRAITORS.
SHUNK
"I AM MAGDA..."

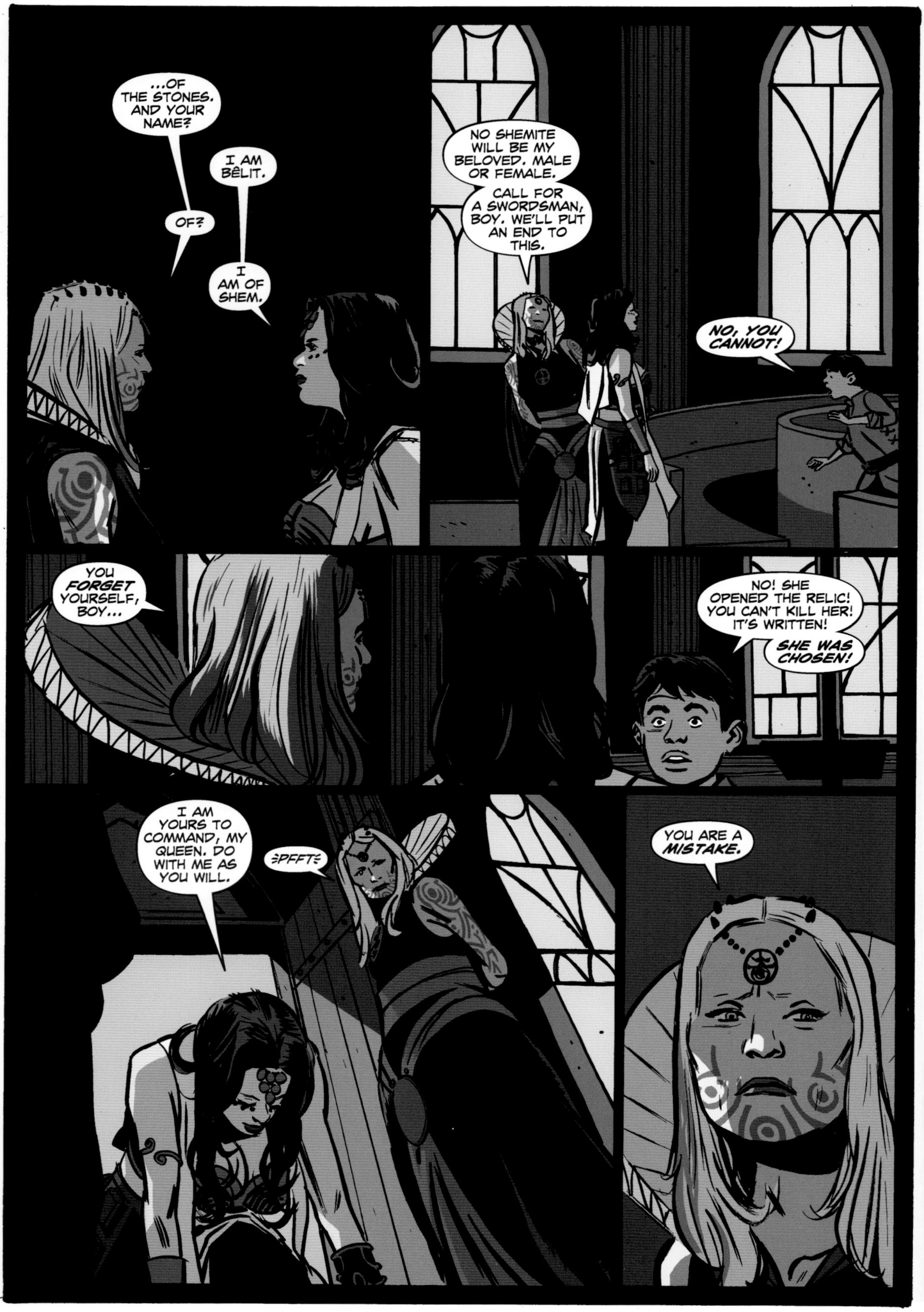
...OF THE STONES. AND YOUR NAME?
I AM BÊLIT.
OF?
I AM OF SHEM.
NO SHEMITE WILL BE MY BELOVED. MALE OR FEMALE.
CALL FOR A SWORDSMAN, BOY. WE'LL PUT AN END TO THIS.
NO, YOU CANNOT!
YOU FORGET YOURSELF, BOY...
NO! SHE OPENED THE RELIC! YOU CAN'T KILL HER! IT'S WRITTEN!
SHE WAS CHOSEN!
I AM YOURS TO COMMAND, MY QUEEN. DO WITH ME AS YOU WILL.
PFFT
YOU ARE A MISTAKE.

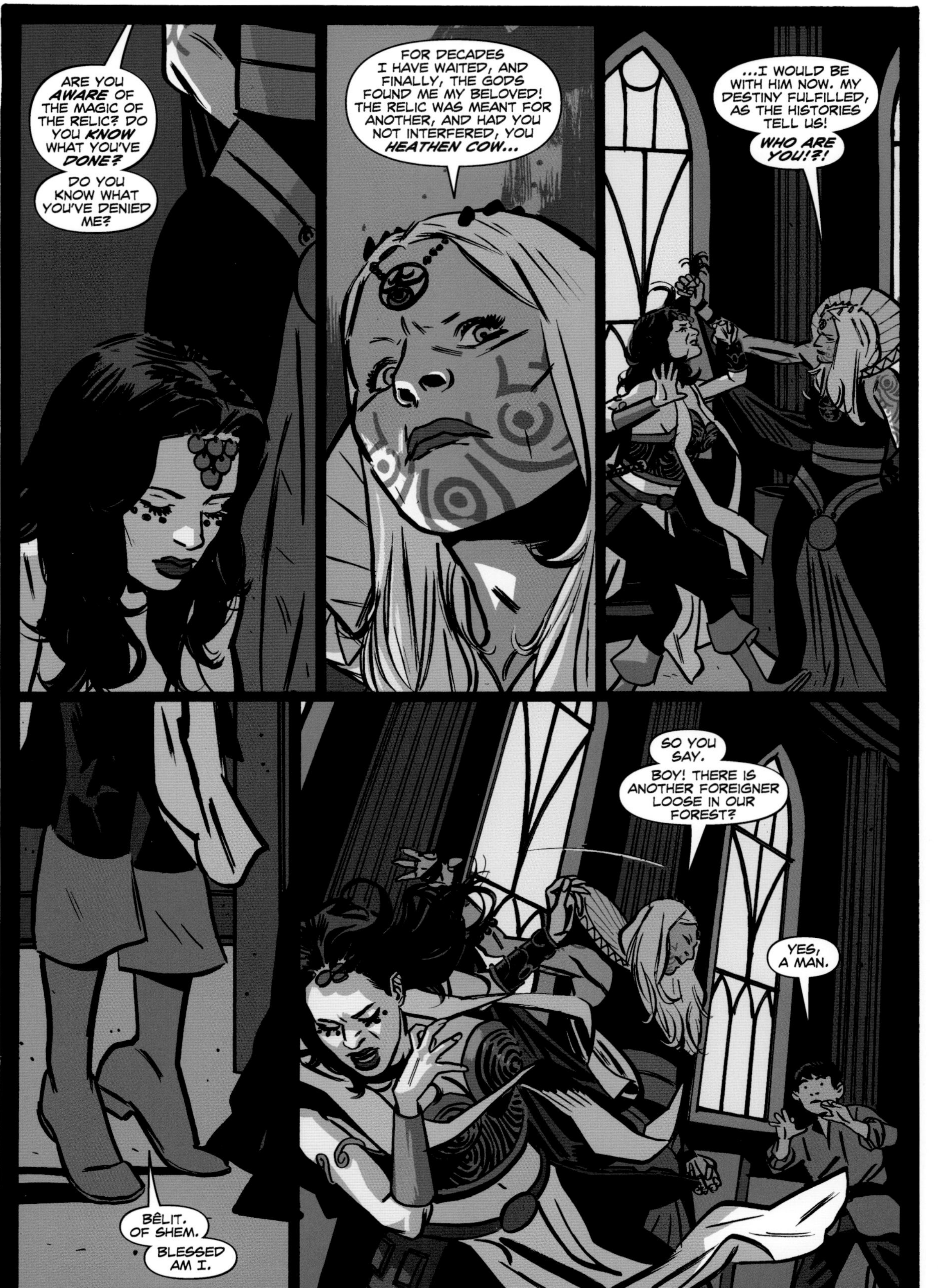

ARE YOU AWARE OF THE MAGIC OF THE RELIC? DO YOU KNOW WHAT YOU'VE DONE?
DO YOU KNOW WHAT YOU'VE DENIED ME?
FOR DECADES I HAVE WAITED, AND FINALLY, THE GODS FOUND ME MY BELOVED! THE RELIC WAS MEANT FOR ANOTHER, AND HAD YOU NOT INTERFERED, YOU HEATHEN COW...
...I WOULD BE WITH HIM NOW. MY DESTINY FULFILLED, AS THE HISTORIES TELL US!
WHO ARE YOU!?!
BÊLIT. OF SHEM.
BLESSED AM I.
SO YOU SAY.
BOY! THERE IS ANOTHER FOREIGNER LOOSE IN OUR FOREST?
YES, A MAN.

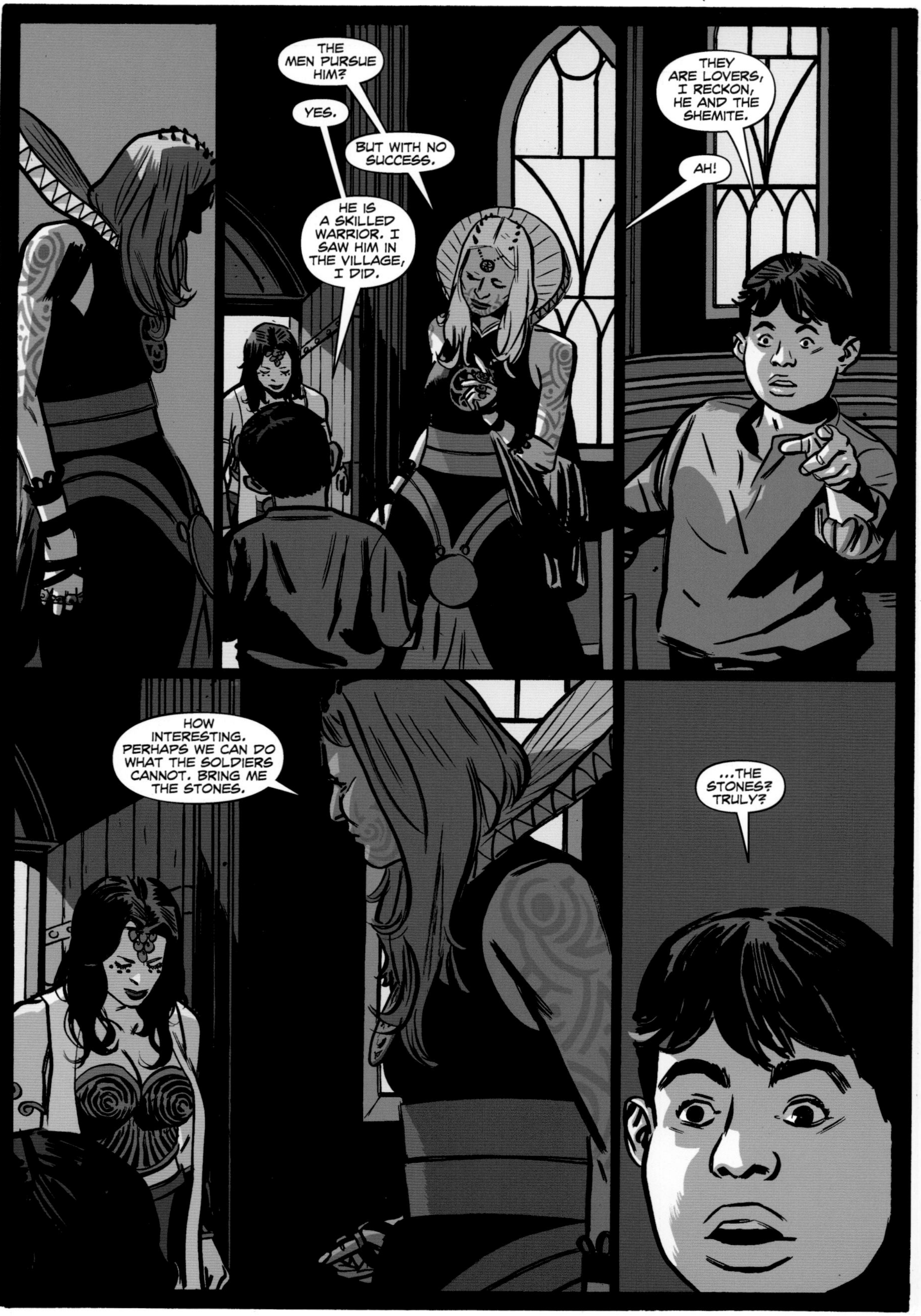
THE MEN PURSUE HIM?
YES.
BUT WITH NO SUCCESS.
HE IS A SKILLED WARRIOR. I SAW HIM IN THE VILLAGE, I DID.
THEY ARE LOVERS, I RECKON, HE AND THE SHEMITE.
AH!
HOW INTERESTING. PERHAPS WE CAN DO WHAT THE SOLDIERS CANNOT. BRING ME THE STONES.
...THE STONES? TRULY?

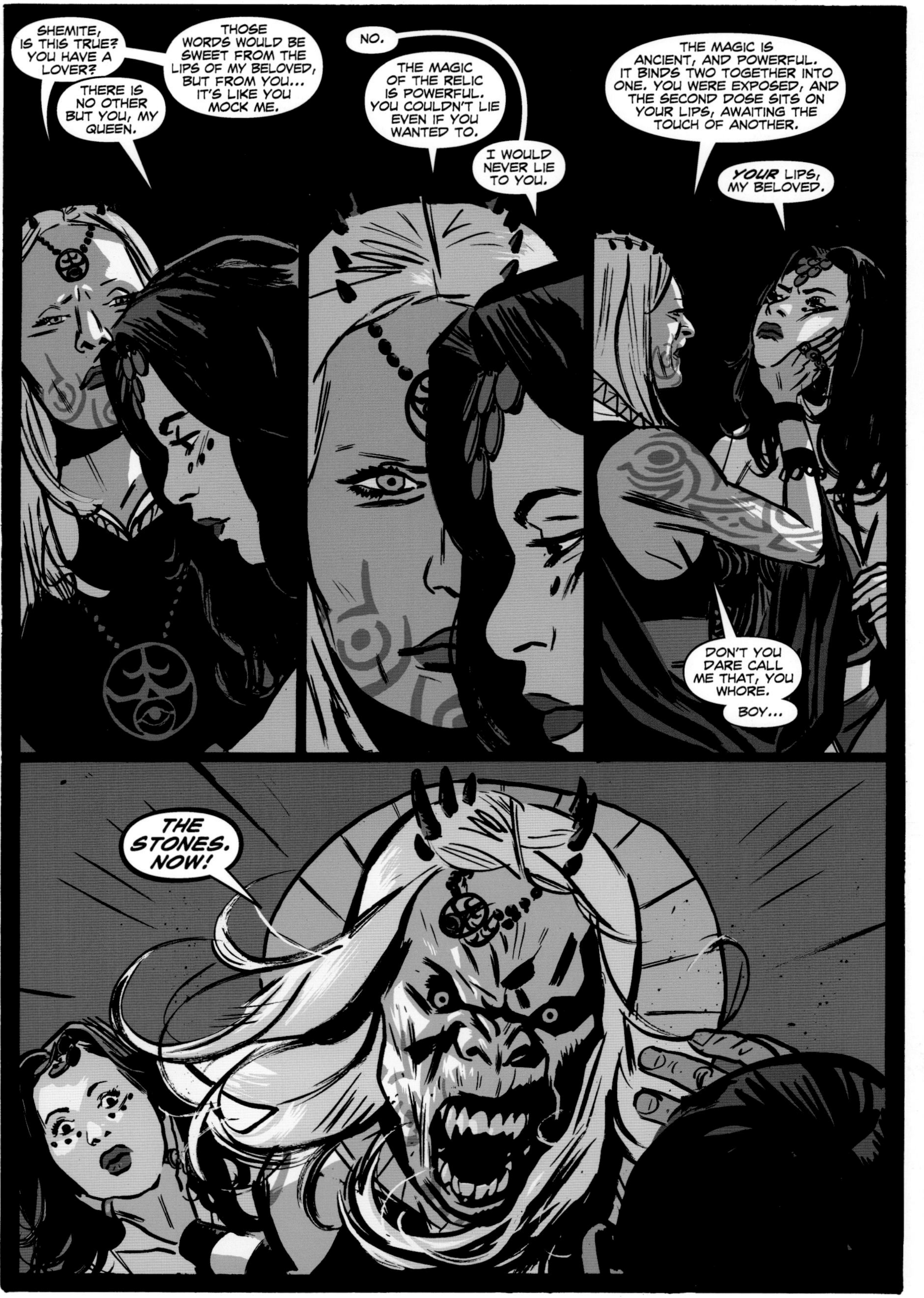
SHEMITE, IS THIS TRUE? YOU HAVE A LOVER?
THERE IS NO OTHER BUT YOU, MY QUEEN.
THOSE WORDS WOULD BE SWEET FROM THE LIPS OF MY BELOVED, BUT FROM YOU... IT'S LIKE YOU MOCK ME.
NO.
THE MAGIC OF THE RELIC IS POWERFUL. YOU COULDN'T LIE EVEN IF YOU WANTED TO.
I WOULD NEVER LIE TO YOU.
THE MAGIC IS ANCIENT, AND POWERFUL. IT BINDS TWO TOGETHER INTO ONE. YOU WERE EXPOSED, AND THE SECOND DOSE SITS ON YOUR LIPS, AWAITING THE TOUCH OF ANOTHER.
YOUR LIPS, MY BELOVED.
DON'T YOU DARE CALL ME THAT, YOU WHORE.
BOY...
THE STONES. NOW!

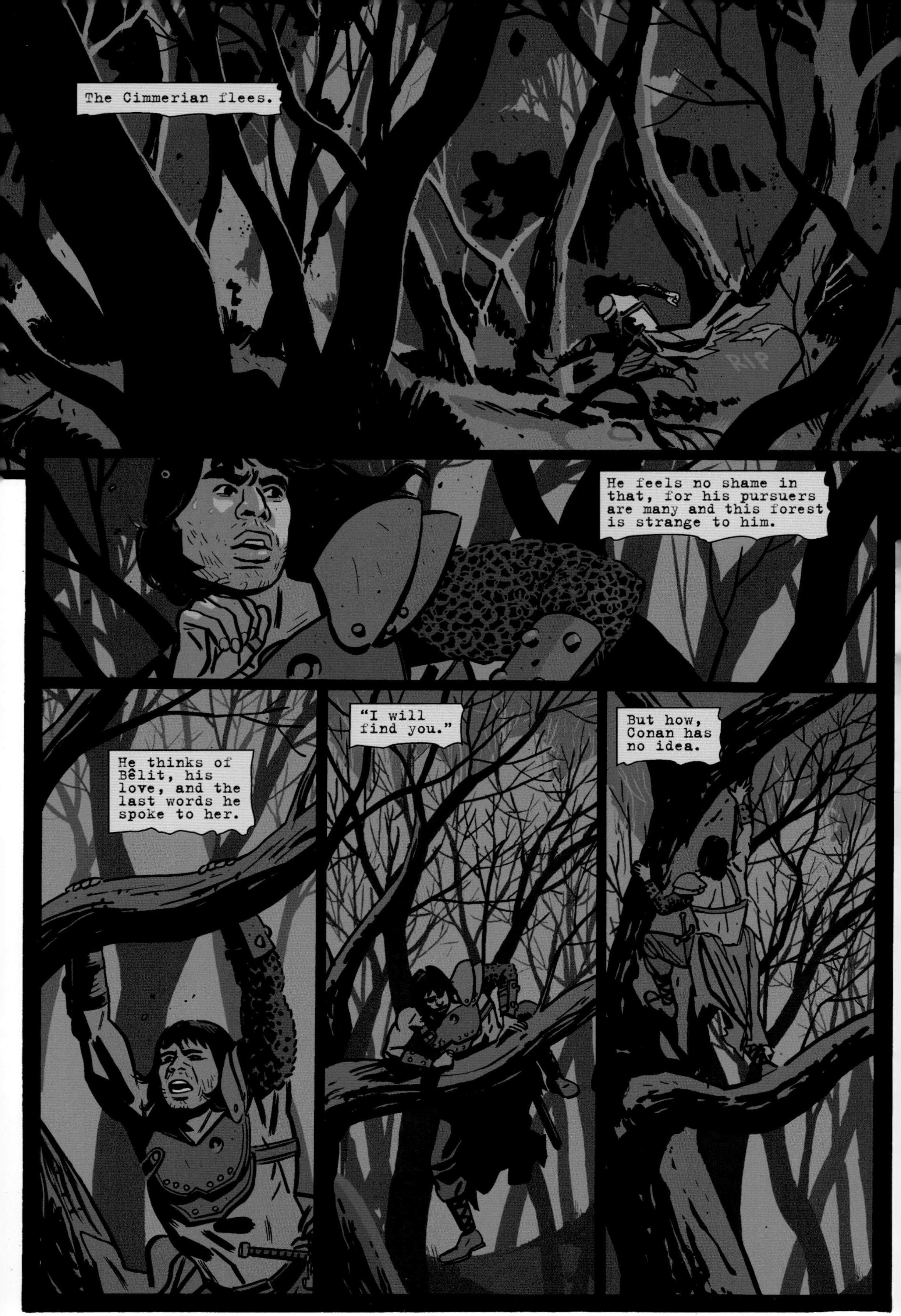
The Cimmerian flees.
RIP
He feels no shame in that, for his pursuers are many and this forest is strange to him.
He thinks of Bêlit, his love, and the last words he spoke to her.
"I will find you."
But how, Conan has no idea.

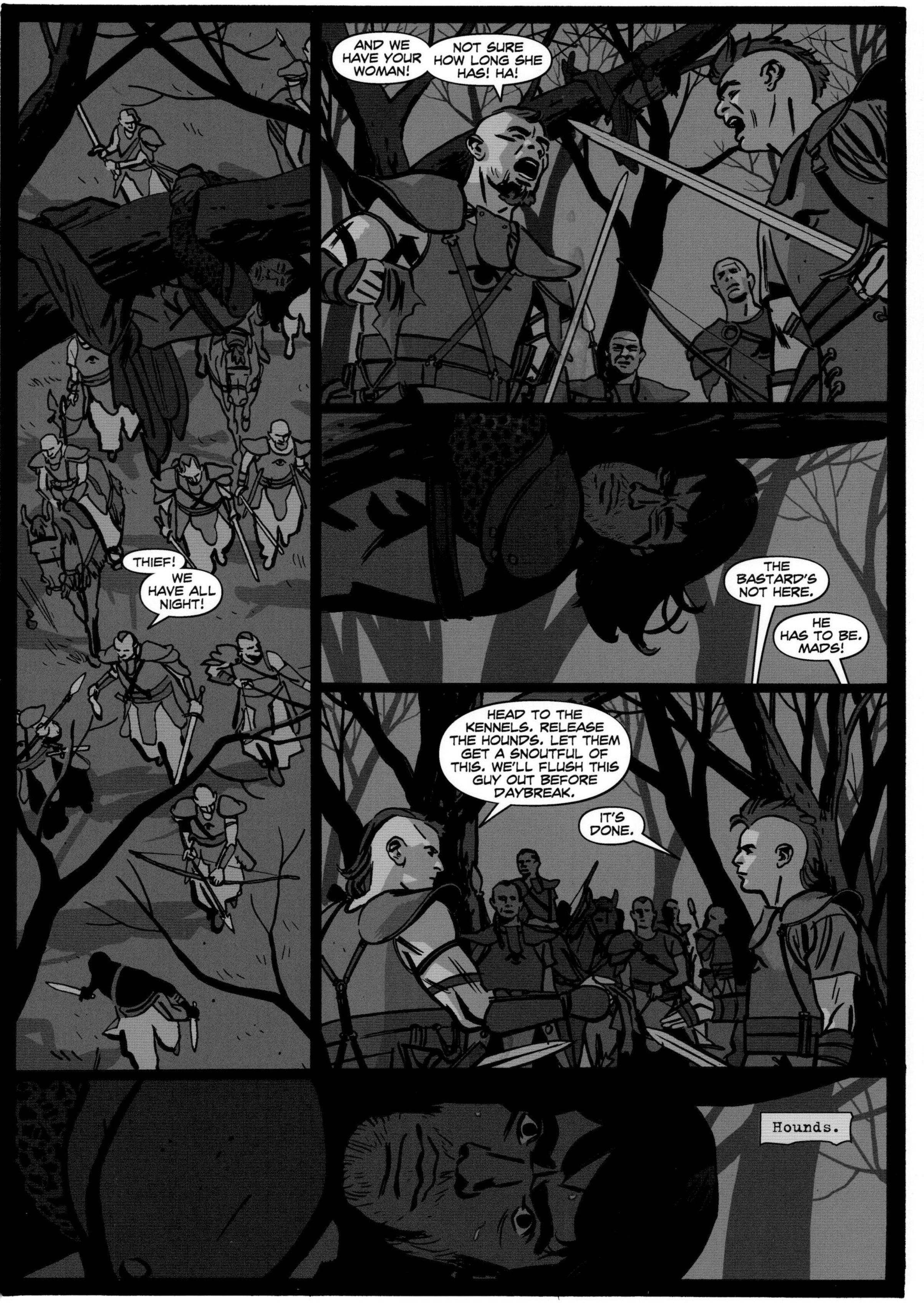
AND WE HAVE YOUR WOMAN!
NOT SURE HOW LONG SHE HAS! HA!
THIEF! WE HAVE ALL NIGHT!
THE BASTARD'S NOT HERE.
HE HAS TO BE. MADS!
HEAD TO THE KENNELS. RELEASE THE HOUNDS. LET THEM GET A SNOUTFUL OF THIS. WE'LL FLUSH THIS GUY OUT BEFORE DAYBREAK.
IT'S DONE.
Hounds.

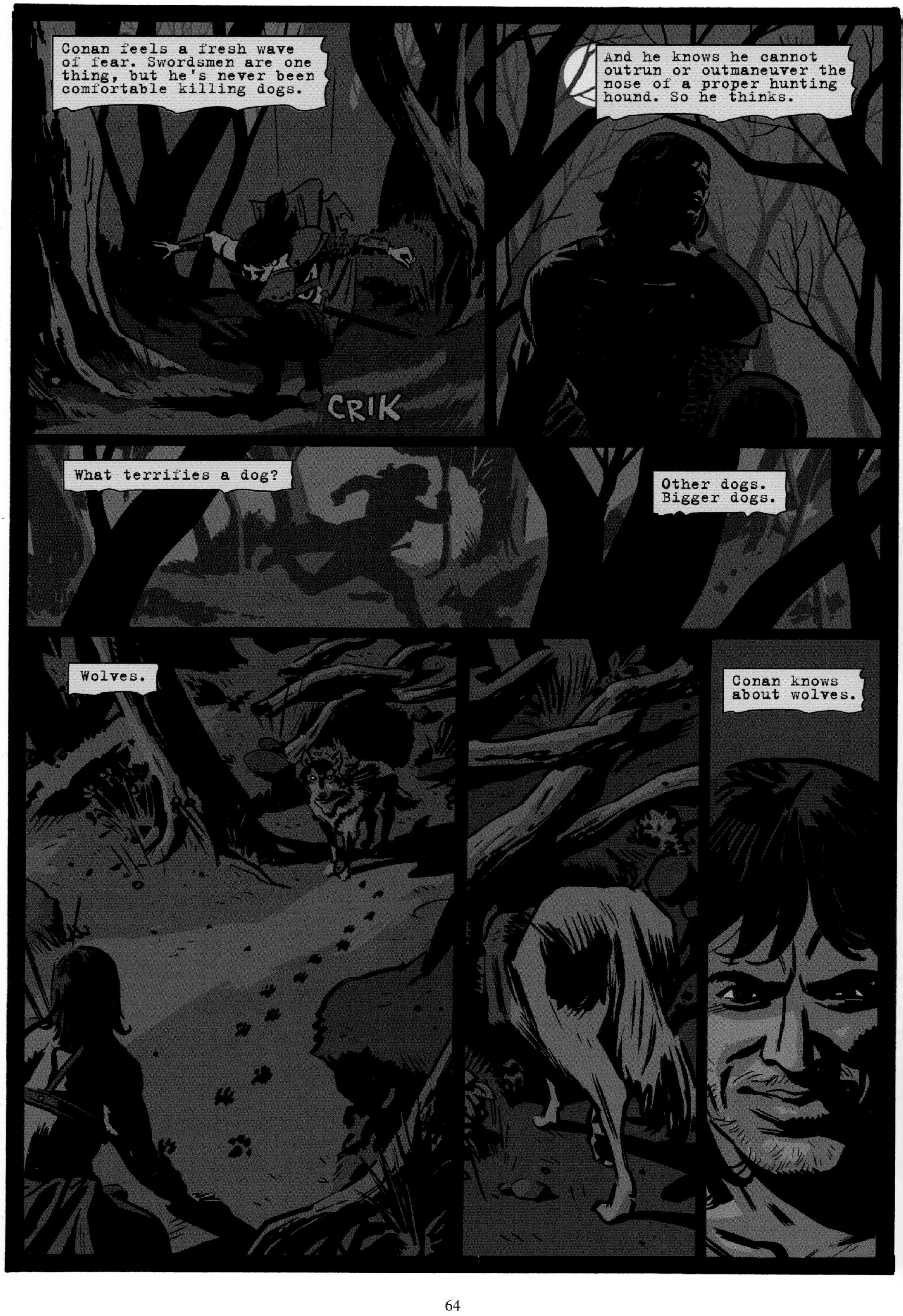
Conan feels a fresh wave of fear. Swordsmen are one thing, but he's never been comfortable killing dogs.
CRIK
And he knows he cannot outrun or outmaneuver the nose of a proper hunting hound. So he thinks.
What terrifies a dog?
Other dogs. Bigger dogs.
Wolves.
Conan knows about wolves.

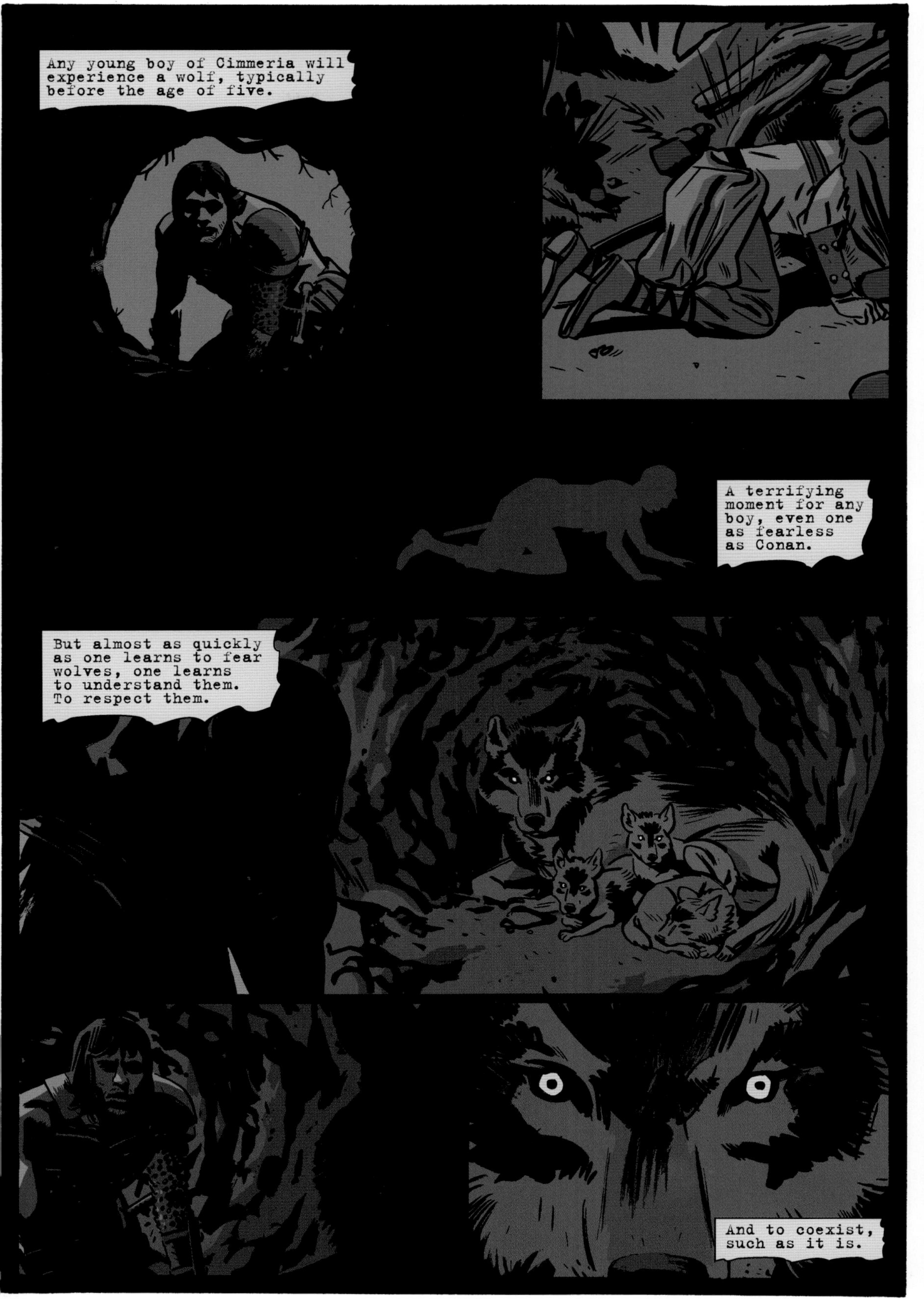
Any young boy of Cimmeria will experience a wolf, typically before the age of five.
A terrifying moment for any boy, even one as fearless as Conan.
But almost as quickly as one learns to fear wolves, one learns to understand them. To respect them.
And to coexist, such as it is.

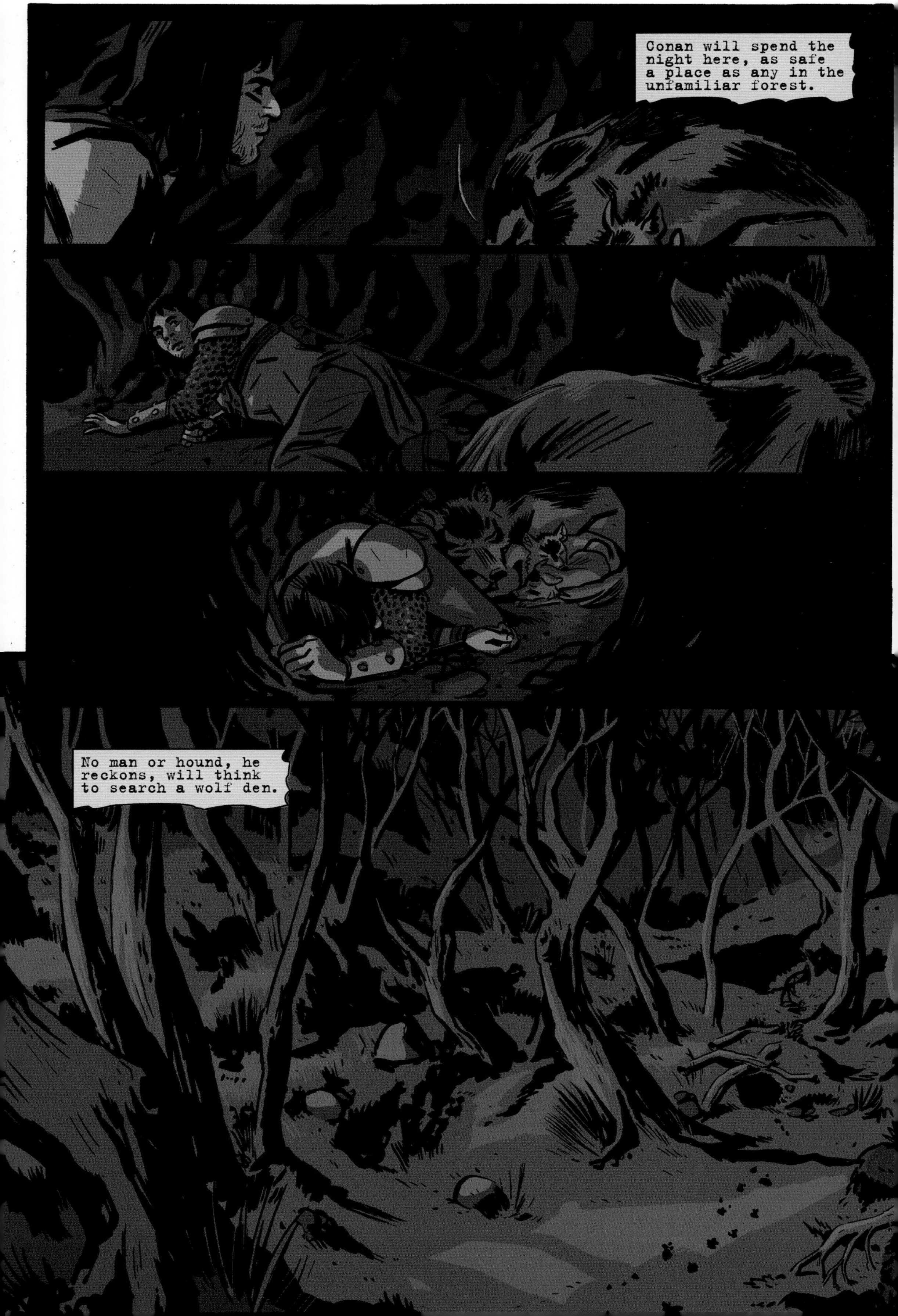
Conan will spend the night here, as safe a place as any in the unfamiliar forest.
No man or hound, he reckons, will think to search a wolf den.

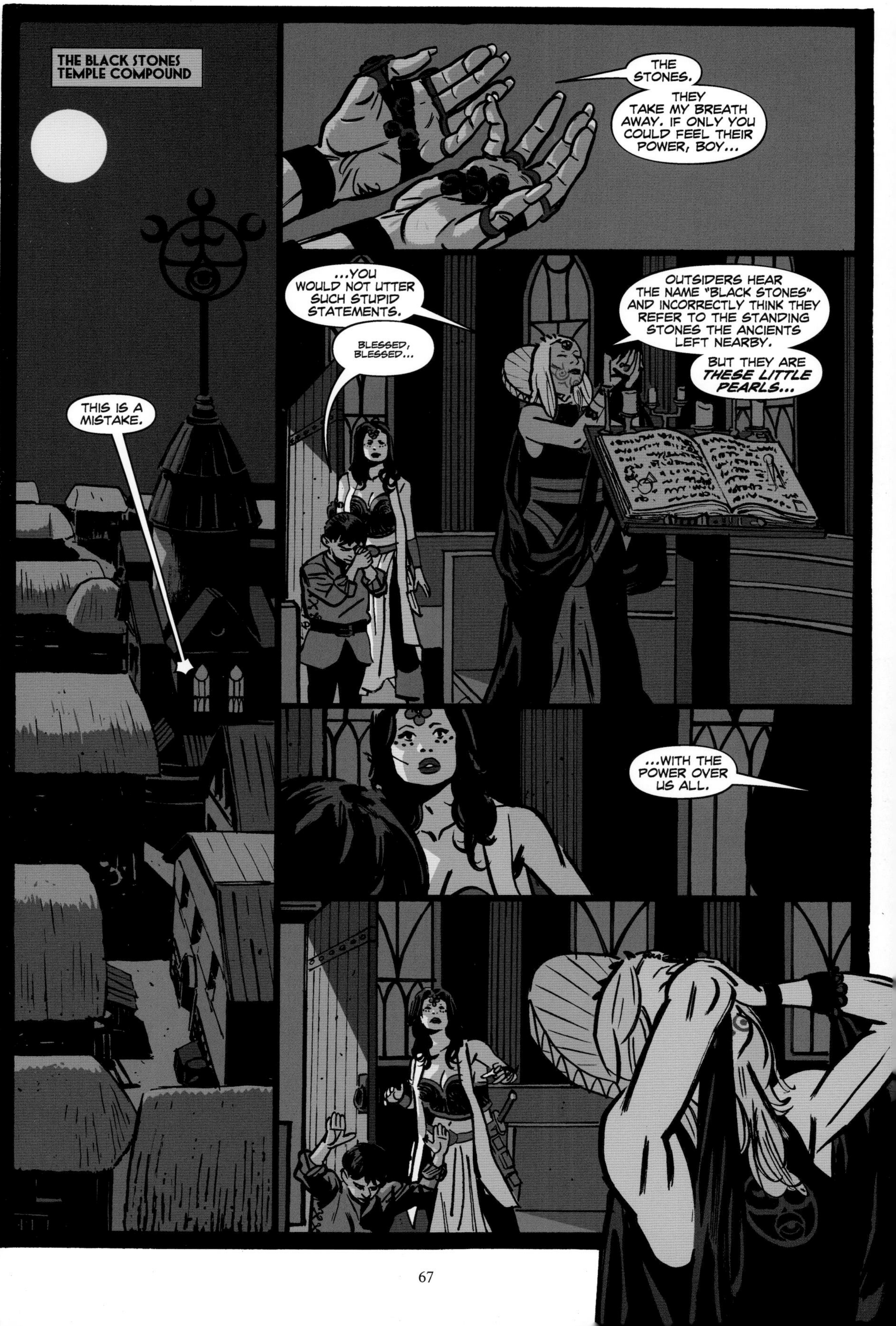
THE BLACK STONES TEMPLE COMPOUND
THIS IS A MISTAKE.
THE STONES.
THEY TAKE MY BREATH AWAY. IF ONLY YOU COULD FEEL THEIR POWER, BOY...
...YOU WOULD NOT UTTER SUCH STUPID STATEMENTS.
BLESSED, BLESSED...
OUTSIDERS HEAR THE NAME "BLACK STONES" AND INCORRECTLY THINK THEY REFER TO THE STANDING STONES THE ANCIENTS LEFT NEARBY.
BUT THEY ARE *THESE LITTLE PEARLS...*
...WITH THE POWER OVER US ALL.

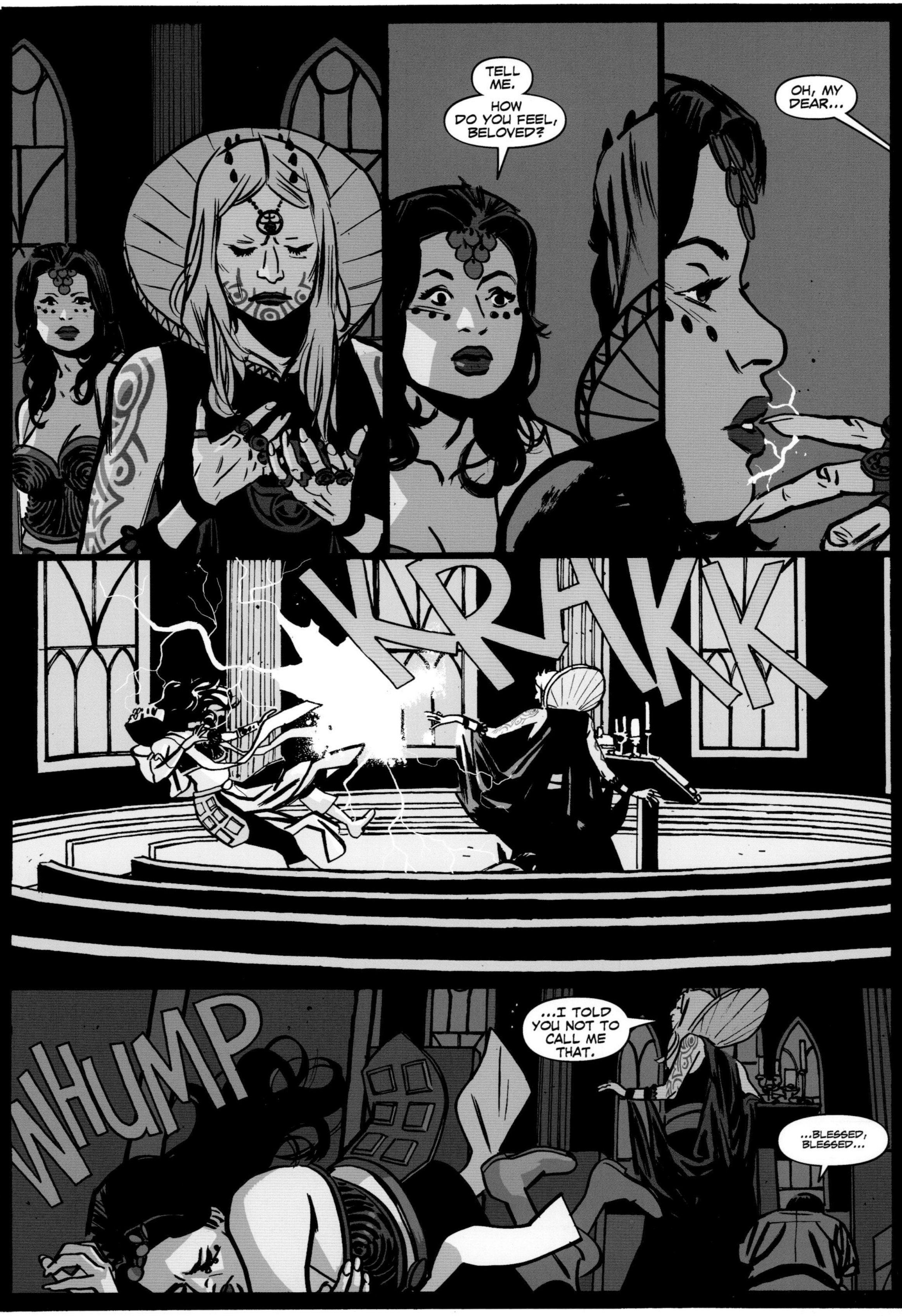

TELL ME.
HOW DO YOU FEEL, BELOVED?
OH, MY DEAR...
KRAKK
WHUMP
...I TOLD YOU NOT TO CALL ME THAT.
...BLESSED, BLESSED...

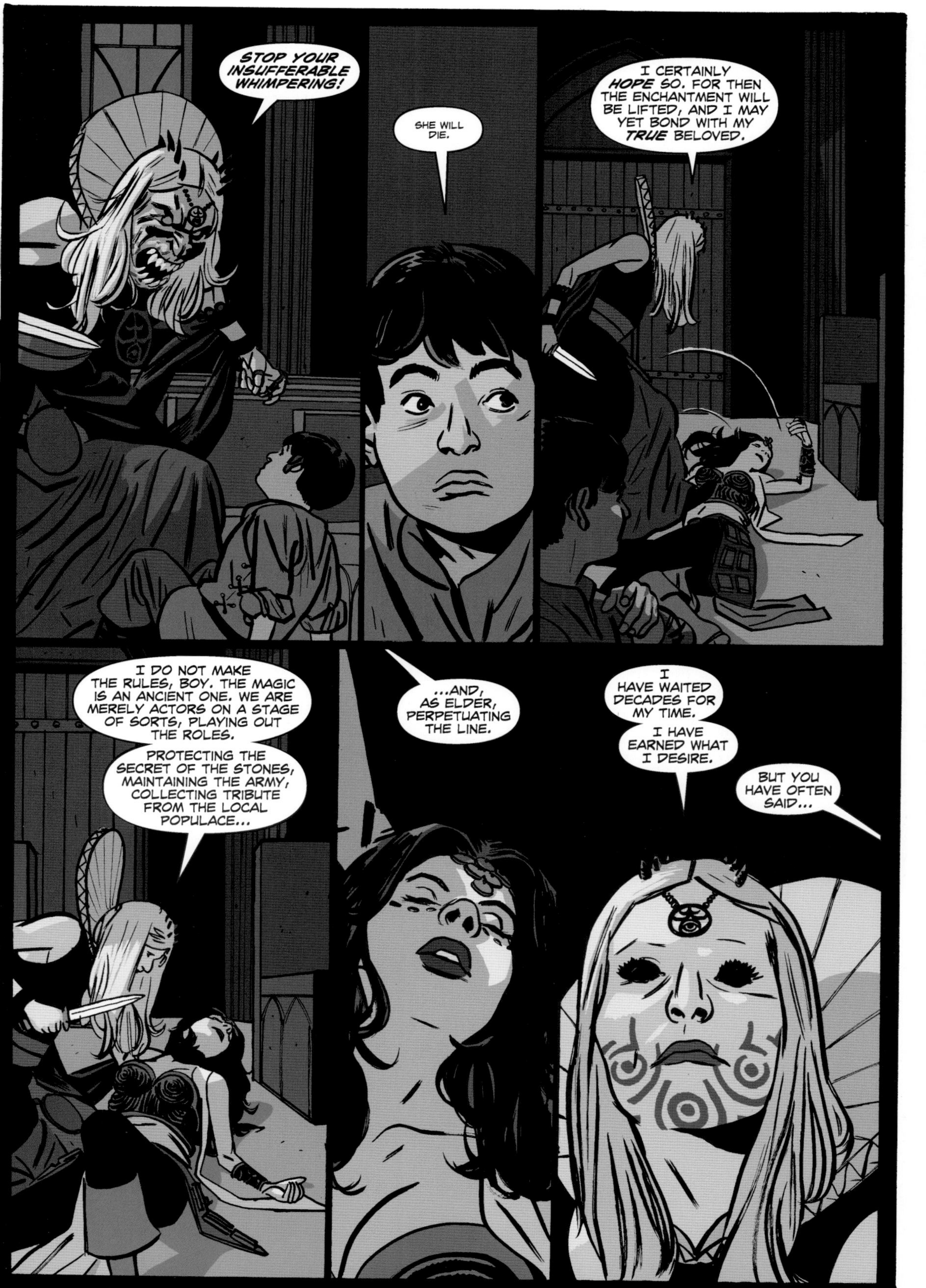
STOP YOUR INSUFFERABLE WHIMPERING!
SHE WILL DIE.
I CERTAINLY HOPE SO. FOR THEN THE ENCHANTMENT WILL BE LIFTED, AND I MAY YET BOND WITH MY TRUE BELOVED.
I DO NOT MAKE THE RULES, BOY. THE MAGIC IS AN ANCIENT ONE. WE ARE MERELY ACTORS ON A STAGE OF SORTS, PLAYING OUT THE ROLES.
PROTECTING THE SECRET OF THE STONES, MAINTAINING THE ARMY, COLLECTING TRIBUTE FROM THE LOCAL POPULACE...
...AND, AS ELDER, PERPETUATING THE LINE.
I HAVE WAITED DECADES FOR MY TIME.
I HAVE EARNED WHAT I DESIRE.
BUT YOU HAVE OFTEN SAID...

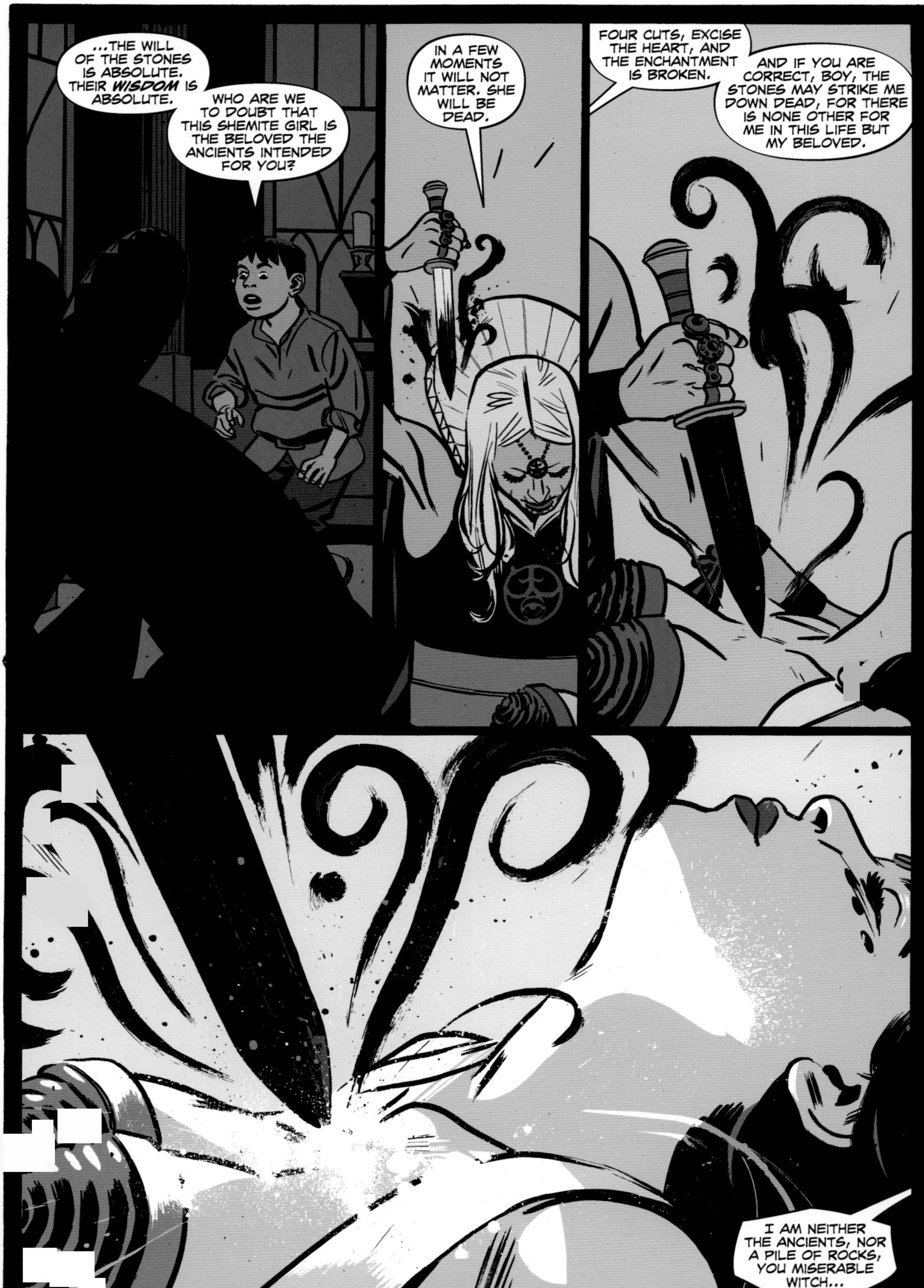
...THE WILL OF THE STONES IS ABSOLUTE. THEIR *WISDOM* IS ABSOLUTE.
WHO ARE WE TO DOUBT THAT THIS SHEMITE GIRL IS THE BELOVED THE ANCIENTS INTENDED FOR YOU?
IN A FEW MOMENTS IT WILL NOT MATTER. SHE WILL BE DEAD.
FOUR CUTS, EXCISE THE HEART, AND THE ENCHANTMENT IS BROKEN.
AND IF YOU ARE CORRECT, BOY, THE STONES MAY STRIKE ME DOWN DEAD, FOR THERE IS NONE OTHER FOR ME IN THIS LIFE BUT MY BELOVED.
I AM NEITHER THE ANCIENTS, NOR A PILE OF ROCKS, YOU MISERABLE WITCH...

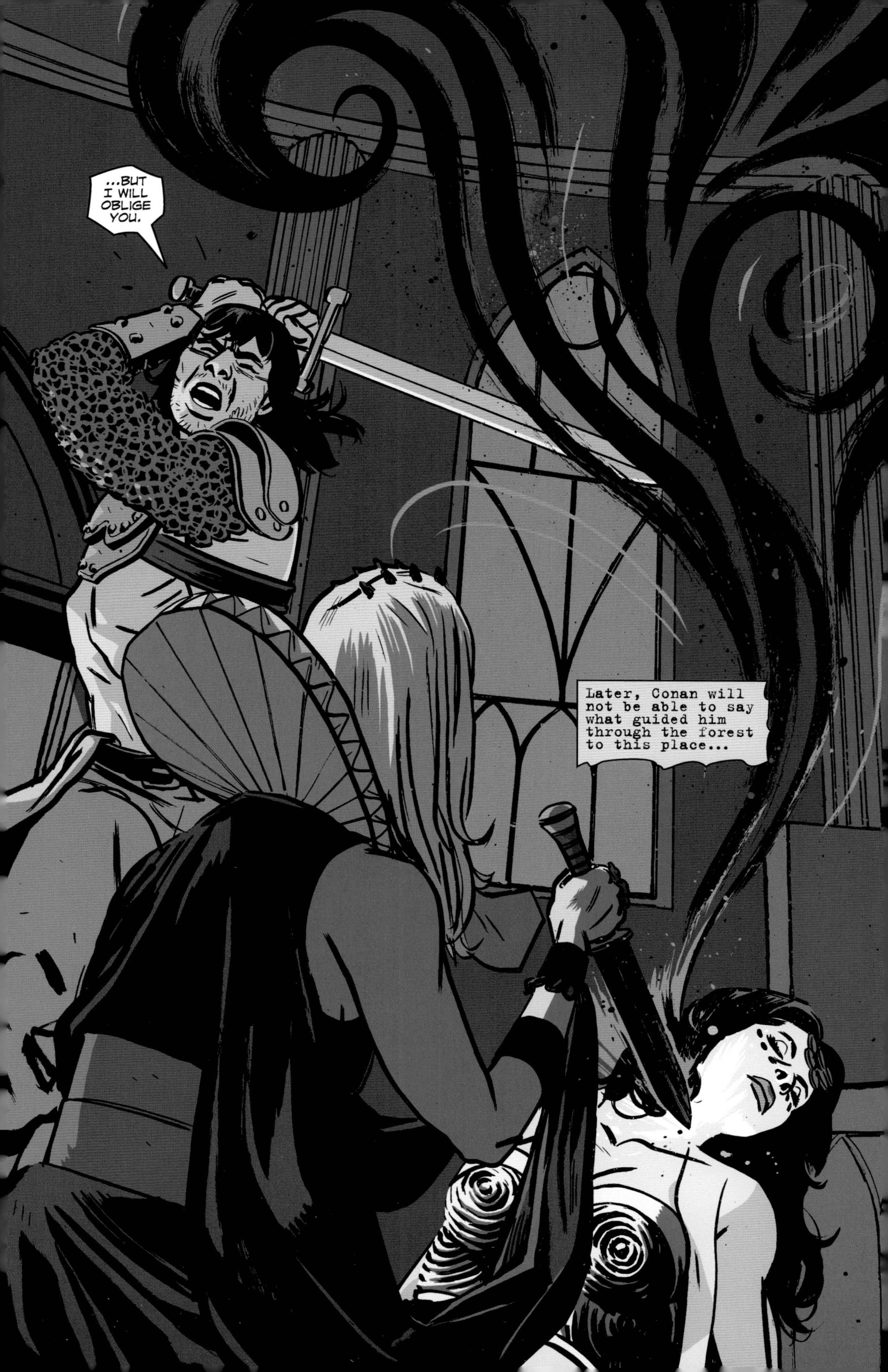
...BUT I WILL OBLIGE YOU.
Later, Conan will not be able to say what guided him through the forest to this place...

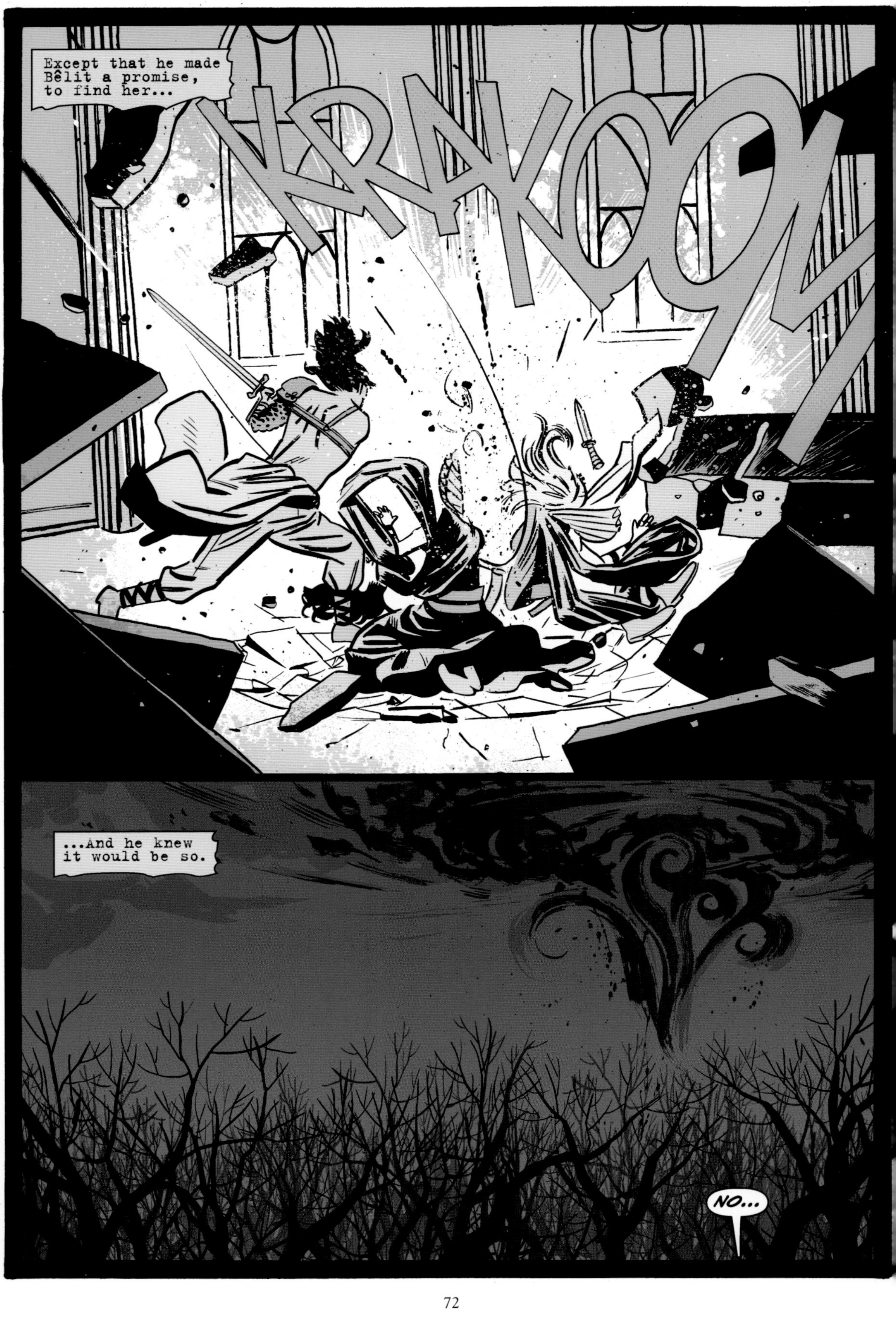
Except that he made Bêlit a promise, to find her...
KRAKOOM
...And he knew it would be so.
NO...

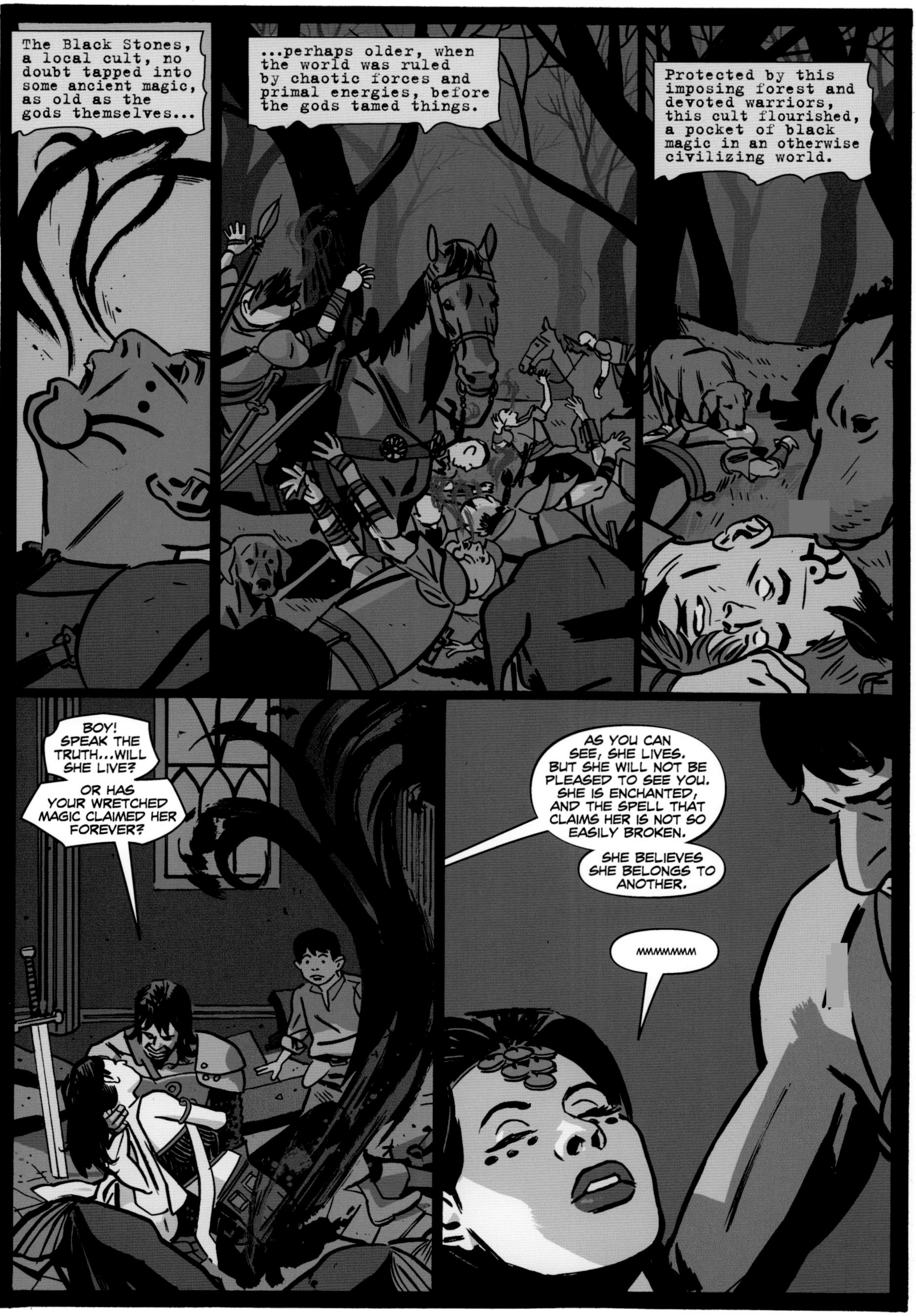

The Black Stones, a local cult, no doubt tapped into some ancient magic, as old as the gods themselves...
...perhaps older, when the world was ruled by chaotic forces and primal energies, before the gods tamed things.
Protected by this imposing forest and devoted warriors, this cult flourished, a pocket of black magic in an otherwise civilizing world.
BOY! SPEAK THE TRUTH...WILL SHE LIVE?
OR HAS YOUR WRETCHED MAGIC CLAIMED HER FOREVER?
AS YOU CAN SEE, SHE LIVES. BUT SHE WILL NOT BE PLEASED TO SEE YOU. SHE IS ENCHANTED, AND THE SPELL THAT CLAIMS HER IS NOT SO EASILY BROKEN.
SHE BELIEVES SHE BELONGS TO ANOTHER.
MMMMMMM

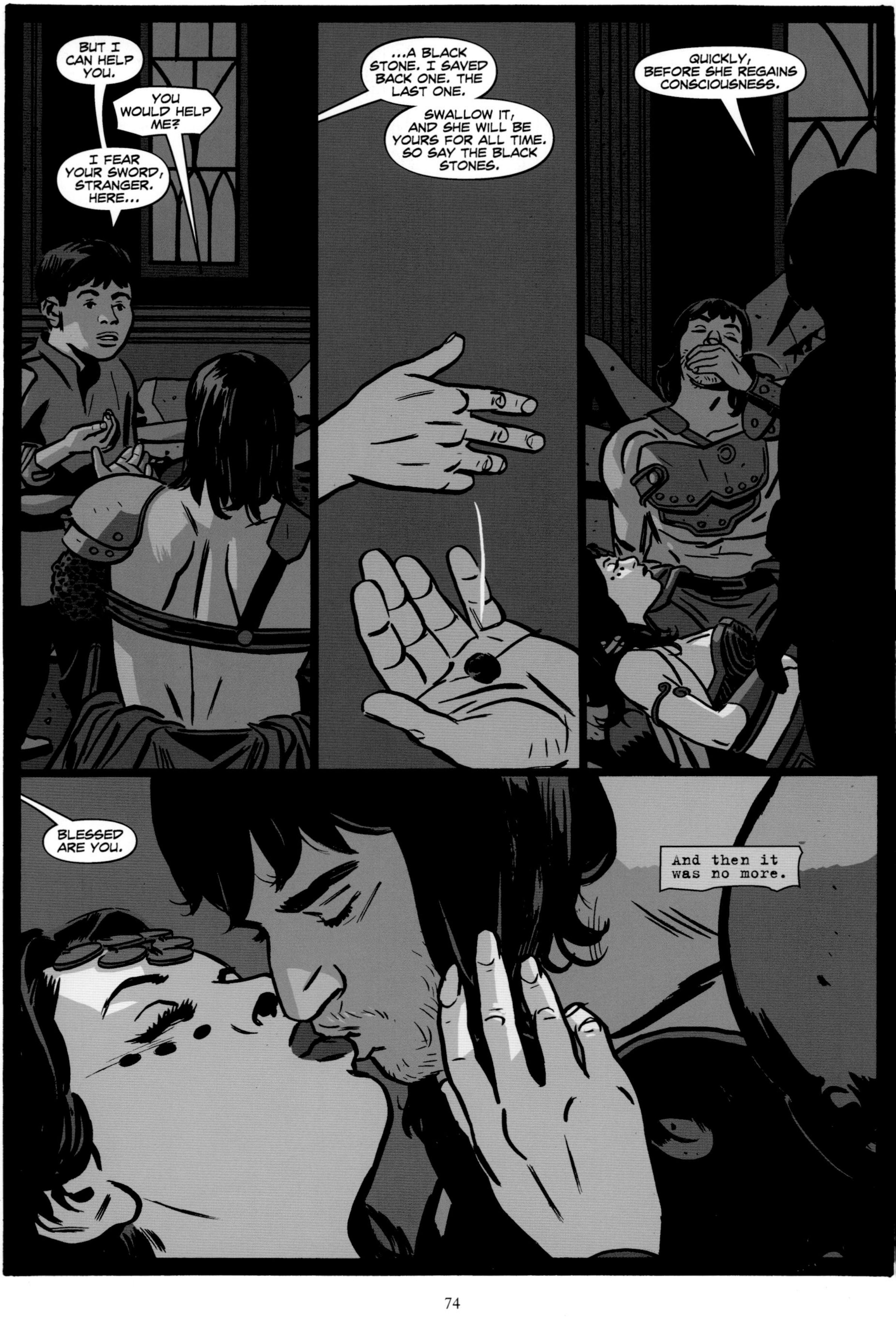
BUT I CAN HELP YOU.
YOU WOULD HELP ME?
I FEAR YOUR SWORD, STRANGER. HERE...
...A BLACK STONE. I SAVED BACK ONE. THE LAST ONE.
SWALLOW IT, AND SHE WILL BE YOURS FOR ALL TIME. SO SAY THE BLACK STONES.
QUICKLY, BEFORE SHE REGAINS CONSCIOUSNESS.
BLESSED ARE YOU.
And then it was no more.

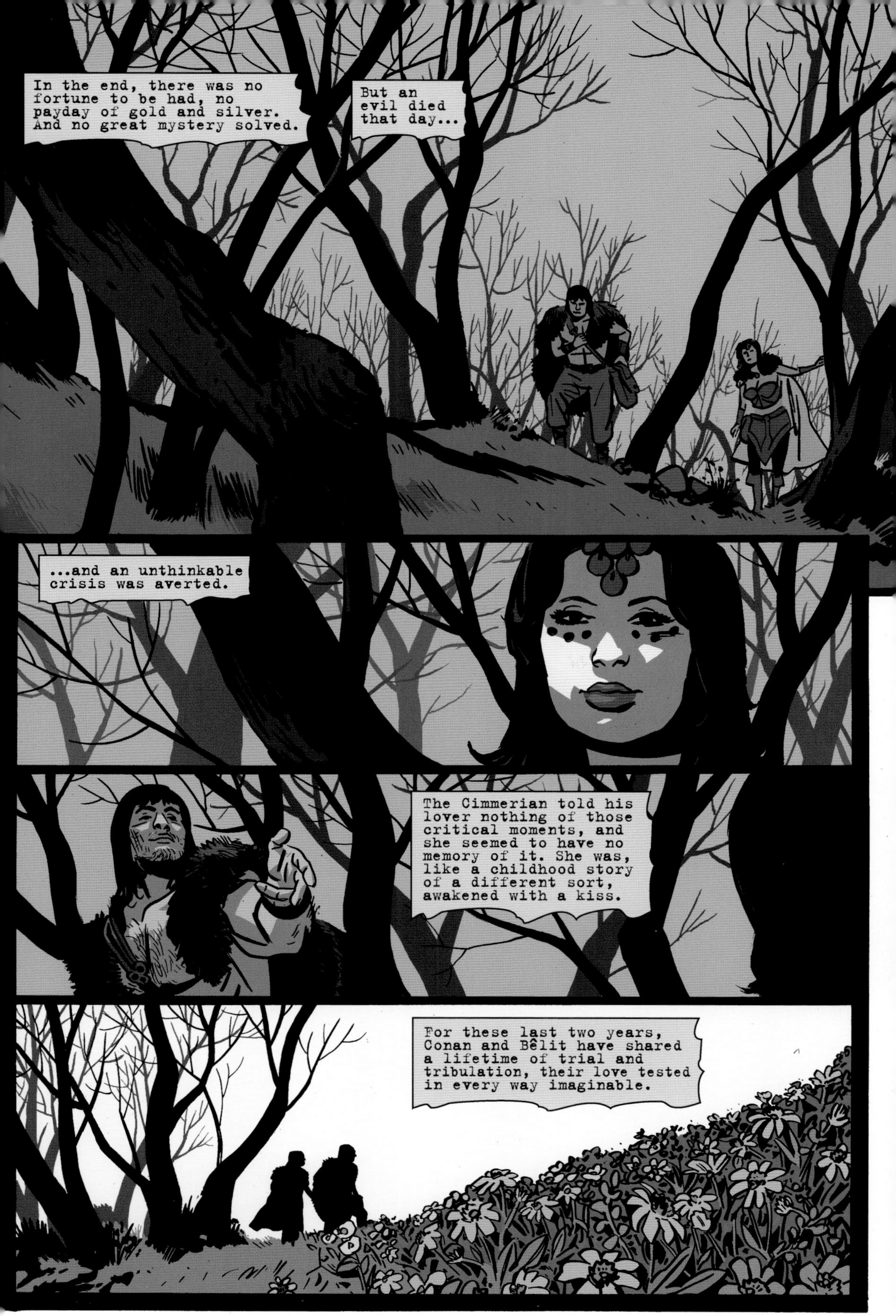
In the end, there was no fortune to be had, no payday of gold and silver. And no great mystery solved.
But an evil died that day...
...and an unthinkable crisis was averted.
The Cimmerian told his lover nothing of those critical moments, and she seemed to have no memory of it. She was, like a childhood story of a different sort, awakened with a kiss.
For these last two years, Conan and Bêlit have shared a lifetime of trial and tribulation, their love tested in every way imaginable.

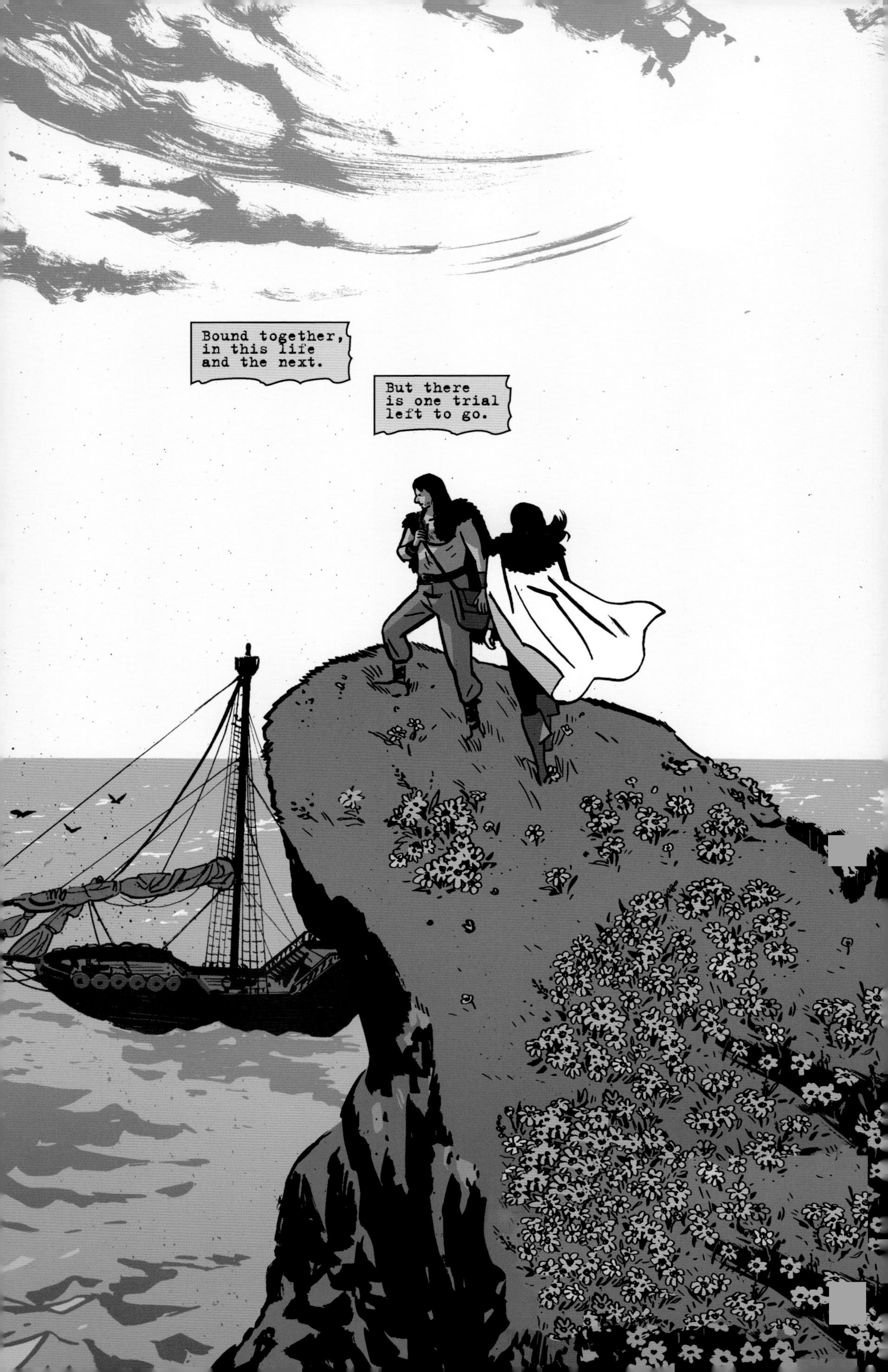
Bound together, in this life and the next.
But there is one trial left to go.

CHAPTER FOUR

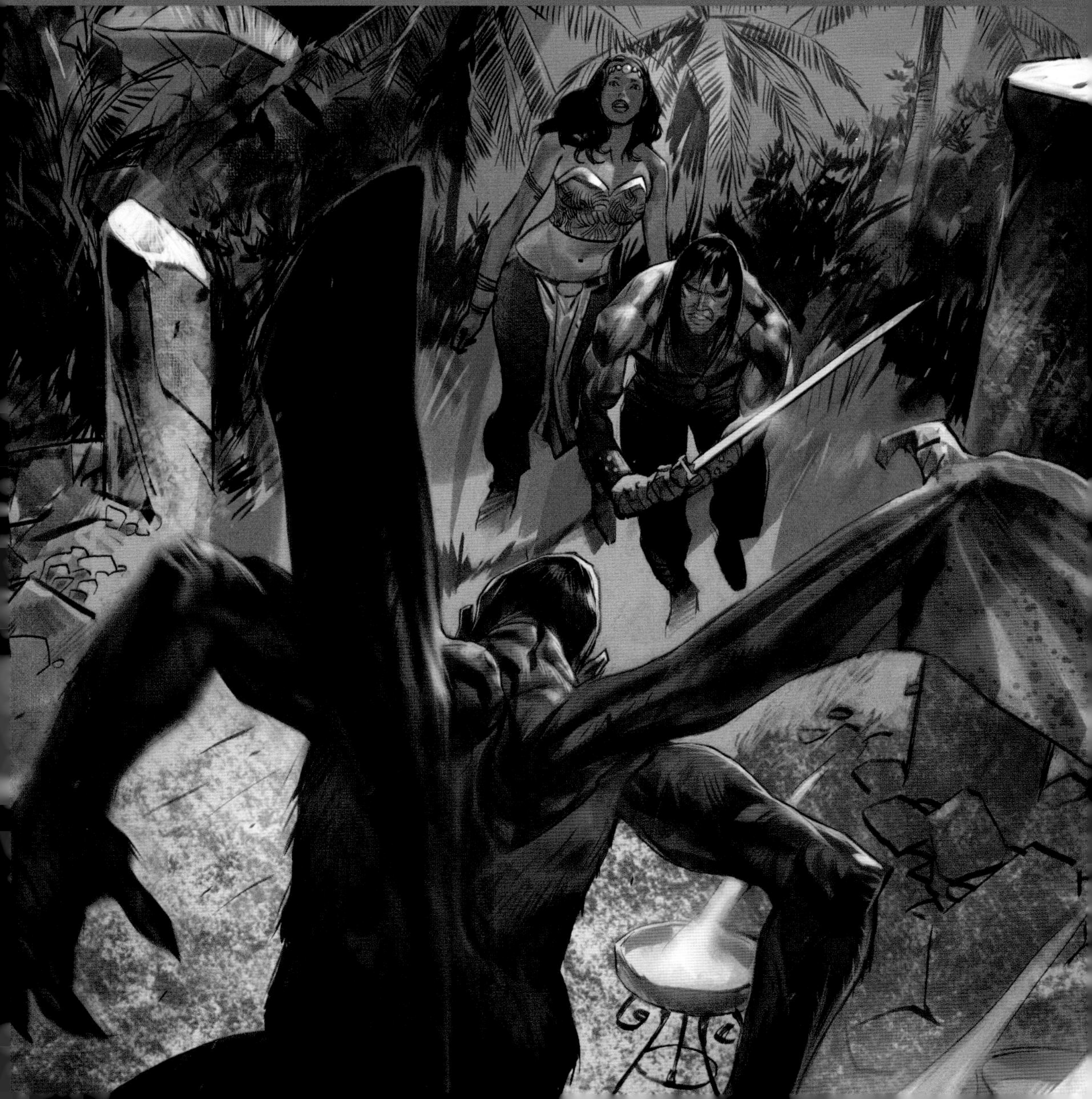

"I am yours, and all the gods and all
their eternities shall not sever us."

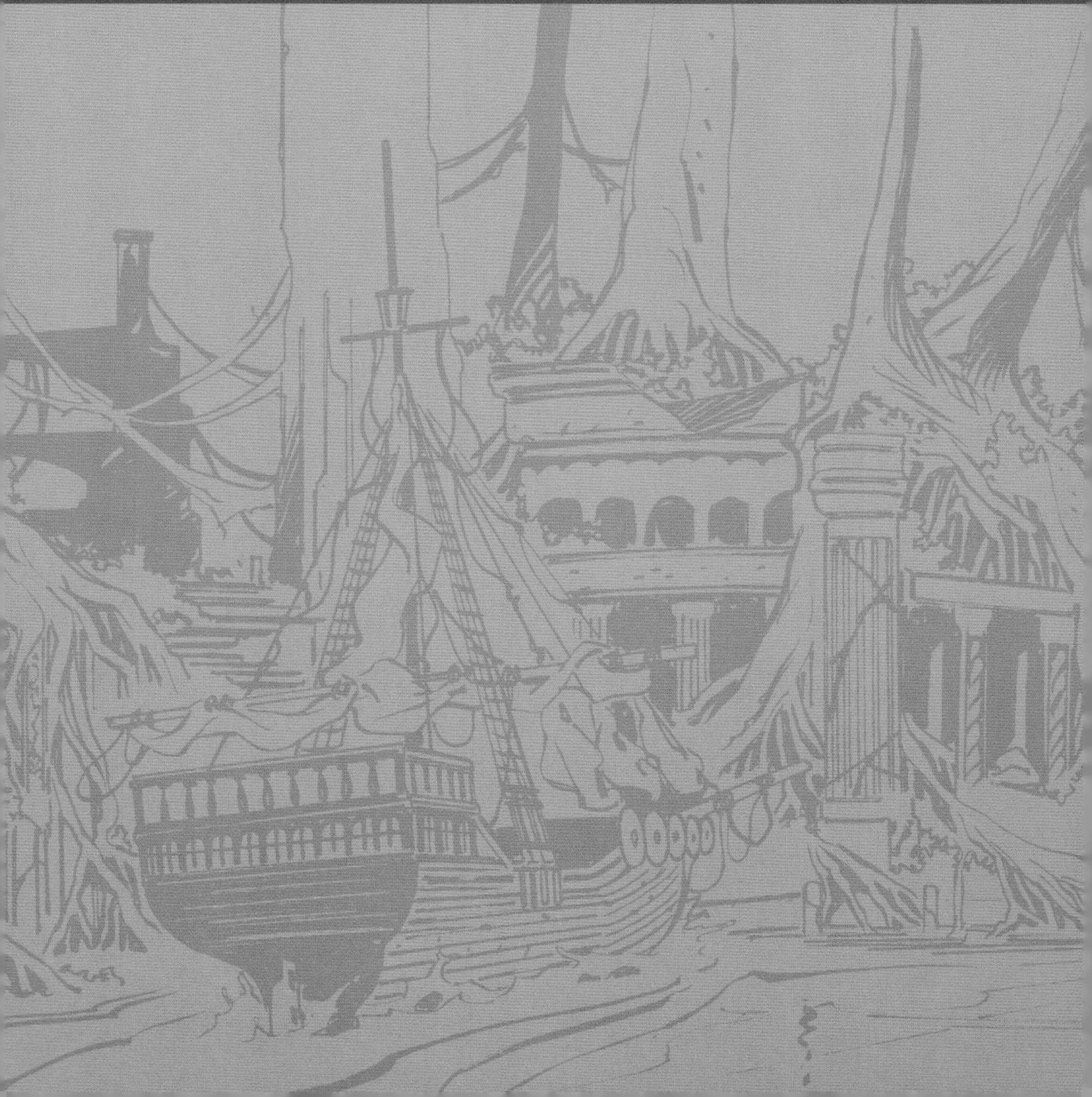

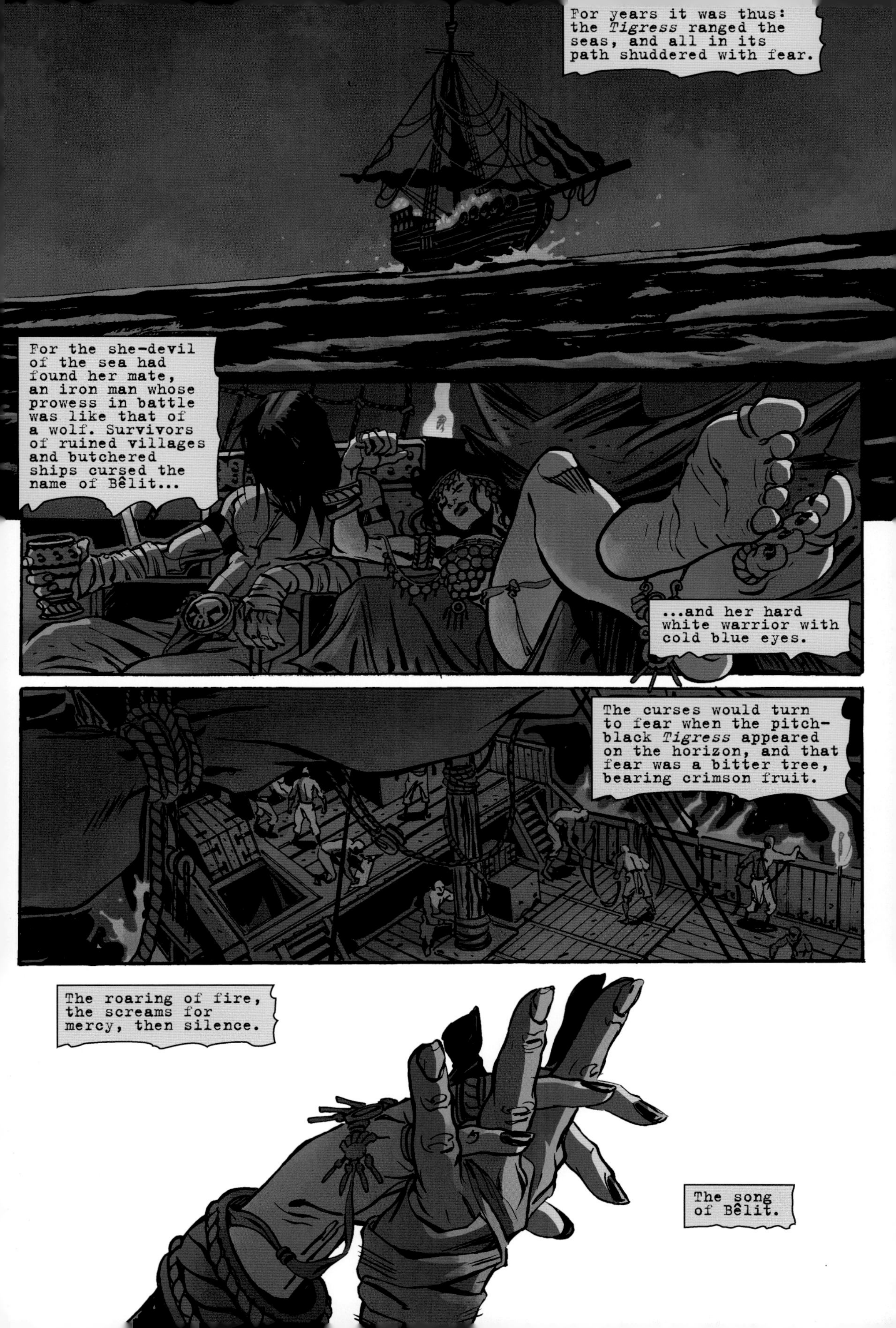
For years it was thus: the *Tigress* ranged the seas, and all in its path shuddered with fear.
For the she-devil of the sea had found her mate, an iron man whose prowess in battle was like that of a wolf. Survivors of ruined villages and butchered ships cursed the name of Bêlit...
...and her hard white warrior with cold blue eyes.
The curses would turn to fear when the pitch-black *Tigress* appeared on the horizon, and that fear was a bitter tree, bearing crimson fruit.
The roaring of fire, the screams for mercy, then silence.
The song of Bêlit.

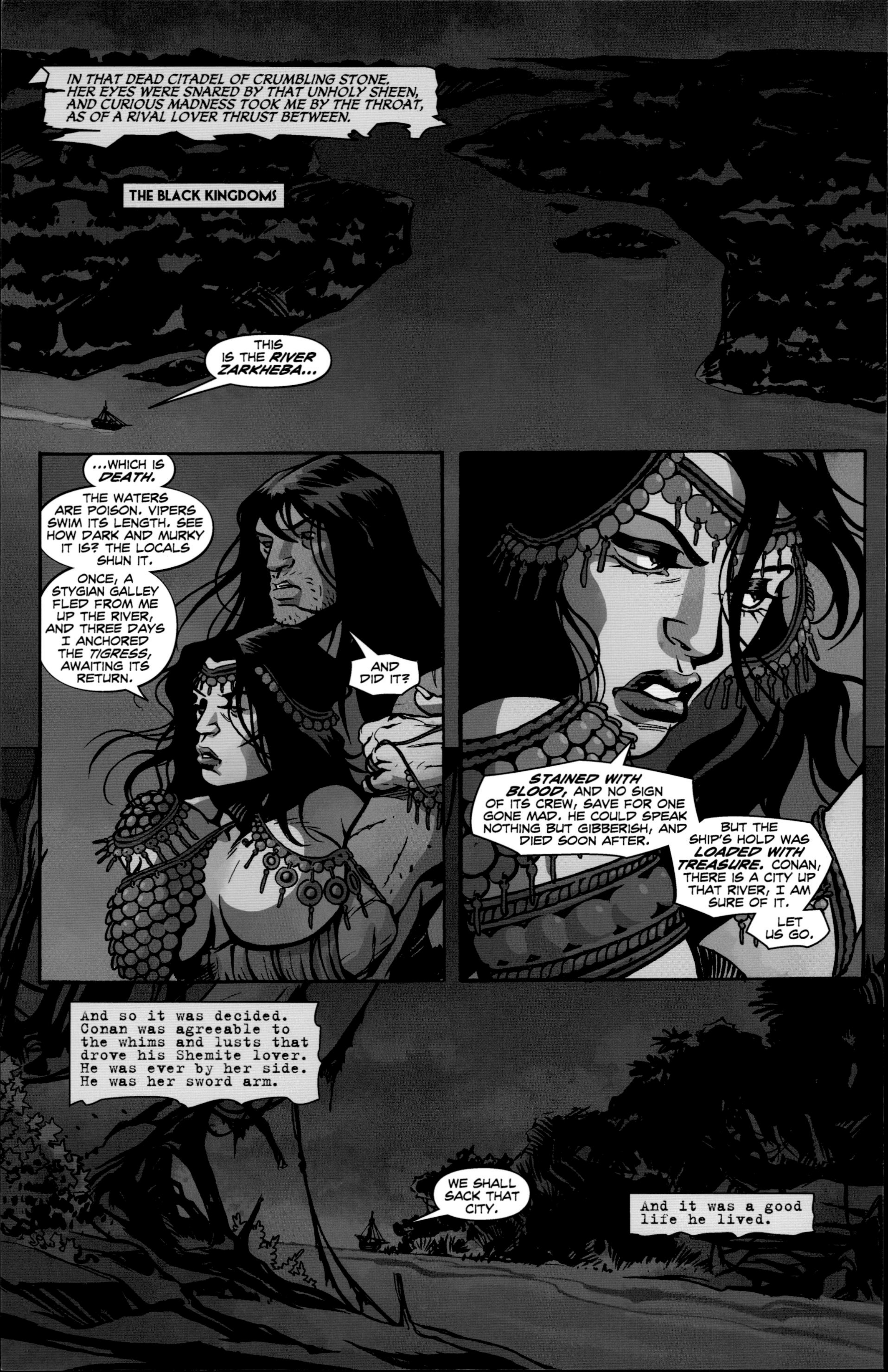
IN THAT DEAD CITADEL OF CRUMBLING STONE, HER EYES WERE SNARED BY THAT UNHOLY SHEEN, AND CURIOUS MADNESS TOOK ME BY THE THROAT, AS OF A RIVAL LOVER THRUST BETWEEN.
THE BLACK KINGDOMS
THIS IS THE RIVER ZARKHEBA...
...WHICH IS DEATH.
THE WATERS ARE POISON. VIPERS SWIM ITS LENGTH. SEE HOW DARK AND MURKY IT IS? THE LOCALS SHUN IT.
ONCE, A STYGIAN GALLEY FLED FROM ME UP THE RIVER, AND THREE DAYS I ANCHORED THE TIGRESS, AWAITING ITS RETURN.
AND DID IT?
STAINED WITH BLOOD, AND NO SIGN OF ITS CREW, SAVE FOR ONE GONE MAD. HE COULD SPEAK NOTHING BUT GIBBERISH, AND DIED SOON AFTER.
BUT THE SHIP'S HOLD WAS LOADED WITH TREASURE. CONAN, THERE IS A CITY UP THAT RIVER, I AM SURE OF IT.
LET US GO.
And so it was decided. Conan was agreeable to the whims and lusts that drove his Shemite lover. He was ever by her side. He was her sword arm.
WE SHALL SACK THAT CITY.
And it was a good life he lived.

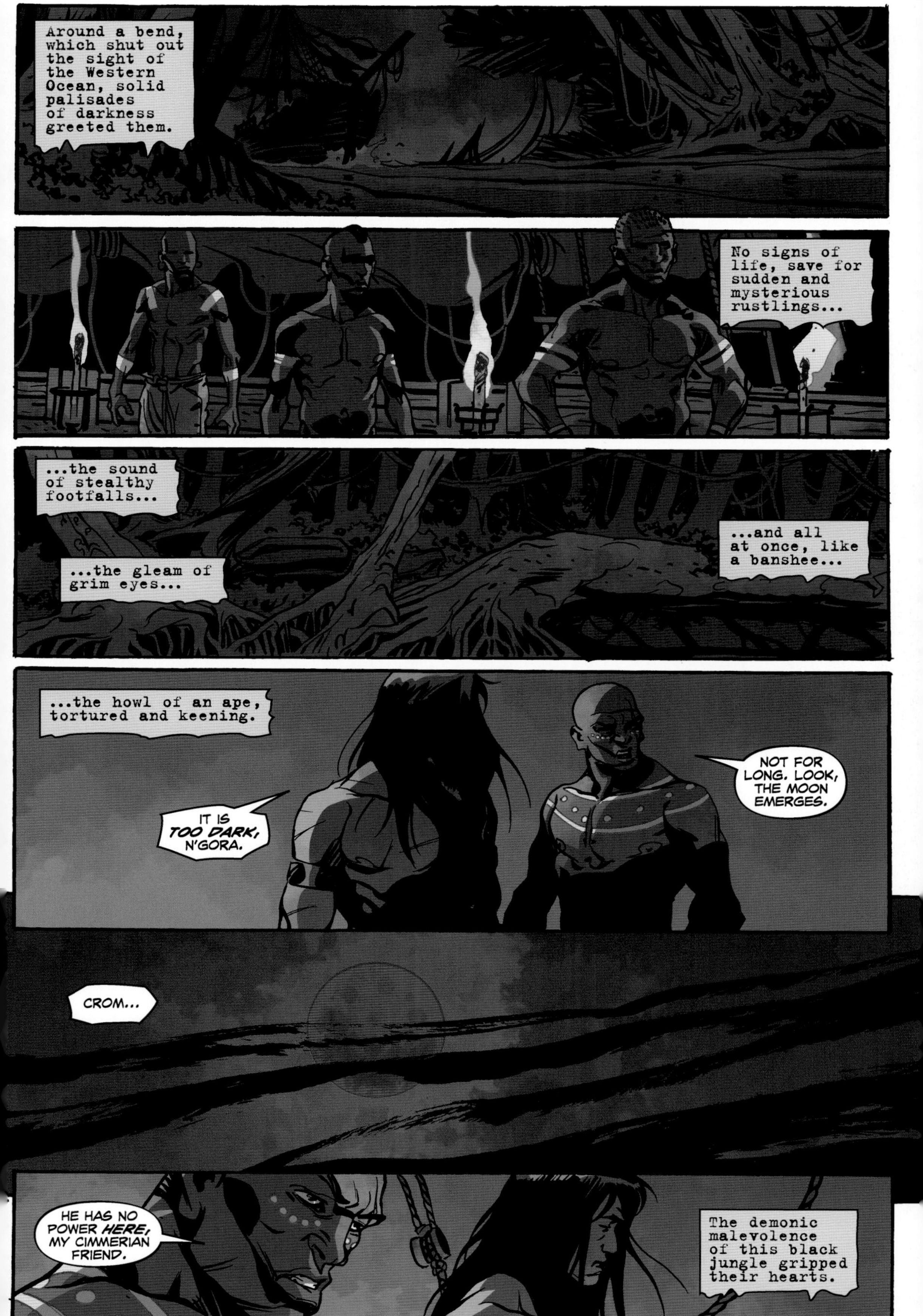
Around a bend, which shut out the sight of the Western Ocean, solid palisades of darkness greeted them.
No signs of life, save for sudden and mysterious rustlings...
...the sound of stealthy footfalls...
...the gleam of grim eyes...
...and all at once, like a banshee...
...the howl of an ape, tortured and keening.
IT IS TOO DARK, N'GORA.
NOT FOR LONG. LOOK, THE MOON EMERGES.
CROM...
HE HAS NO POWER HERE, MY CIMMERIAN FRIEND.
The demonic malevolence of this black jungle gripped their hearts.

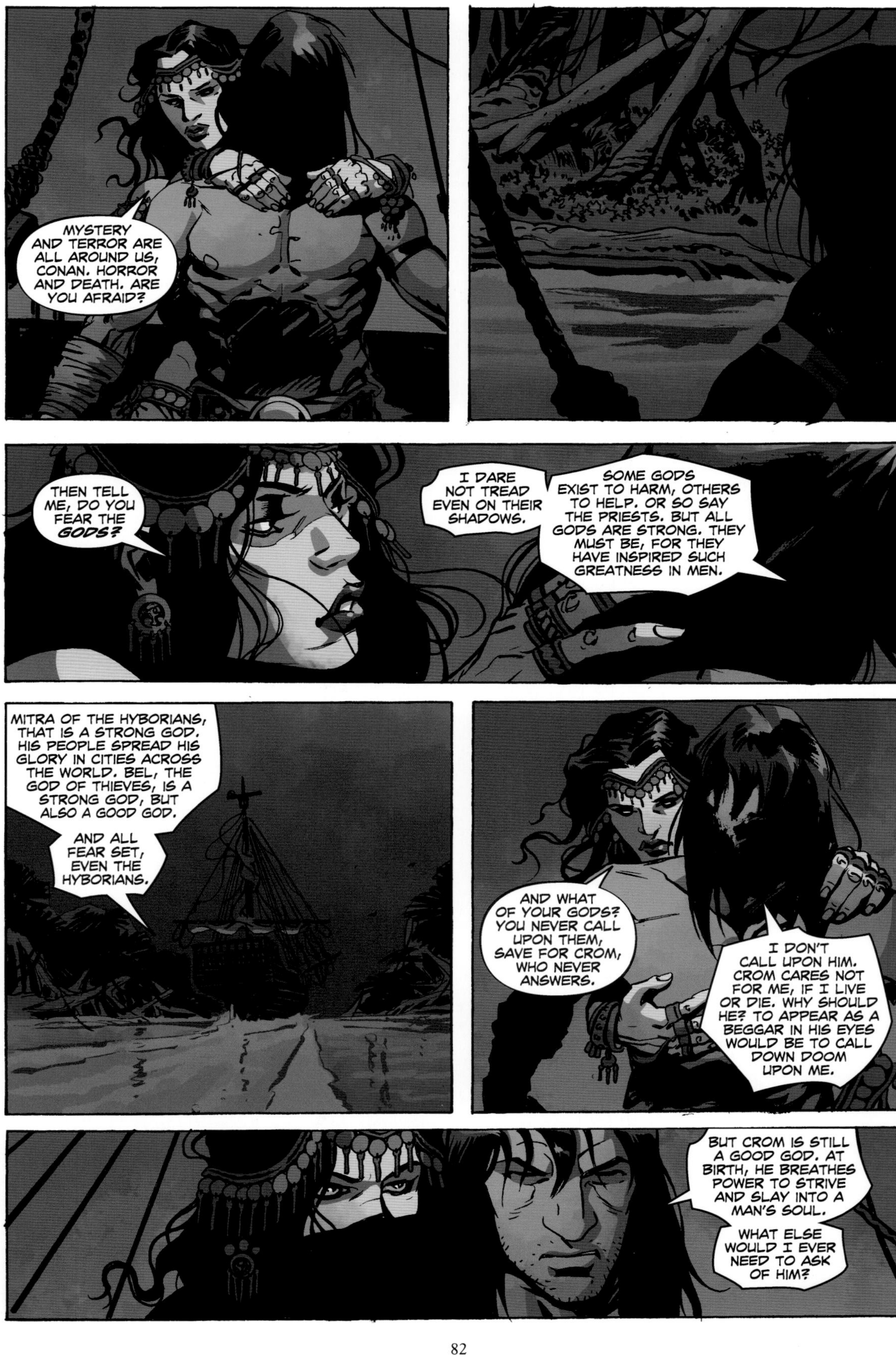
MYSTERY AND TERROR ARE ALL AROUND US, CONAN. HORROR AND DEATH. ARE YOU AFRAID?
THEN TELL ME, DO YOU FEAR THE *GODS?*
I DARE NOT TREAD EVEN ON THEIR SHADOWS.
SOME GODS EXIST TO HARM, OTHERS TO HELP. OR SO SAY THE PRIESTS. BUT ALL GODS ARE STRONG. THEY MUST BE, FOR THEY HAVE INSPIRED SUCH GREATNESS IN MEN.
MITRA OF THE HYBORIANS, THAT IS A STRONG GOD. HIS PEOPLE SPREAD HIS GLORY IN CITIES ACROSS THE WORLD. BEL, THE GOD OF THIEVES, IS A STRONG GOD, BUT ALSO A GOOD GOD.
AND ALL FEAR SET, EVEN THE HYBORIANS.
AND WHAT OF YOUR GODS? YOU NEVER CALL UPON THEM, SAVE FOR CROM, WHO NEVER ANSWERS.
I DON'T CALL UPON HIM. CROM CARES NOT FOR ME, IF I LIVE OR DIE. WHY SHOULD HE? TO APPEAR AS A BEGGAR IN HIS EYES WOULD BE TO CALL DOWN DOOM UPON ME.
BUT CROM IS STILL A GOOD GOD. AT BIRTH, HE BREATHES POWER TO STRIVE AND SLAY INTO A MAN'S SOUL.
WHAT ELSE WOULD I EVER NEED TO ASK OF HIM?

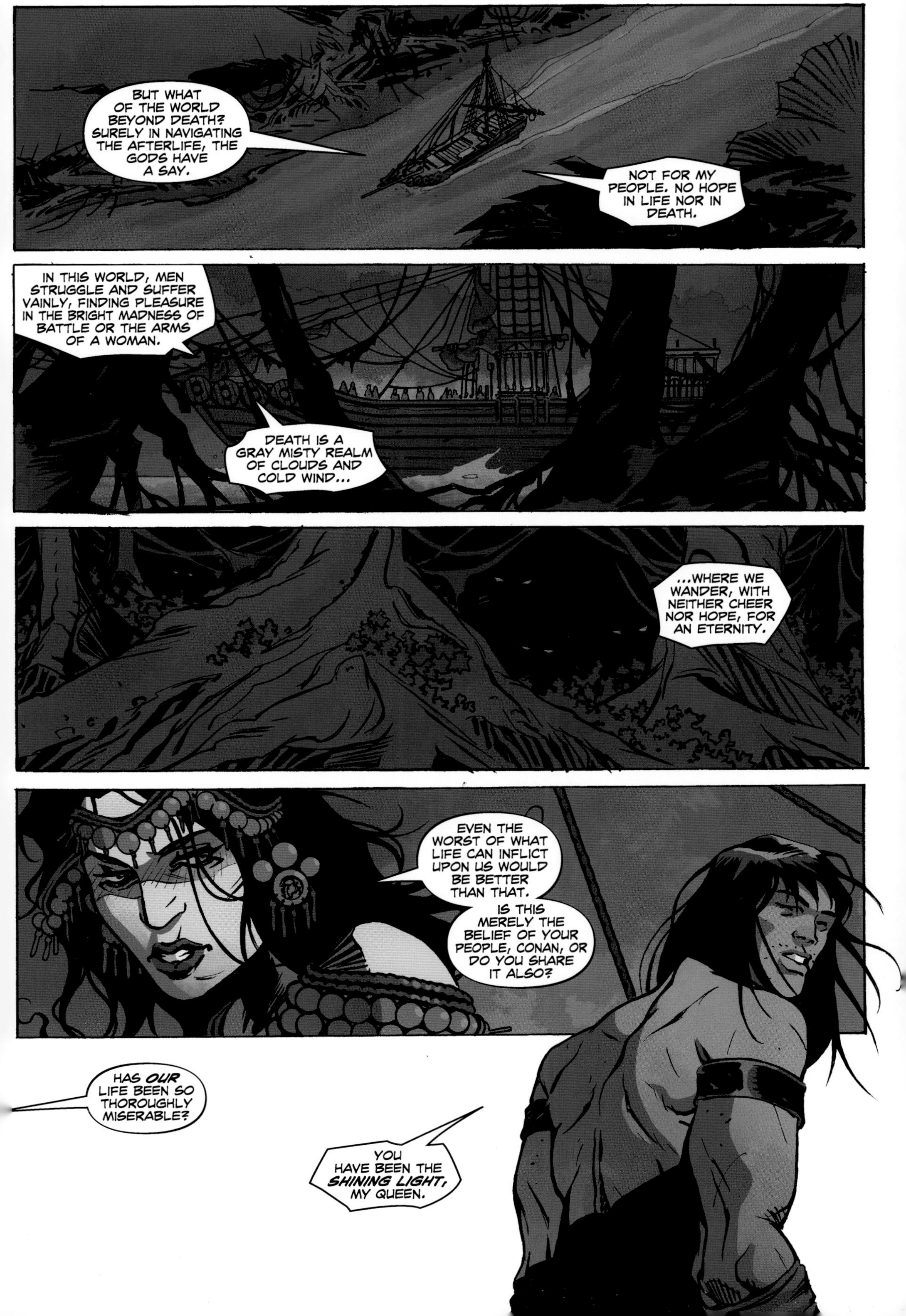
BUT WHAT OF THE WORLD BEYOND DEATH? SURELY IN NAVIGATING THE AFTERLIFE, THE GODS HAVE A SAY.
NOT FOR MY PEOPLE. NO HOPE IN LIFE NOR IN DEATH.
IN THIS WORLD, MEN STRUGGLE AND SUFFER VAINLY, FINDING PLEASURE IN THE BRIGHT MADNESS OF BATTLE OR THE ARMS OF A WOMAN.
DEATH IS A GRAY MISTY REALM OF CLOUDS AND COLD WIND...
...WHERE WE WANDER, WITH NEITHER CHEER NOR HOPE, FOR AN ETERNITY.
EVEN THE WORST OF WHAT LIFE CAN INFLICT UPON US WOULD BE BETTER THAN THAT.
IS THIS MERELY THE BELIEF OF YOUR PEOPLE, CONAN, OR DO YOU SHARE IT ALSO?
HAS *OUR* LIFE BEEN SO THOROUGHLY MISERABLE?
YOU HAVE BEEN THE *SHINING LIGHT,* MY QUEEN.

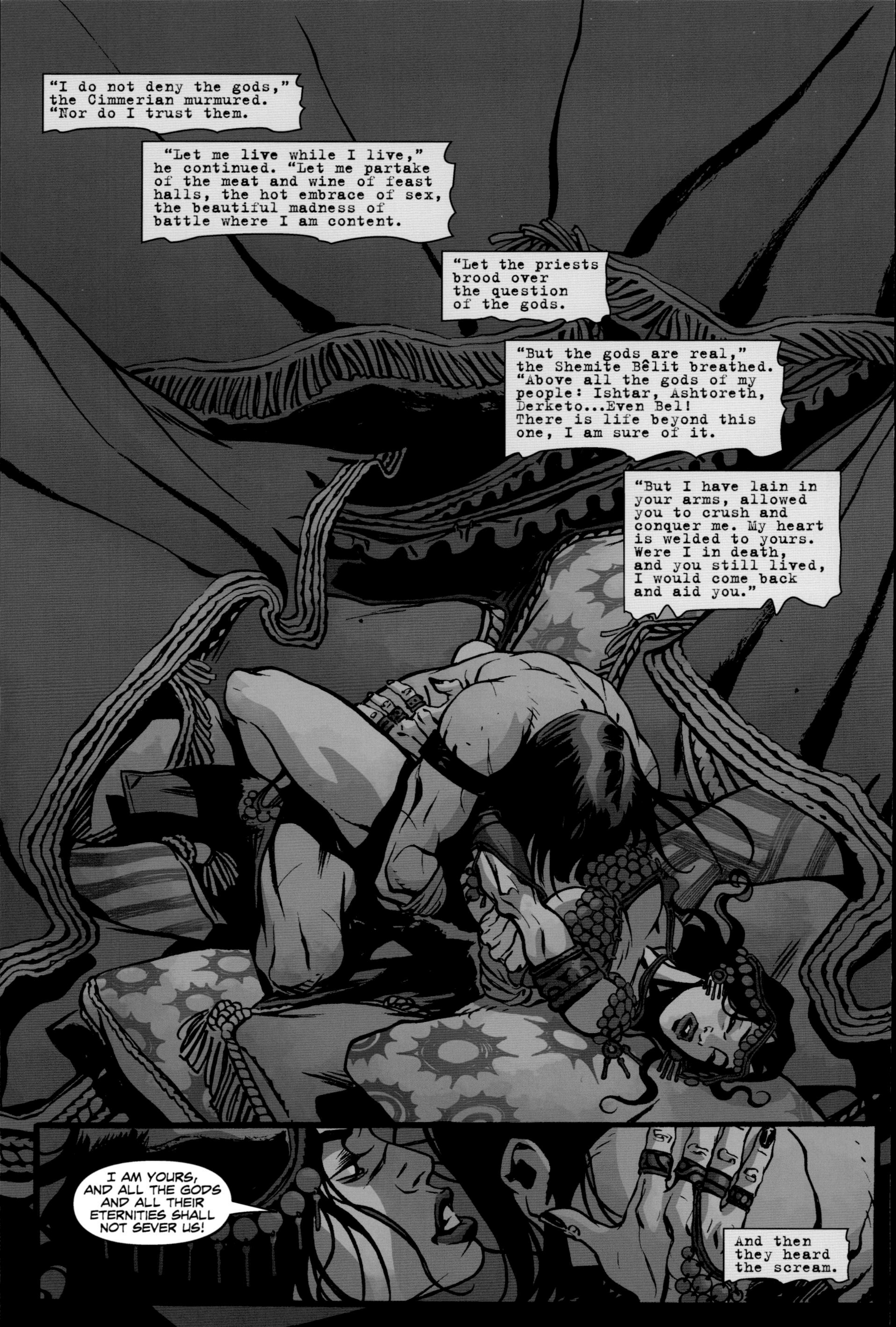
"I do not deny the gods," the Cimmerian murmured. "Nor do I trust them.
"Let me live while I live," he continued. "Let me partake of the meat and wine of feast halls, the hot embrace of sex, the beautiful madness of battle where I am content.
"Let the priests brood over the question of the gods.
"But the gods are real," the Shemite Bêlit breathed. "Above all the gods of my people: Ishtar, Ashtoreth, Derketo...Even Bel! There is life beyond this one, I am sure of it.
"But I have lain in your arms, allowed you to crush and conquer me. My heart is welded to yours. Were I in death, and you still lived, I would come back and aid you."
I AM YOURS, AND ALL THE GODS AND ALL THEIR ETERNITIES SHALL NOT SEVER US!
And then they heard the scream.

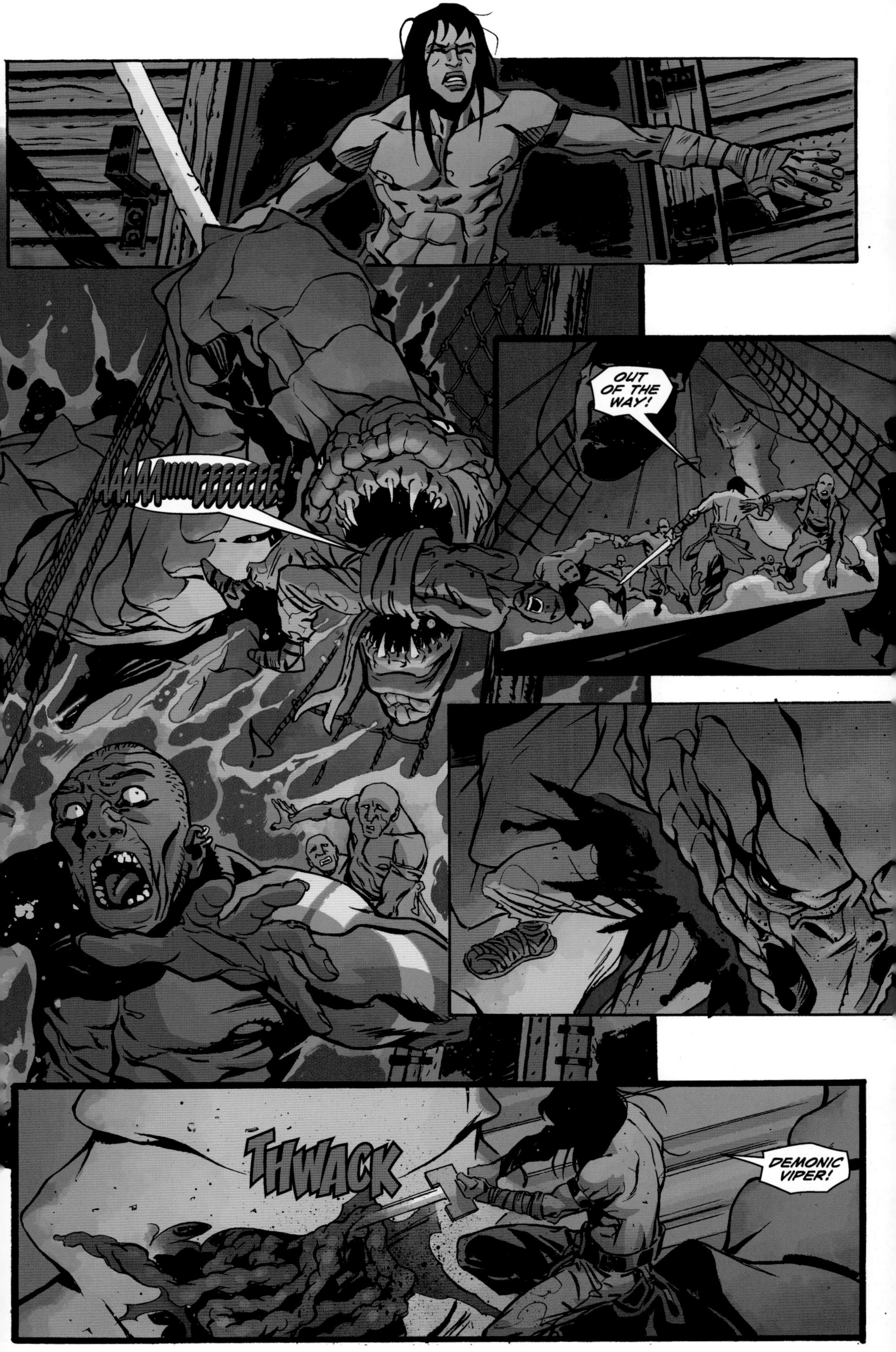
AAAAAIIIIIEEEEEEE!
OUT OF THE WAY!
THWACK
DEMONIC VIPER!

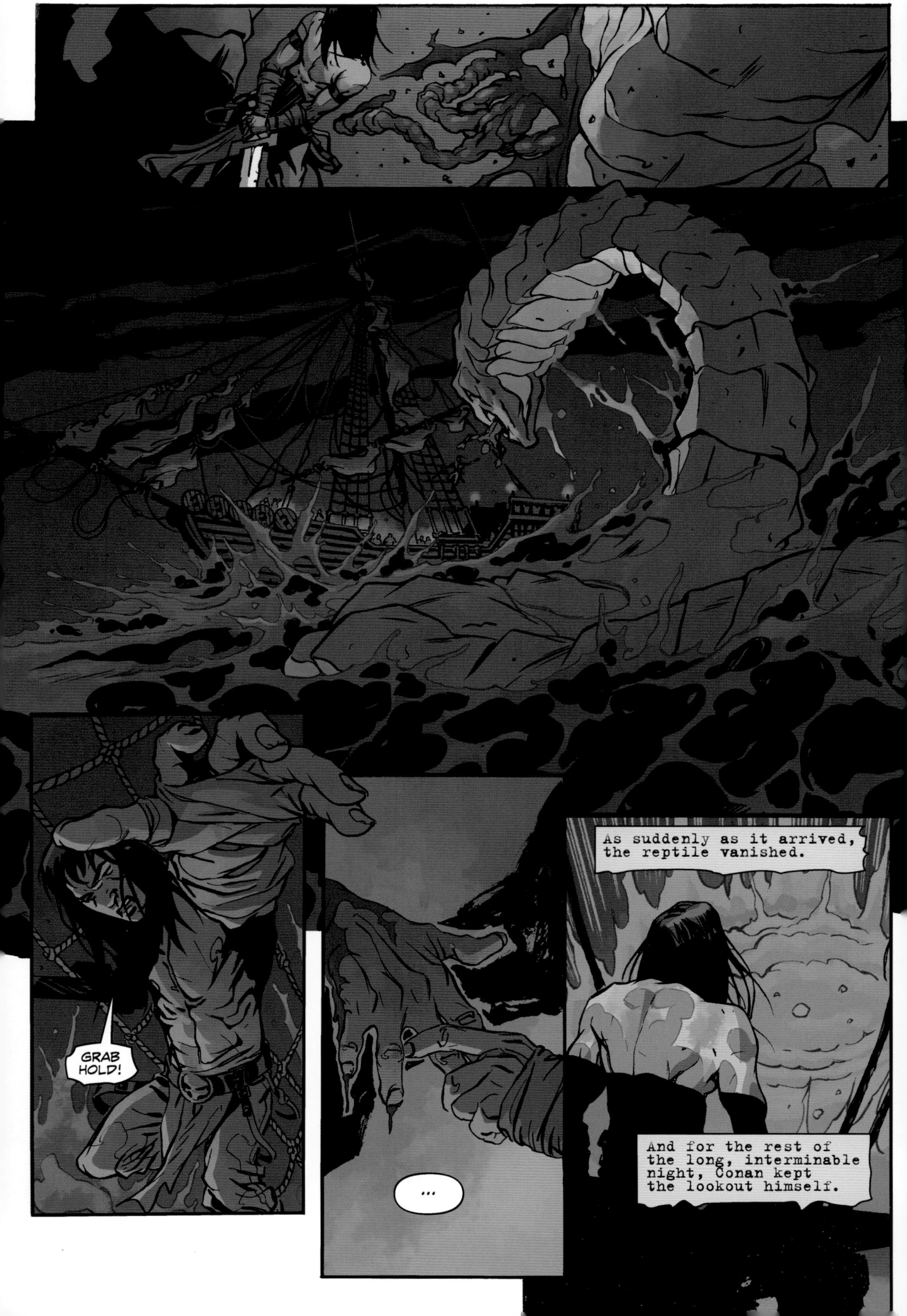
GRAB HOLD!
...
As suddenly as it arrived, the reptile vanished.
And for the rest of the long, interminable night, Conan kept the lookout himself.

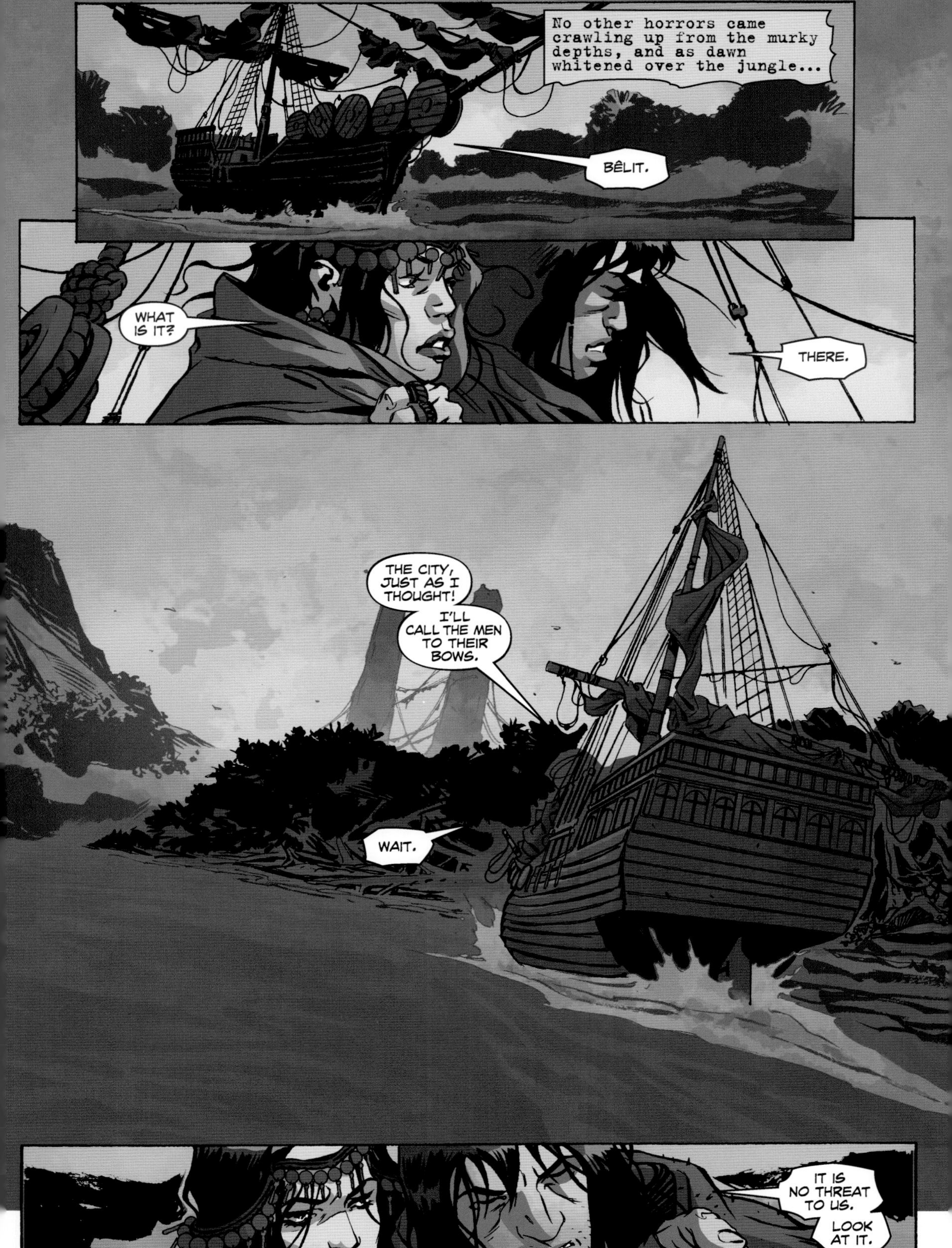
No other horrors came crawling up from the murky depths, and as dawn whitened over the jungle...
BÊLIT.
WHAT IS IT?
THERE.
THE CITY, JUST AS I THOUGHT!
I'LL CALL THE MEN TO THEIR BOWS.
WAIT.
IT IS NO THREAT TO US.
LOOK AT IT.

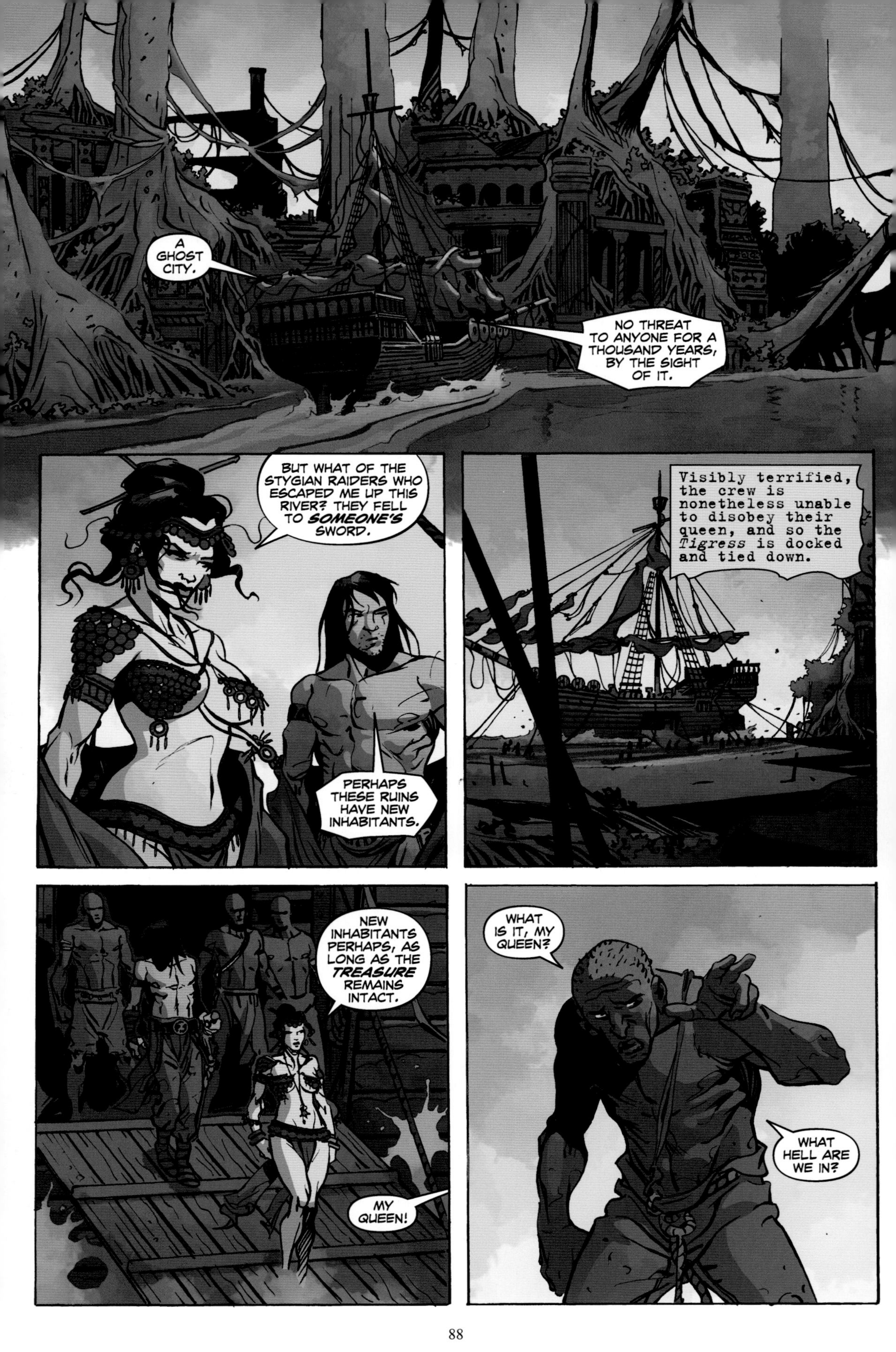
A GHOST CITY.
NO THREAT TO ANYONE FOR A THOUSAND YEARS, BY THE SIGHT OF IT.
BUT WHAT OF THE STYGIAN RAIDERS WHO ESCAPED ME UP THIS RIVER? THEY FELL TO SOMEONE'S SWORD.
PERHAPS THESE RUINS HAVE NEW INHABITANTS.
Visibly terrified, the crew is nonetheless unable to disobey their queen, and so the Tigress is docked and tied down.
NEW INHABITANTS PERHAPS, AS LONG AS THE TREASURE REMAINS INTACT.
MY QUEEN!
WHAT IS IT, MY QUEEN?
WHAT HELL ARE WE IN?

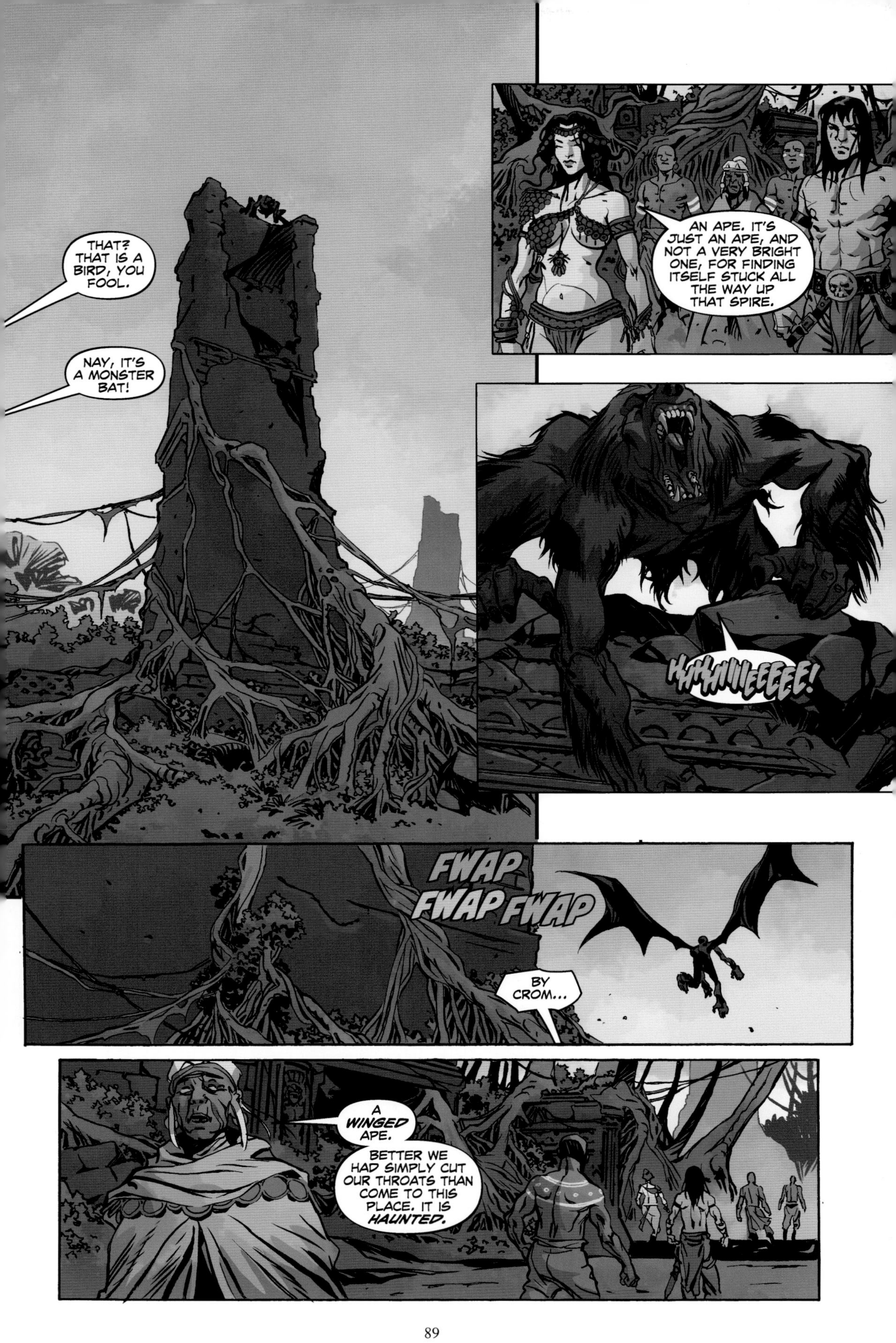
THAT? THAT IS A BIRD, YOU FOOL.
NAY, IT'S A MONSTER BAT!
AN APE. IT'S JUST AN APE, AND NOT A VERY BRIGHT ONE, FOR FINDING ITSELF STUCK ALL THE WAY UP THAT SPIRE.
HHHHIIIIEEEEE!
FWAP FWAP FWAP
BY CROM...
A WINGED APE.
BETTER WE HAD SIMPLY CUT OUR THROATS THAN COME TO THIS PLACE. IT IS HAUNTED.

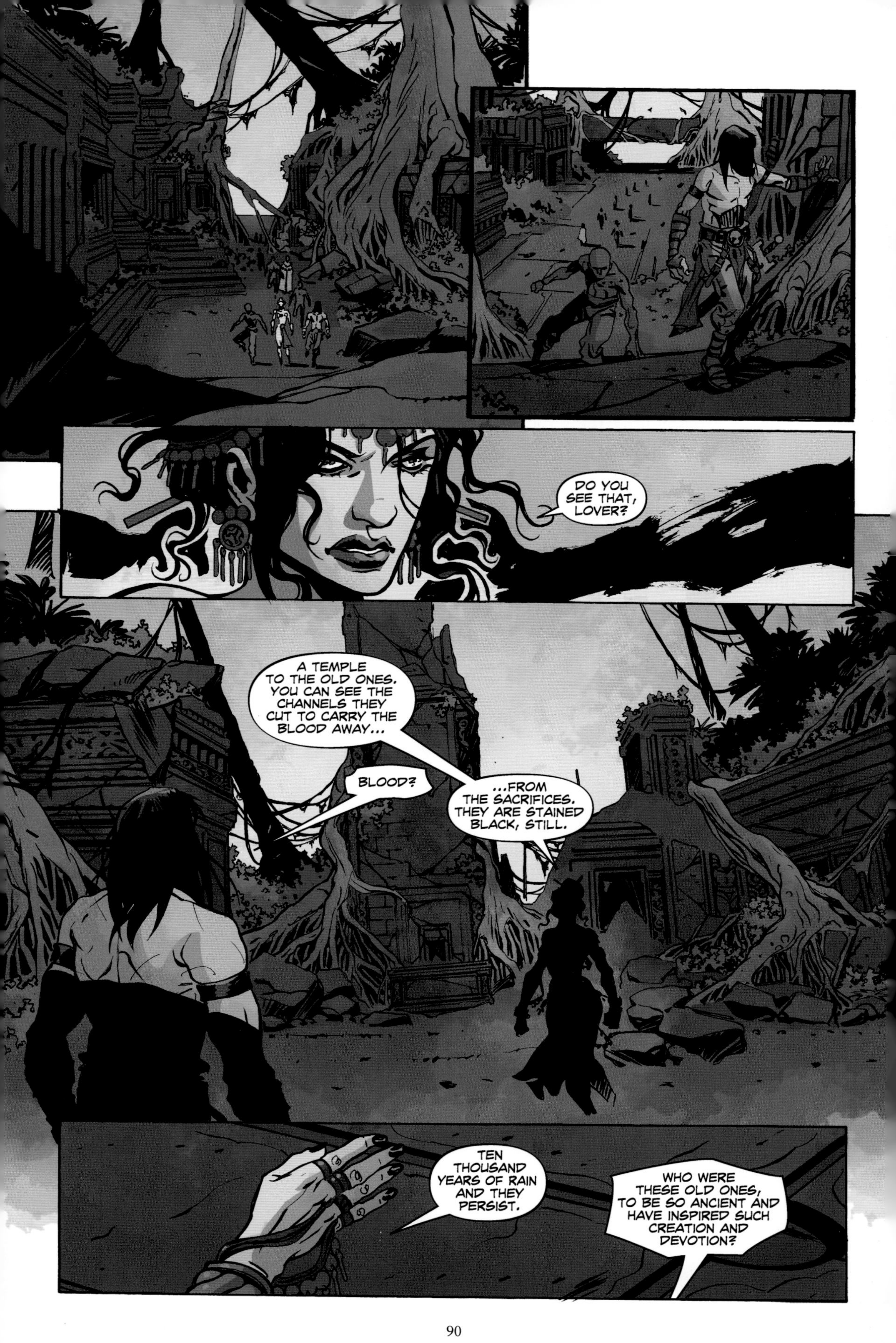
DO YOU SEE THAT, LOVER?
A TEMPLE TO THE OLD ONES. YOU CAN SEE THE CHANNELS THEY CUT TO CARRY THE BLOOD AWAY...
BLOOD?
...FROM THE SACRIFICES. THEY ARE STAINED BLACK, STILL.
TEN THOUSAND YEARS OF RAIN AND THEY PERSIST.
WHO WERE THESE OLD ONES, TO BE SO ANCIENT AND HAVE INSPIRED SUCH CREATION AND DEVOTION?

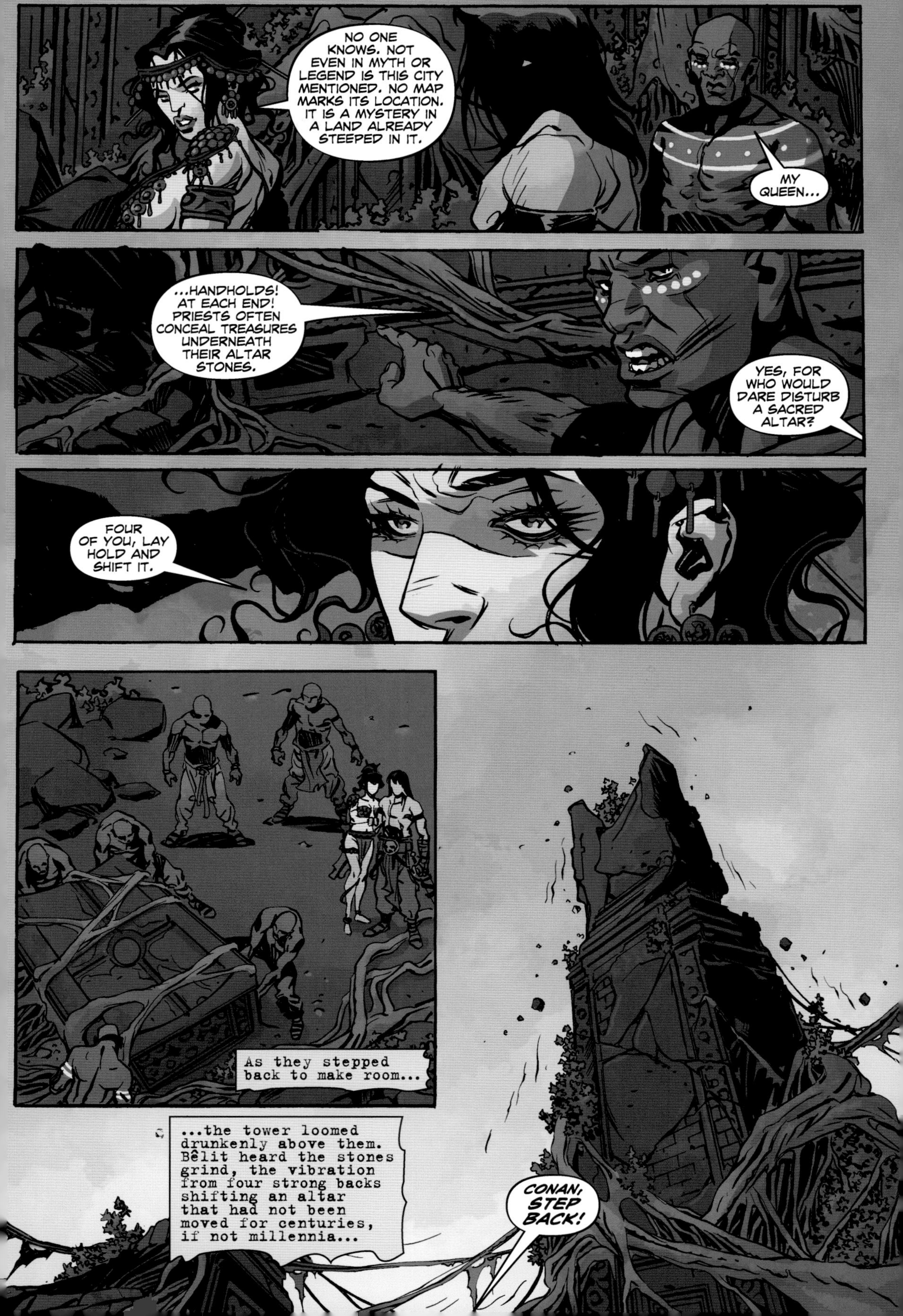
NO ONE KNOWS. NOT EVEN IN MYTH OR LEGEND IS THIS CITY MENTIONED. NO MAP MARKS ITS LOCATION. IT IS A MYSTERY IN A LAND ALREADY STEEPED IN IT.
MY QUEEN...
...HANDHOLDS! AT EACH END! PRIESTS OFTEN CONCEAL TREASURES UNDERNEATH THEIR ALTAR STONES.
YES, FOR WHO WOULD DARE DISTURB A SACRED ALTAR?
FOUR OF YOU, LAY HOLD AND SHIFT IT.
As they stepped back to make room...
...the tower loomed drunkenly above them. Bêlit heard the stones grind, the vibration from four strong backs shifting an altar that had not been moved for centuries, if not millennia...
CONAN, STEP BACK!

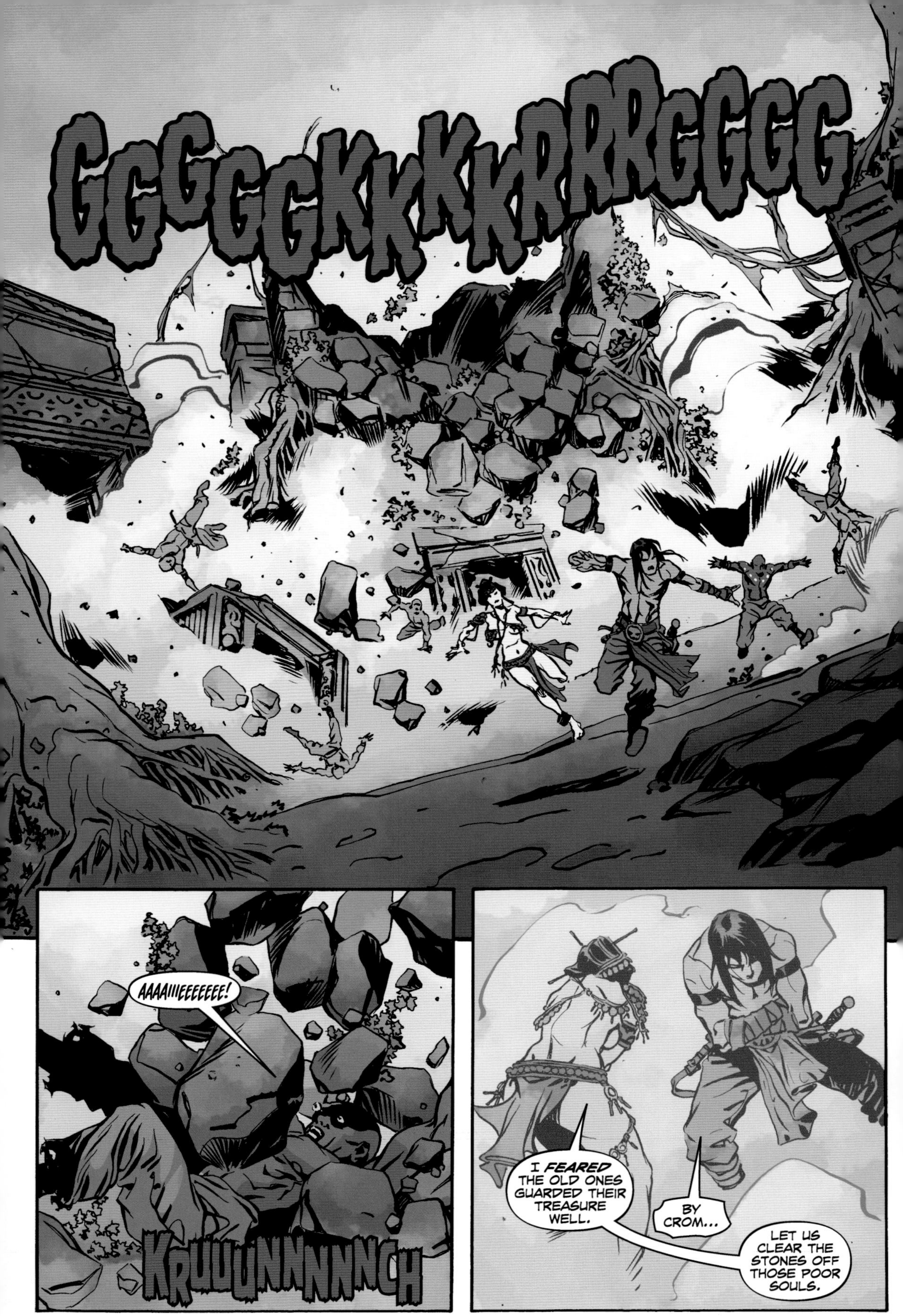
GGGGGKKKKRRRGGGG
AAAAIIIEEEEEEE!
KRUUGNNNNNCH
I FEARED THE OLD ONES GUARDED THEIR TREASURE WELL.
BY CROM...
LET US CLEAR THE STONES OFF THOSE POOR SOULS.

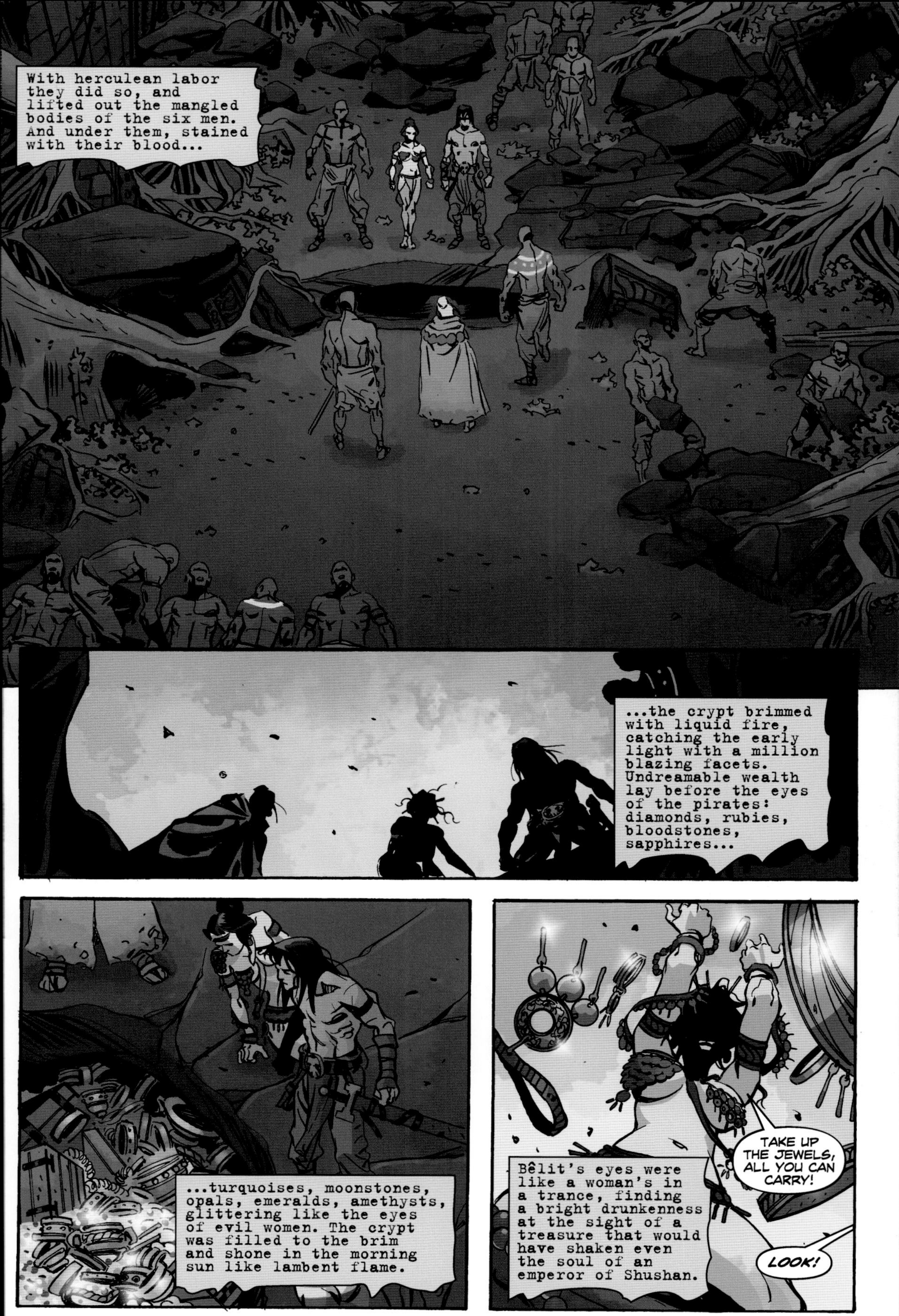

With herculean labor they did so, and lifted out the mangled bodies of the six men. And under them, stained with their blood...
...the crypt brimmed with liquid fire, catching the early light with a million blazing facets. Undreamable wealth lay before the eyes of the pirates: diamonds, rubies, bloodstones, sapphires...
...turquoises, moonstones, opals, emeralds, amethysts, glittering like the eyes of evil women. The crypt was filled to the brim and shone in the morning sun like lambent flame.
Bêlit's eyes were like a woman's in a trance, finding a bright drunkenness at the sight of a treasure that would have shaken even the soul of an emperor of Shushan.
TAKE UP THE JEWELS, ALL YOU CAN CARRY!
LOOK!

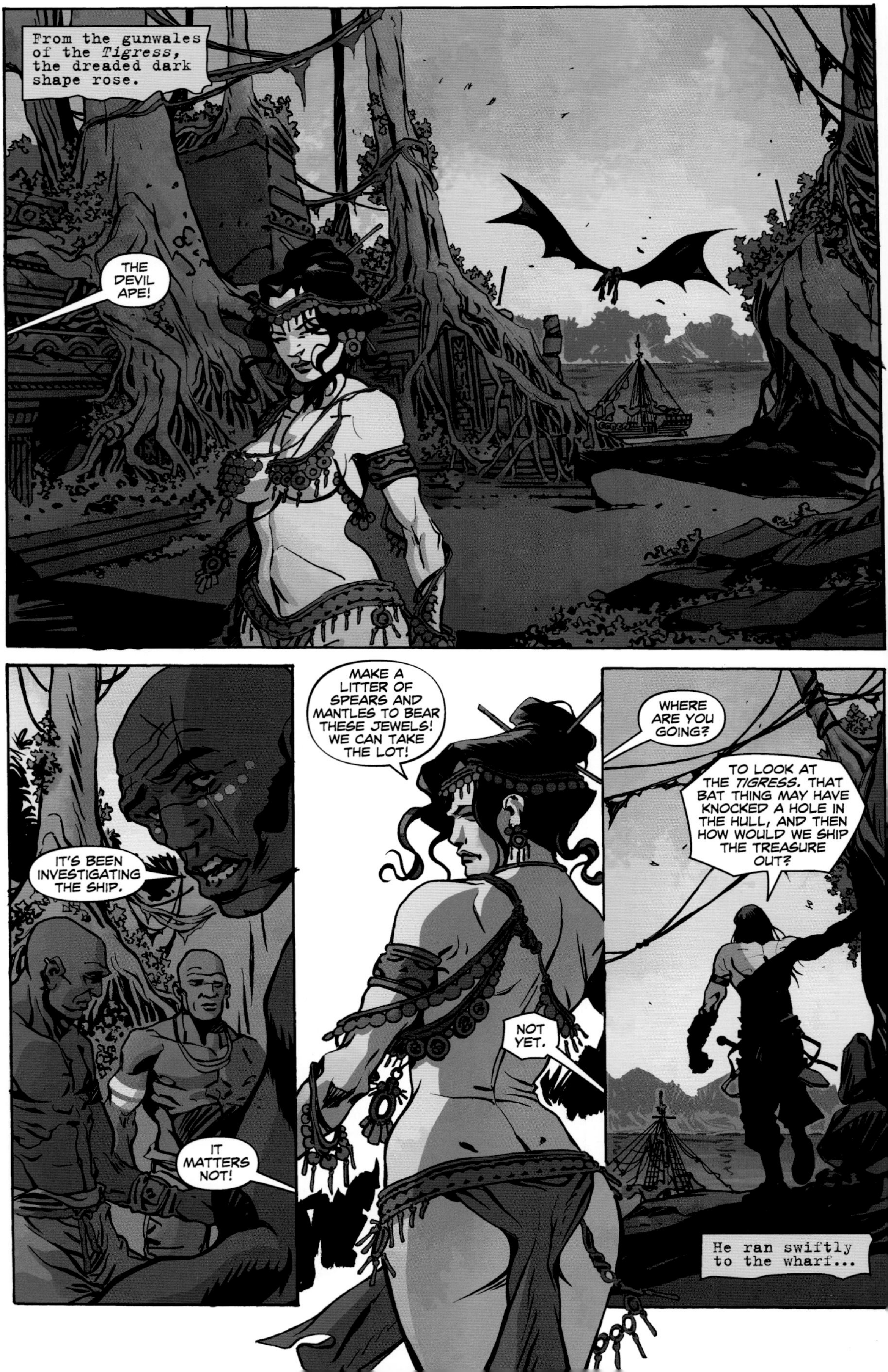
From the gunwales of the *Tigress*, the dreaded dark shape rose.
THE DEVIL APE!
IT'S BEEN INVESTIGATING THE SHIP.
IT MATTERS NOT!
MAKE A LITTER OF SPEARS AND MANTLES TO BEAR THESE JEWELS! WE CAN TAKE THE LOT!
NOT YET.
WHERE ARE YOU GOING?
TO LOOK AT THE *TIGRESS*. THAT BAT THING MAY HAVE KNOCKED A HOLE IN THE HULL, AND THEN HOW WOULD WE SHIP THE TREASURE OUT?
He ran swiftly to the wharf...

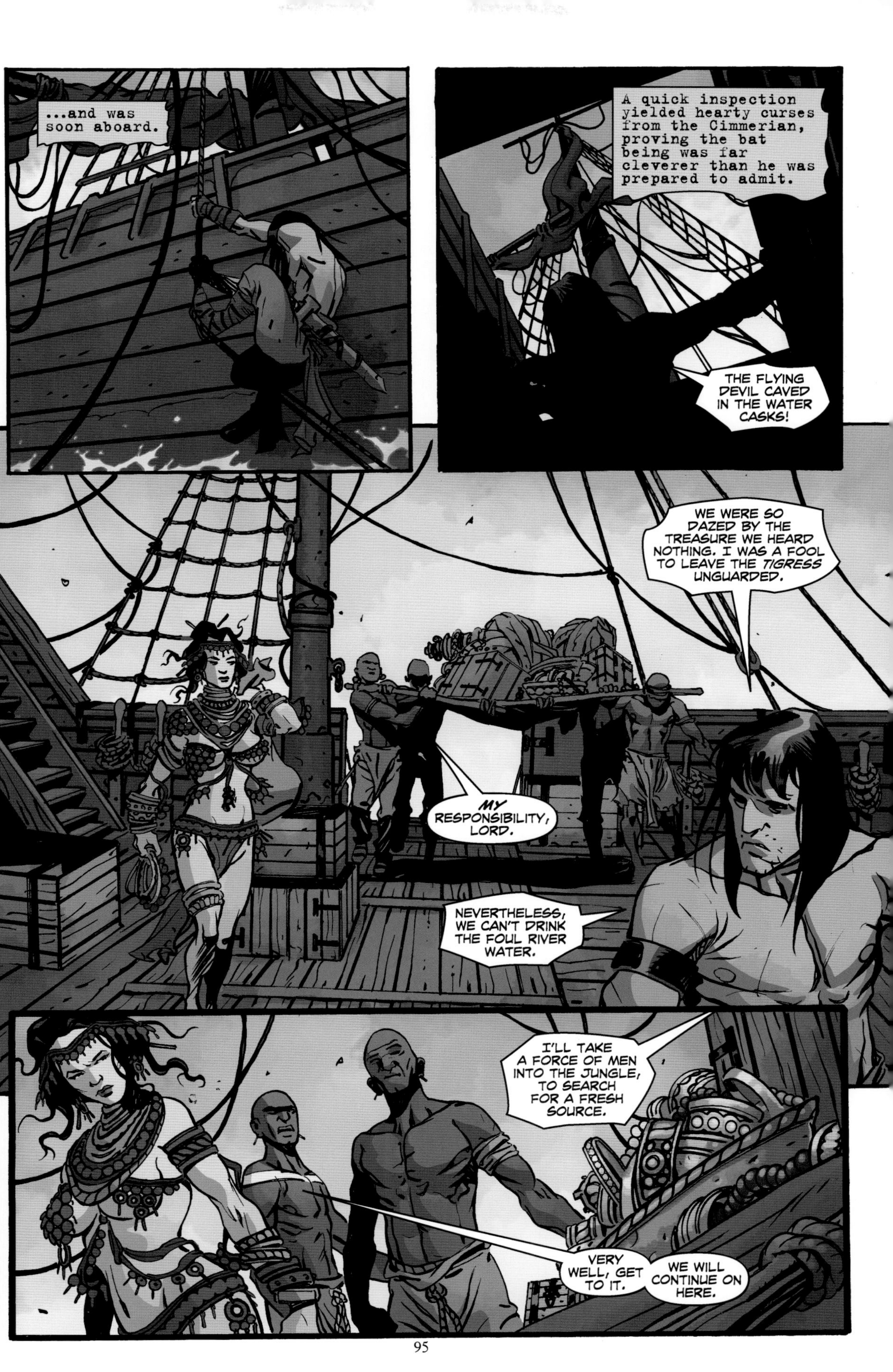
...and was soon aboard.
A quick inspection yielded hearty curses from the Cimmerian, proving the bat being was far cleverer than he was prepared to admit.
THE FLYING DEVIL CAVED IN THE WATER CASKS!
WE WERE SO DAZED BY THE TREASURE WE HEARD NOTHING. I WAS A FOOL TO LEAVE THE *TIGRESS* UNGUARDED.
MY RESPONSIBILITY, LORD.
NEVERTHELESS, WE CAN'T DRINK THE FOUL RIVER WATER.
I'LL TAKE A FORCE OF MEN INTO THE JUNGLE, TO SEARCH FOR A FRESH SOURCE.
VERY WELL, GET TO IT.
WE WILL CONTINUE ON HERE.

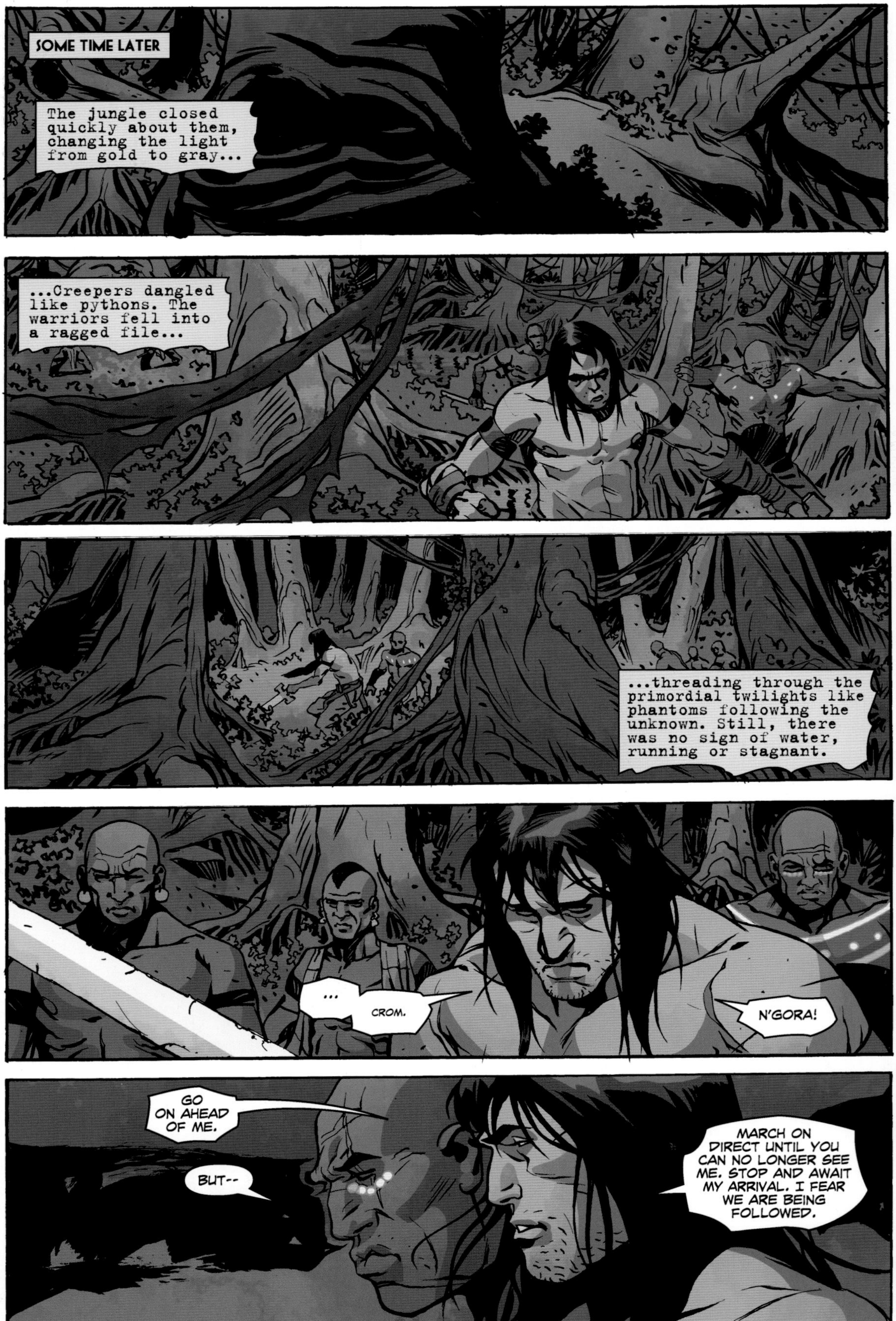
SOME TIME LATER
The jungle closed quickly about them, changing the light from gold to gray...
...Creepers dangled like pythons. The warriors fell into a ragged file...
...threading through the primordial twilights like phantoms following the unknown. Still, there was no sign of water, running or stagnant.
...
CROM.
N'GORA!
GO ON AHEAD OF ME.
BUT--
MARCH ON DIRECT UNTIL YOU CAN NO LONGER SEE ME. STOP AND AWAIT MY ARRIVAL. I FEAR WE ARE BEING FOLLOWED.

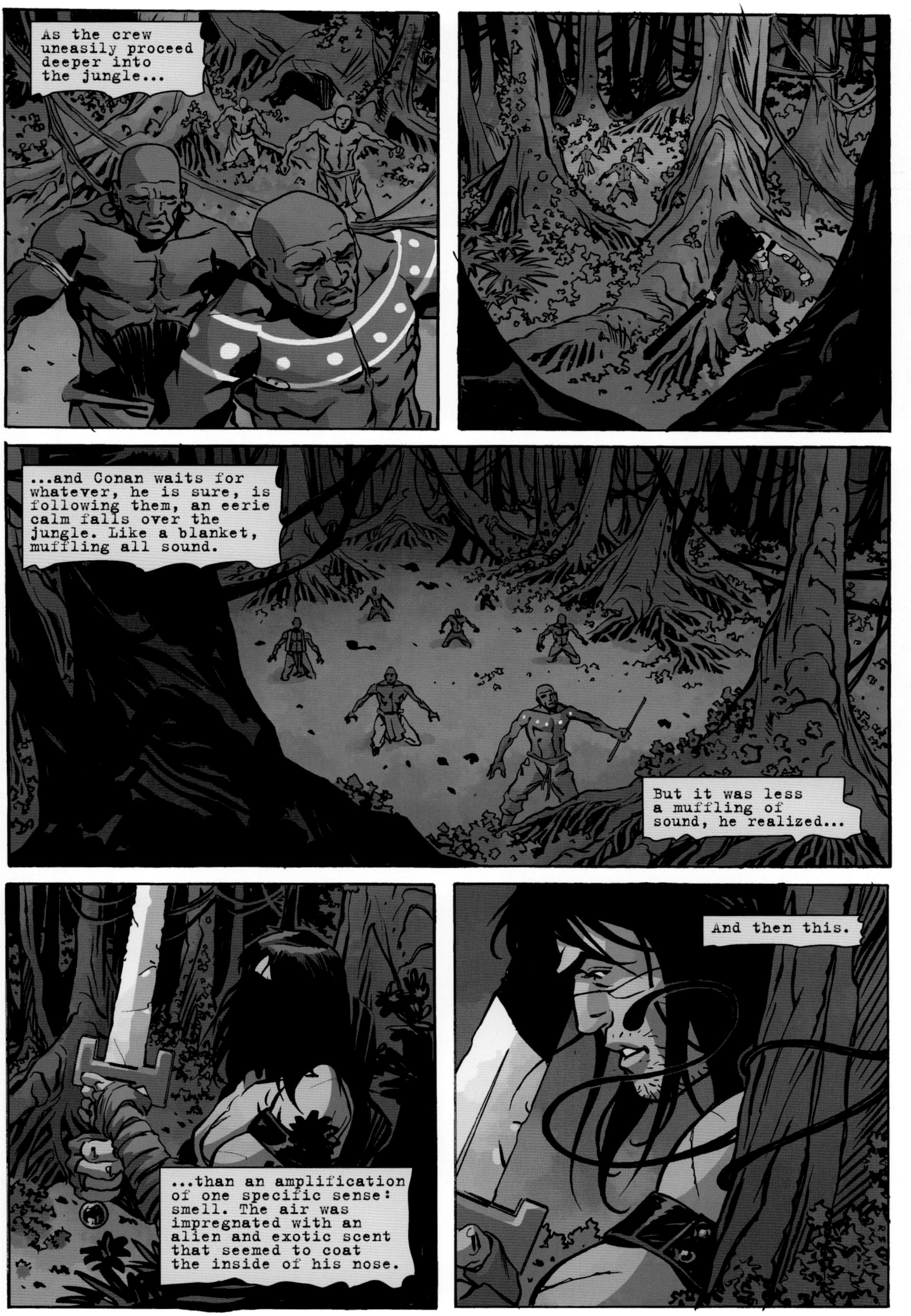
As the crew uneasily proceed deeper into the jungle...
...and Conan waits for whatever, he is sure, is following them, an eerie calm falls over the jungle. Like a blanket, muffling all sound.
But it was less a muffling of sound, he realized...
...than an amplification of one specific sense: smell. The air was impregnated with an alien and exotic scent that seemed to coat the inside of his nose.
And then this.

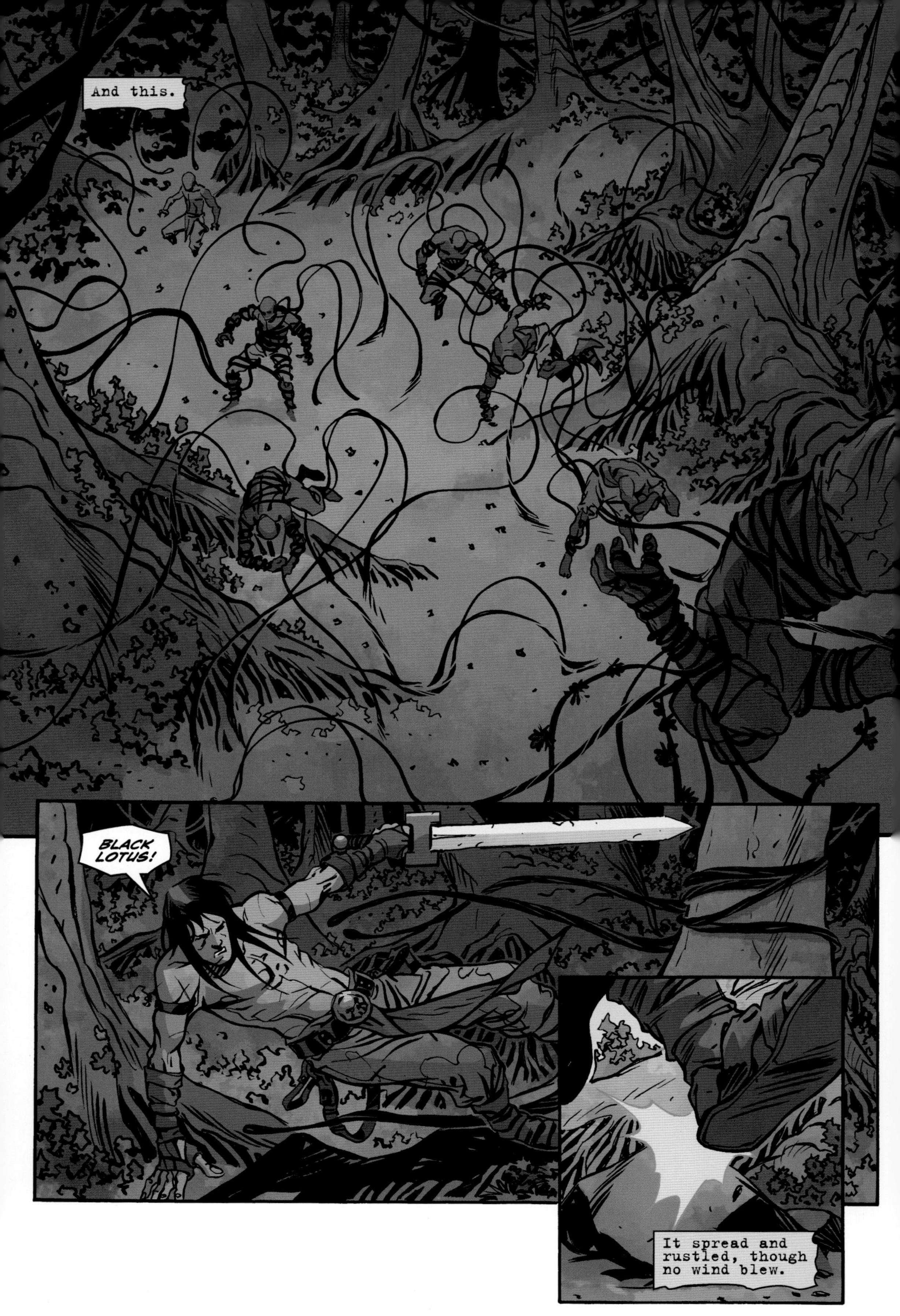
And this.
BLACK LOTUS!
It spread and rustled, though no wind blew.

To ingest the blossom meant death. To breathe its pollen meant something potentially far worse: a dream-haunted slumber.

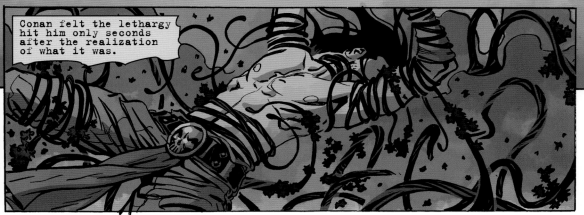

Conan felt the lethargy hit him only seconds after the realization of what it was.

He made a massive attempt to reach his sword, but his limbs were lifeless. He went to shout, but produced little more than a faint rattle.

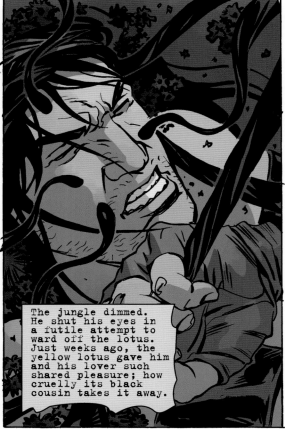

The jungle dimmed. He shut his eyes in a futile attempt to ward off the lotus. Just weeks ago, the yellow lotus gave him and his lover such shared pleasure; how cruelly its black cousin takes it away.

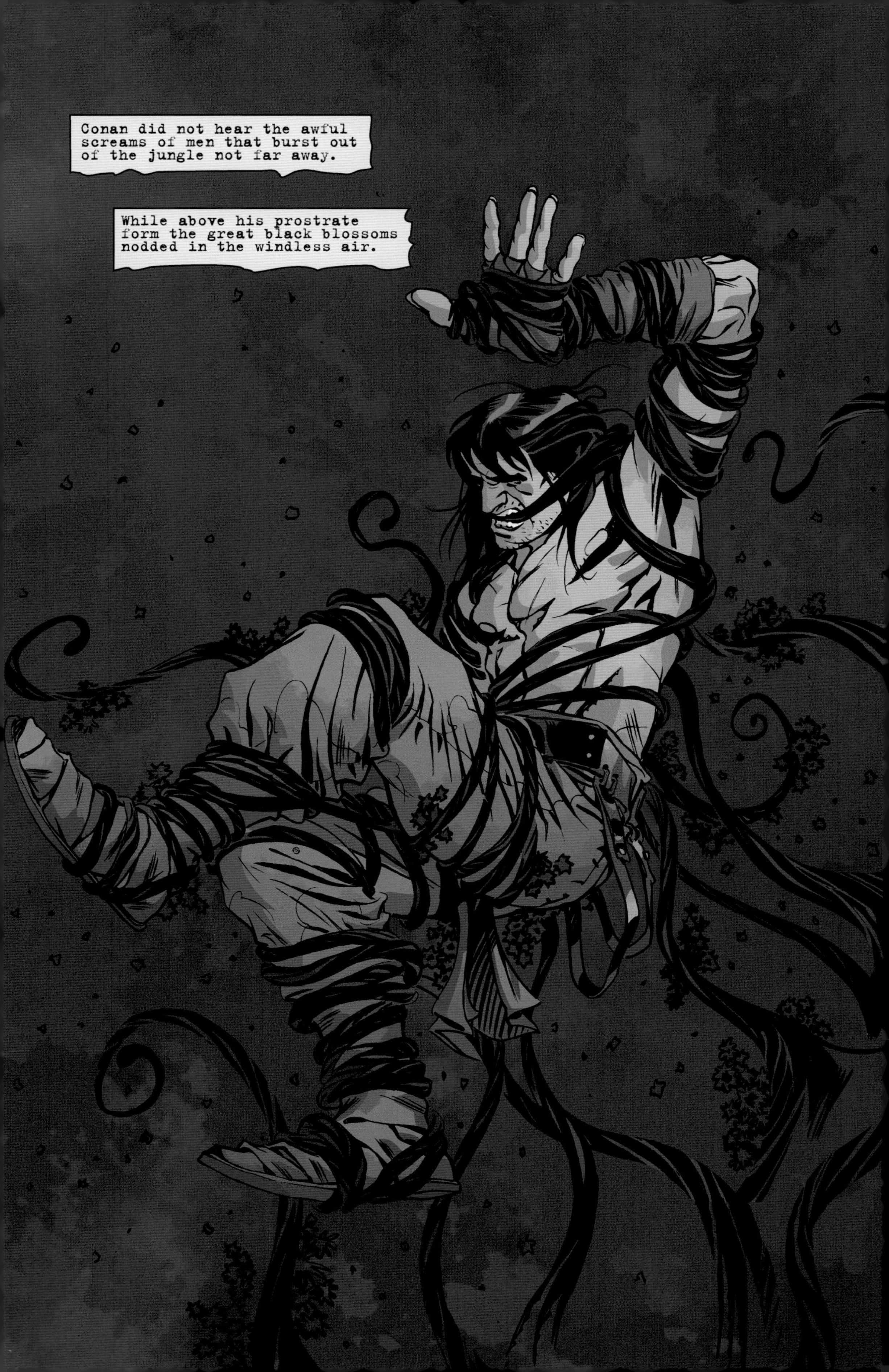
Conan did not hear the awful screams of men that burst out of the jungle not far away.
While above his prostrate form the great black blossoms nodded in the windless air.

CHAPTER FIVE

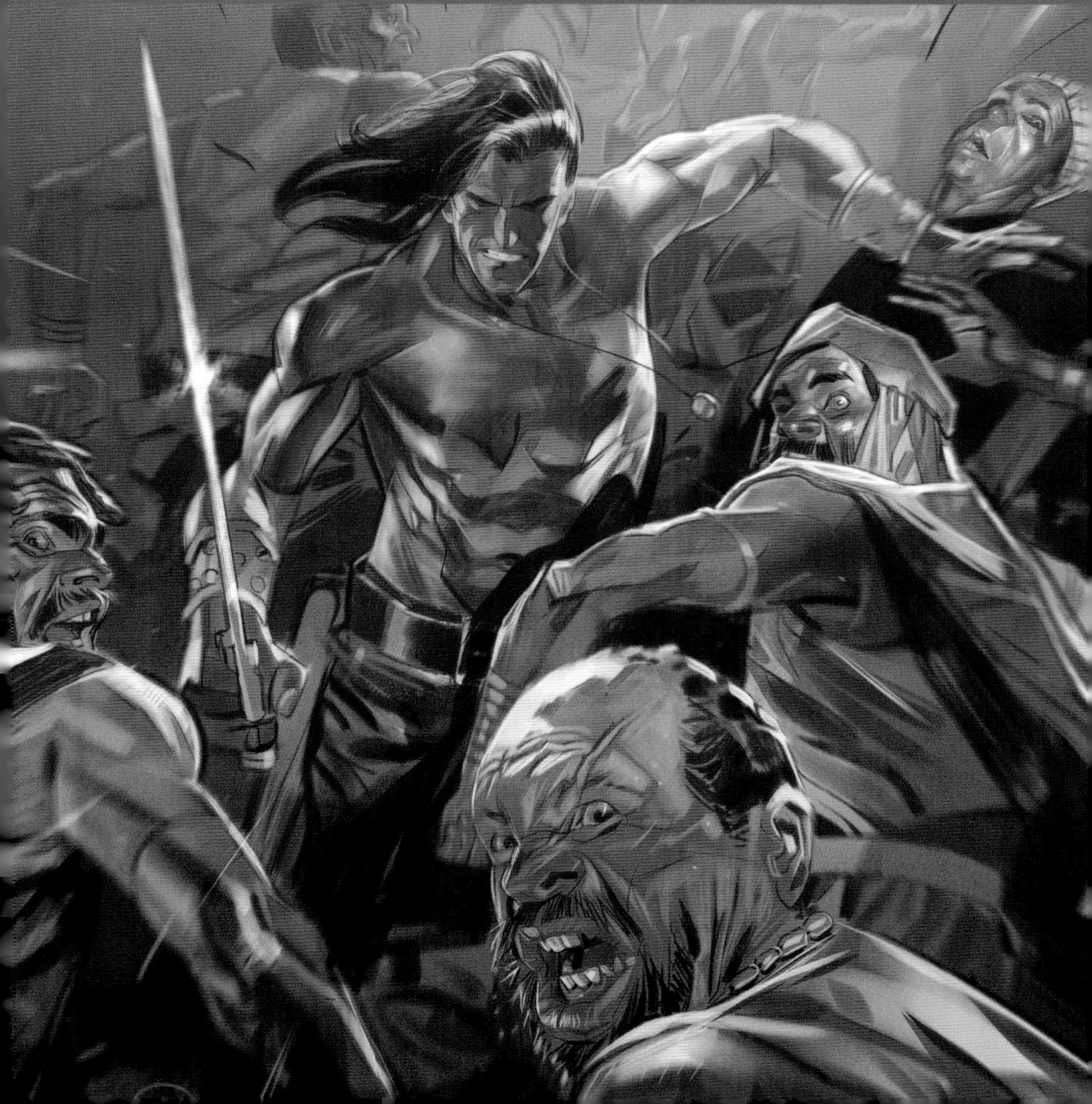

"What shapes would emerge from the blackness he knew not. Nor did he care."

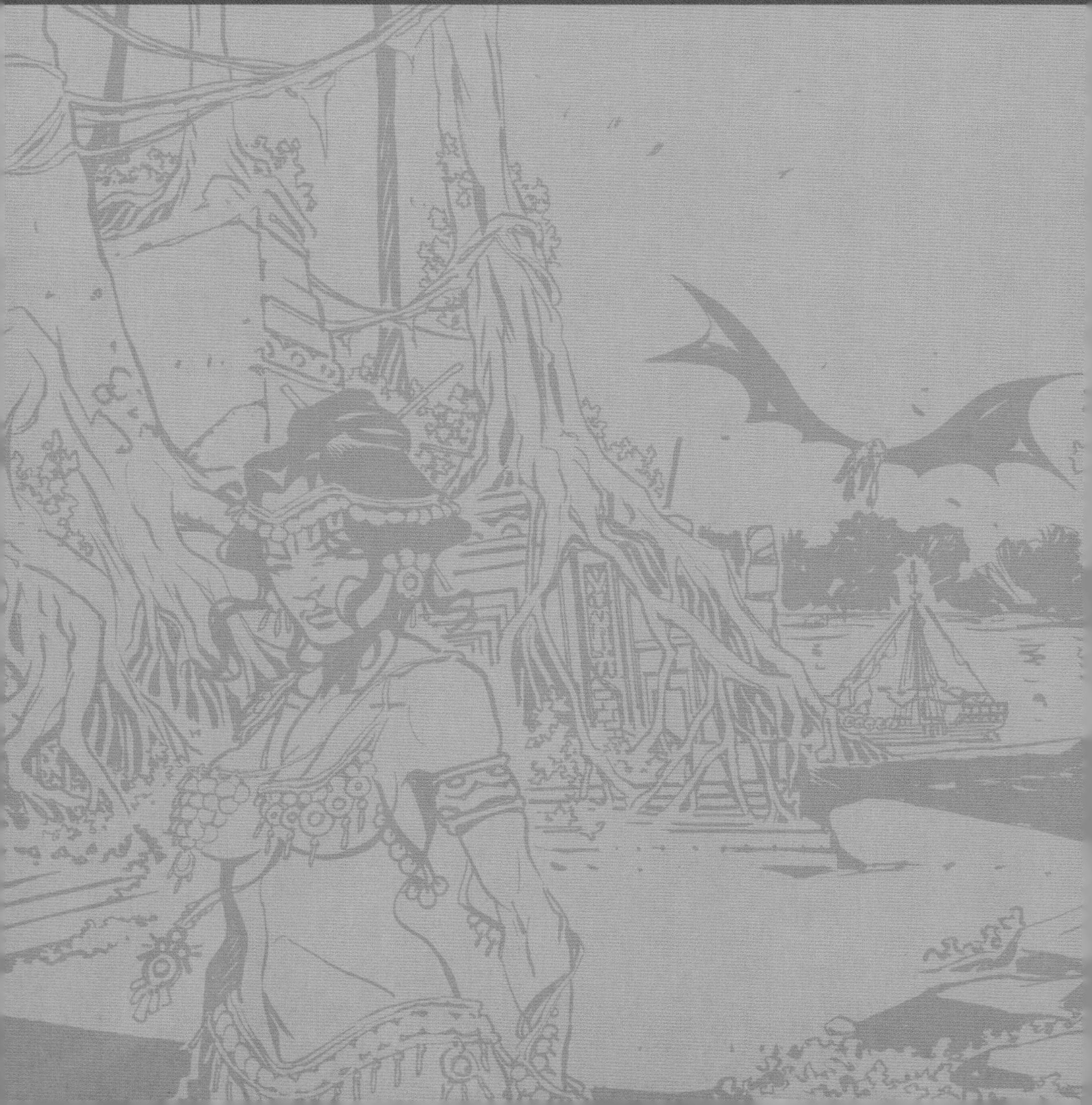

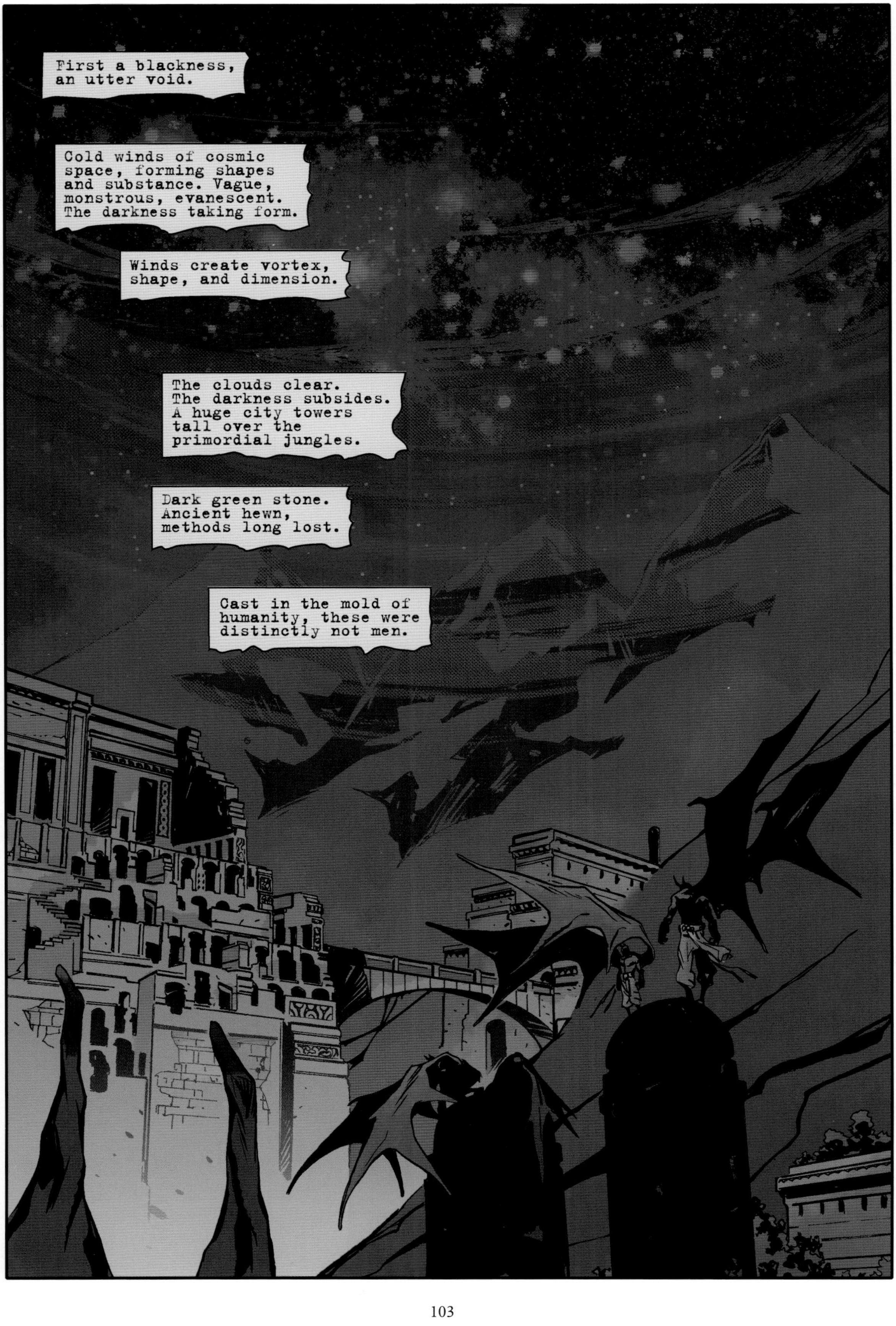
First a blackness, an utter void.
Cold winds of cosmic space, forming shapes and substance. Vague, monstrous, evanescent. The darkness taking form.
Winds create vortex, shape, and dimension.
The clouds clear. The darkness subsides. A huge city towers tall over the primordial jungles.
Dark green stone. Ancient hewn, methods long lost.
Cast in the mold of humanity, these were distinctly not men.

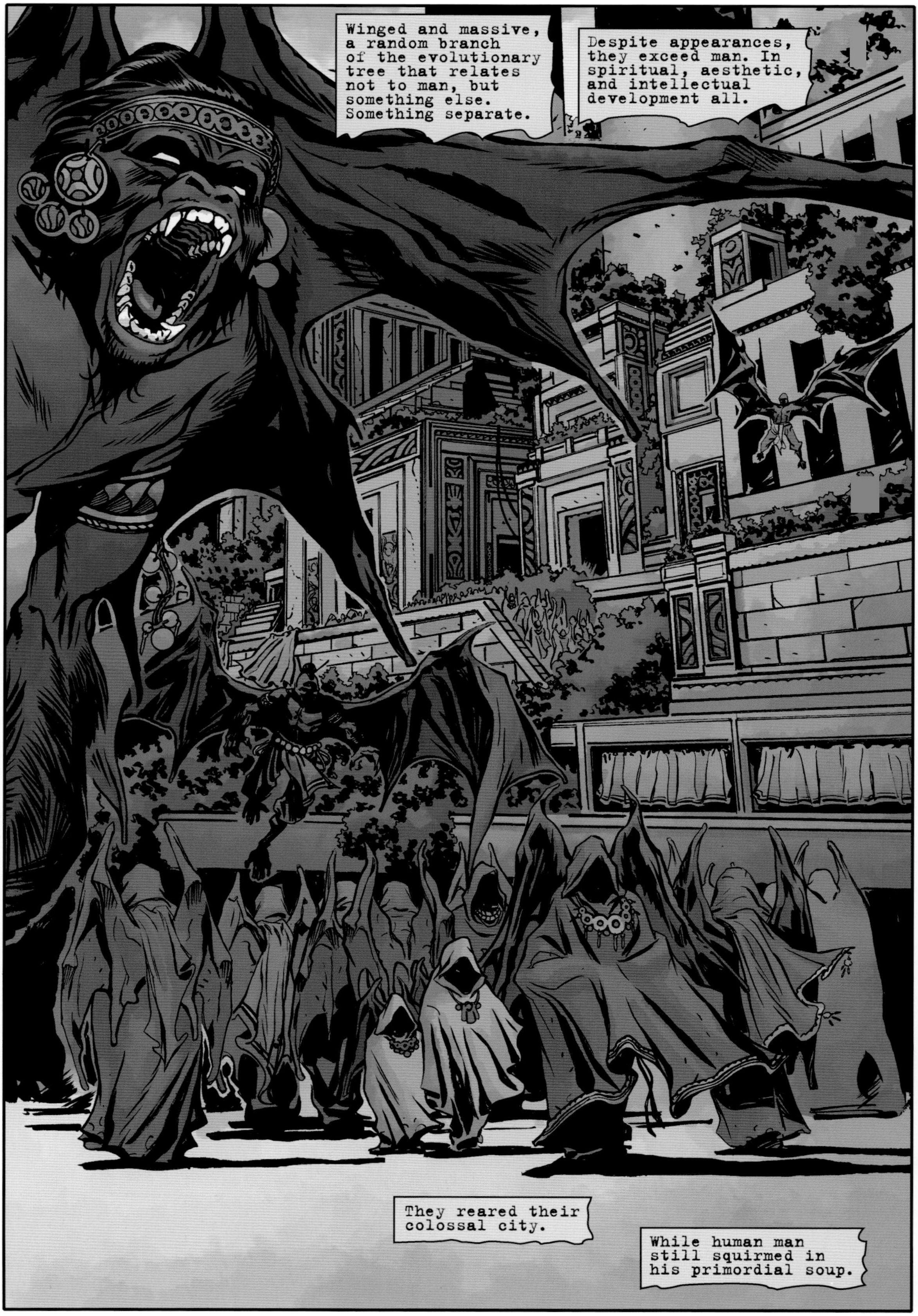
Winged and massive, a random branch of the evolutionary tree that relates not to man, but something else. Something separate.
Despite appearances, they exceed man. In spiritual, aesthetic, and intellectual development all.
They reared their colossal city.
While human man still squirmed in his primordial soup.

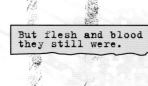

But flesh and blood they still were.

They lived and loved, and when the ice came, they died en masse.

Millions of years of change. The vista shimmers and waves, heats up and cools down. Each wave brings alterations and iterations.

New species rise up, and others fall. The ecosystem is replenished countless times.

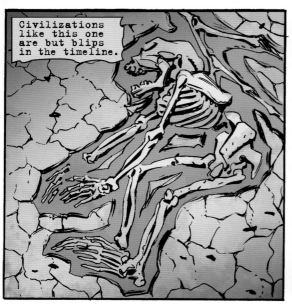

Civilizations like this one are but blips in the timeline.

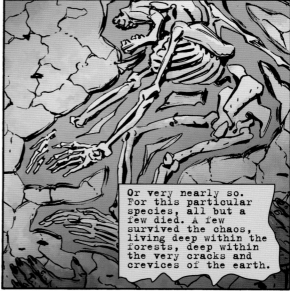

Or very nearly so. For this particular species, all but a few died. A few survived the chaos, living deep within the forests, deep within the very cracks and crevices of the earth.

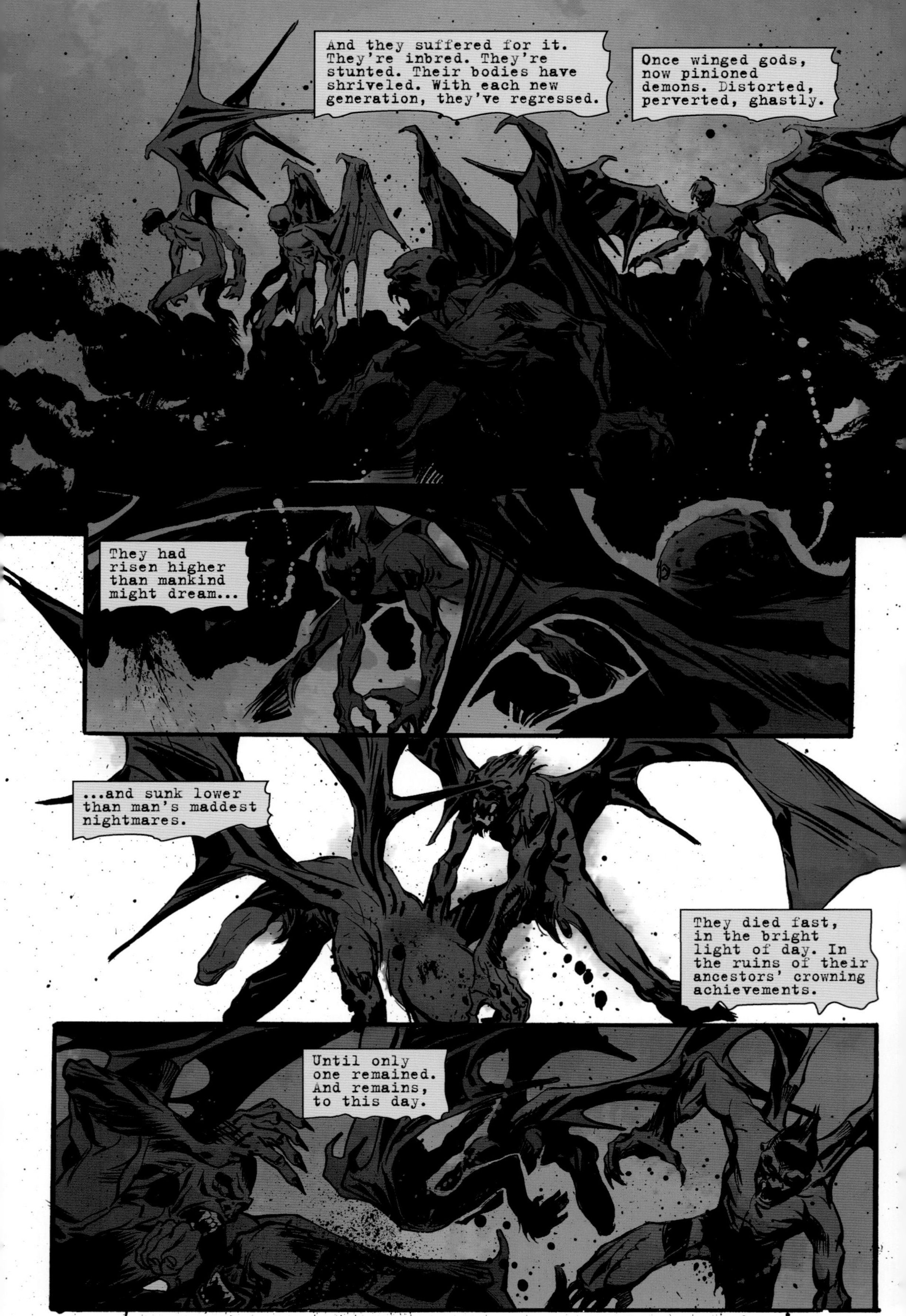
And they suffered for it. They're inbred. They're stunted. Their bodies have shriveled. With each new generation, they've regressed.
Once winged gods, now pinioned demons. Distorted, perverted, ghastly.
They had risen higher than mankind might dream...
...and sunk lower than man's maddest nightmares.
They died fast, in the bright light of day. In the ruins of their ancestors' crowning achievements.
Until only one remained. And remains, to this day.

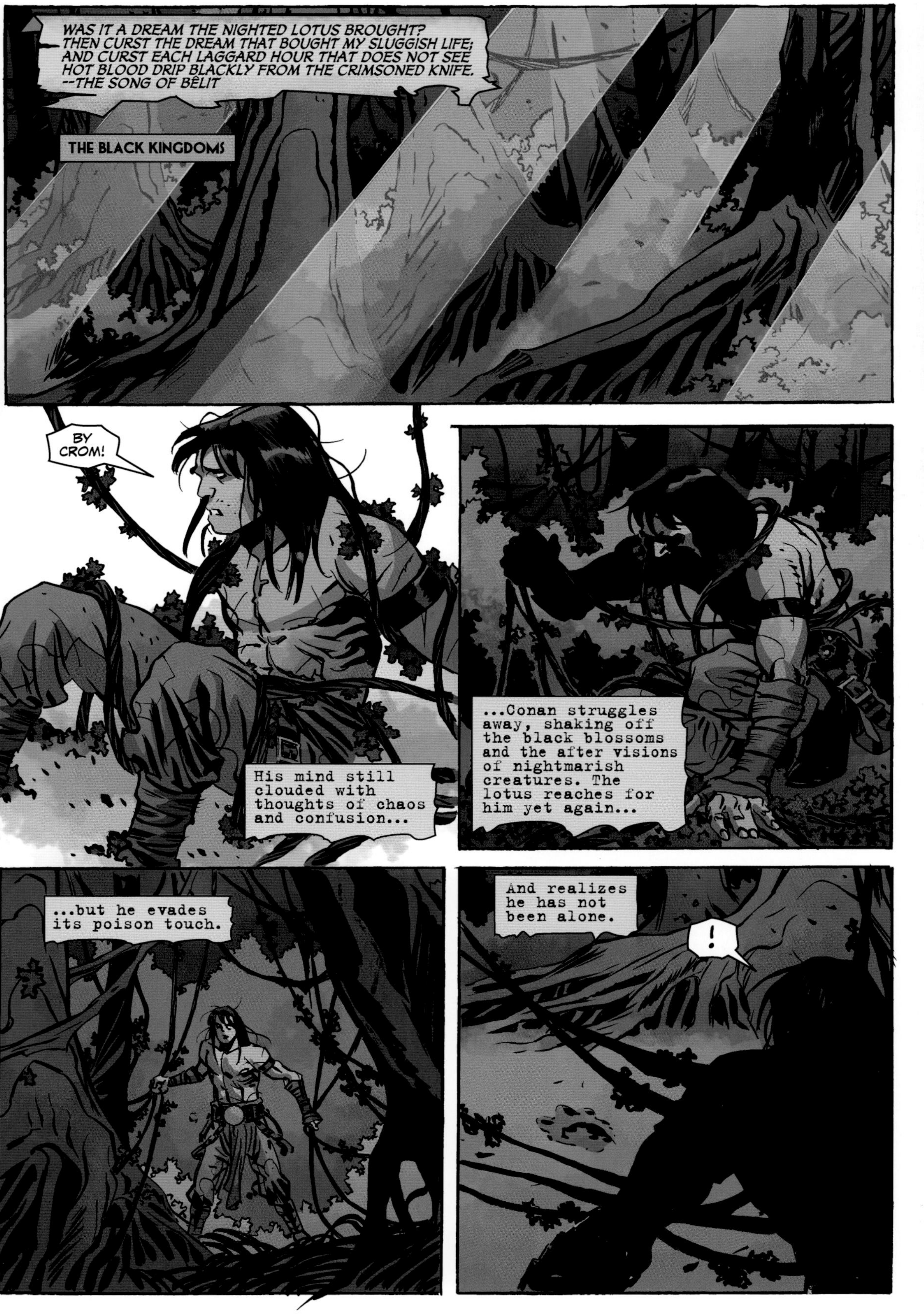
WAS IT A DREAM THE NIGHTED LOTUS BROUGHT?
THEN CURST THE DREAM THAT BOUGHT MY SLUGGISH LIFE;
AND CURST EACH LAGGARD HOUR THAT DOES NOT SEE
HOT BLOOD DRIP BLACKLY FROM THE CRIMSONED KNIFE.
--THE SONG OF BÊLIT
THE BLACK KINGDOMS
BY CROM!
His mind still clouded with thoughts of chaos and confusion...
...Conan struggles away, shaking off the black blossoms and the after visions of nightmarish creatures. The lotus reaches for him yet again...
...but he evades its poison touch.
And realizes he has not been alone.
!

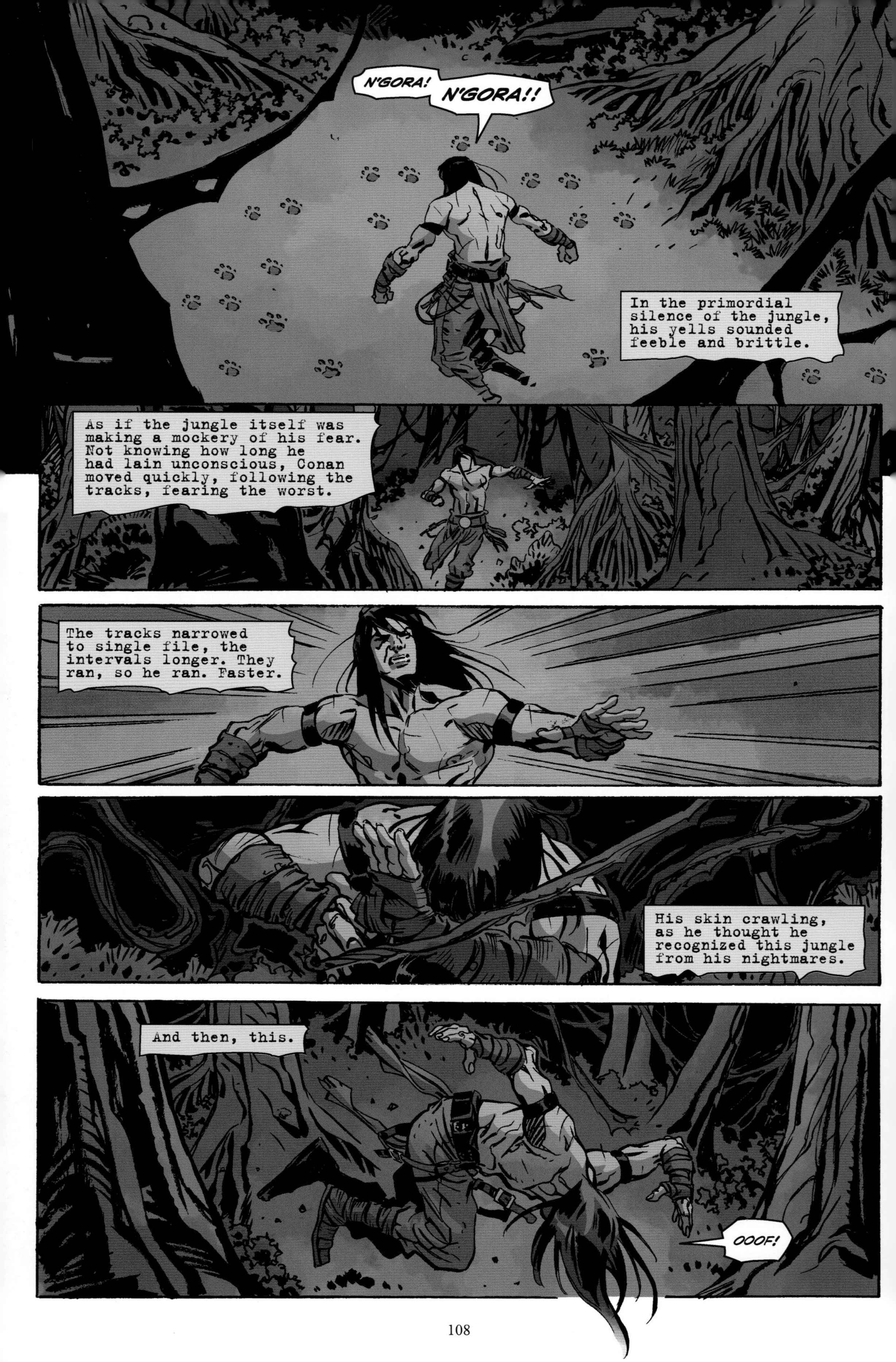
N'GORA!
N'GORA!!
In the primordial silence of the jungle, his yells sounded feeble and brittle.
As if the jungle itself was making a mockery of his fear. Not knowing how long he had lain unconscious, Conan moved quickly, following the tracks, fearing the worst.
The tracks narrowed to single file, the intervals longer. They ran, so he ran. Faster.
His skin crawling, as he thought he recognized this jungle from his nightmares.
And then, this.
OOOF!

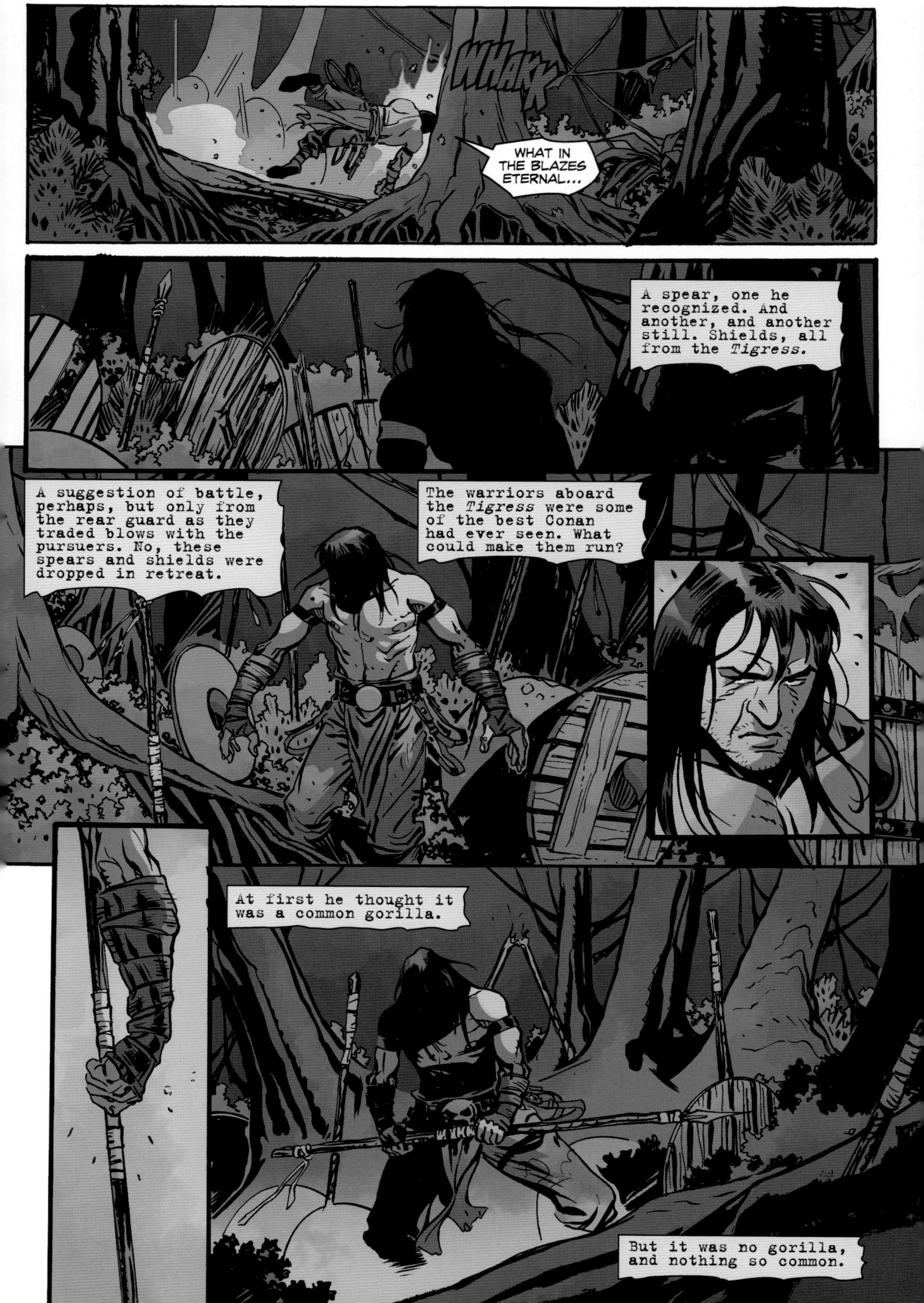
WHAKK
WHAT IN THE BLAZES ETERNAL...
A spear, one he recognized. And another, and another still. Shields, all from the *Tigress.*
A suggestion of battle, perhaps, but only from the rear guard as they traded blows with the pursuers. No, these spears and shields were dropped in retreat.
The warriors aboard the *Tigress* were some of the best Conan had ever seen. What could make them run?
At first he thought it was a common gorilla.
But it was no gorilla, and nothing so common.

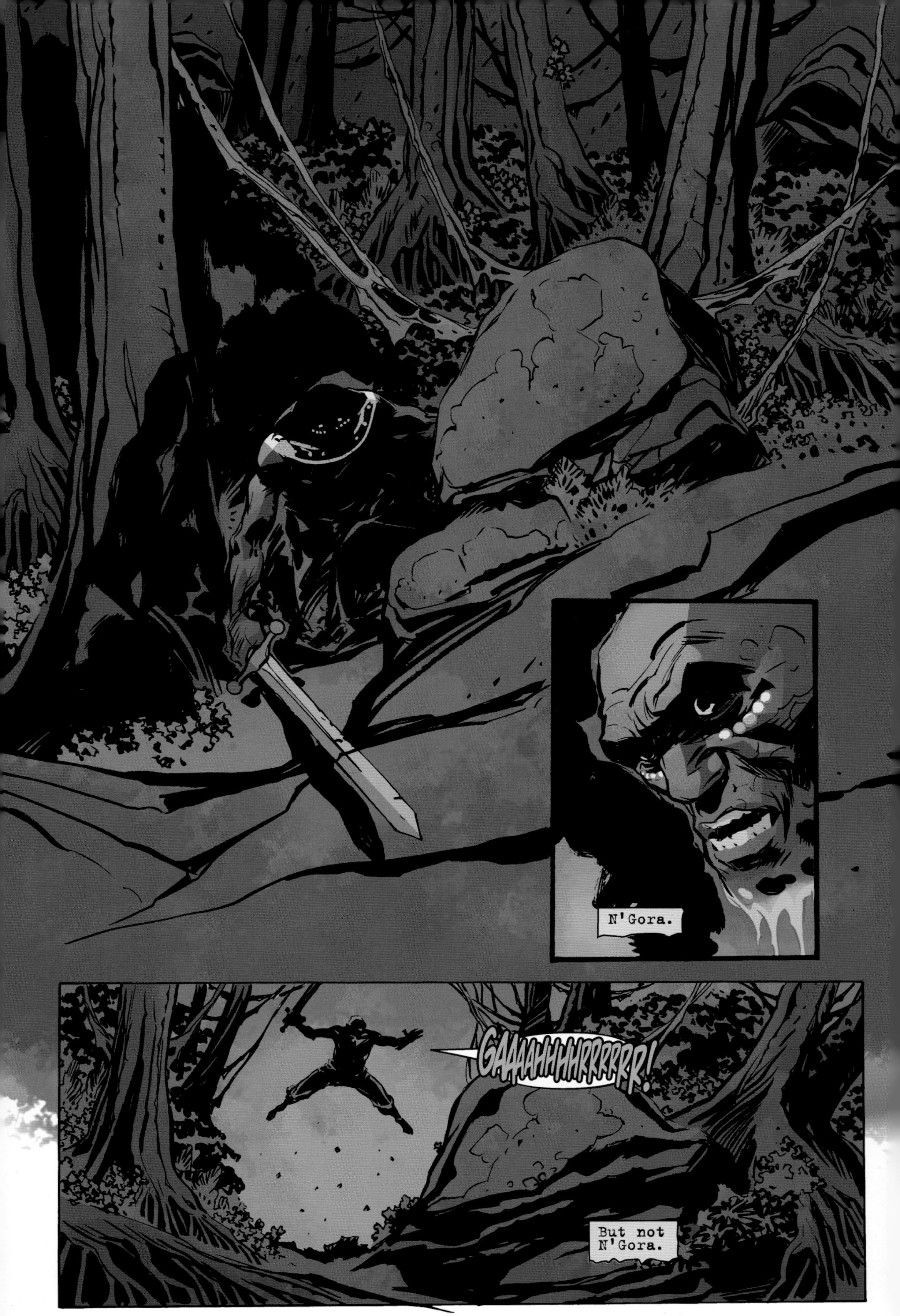
N'Gora.
GAAAAHHHHRRRRRR!
But not
N'Gora.

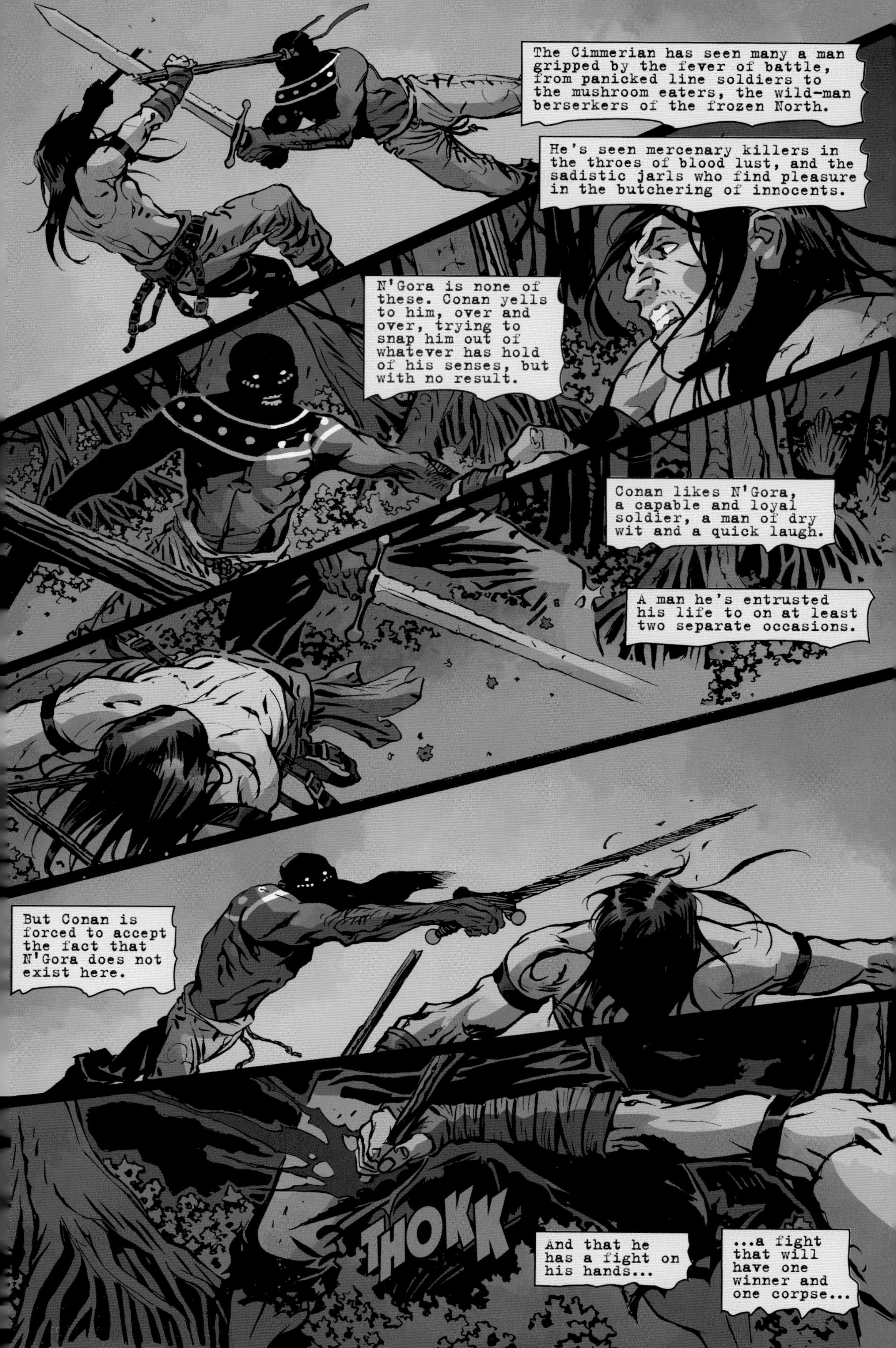
The Cimmerian has seen many a man gripped by the fever of battle, from panicked line soldiers to the mushroom eaters, the wild-man berserkers of the frozen North.
He's seen mercenary killers in the throes of blood lust, and the sadistic jarls who find pleasure in the butchering of innocents.
N'Gora is none of these. Conan yells to him, over and over, trying to snap him out of whatever has hold of his senses, but with no result.
Conan likes N'Gora, a capable and loyal soldier, a man of dry wit and a quick laugh.
A man he's entrusted his life to on at least two separate occasions.
But Conan is forced to accept the fact that N'Gora does not exist here.
THOKK
And that he has a fight on his hands...
...a fight that will have one winner and one corpse...

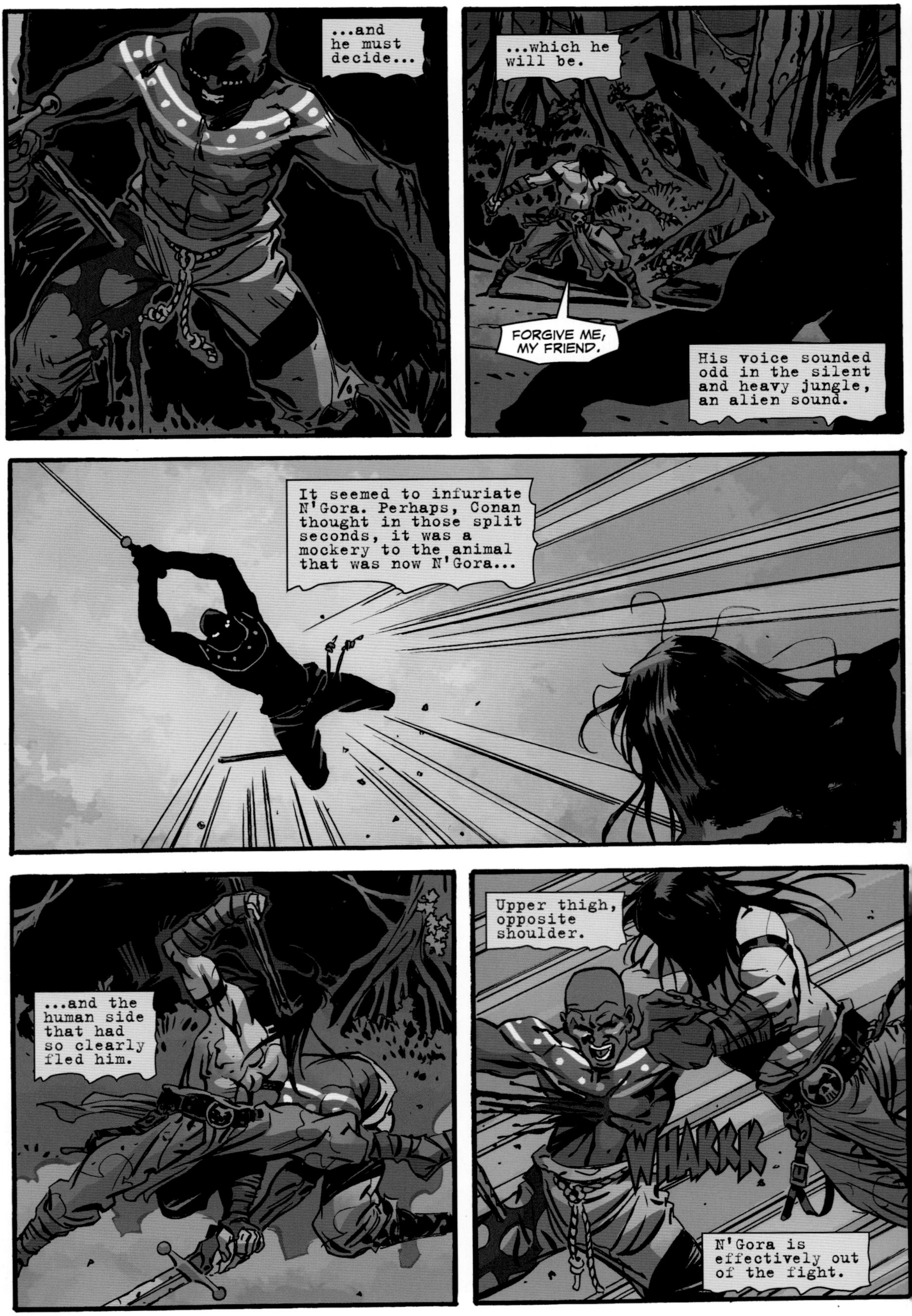
...and he must decide...
...which he will be.
FORGIVE ME, MY FRIEND.
His voice sounded odd in the silent and heavy jungle, an alien sound.
It seemed to infuriate N'Gora. Perhaps, Conan thought in those split seconds, it was a mockery to the animal that was now N'Gora...
...and the human side that had so clearly fled him.
Upper thigh, opposite shoulder.
WHAKKK
N'Gora is effectively out of the fight.

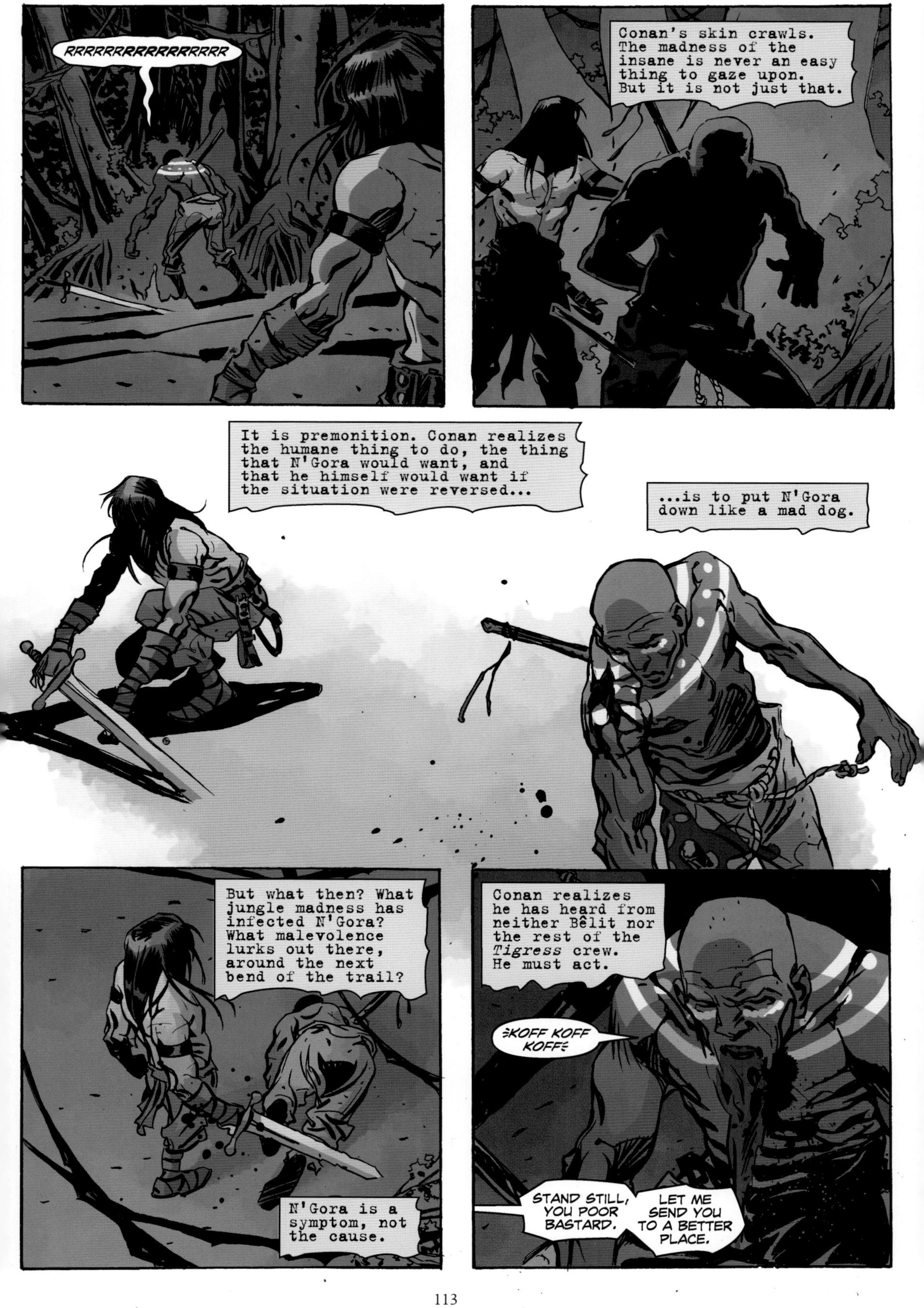
RRRRRRRRRRRRRRRR
Conan's skin crawls. The madness of the insane is never an easy thing to gaze upon. But it is not just that.
It is premonition. Conan realizes the humane thing to do, the thing that N'Gora would want, and that he himself would want if the situation were reversed...
...is to put N'Gora down like a mad dog.
But what then? What jungle madness has infected N'Gora? What malevolence lurks out there, around the next bend of the trail?
N'Gora is a symptom, not the cause.
Conan realizes he has heard from neither Bêlit nor the rest of the *Tigress* crew. He must act.
KOFF KOFF KOFF
STAND STILL, YOU POOR BASTARD.
LET ME SEND YOU TO A BETTER PLACE.

FEEEEEAAAARGGGGH!!!

SLICCCCCC

UFF!

GAAAHHHR

THAT'S IT. JUST LET IT GO.

SLEEP, YOU MAD DOG.

YOU'VE EARNED SOME PEACE.

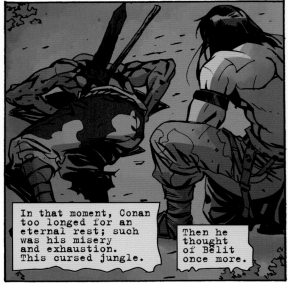

In that moment, Conan too longed for an eternal rest; such was his misery and exhaustion. This cursed jungle.

Then he thought of Bêlit once more.

114

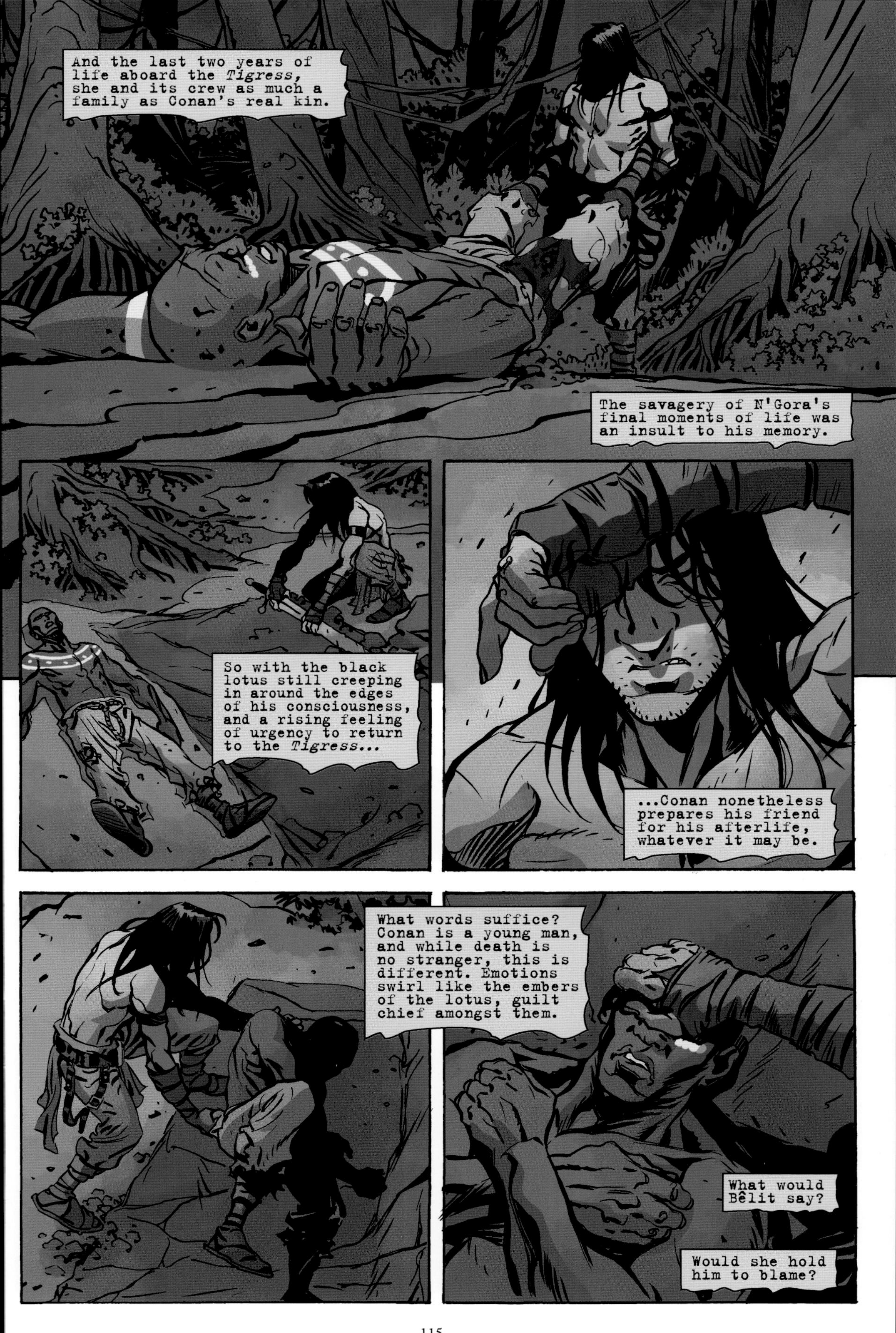
And the last two years of life aboard the *Tigress*, she and its crew as much a family as Conan's real kin.
The savagery of N'Gora's final moments of life was an insult to his memory.
So with the black lotus still creeping in around the edges of his consciousness, and a rising feeling of urgency to return to the *Tigress*...
...Conan nonetheless prepares his friend for his afterlife, whatever it may be.
What words suffice? Conan is a young man, and while death is no stranger, this is different. Emotions swirl like the embers of the lotus, guilt chief amongst them.
What would Bêlit say?
Would she hold him to blame?

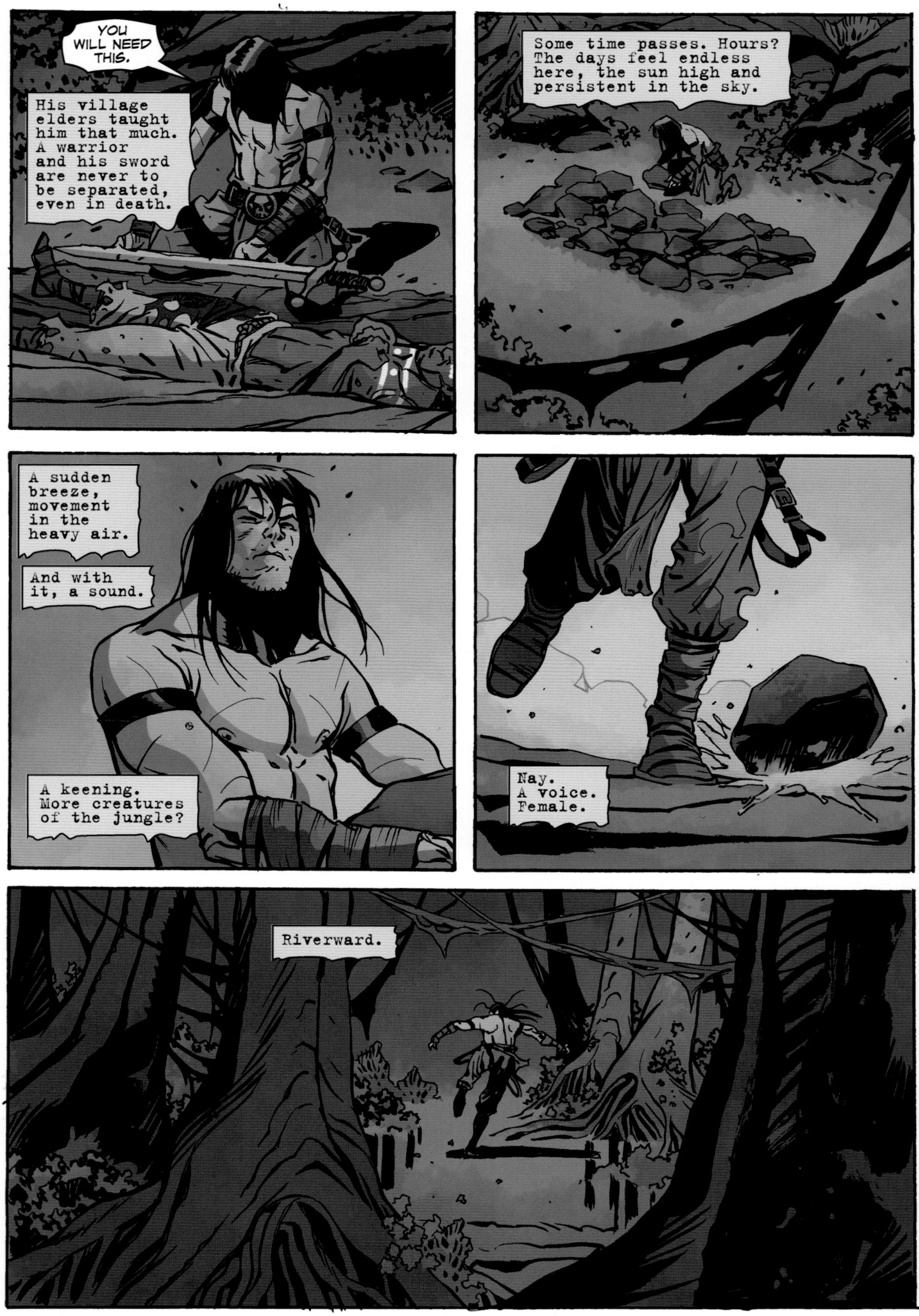
YOU WILL NEED THIS.
His village elders taught him that much. A warrior and his sword are never to be separated, even in death.
Some time passes. Hours? The days feel endless here, the sun high and persistent in the sky.
A sudden breeze, movement in the heavy air.
And with it, a sound.
A keening. More creatures of the jungle?
Nay. A voice. Female.
Riverward.

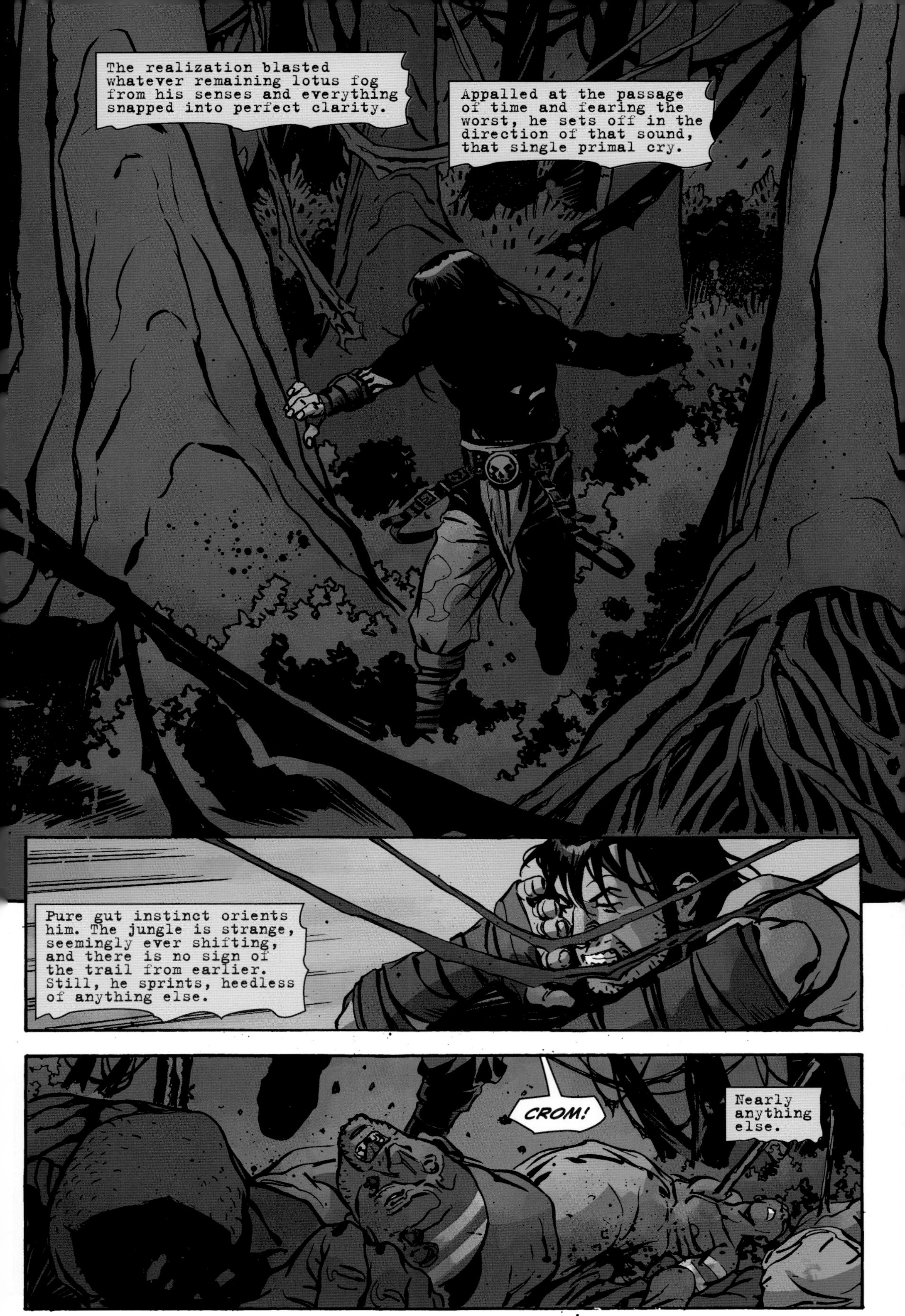
The realization blasted whatever remaining lotus fog from his senses and everything snapped into perfect clarity.
Appalled at the passage of time and fearing the worst, he sets off in the direction of that sound, that single primal cry.
Pure gut instinct orients him. The jungle is strange, seemingly ever shifting, and there is no sign of the trail from earlier. Still, he sprints, heedless of anything else.
CROM!
Nearly anything else.

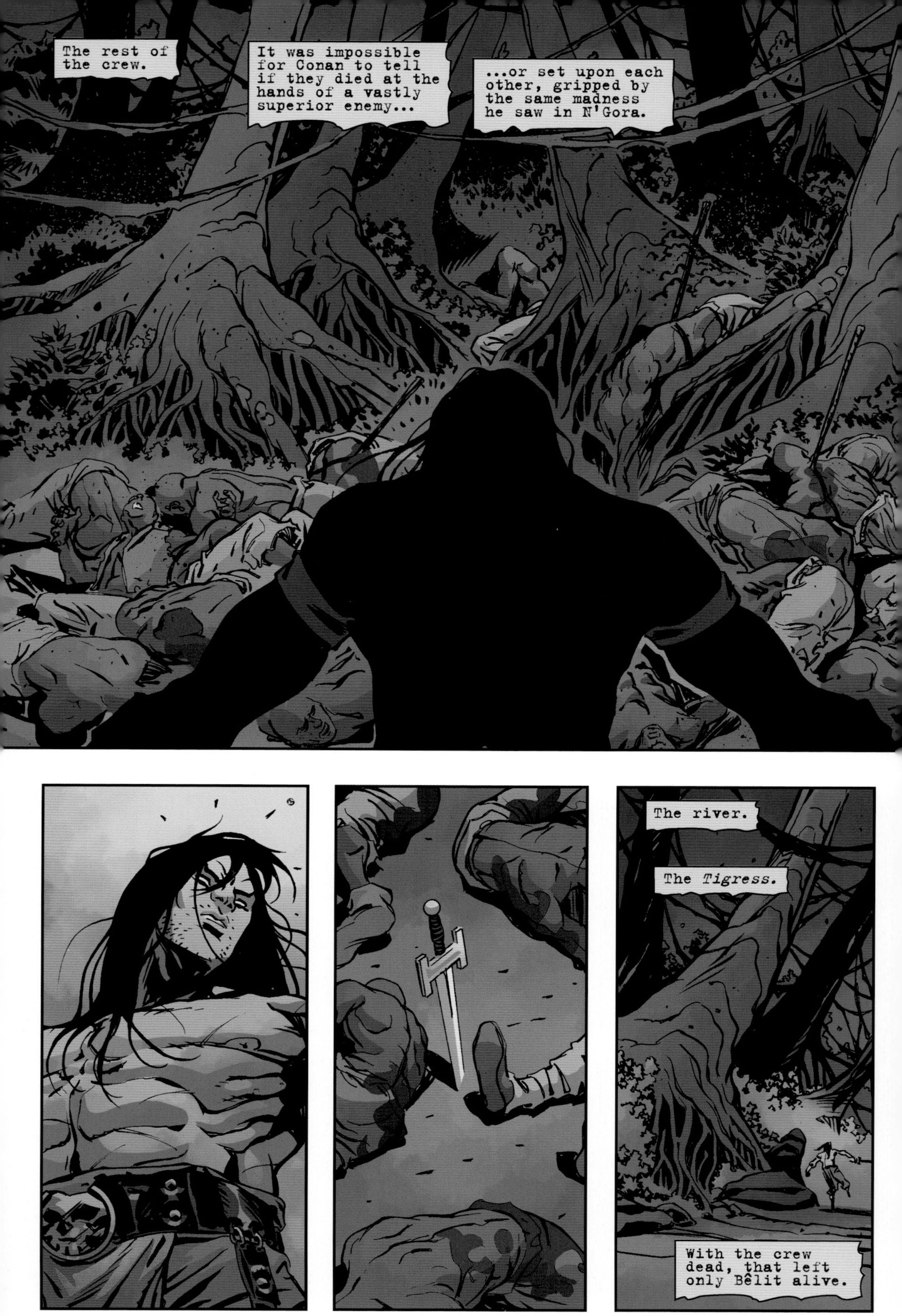
The rest of the crew.
It was impossible for Conan to tell if they died at the hands of a vastly superior enemy...
...or set upon each other, gripped by the same madness he saw in N'Gora.
The river.
The *Tigress.*
With the crew dead, that left only Bêlit alive.

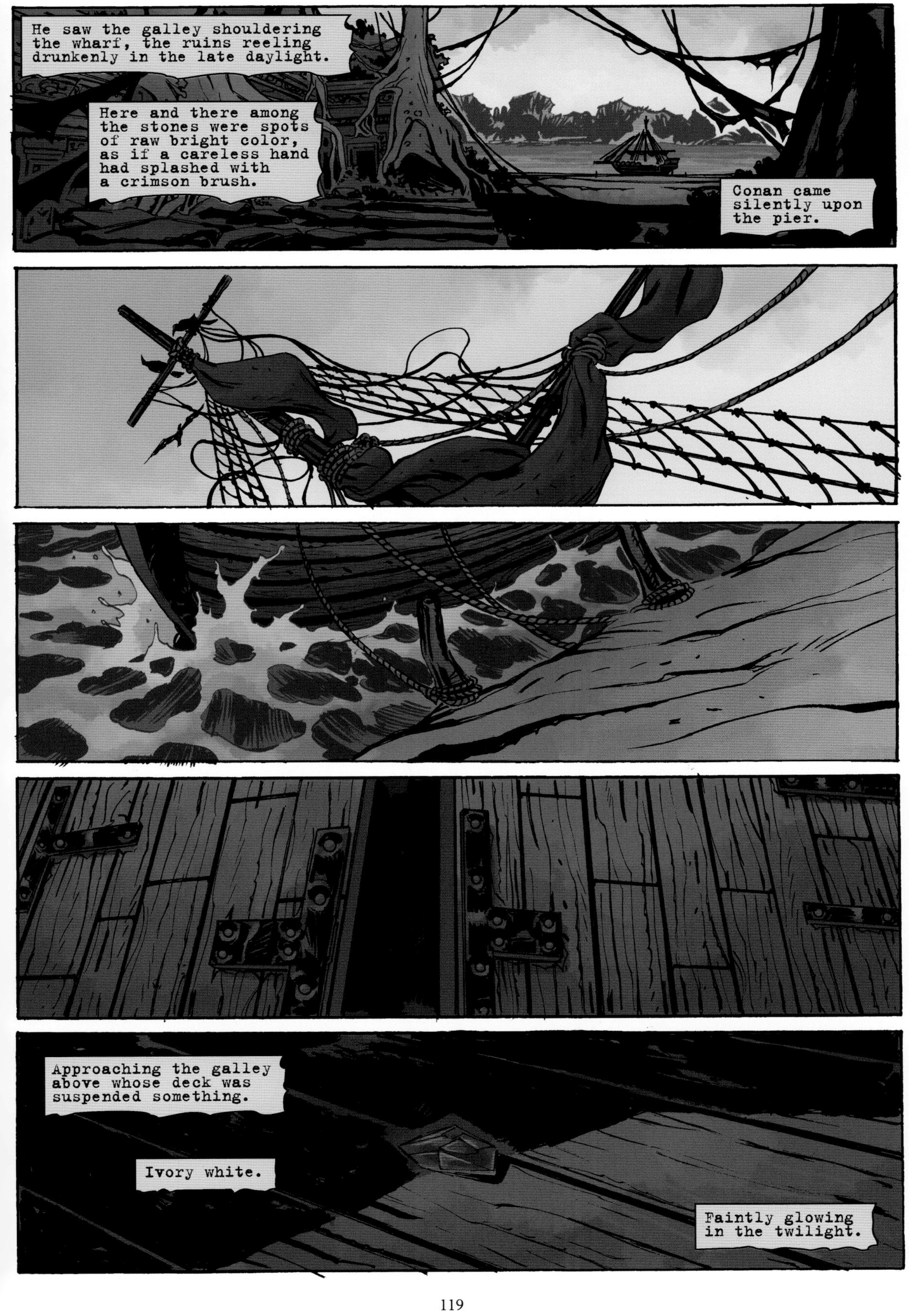
He saw the galley shouldering the wharf, the ruins reeling drunkenly in the late daylight.
Here and there among the stones were spots of raw bright color, as if a careless hand had splashed with a crimson brush.
Conan came silently upon the pier.
Approaching the galley above whose deck was suspended something.
Ivory white.
Faintly glowing in the twilight.

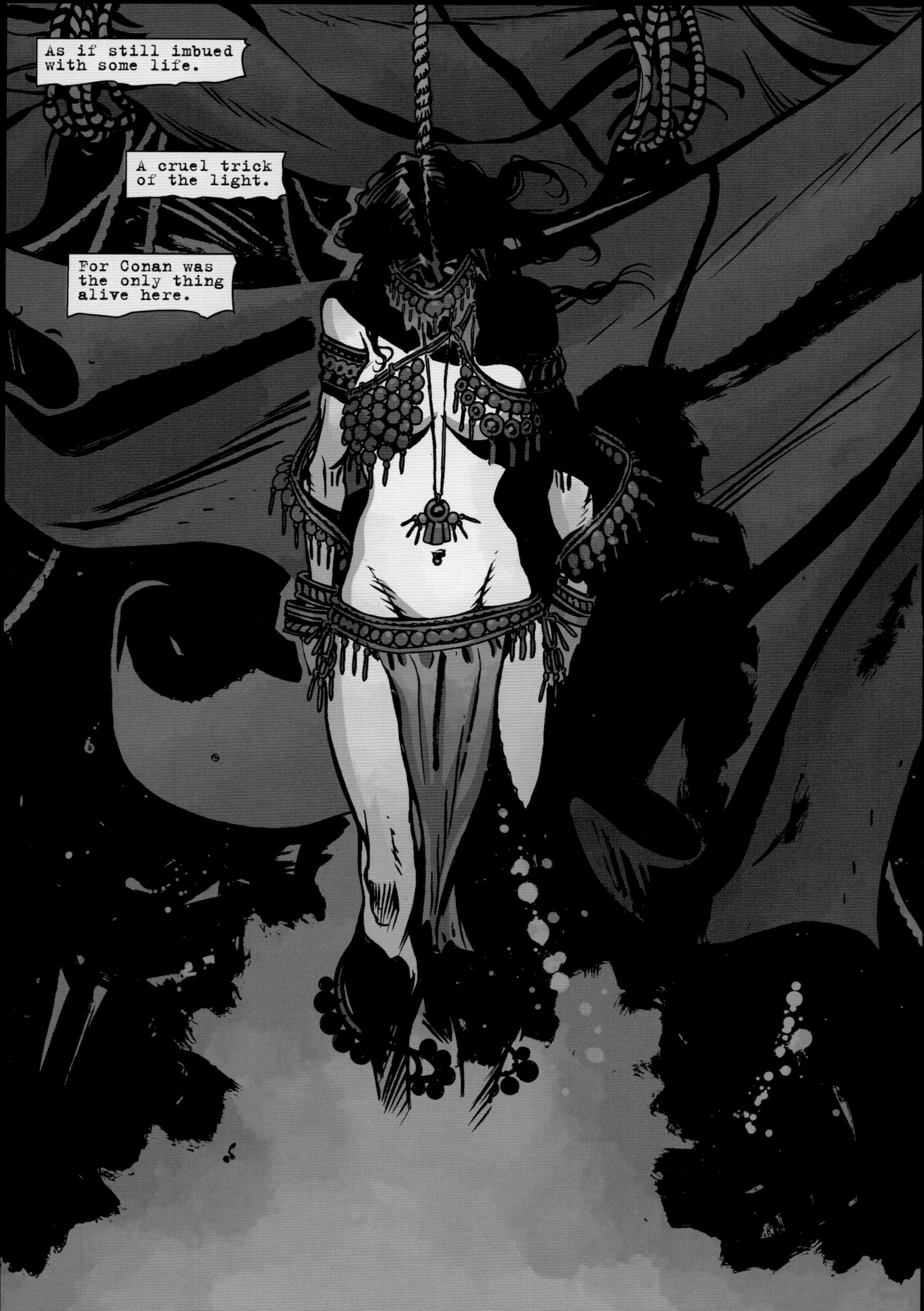
As if still imbued with some life.
A cruel trick of the light.
For Conan was the only thing alive here.

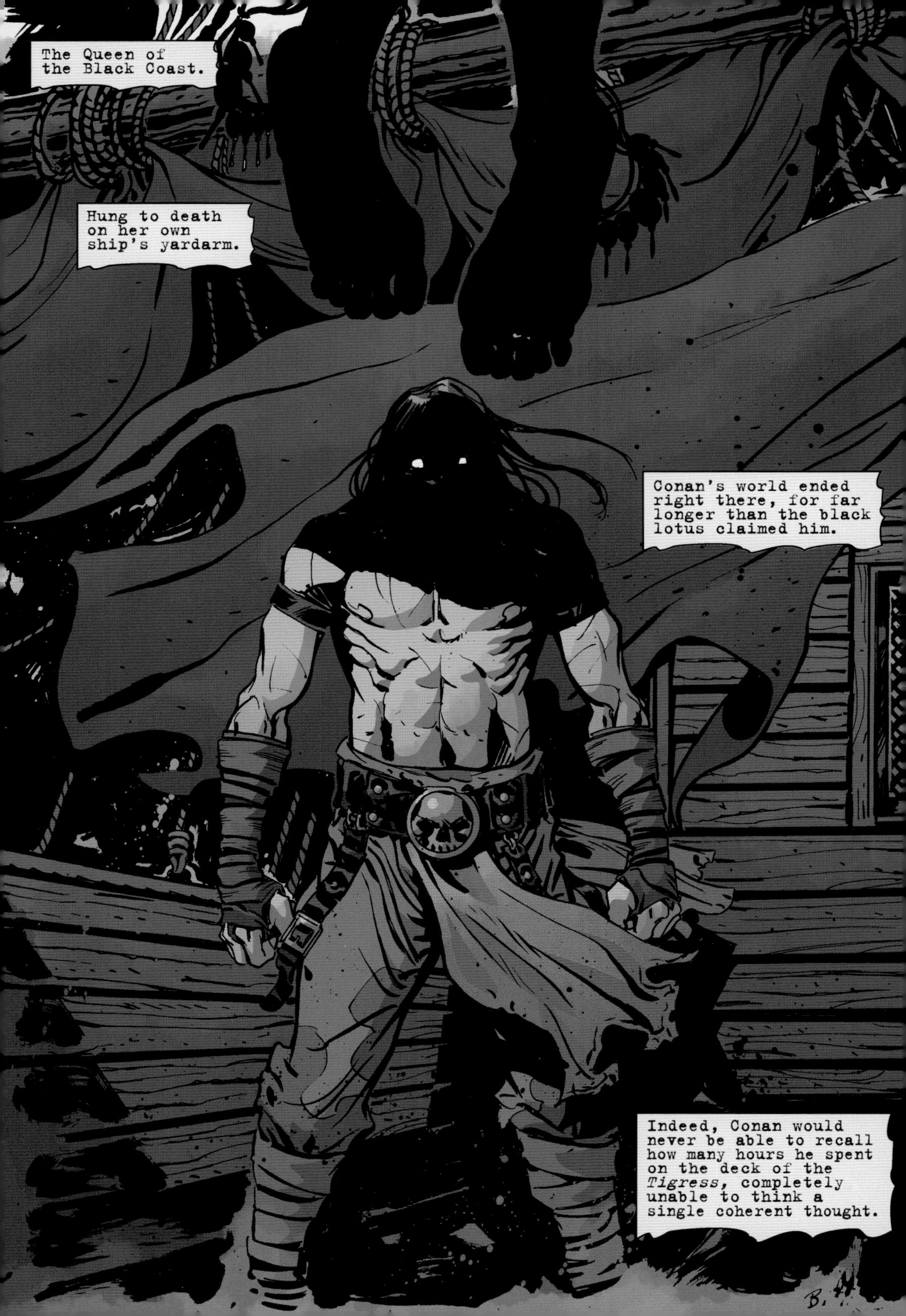
The Queen of the Black Coast.
Hung to death on her own ship's yardarm.
Conan's world ended right there, for far longer than the black lotus claimed him.
Indeed, Conan would never be able to recall how many hours he spent on the deck of the *Tigress*, completely unable to think a single coherent thought.
B.

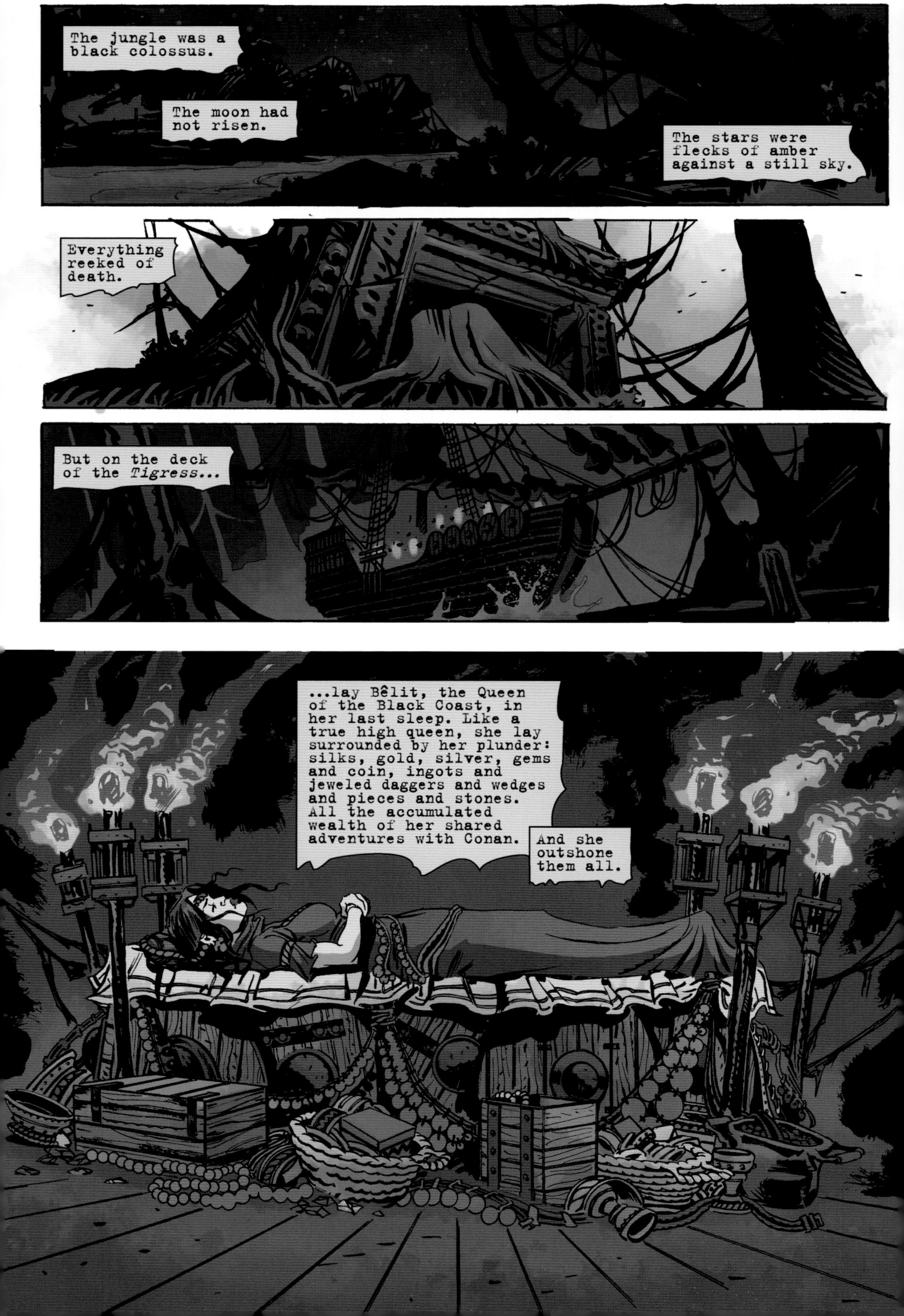
The jungle was a black colossus.
The moon had not risen.
The stars were flecks of amber against a still sky.
Everything reeked of death.
But on the deck of the *Tigress*...
...lay Bêlit, the Queen of the Black Coast, in her last sleep. Like a true high queen, she lay surrounded by her plunder: silks, gold, silver, gems and coin, ingots and jeweled daggers and wedges and pieces and stones. All the accumulated wealth of her shared adventures with Conan.
And she outshone them all.

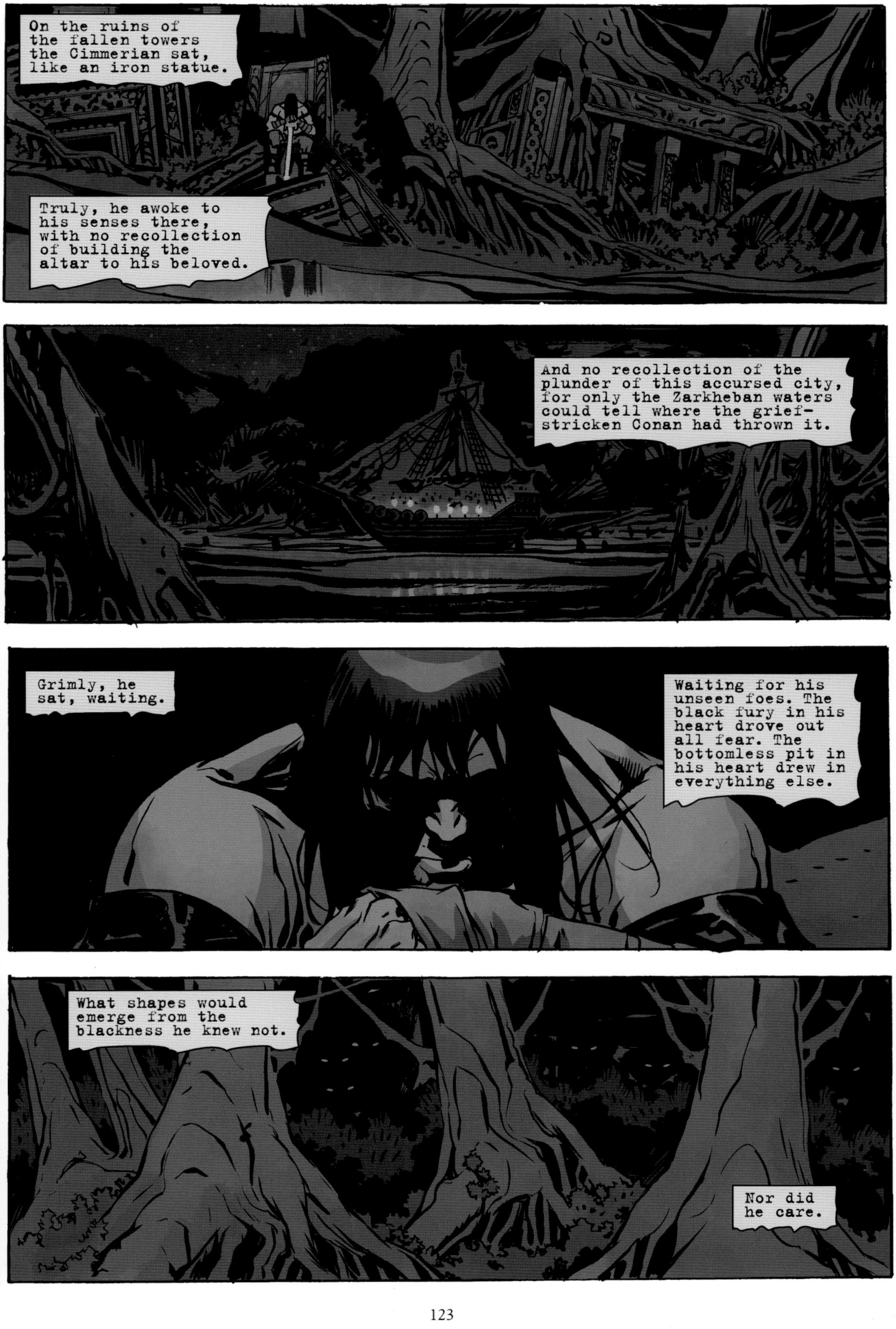
On the ruins of the fallen towers the Cimmerian sat, like an iron statue.
Truly, he awoke to his senses there, with no recollection of building the altar to his beloved.
And no recollection of the plunder of this accursed city, for only the Zarkheban waters could tell where the grief-stricken Conan had thrown it.
Grimly, he sat, waiting.
Waiting for his unseen foes. The black fury in his heart drove out all fear. The bottomless pit in his heart drew in everything else.
What shapes would emerge from the blackness he knew not.
Nor did he care.

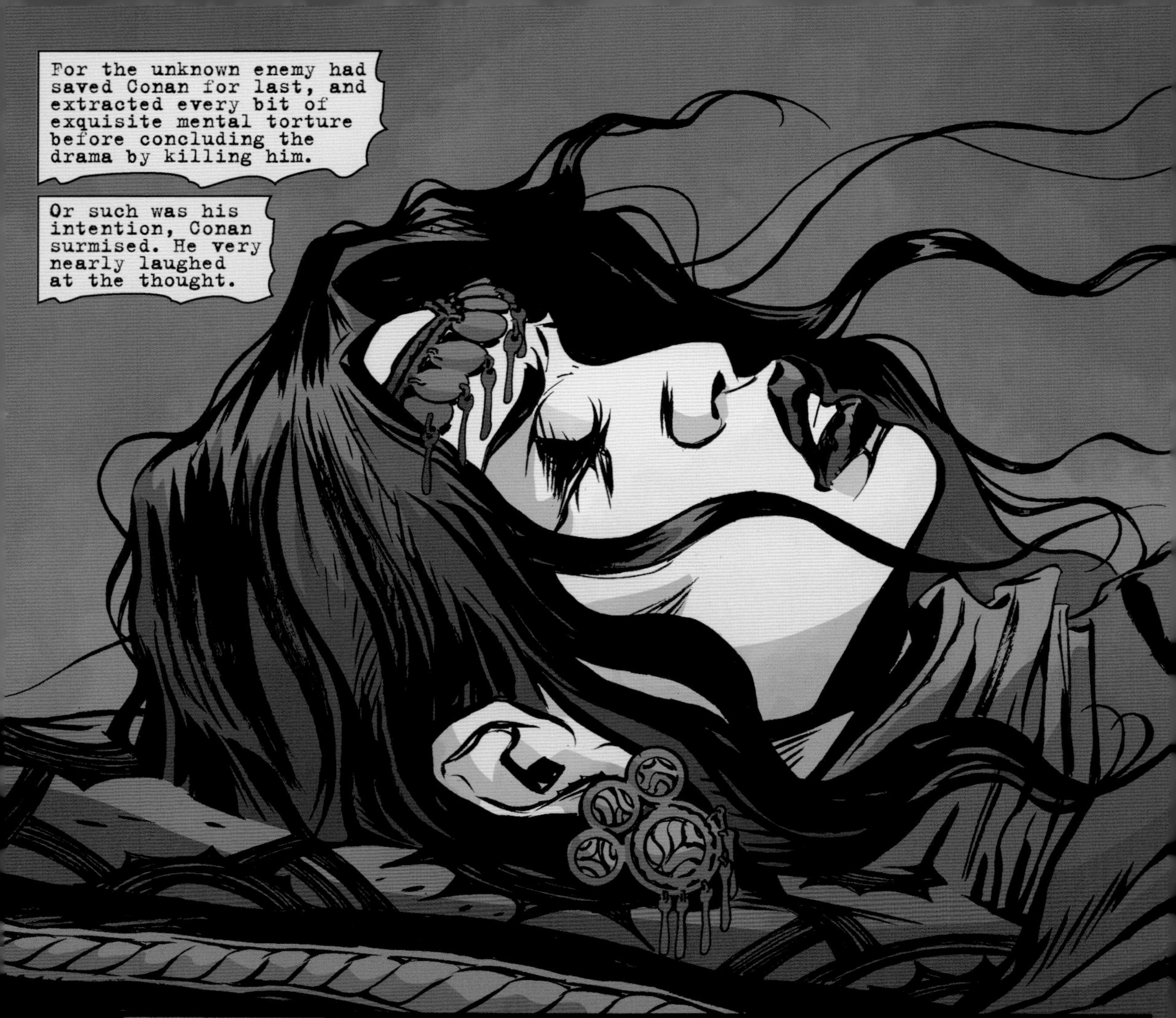
For the unknown enemy had saved Conan for last, and extracted every bit of exquisite mental torture before concluding the drama by killing him.
Or such was his intention, Conan surmised. He very nearly laughed at the thought.

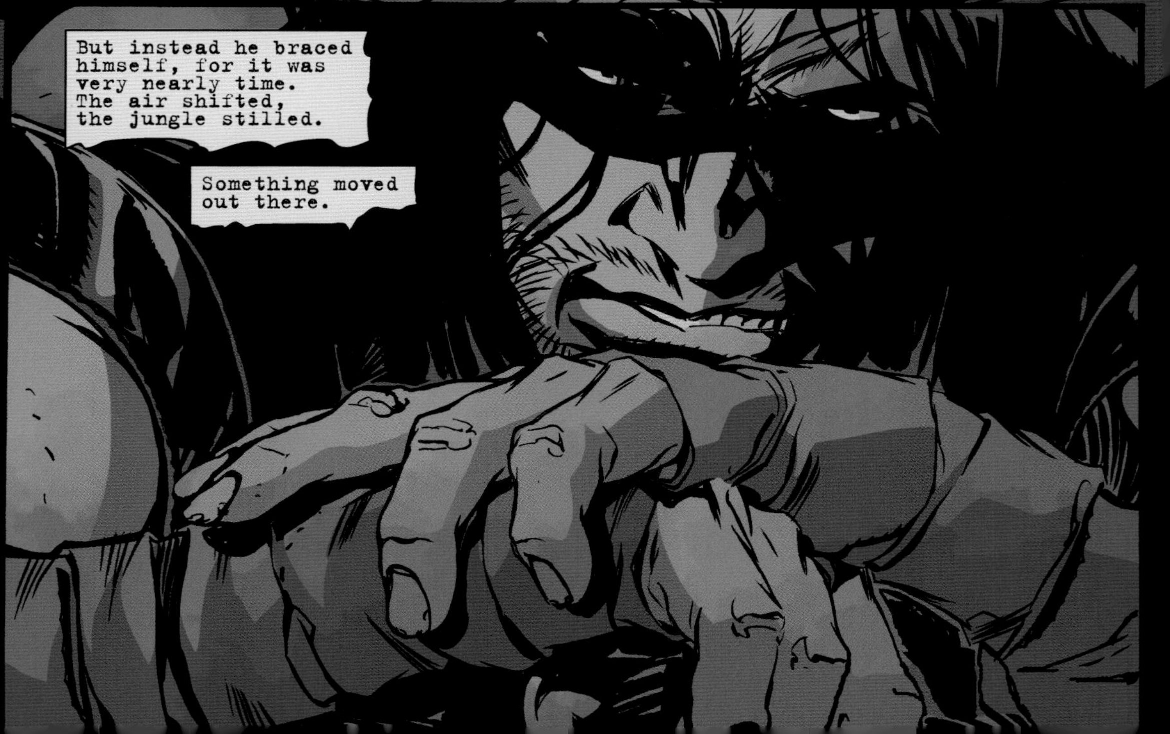
But instead he braced himself, for it was very nearly time. The air shifted, the jungle stilled.
Something moved out there.

CHAPTER SIX

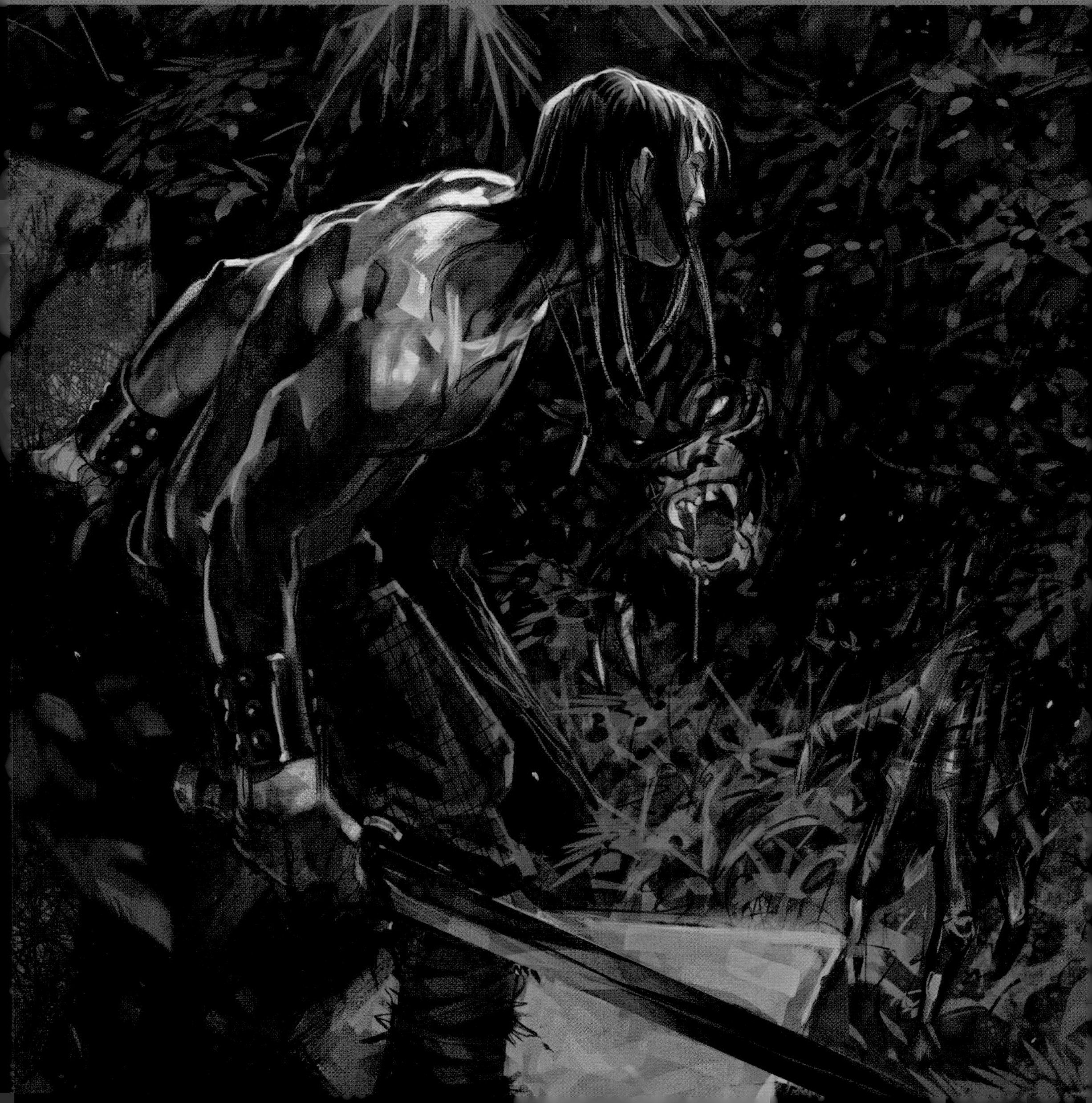

"Let me take you from this accursed place."

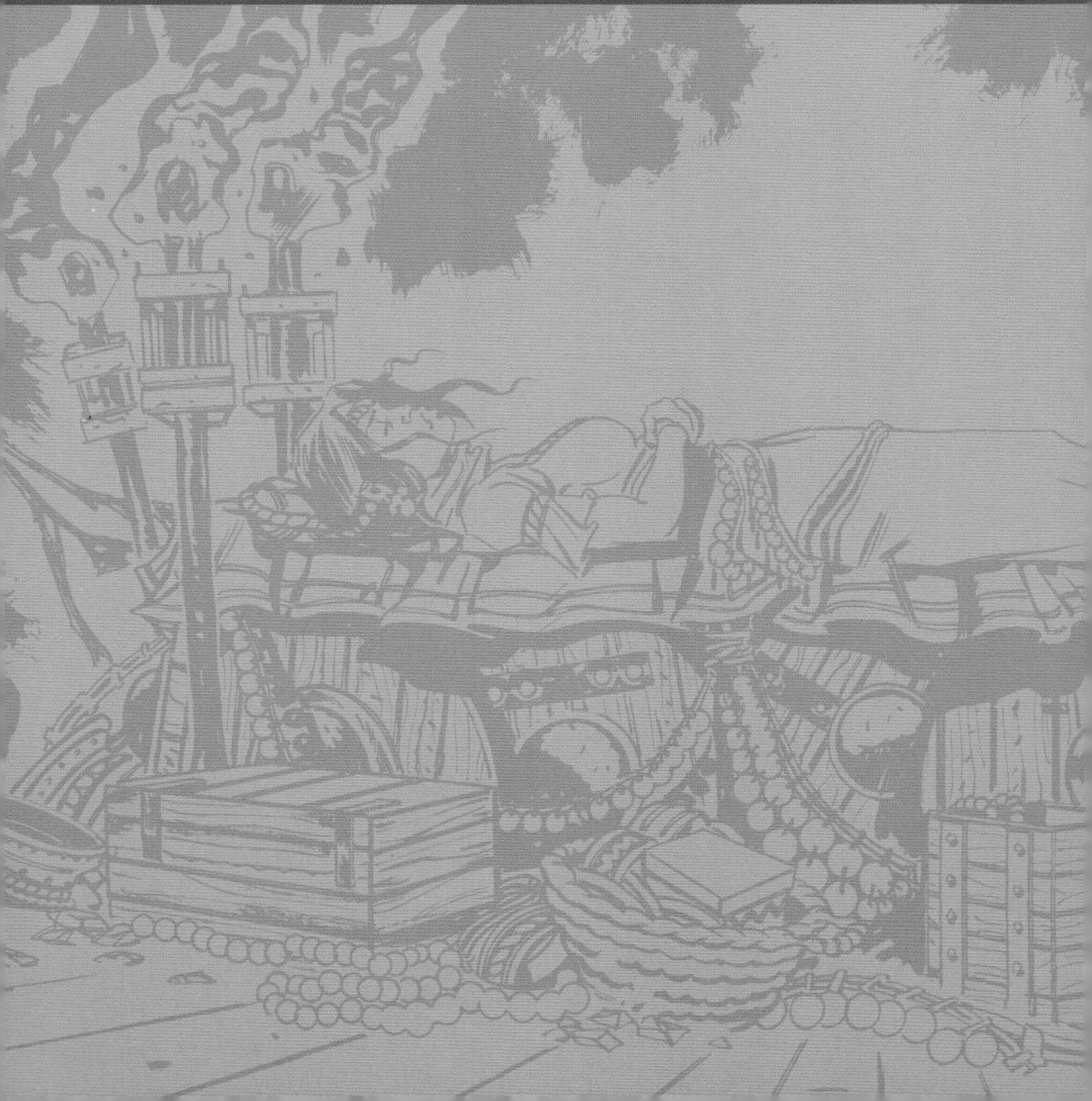

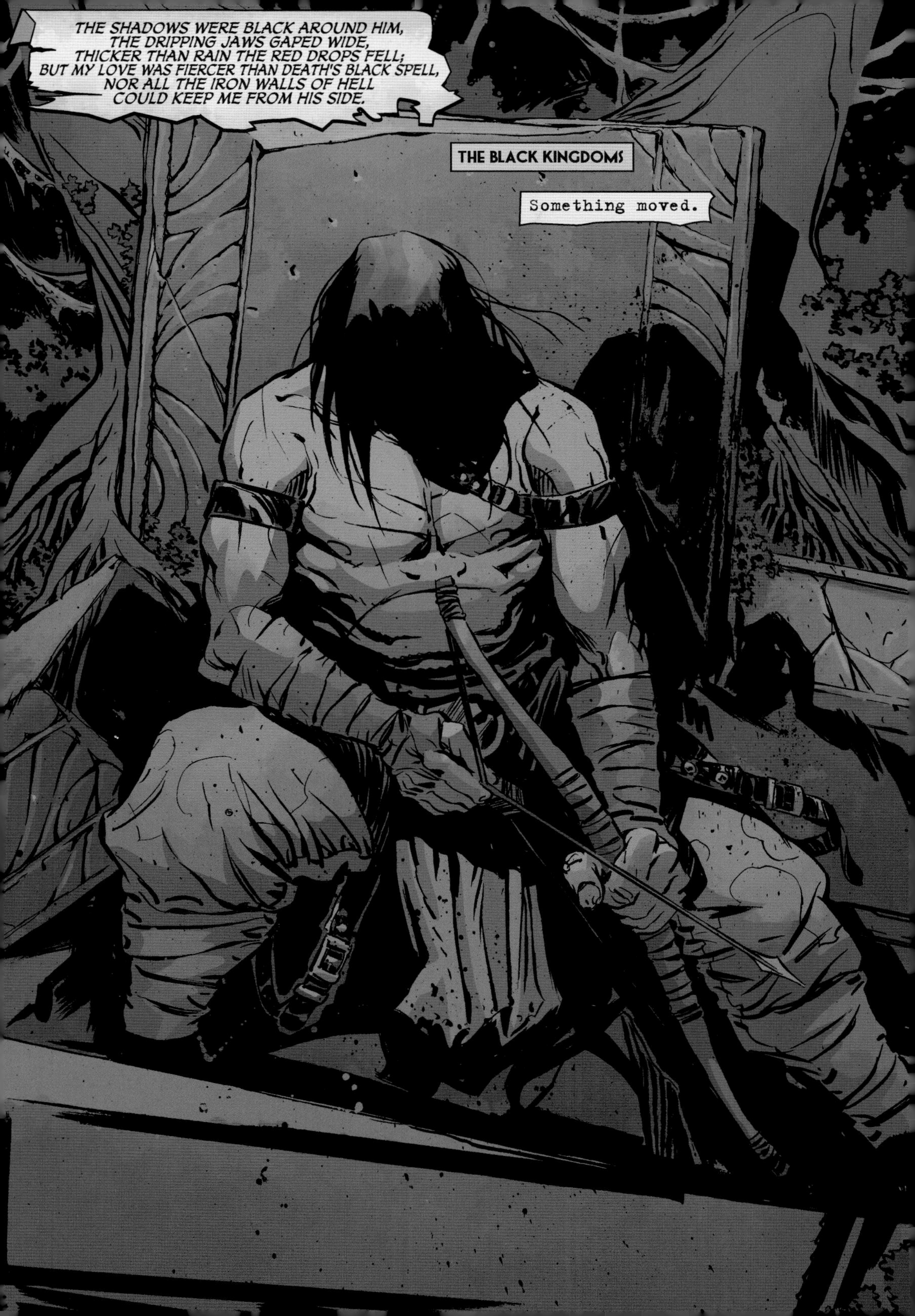
THE SHADOWS WERE BLACK AROUND HIM, THE DRIPPING JAWS GAPED WIDE, THICKER THAN RAIN THE RED DROPS FELL; BUT MY LOVE WAS FIERCER THAN DEATH'S BLACK SPELL, NOR ALL THE IRON WALLS OF HELL COULD KEEP ME FROM HIS SIDE.
THE BLACK KINGDOMS
Something moved.

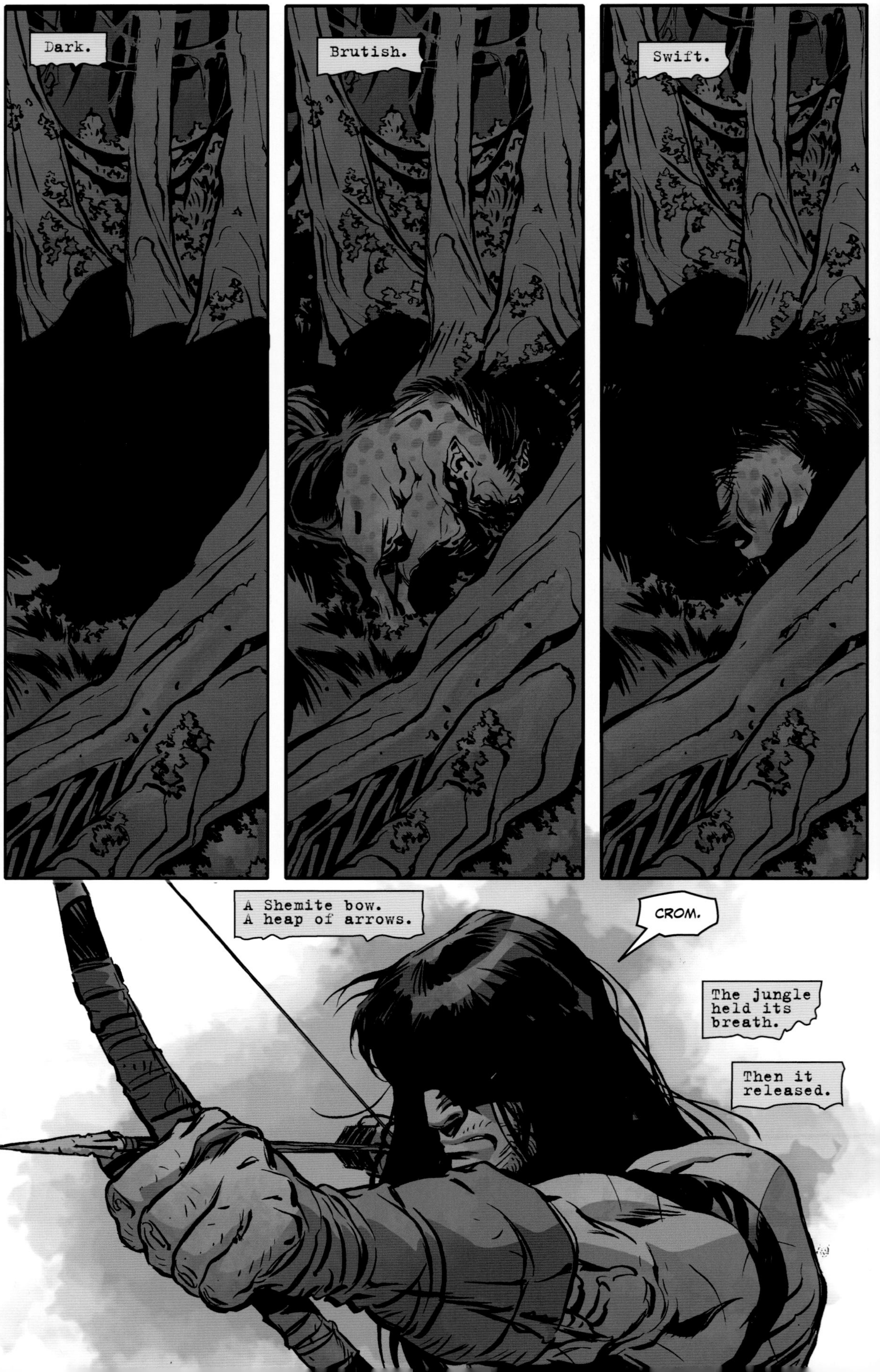
Dark.
Brutish.
Swift.
A Shemite bow. A heap of arrows.
CROM.
The jungle held its breath.
Then it released.

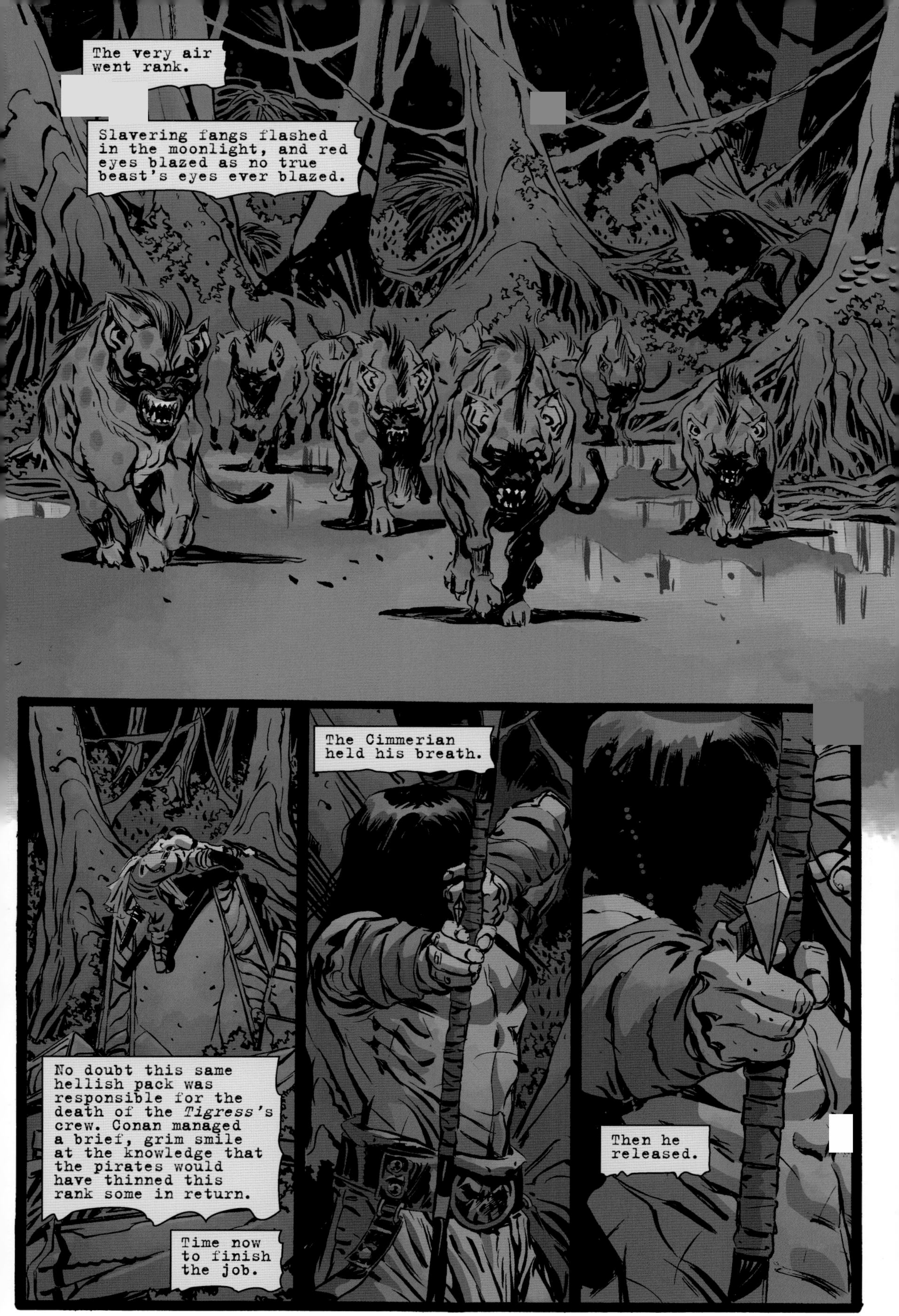
The very air went rank.
Slavering fangs flashed in the moonlight, and red eyes blazed as no true beast's eyes ever blazed.
No doubt this same hellish pack was responsible for the death of the *Tigress*'s crew. Conan managed a brief, grim smile at the knowledge that the pirates would have thinned this rank some in return.
Time now to finish the job.
The Cimmerian held his breath.
Then he released.

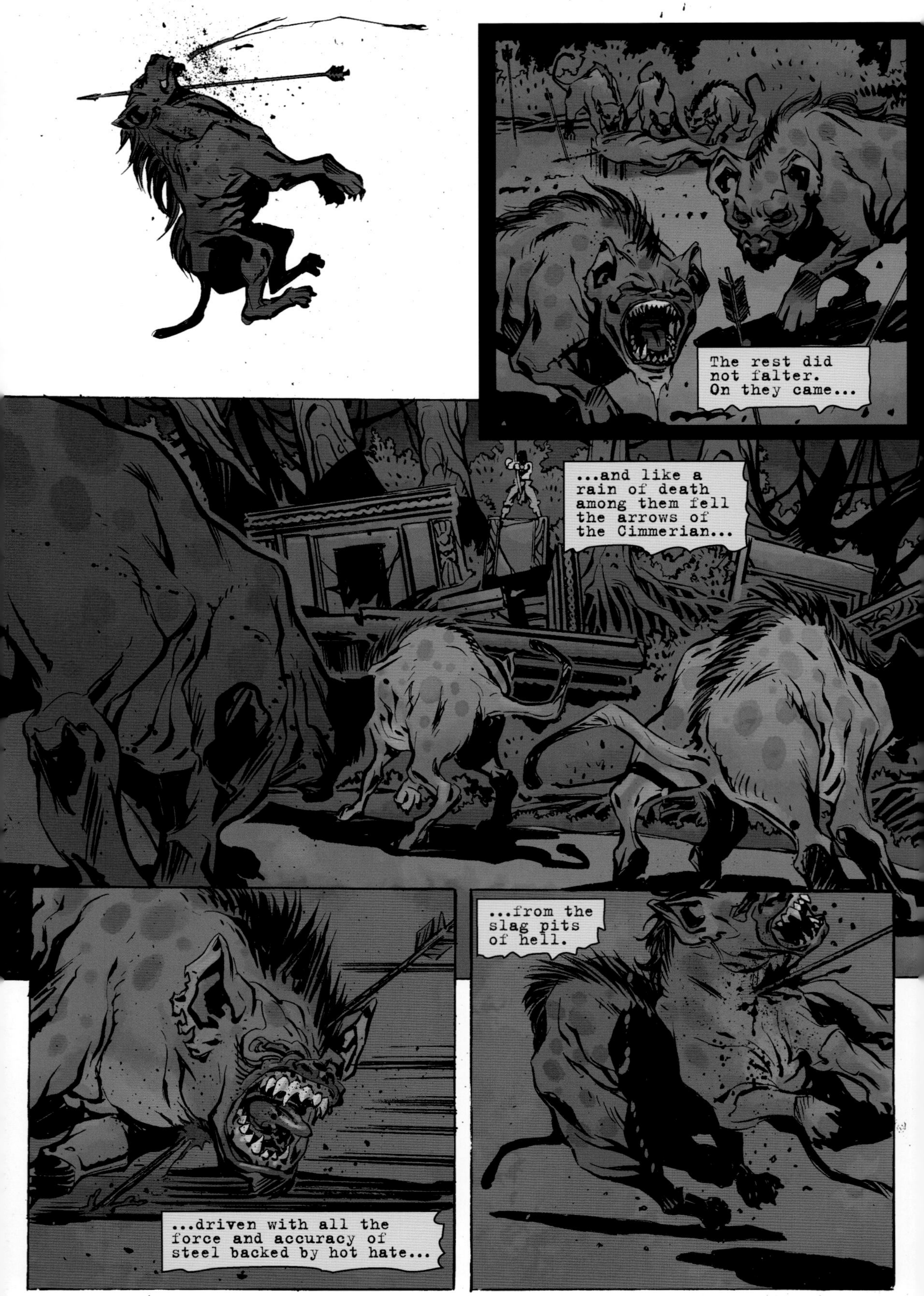
The rest did
not falter.
On they came...
...and like a
rain of death
among them fell
the arrows of
the Cimmerian...
...driven with all the
force and accuracy of
steel backed by hot hate...
...from the
slag pits
of hell.

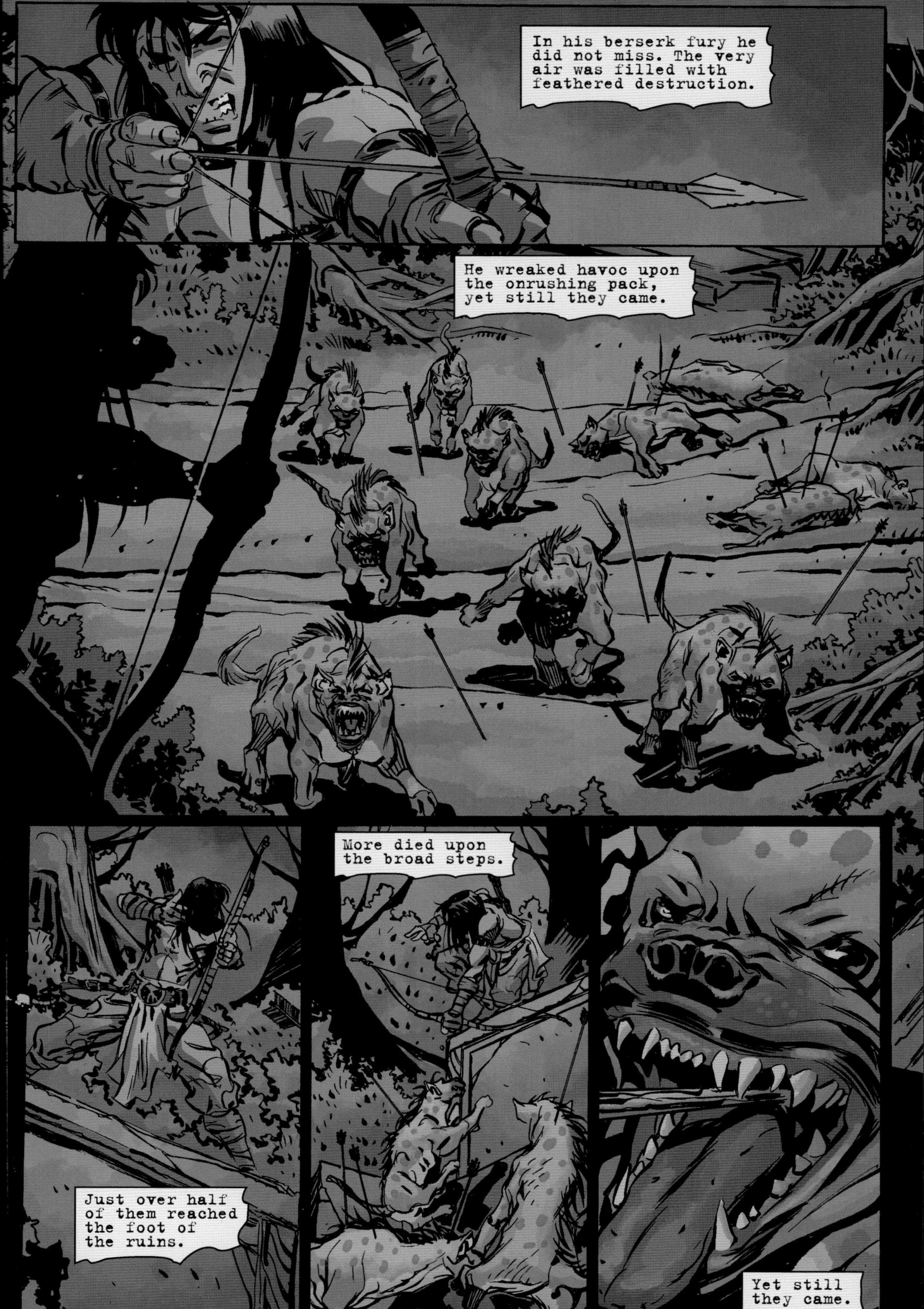
In his berserk fury he did not miss. The very air was filled with feathered destruction.
He wreaked havoc upon the onrushing pack, yet still they came.
Just over half of them reached the foot of the ruins.
More died upon the broad steps.
Yet still they came.

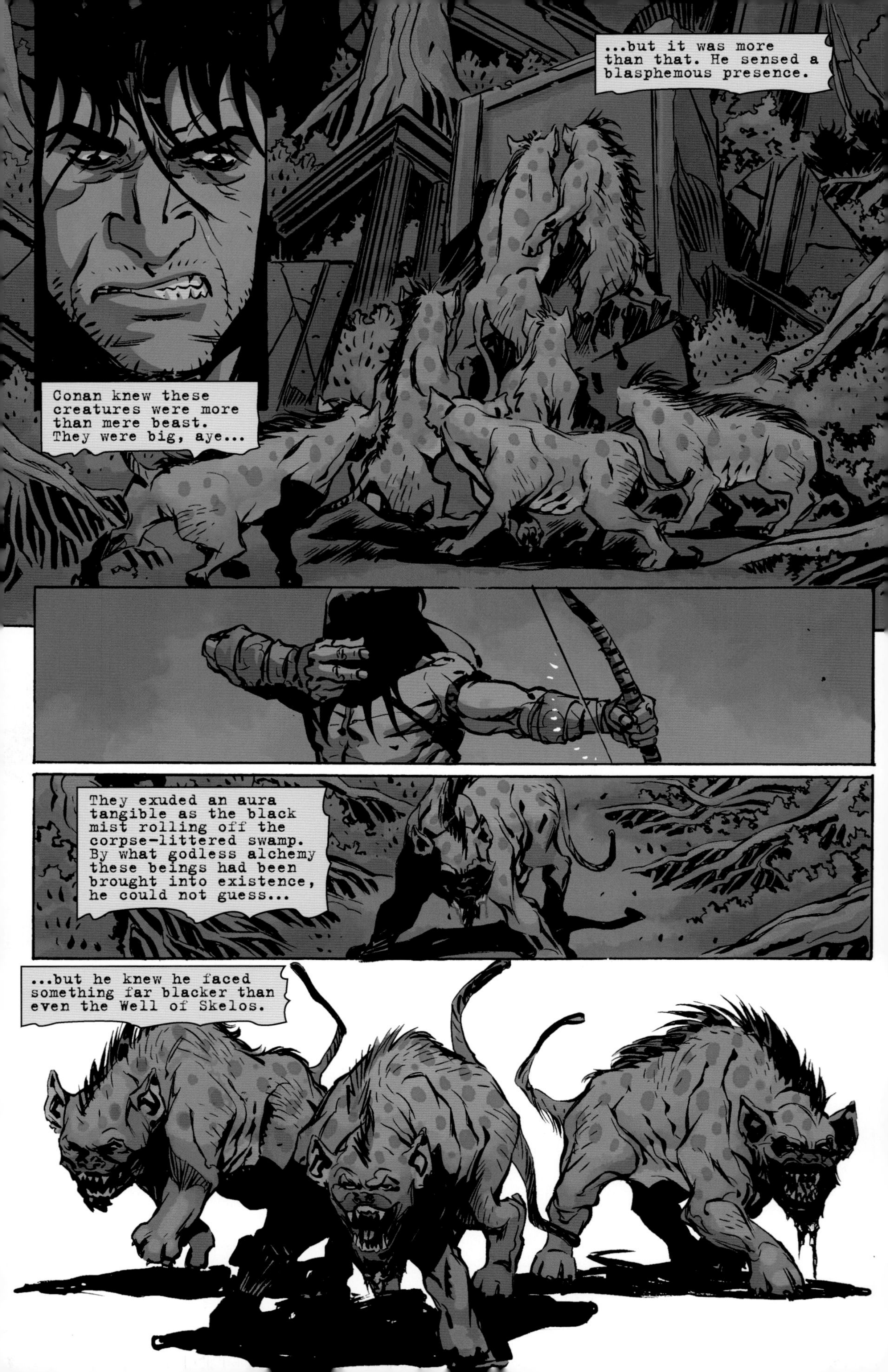
...but it was more than that. He sensed a blasphemous presence.
Conan knew these creatures were more than mere beast. They were big, aye...
They exuded an aura tangible as the black mist rolling off the corpse-littered swamp. By what godless alchemy these beings had been brought into existence, he could not guess...
...but he knew he faced something far blacker than even the Well of Skelos.

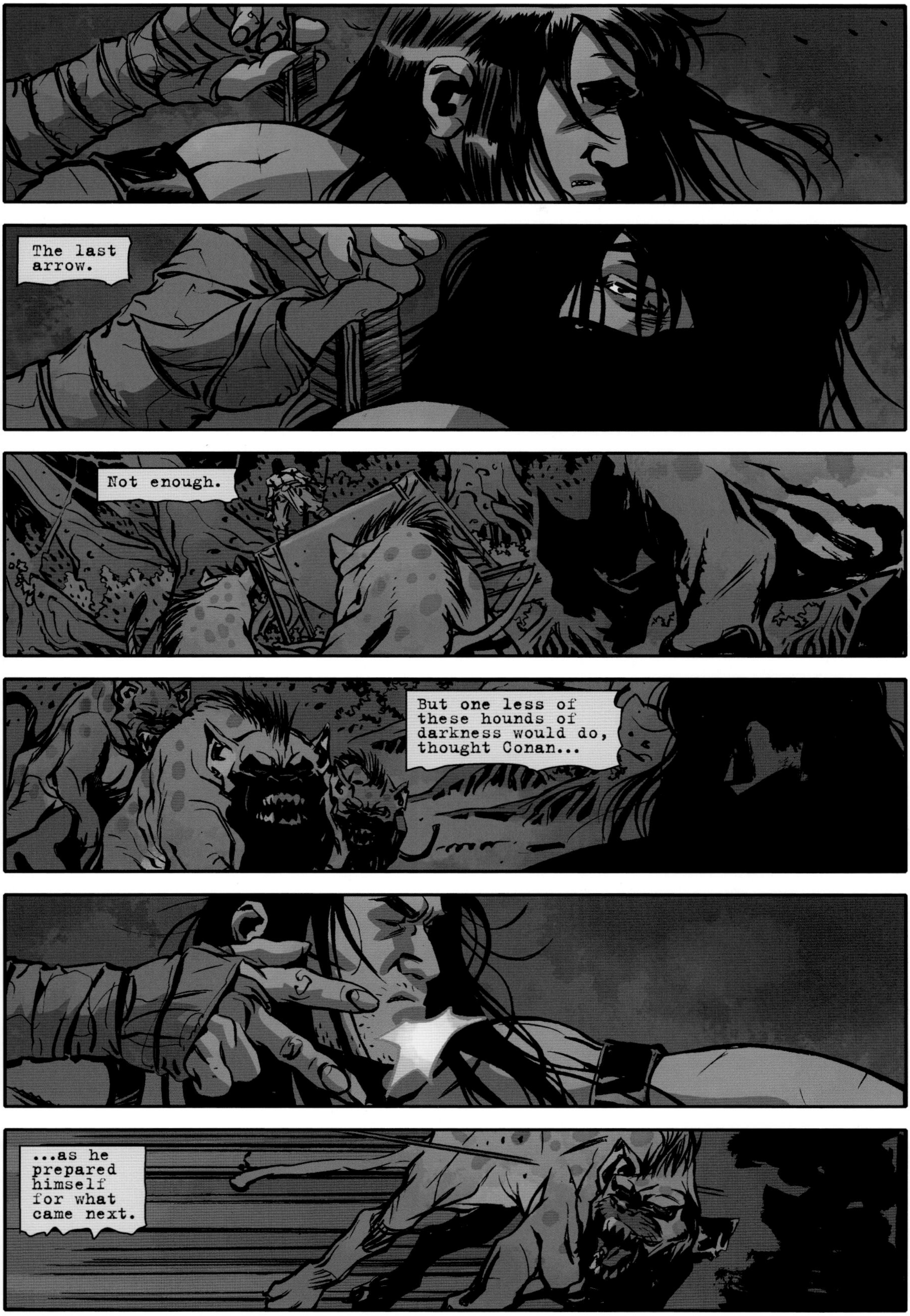
The last arrow.
Not enough.
But one less of these hounds of darkness would do, thought Conan...
...as he prepared himself for what came next.

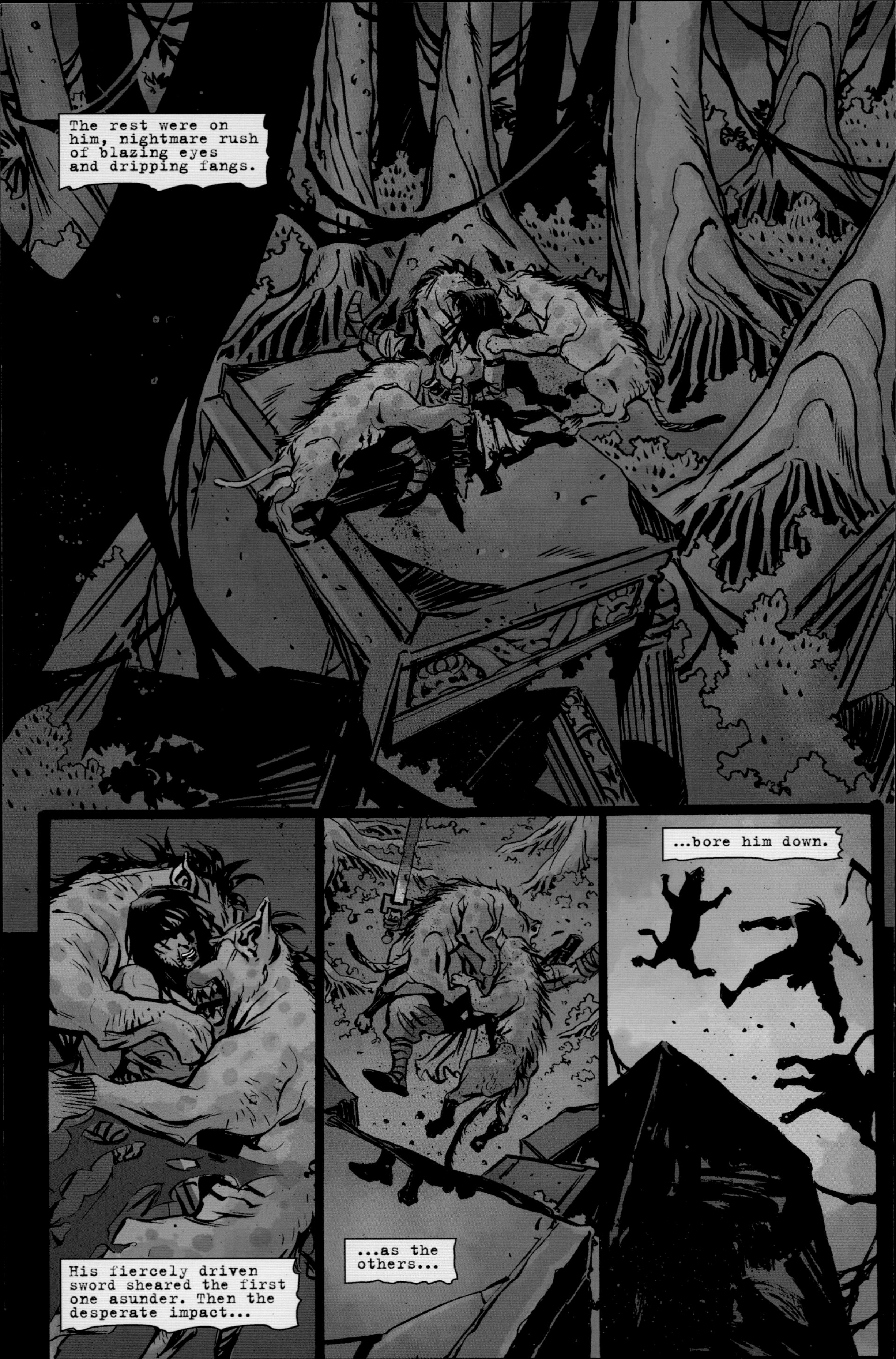

The rest were on him, nightmare rush of blazing eyes and dripping fangs.
His fiercely driven sword sheared the first one asunder. Then the desperate impact...
...as the others...
...bore him down.

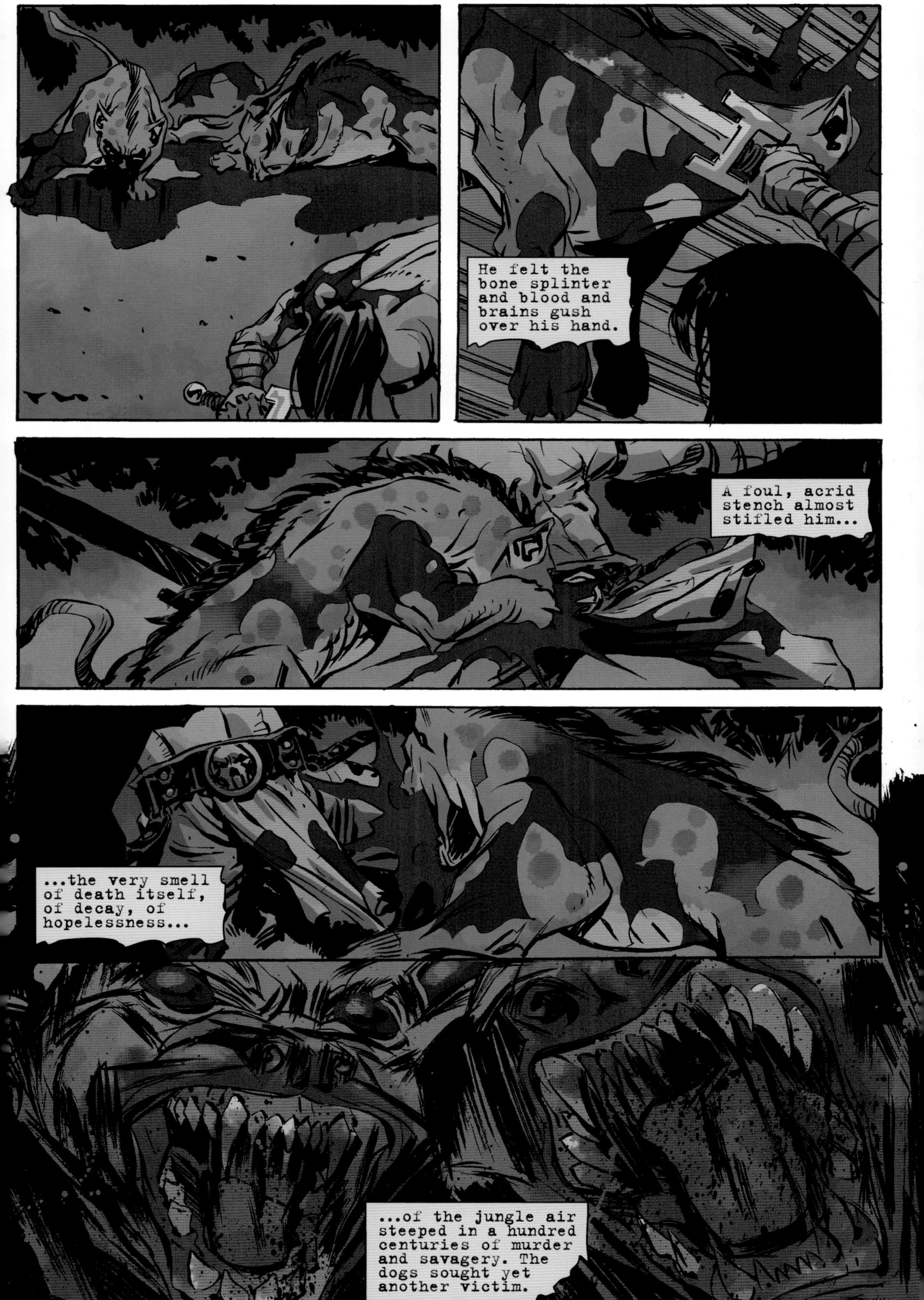
He felt the bone splinter and blood and brains gush over his hand.
A foul, acrid stench almost stifled him...
...the very smell of death itself, of decay, of hopelessness...
...of the jungle air steeped in a hundred centuries of murder and savagery. The dogs sought yet another victim.

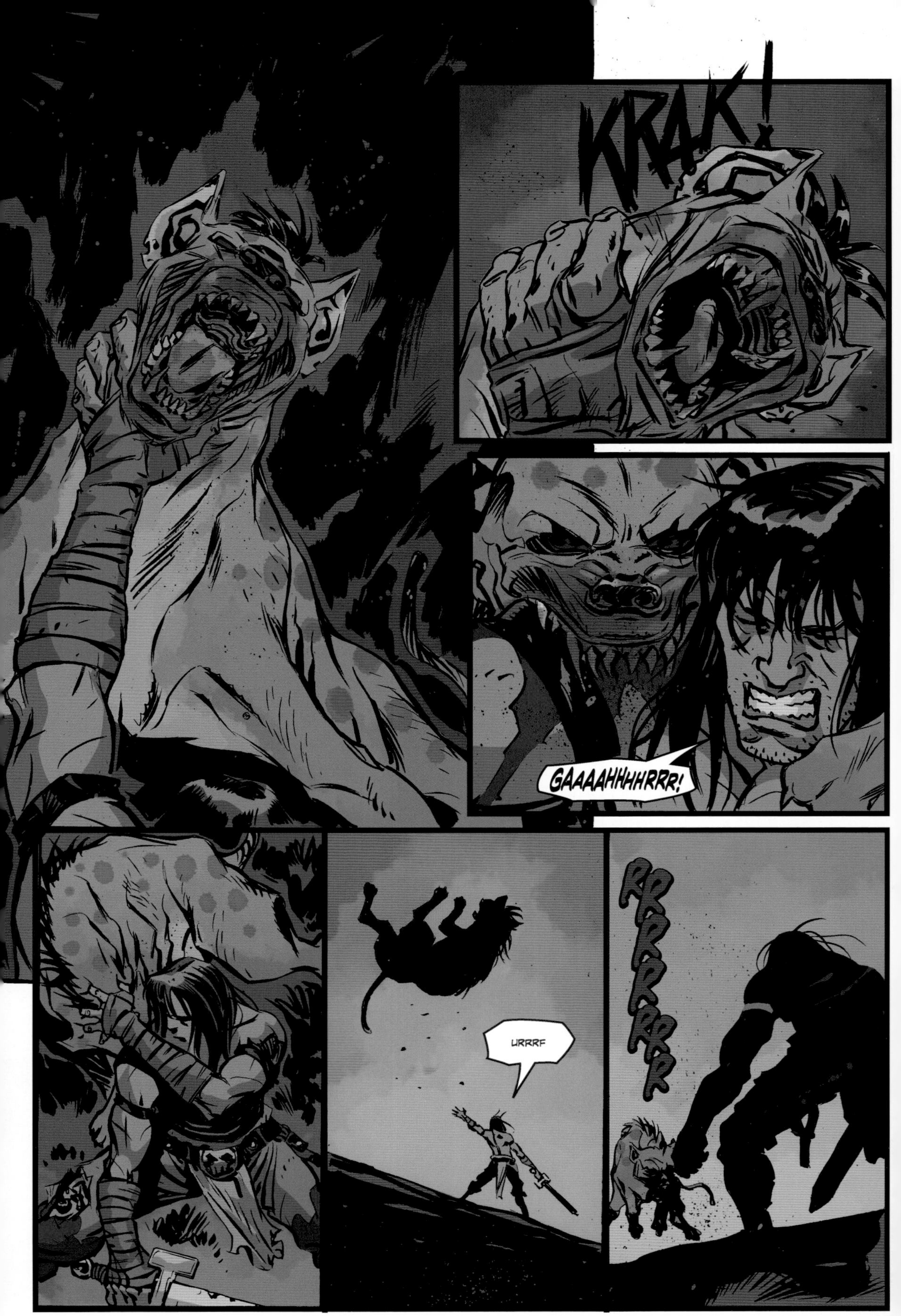
KRAK!
GAAAAHHHHRRR!
URRRF
RRRRRRRR

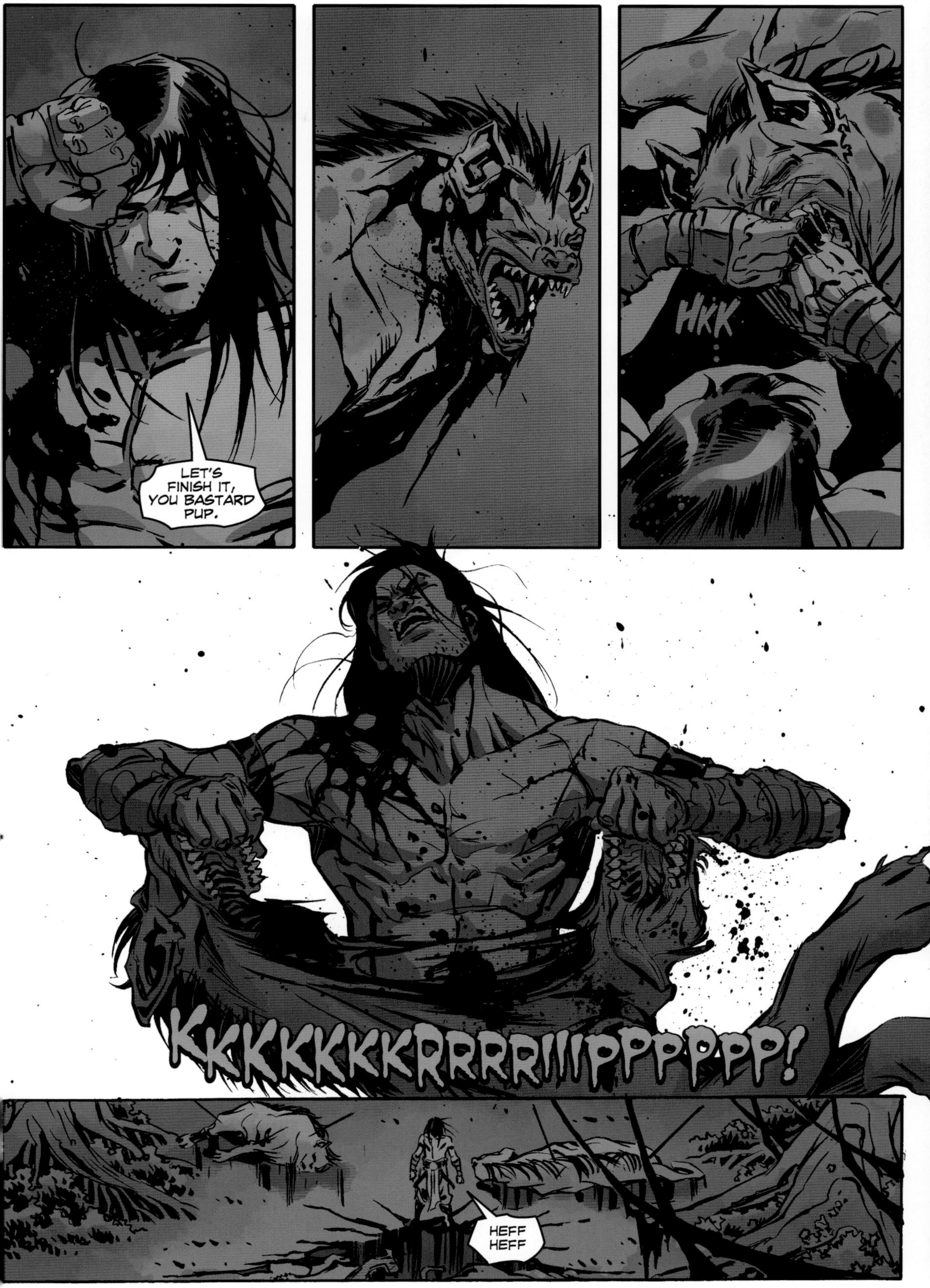
LET'S FINISH IT, YOU BASTARD PUP.
HKK
KKKKKKKRRRRIIIPPPPPP!
HEFF HEFF

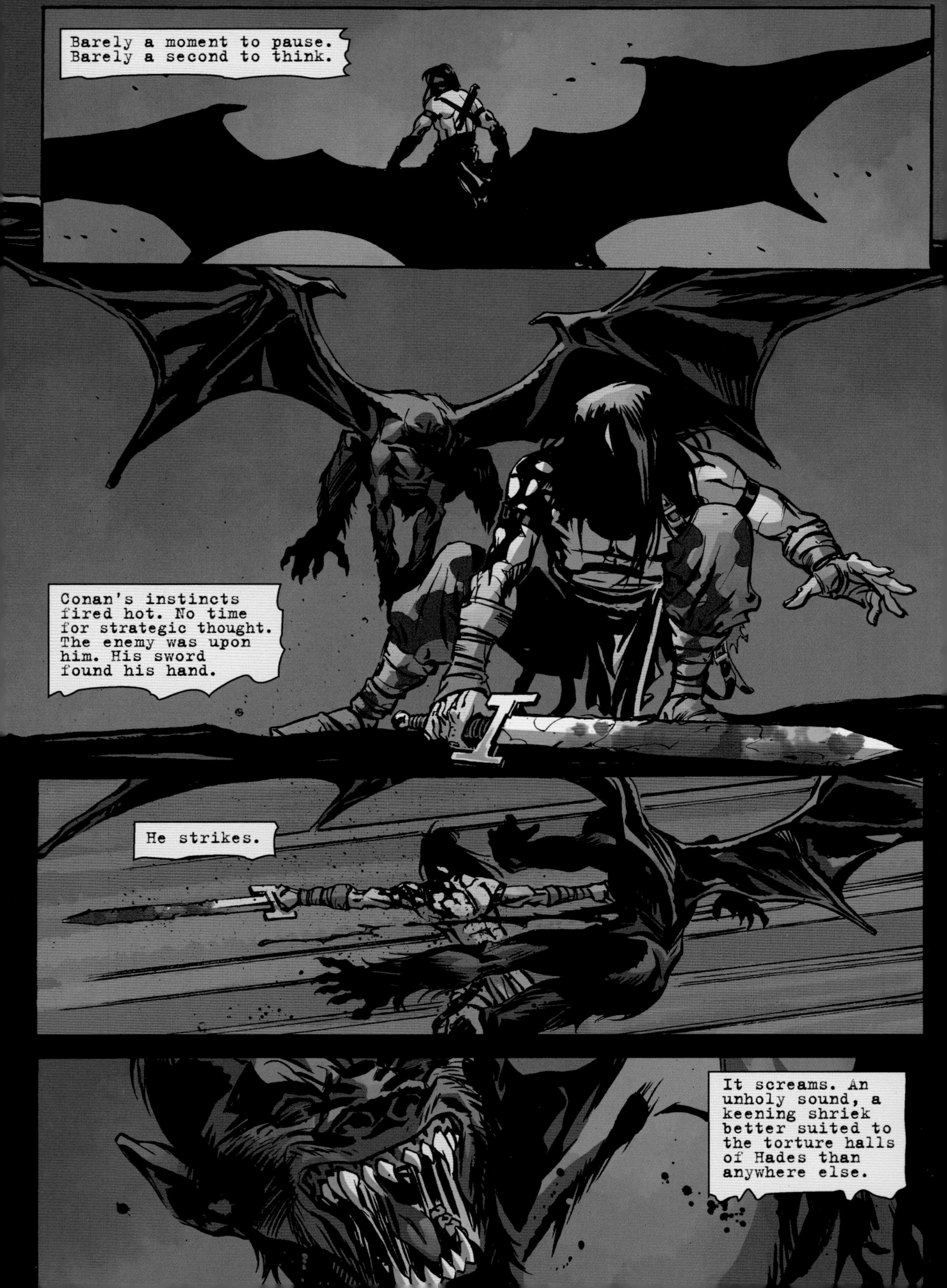
Barely a moment to pause. Barely a second to think.
Conan's instincts fired hot. No time for strategic thought. The enemy was upon him. His sword found his hand.
He strikes.
It screams. An unholy sound, a keening shriek better suited to the torture halls of Hades than anywhere else.

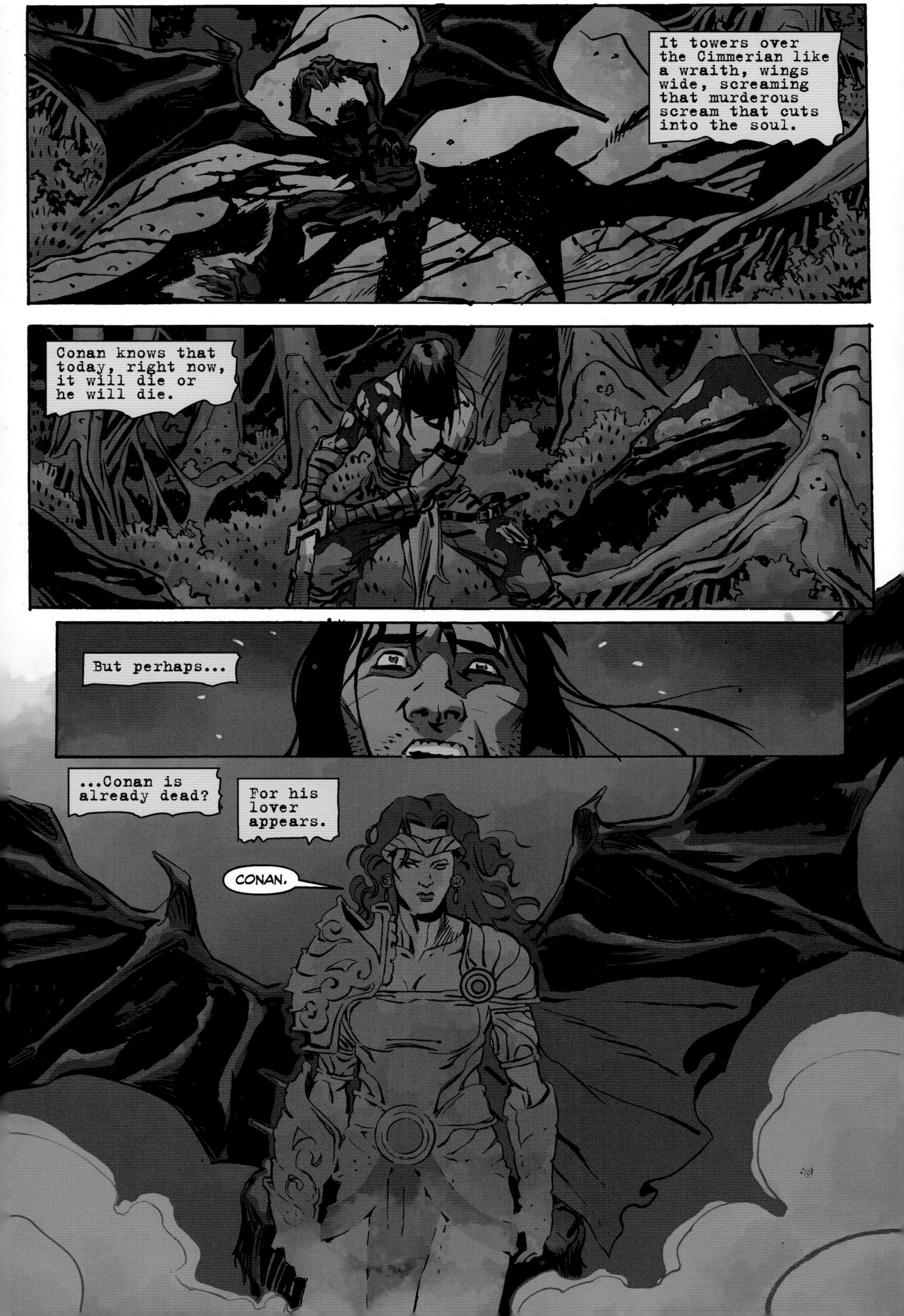

It towers over the Cimmerian like a wraith, wings wide, screaming that murderous scream that cuts into the soul.
Conan knows that today, right now, it will die or he will die.
But perhaps...
...Conan is already dead?
For his lover appears.
CONAN.

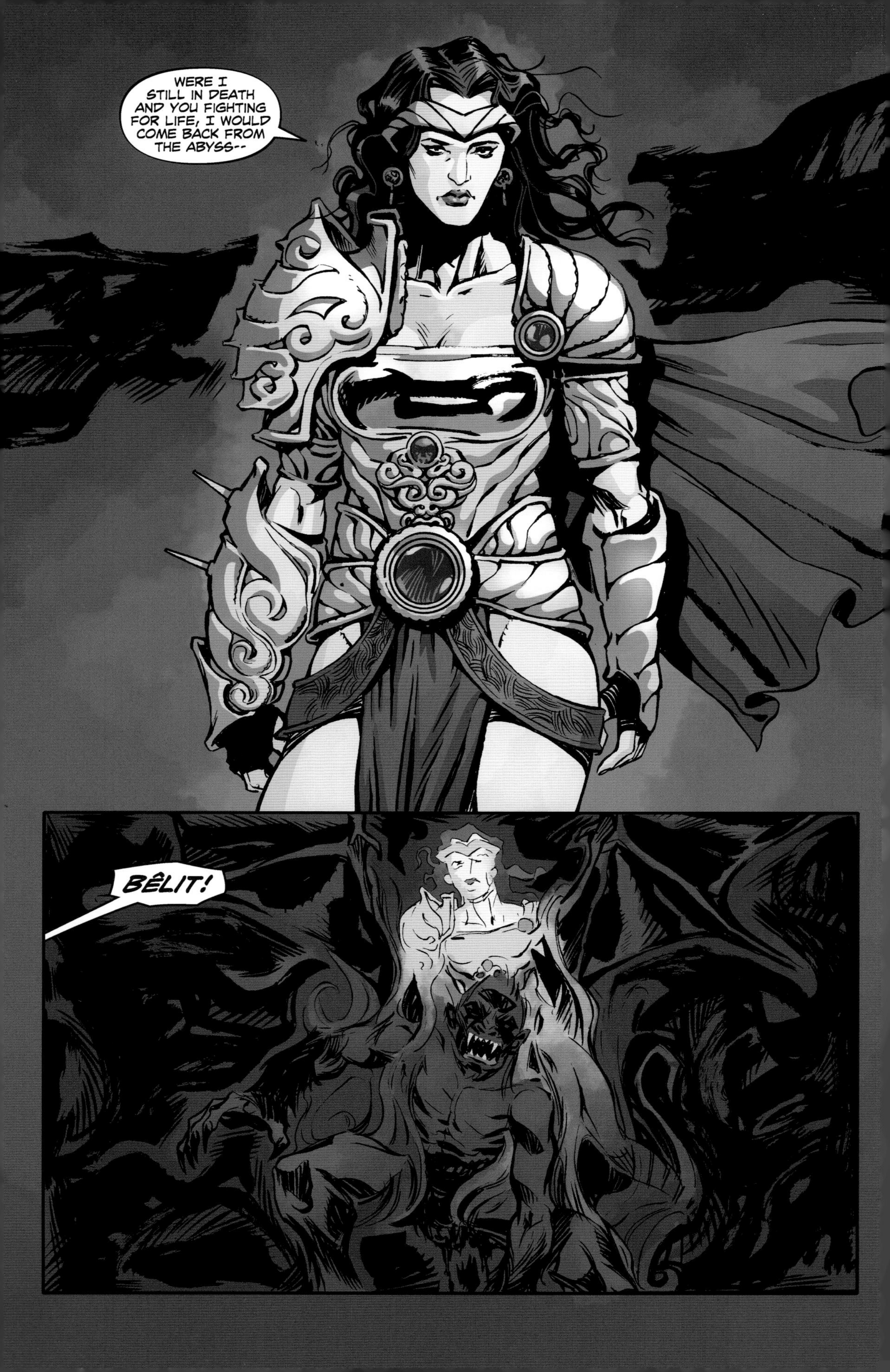
WERE I STILL IN DEATH AND YOU FIGHTING FOR LIFE, I WOULD COME BACK FROM THE ABYSS--
BÊLIT!

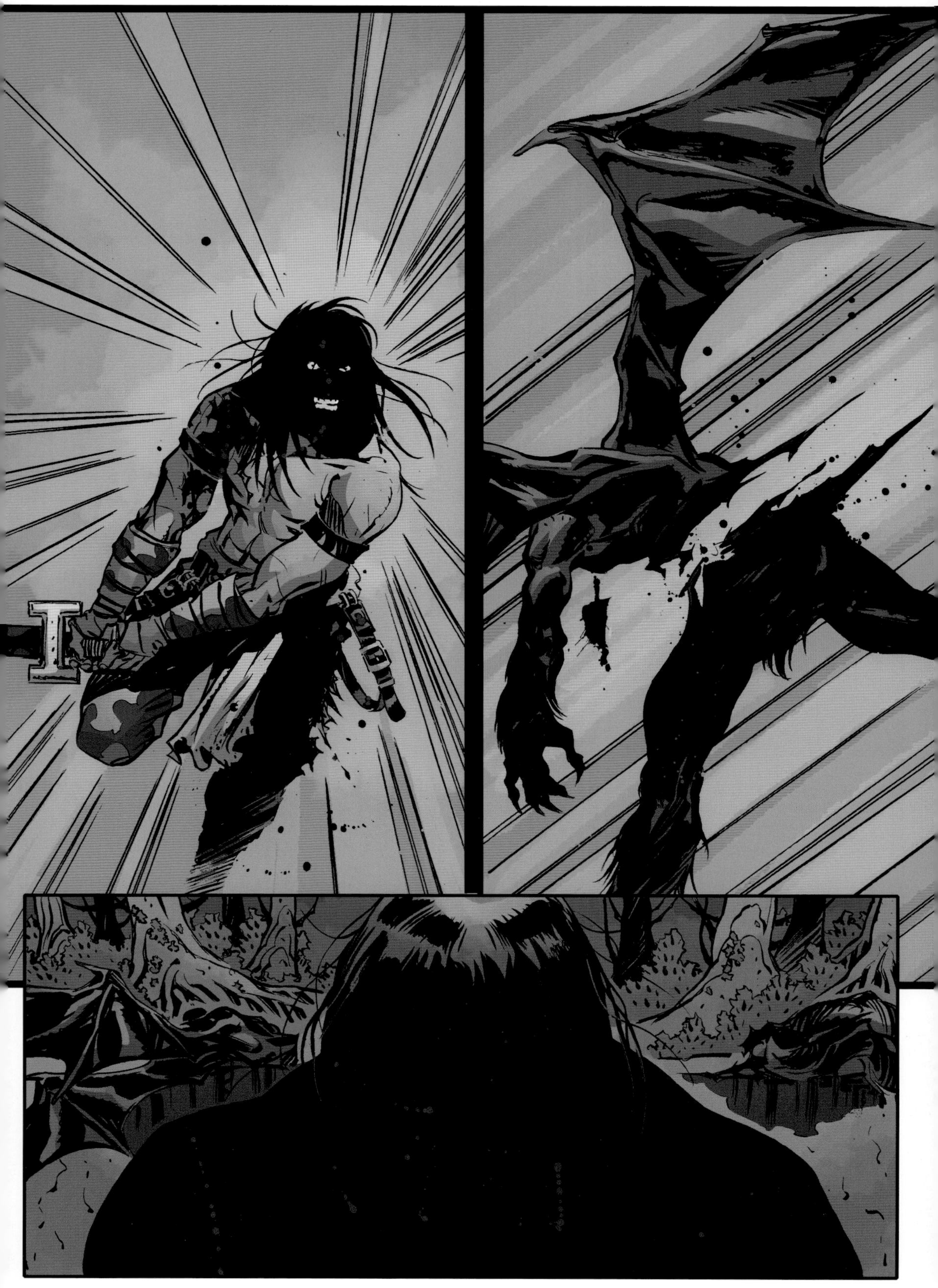

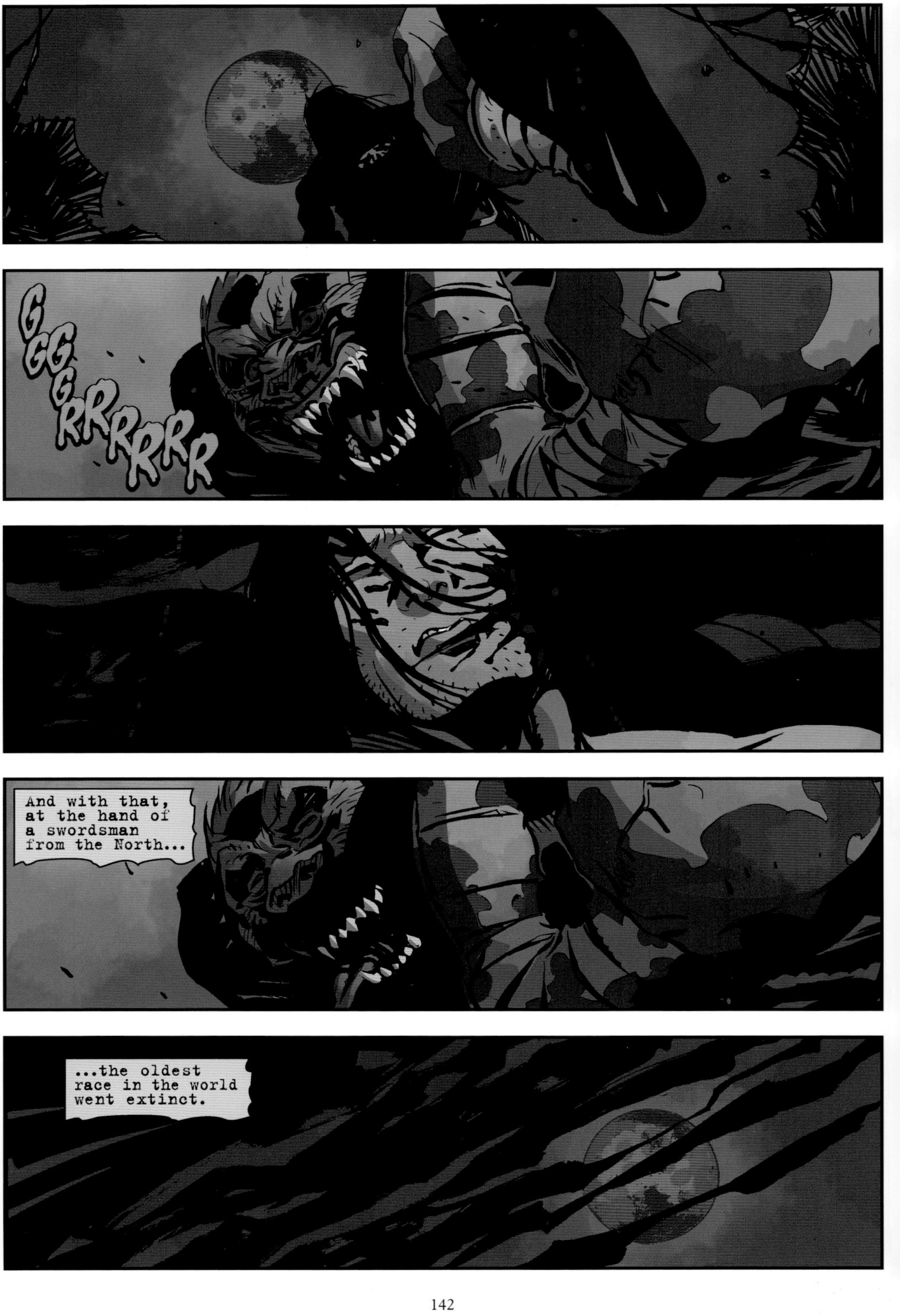
GGGGRRRRRR
And with that, at the hand of a swordsman from the North...
...the oldest race in the world went extinct.

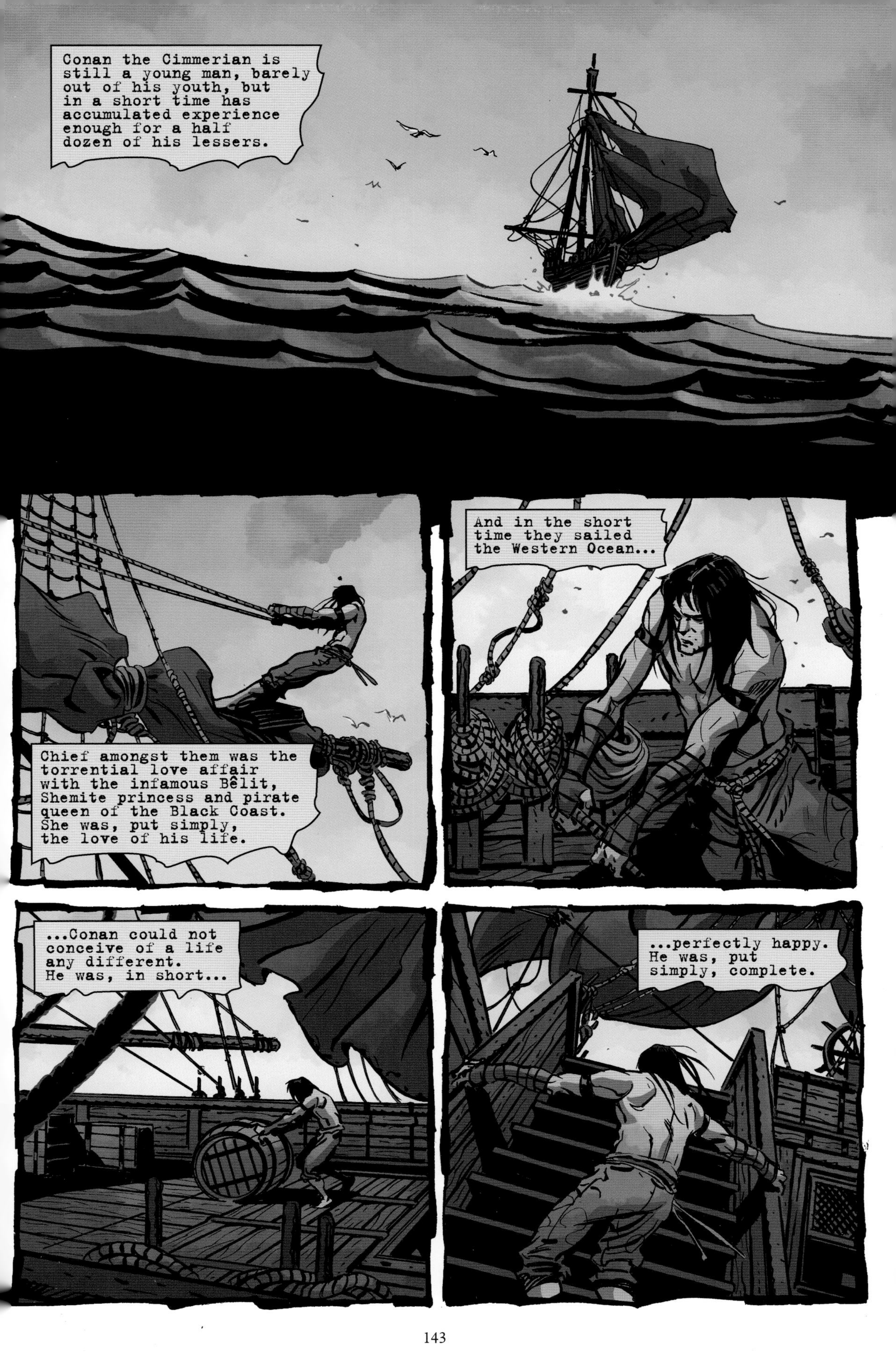
Conan the Cimmerian is still a young man, barely out of his youth, but in a short time has accumulated experience enough for a half dozen of his lessers.
Chief amongst them was the torrential love affair with the infamous Bêlit, Shemite princess and pirate queen of the Black Coast. She was, put simply, the love of his life.
And in the short time they sailed the Western Ocean...
...Conan could not conceive of a life any different. He was, in short...
...perfectly happy. He was, put simply, complete.

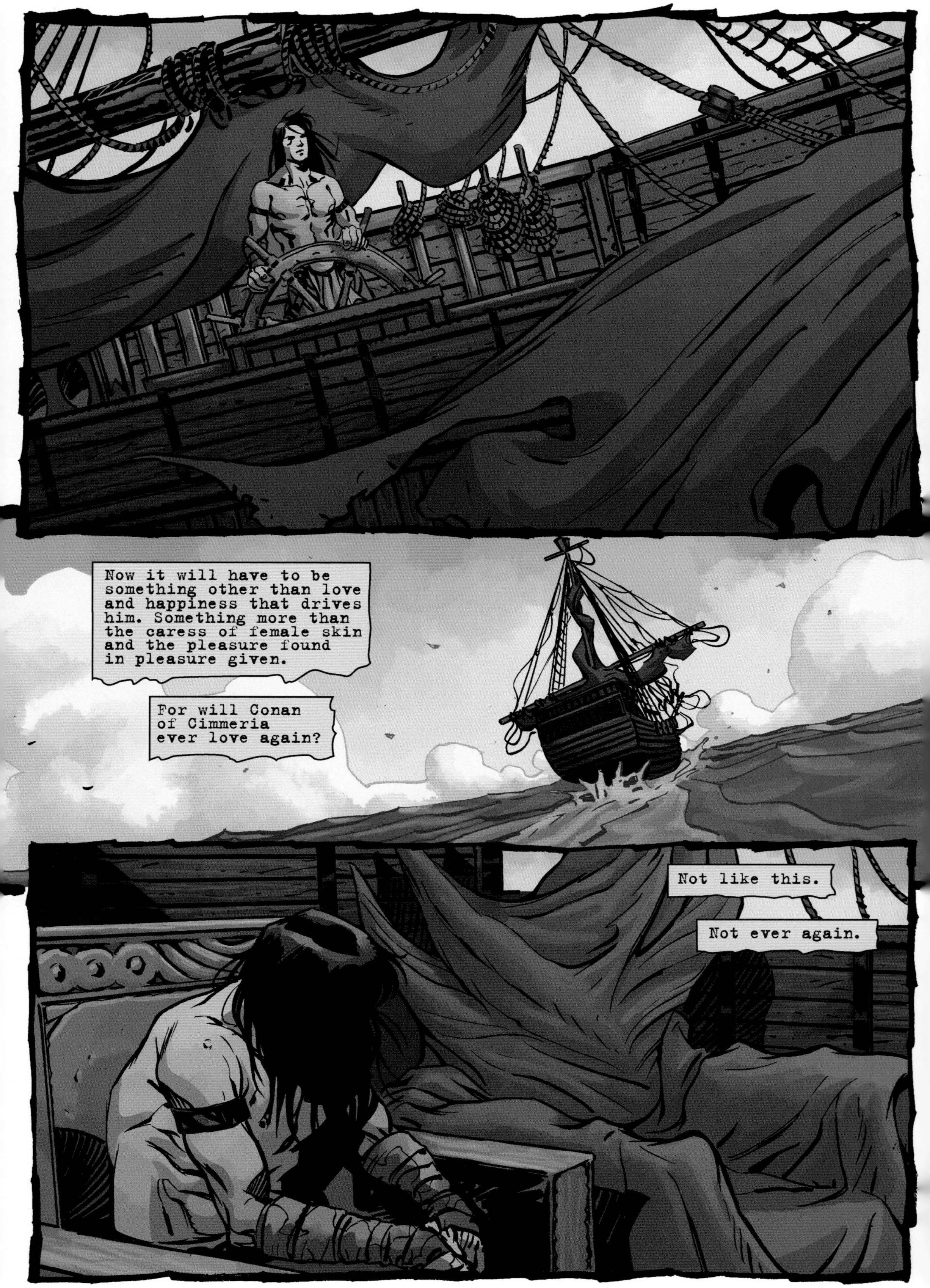
Now it will have to be something other than love and happiness that drives him. Something more than the caress of female skin and the pleasure found in pleasure given.
For will Conan of Cimmeria ever love again?
Not like this.
Not ever again.

It will be a life lived by the sword.

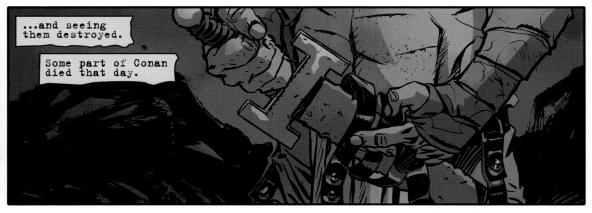

A life lived with harshness and little remorse. A day lived at a time. A life spent seeking out enemies...

...and seeing them destroyed.

Some part of Conan died that day.

Left amongst the carnage of battle. The jungle ruins can claim that much from him.

That...

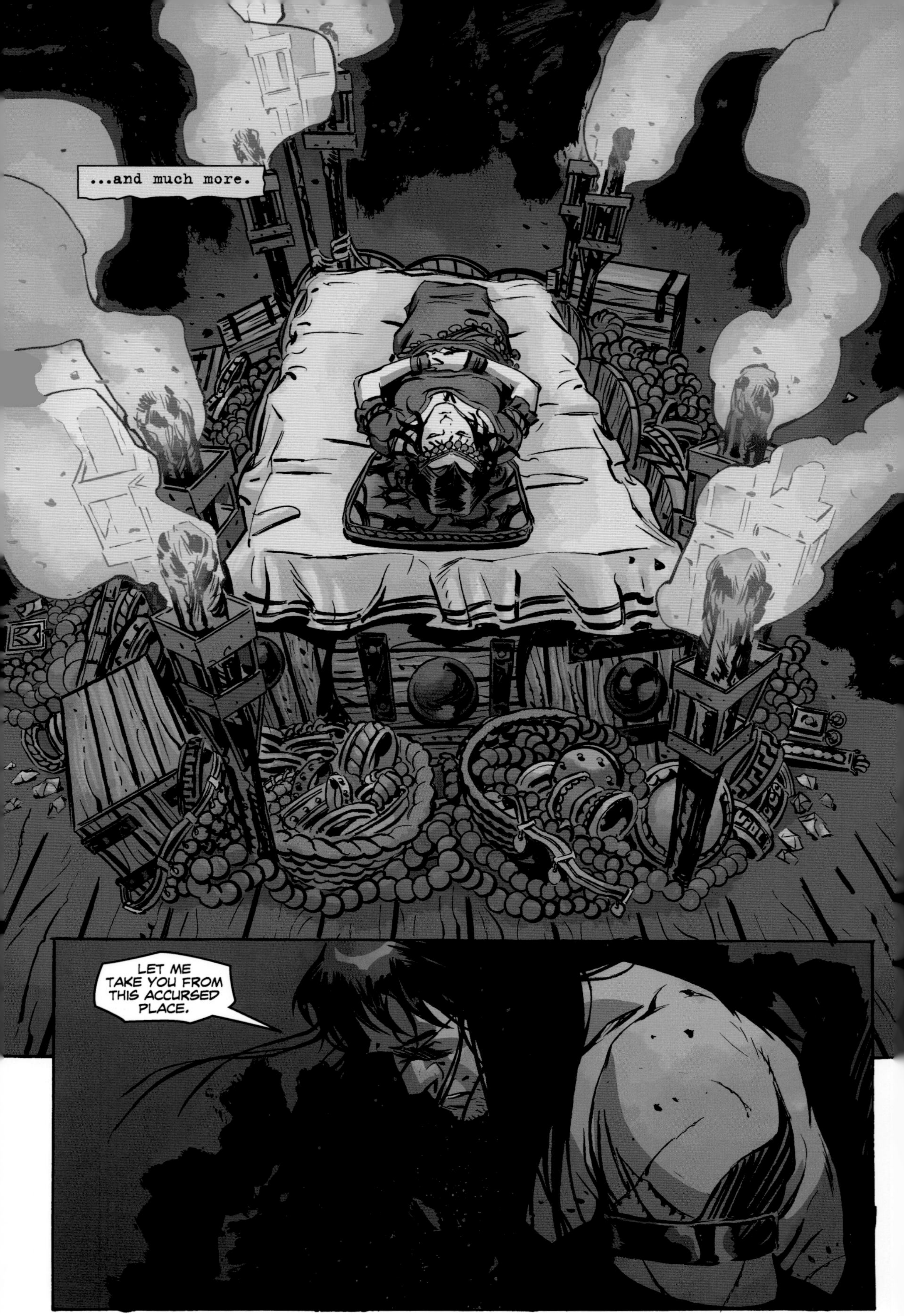
...and much more.
LET ME TAKE YOU FROM THIS ACCURSED PLACE.

He strode to the rotted wharf, and caring not, kicked the moorings free of ancient cleats.

The *Tigress* slid out, sullen and sluggish in the brackish water, until the current caught hold and pulled it along.

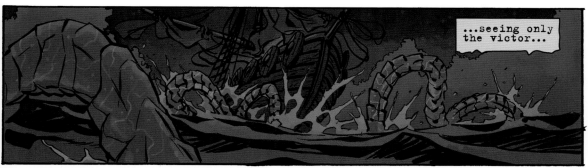

The jungle watched the man who came, killed, pillaged, and left...

...seeing only the victor...

...and not the man who lost too much.

Still, he left with no further trouble. A day and a night on that foul river...

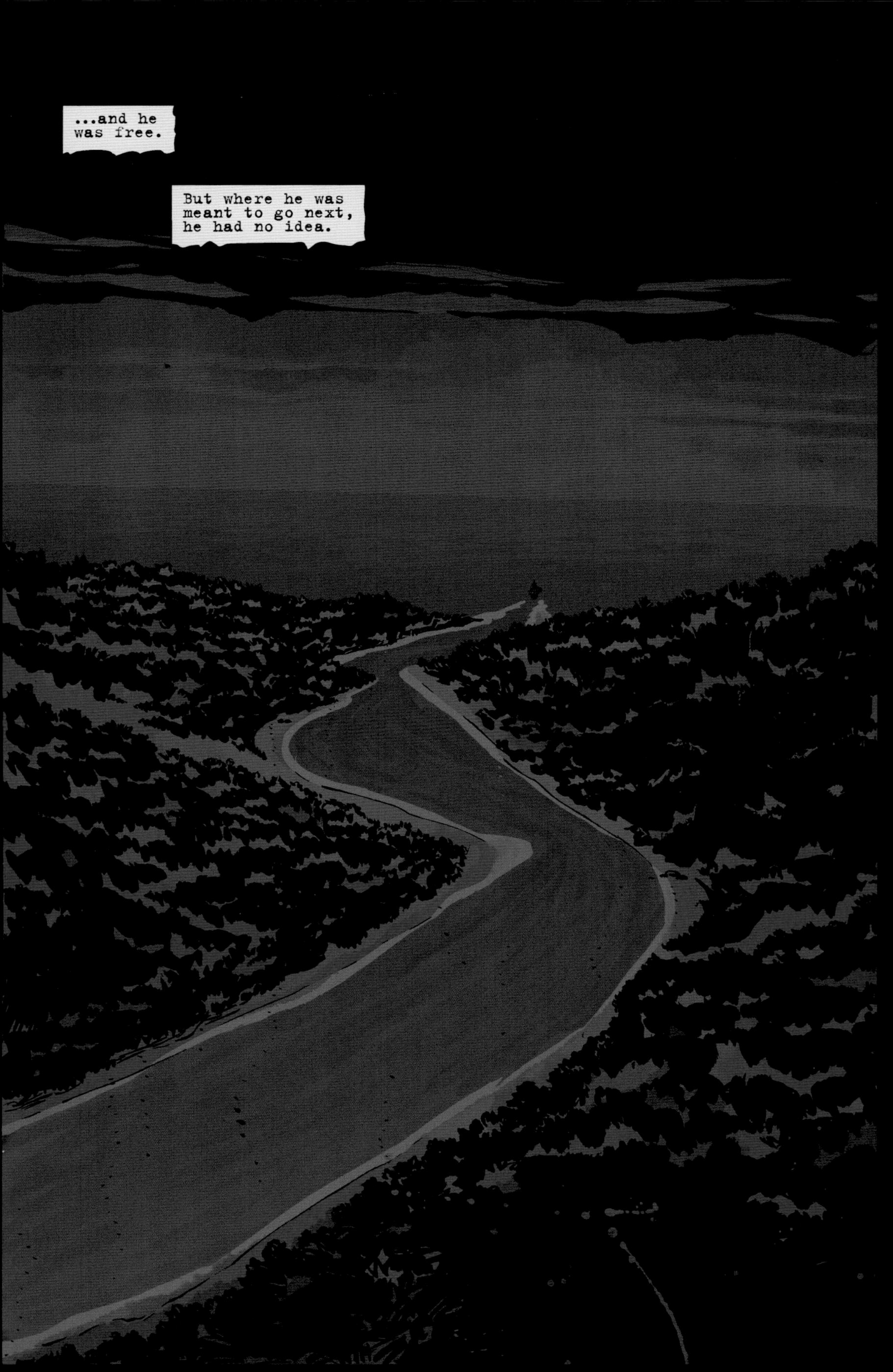
...and he was free.
But where he was meant to go next, he had no idea.

CHAPTER SEVEN

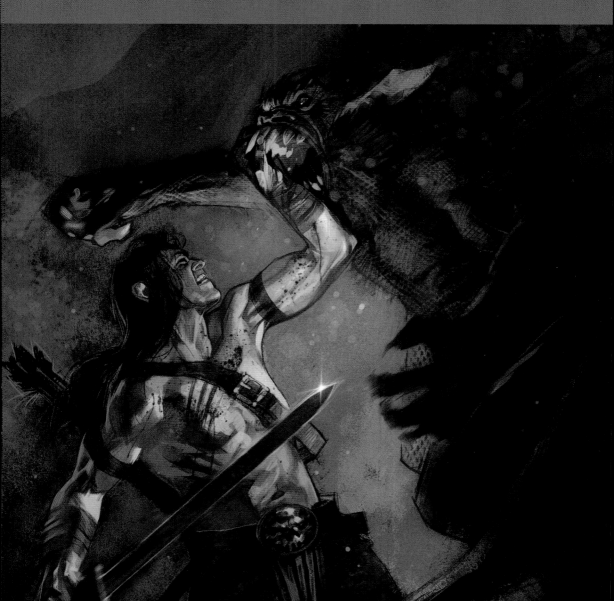

"So passed the Queen of the Black Coast,
from this world to the next."

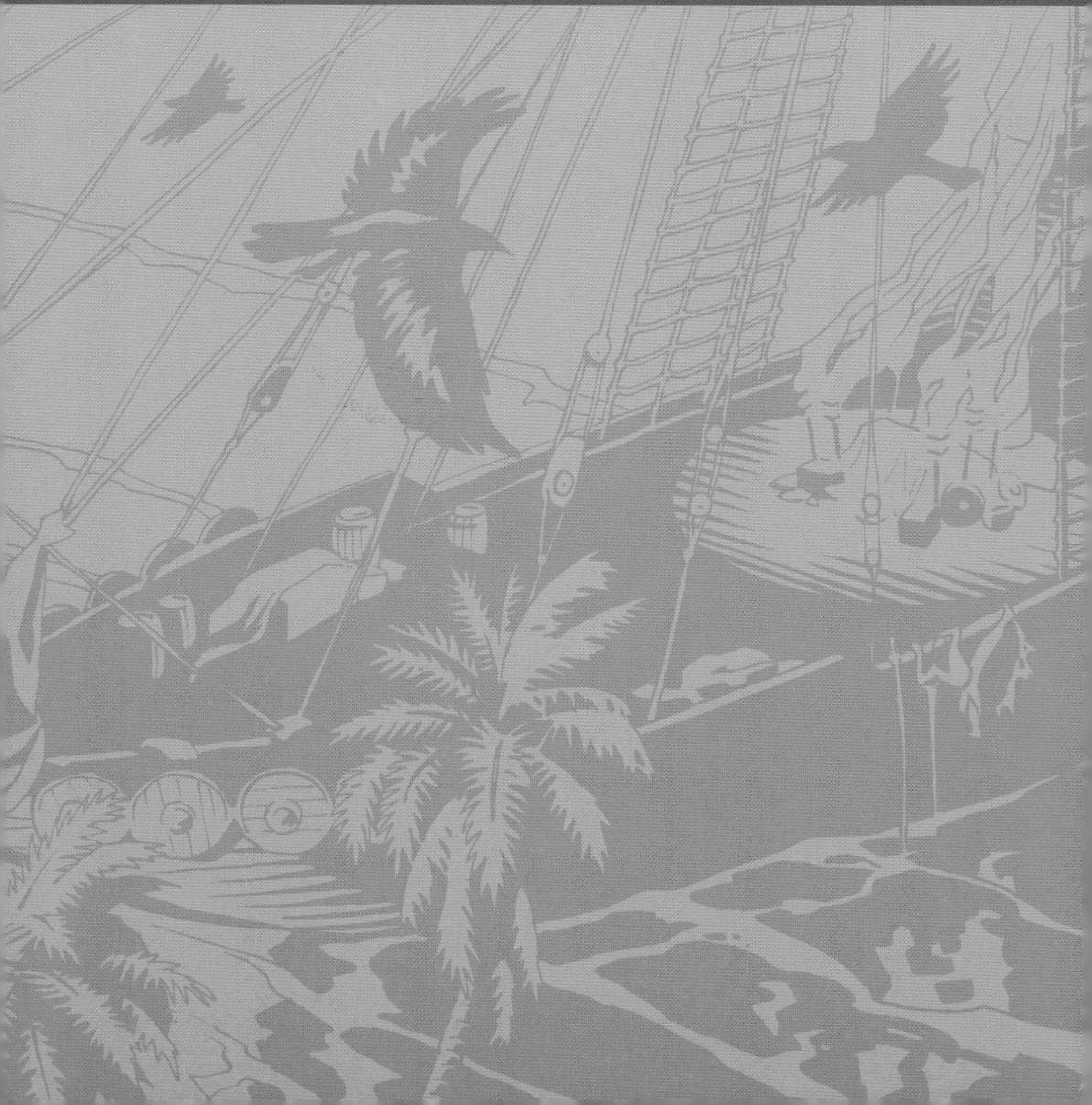

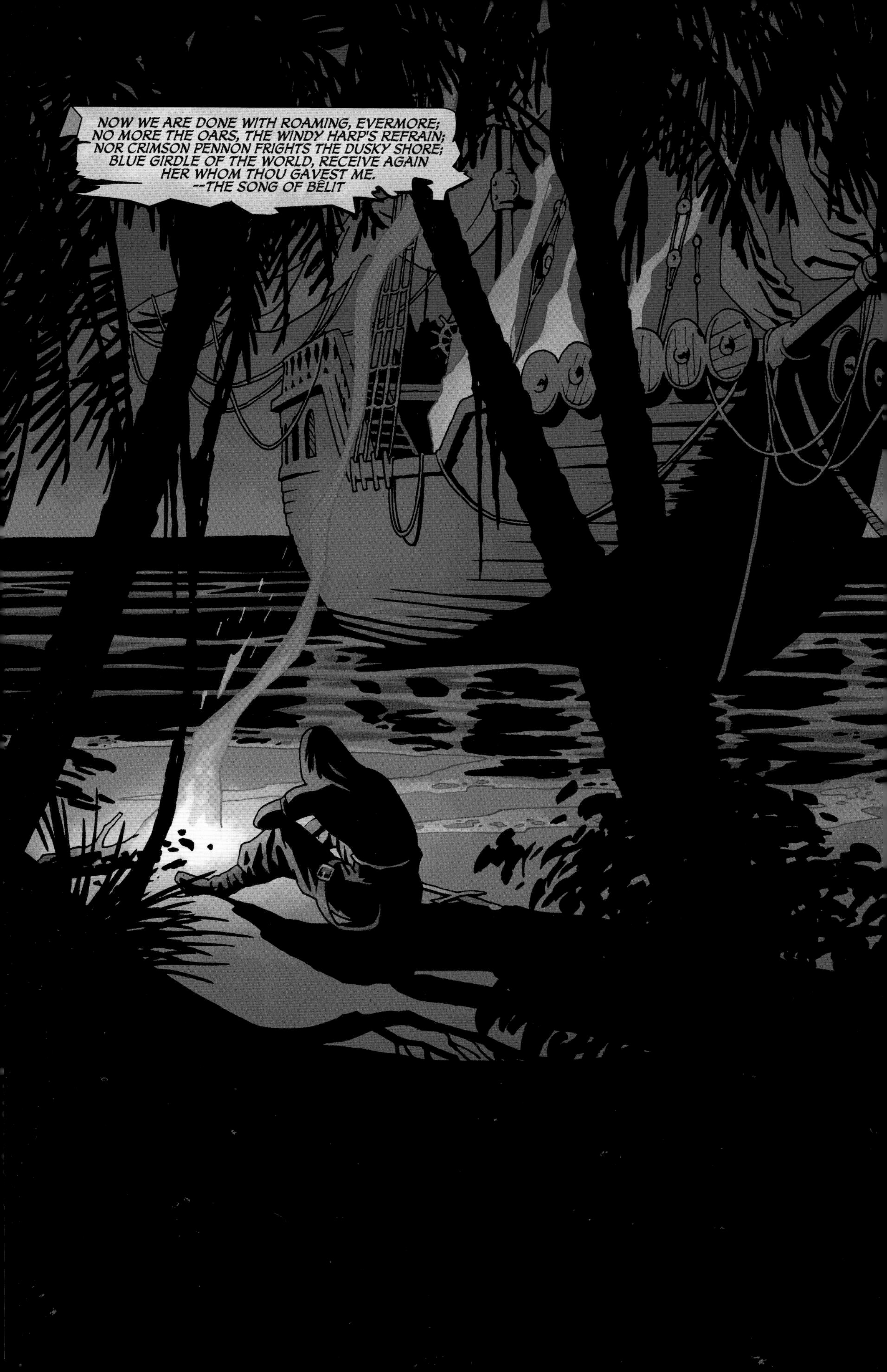
NOW WE ARE DONE WITH ROAMING, EVERMORE;
NO MORE THE OARS, THE WINDY HARP'S REFRAIN;
NOR CRIMSON PENNON FRIGHTS THE DUSKY SHORE;
BLUE GIRDLE OF THE WORLD, RECEIVE AGAIN
HER WHOM THOU GAVEST ME.
--THE SONG OF BÊLIT

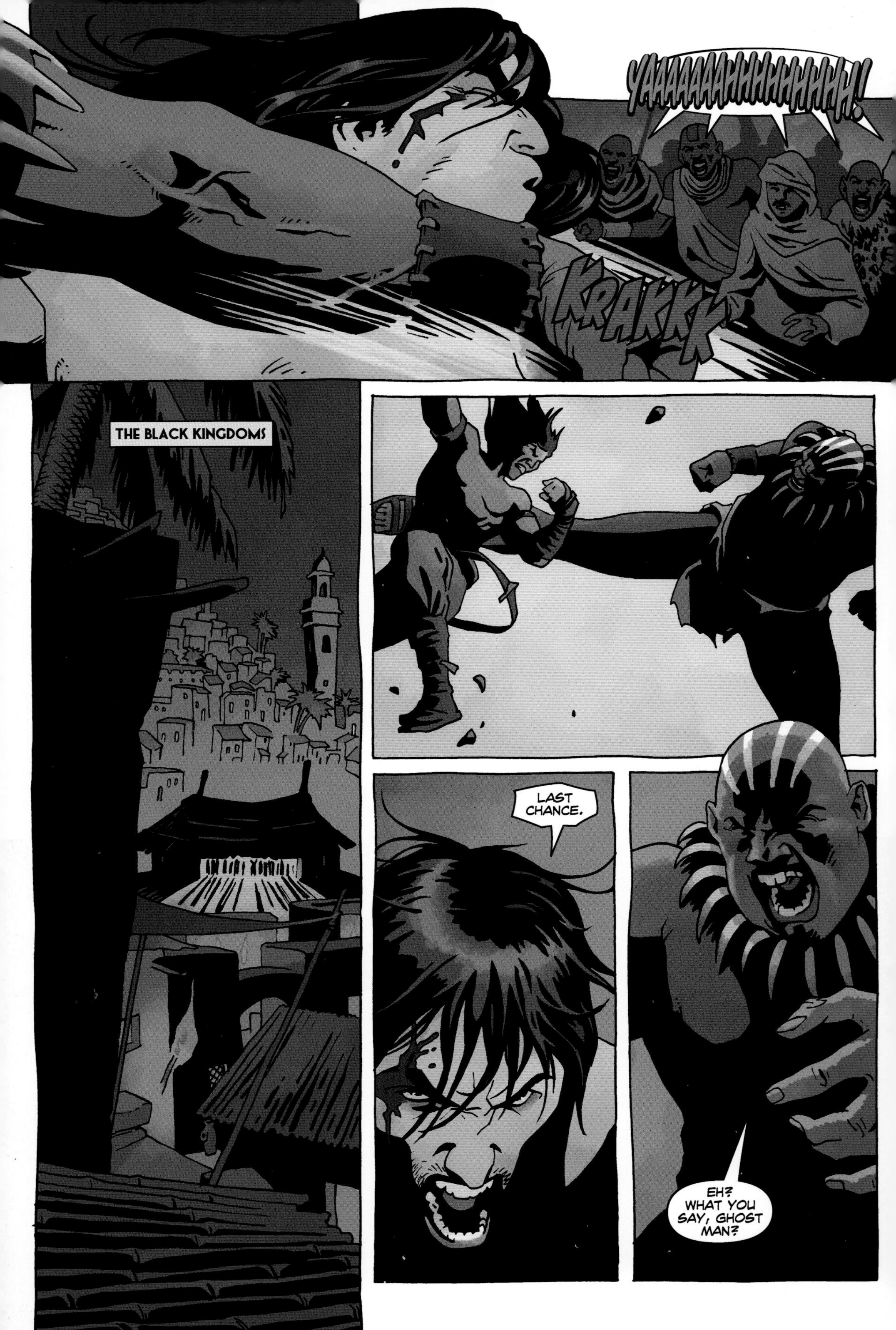

YAAAAAAAHHHHHHHH!
KRAKKK
THE BLACK KINGDOMS
LAST CHANCE.
EH? WHAT YOU SAY, GHOST MAN?

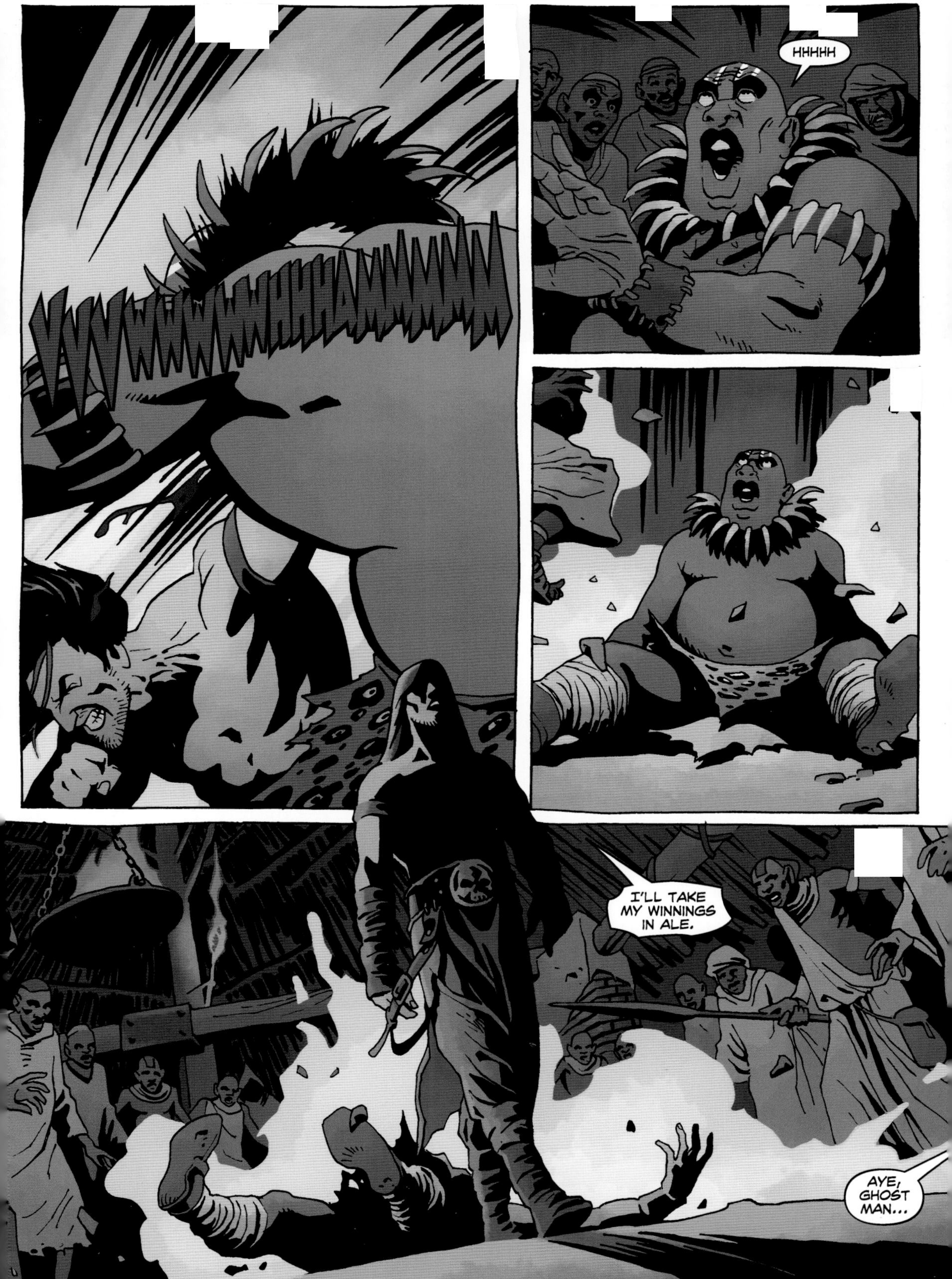
VAVVWHAWWWHHAMMMMM
HHHHH
I'LL TAKE MY WINNINGS IN ALE.
AYE, GHOST MAN...

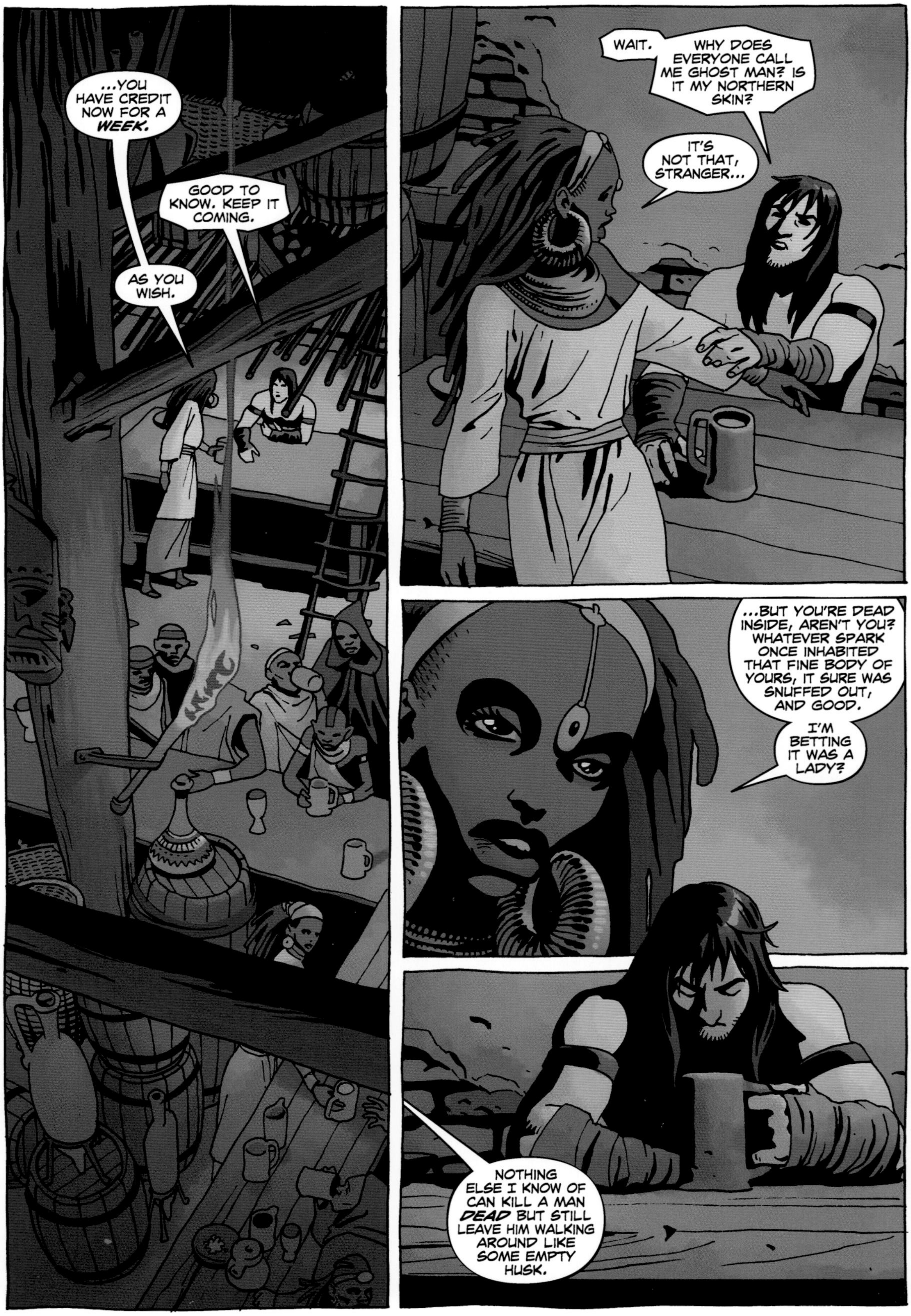
...YOU HAVE CREDIT NOW FOR A *WEEK.*
GOOD TO KNOW. KEEP IT COMING.
AS YOU WISH.
WAIT.
WHY DOES EVERYONE CALL ME GHOST MAN? IS IT MY NORTHERN SKIN?
IT'S NOT THAT, STRANGER...
...BUT YOU'RE DEAD INSIDE, AREN'T YOU? WHATEVER SPARK ONCE INHABITED THAT FINE BODY OF YOURS, IT SURE WAS SNUFFED OUT, AND GOOD.
I'M BETTING IT WAS A LADY?
NOTHING ELSE I KNOW OF CAN KILL A MAN *DEAD* BUT STILL LEAVE HIM WALKING AROUND LIKE SOME EMPTY HUSK.

Again dawn tinged the ocean. The magical hours that precede the rising of the sun, when the world is gray and silver and still.

Conan of Cimmeria felt no magic. He sat upon that white beach, the no-name, anonymous beach along the shores of the Black Coast, the gods-forsaken hellish jungle coast.

He stared at the water.

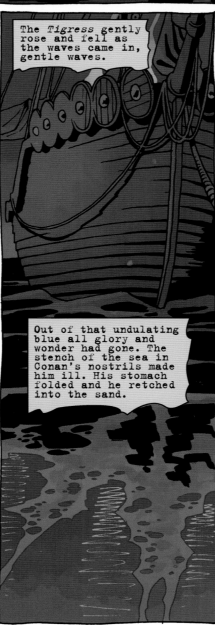

The *Tigress* gently rose and fell as the waves came in, gentle waves.

Out of that undulating blue all glory and wonder had gone. The stench of the sea in Conan's nostrils made him ill. His stomach folded and he retched into the sand.

CROM.

All light had gone out of his eyes. All spark of life had left him.

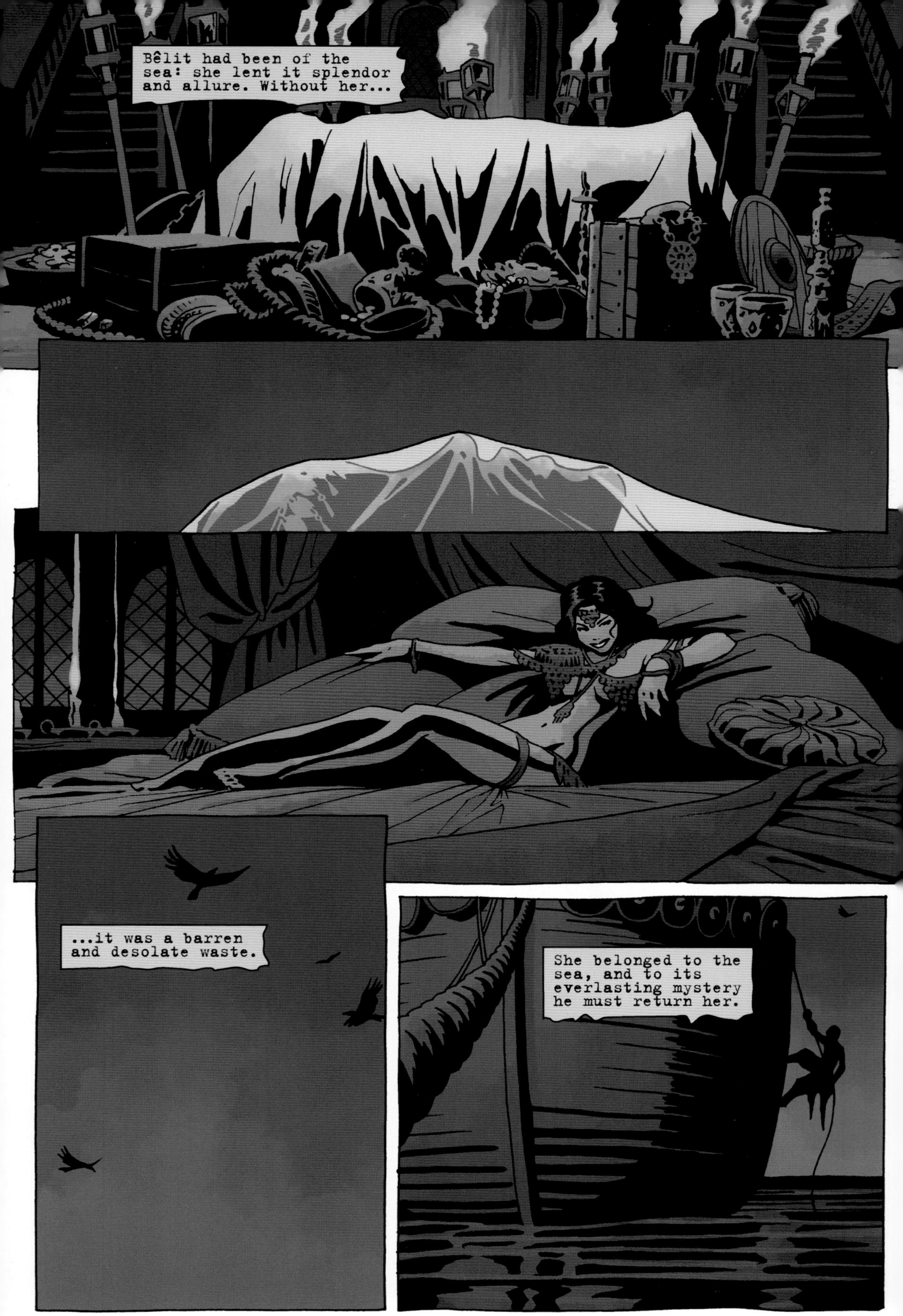
Bêlit had been of the sea: she lent it splendor and allure. Without her...
...it was a barren and desolate waste.
She belonged to the sea, and to its everlasting mystery he must return her.

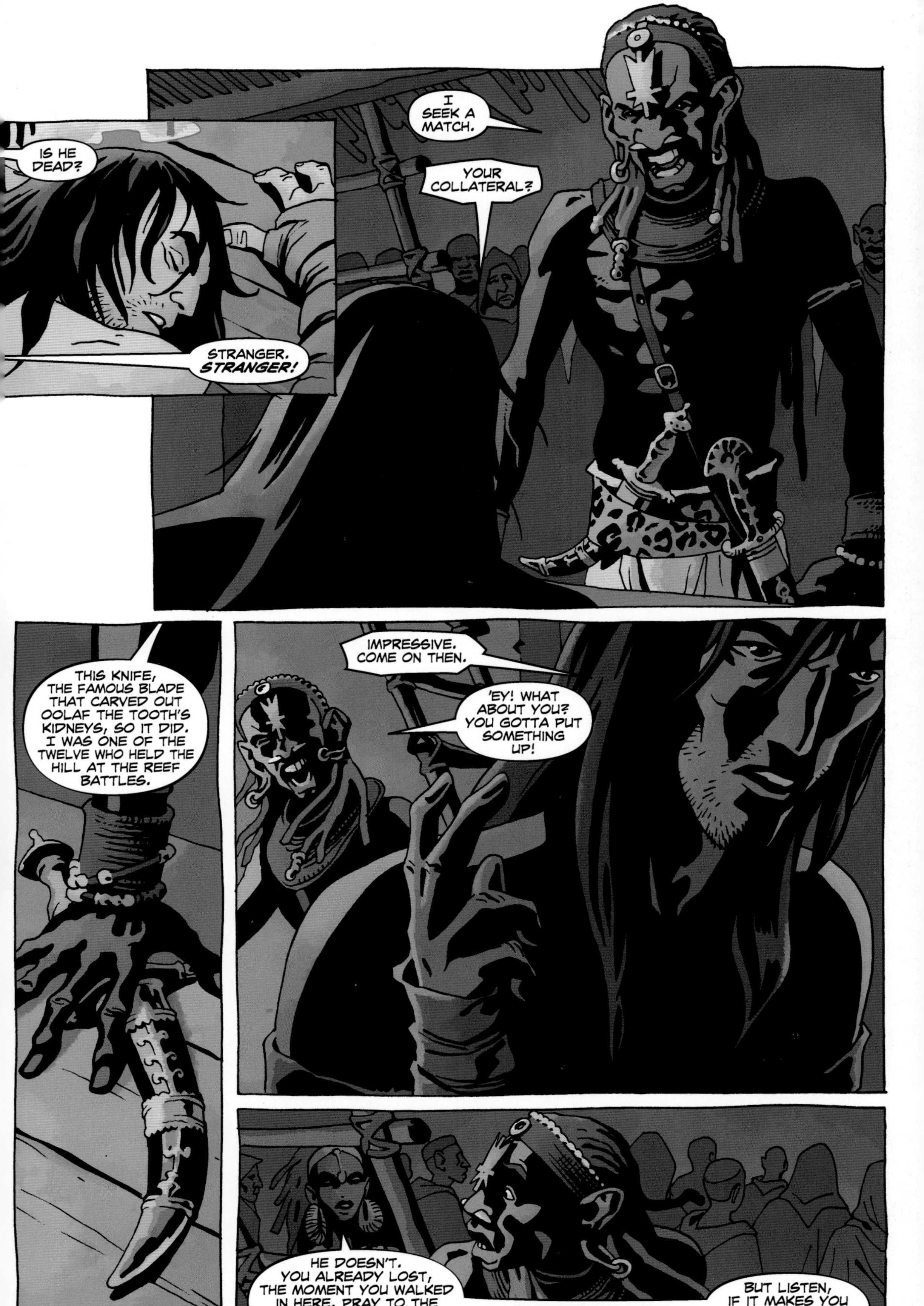
IS HE DEAD?
STRANGER. STRANGER!
I SEEK A MATCH.
YOUR COLLATERAL?
THIS KNIFE, THE FAMOUS BLADE THAT CARVED OUT OOLAF THE TOOTH'S KIDNEYS, SO IT DID. I WAS ONE OF THE TWELVE WHO HELD THE HILL AT THE REEF BATTLES.
IMPRESSIVE. COME ON THEN.
'EY! WHAT ABOUT YOU? YOU GOTTA PUT SOMETHING UP!
HE DOESN'T. YOU ALREADY LOST, THE MOMENT YOU WALKED IN HERE. PRAY TO THE MAKER YOU DIE QUICKLY.
BUT LISTEN, IF IT MAKES YOU FEEL ANY BETTER...

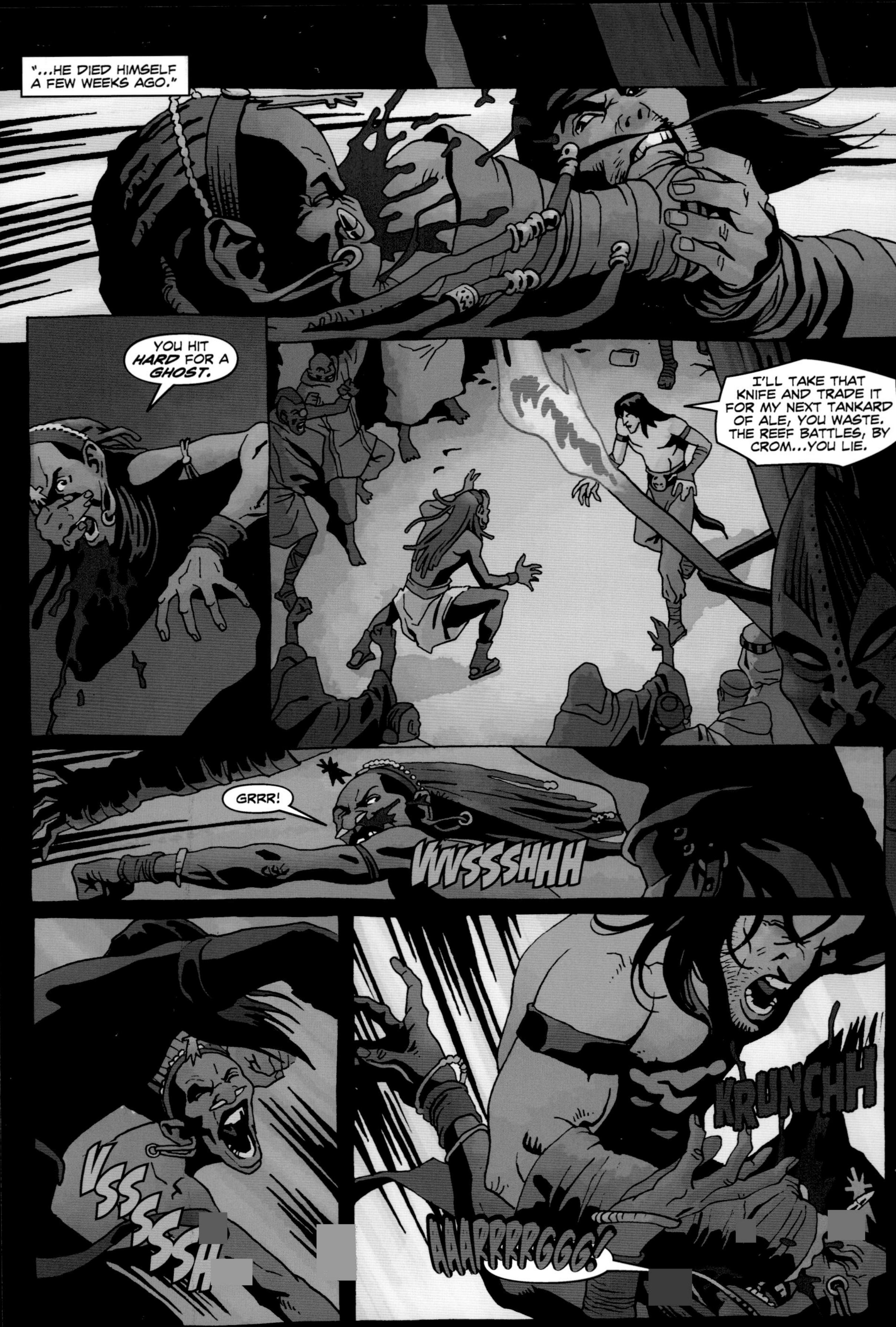
"...HE DIED HIMSELF A FEW WEEKS AGO."
YOU HIT HARD FOR A GHOST.
I'LL TAKE THAT KNIFE AND TRADE IT FOR MY NEXT TANKARD OF ALE, YOU WASTE. THE REEF BATTLES, BY CROM...YOU LIE.
GRRR!
VVSSSHHH
VSSSSH
KRUNCHH
AAARRRRGGG!

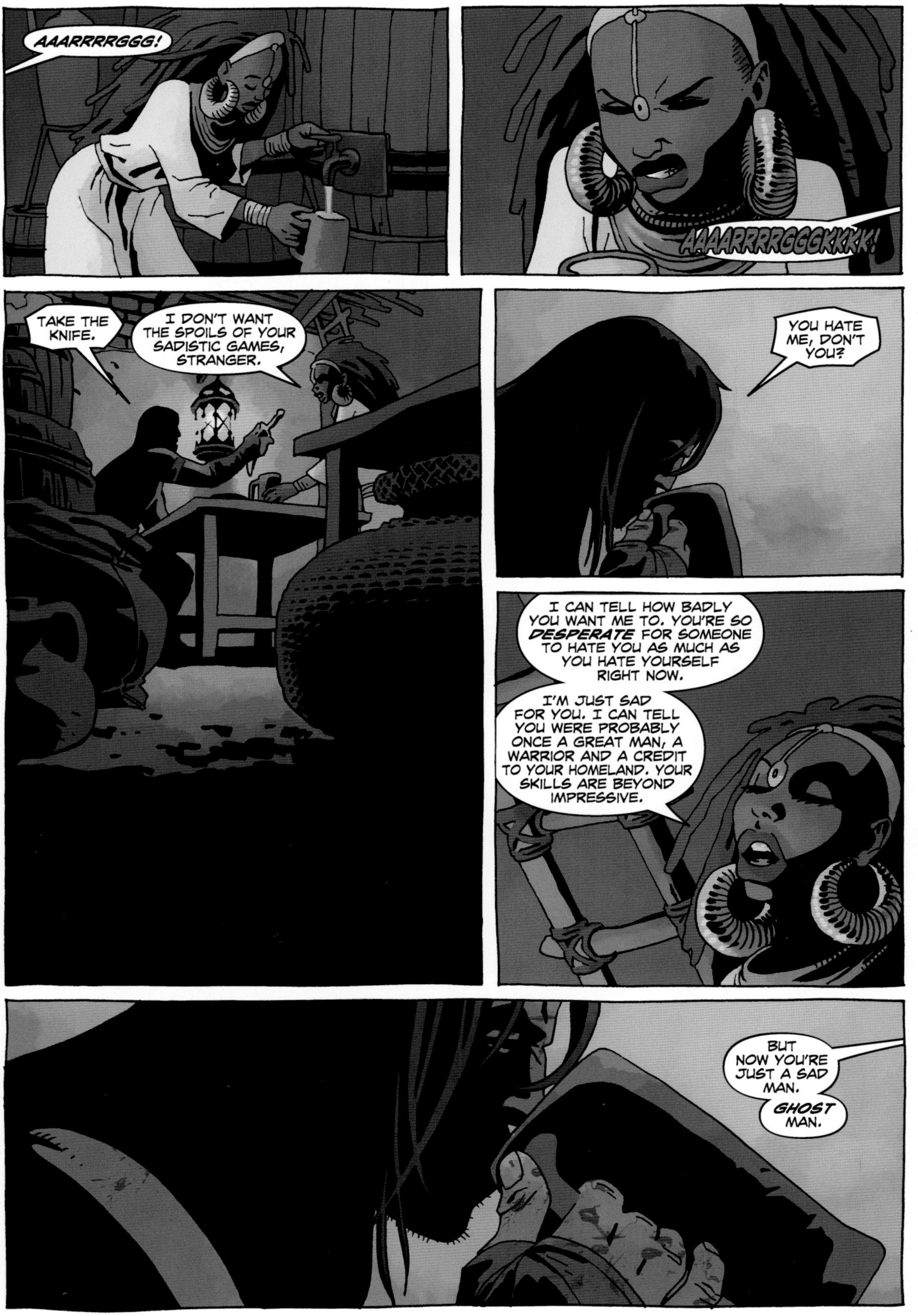
AAARRRRGGG!
AAAARRRRGGGKKKK!
TAKE THE KNIFE.
I DON'T WANT THE SPOILS OF YOUR SADISTIC GAMES, STRANGER.
YOU HATE ME, DON'T YOU?
I CAN TELL HOW BADLY YOU WANT ME TO. YOU'RE SO *DESPERATE* FOR SOMEONE TO HATE YOU AS MUCH AS YOU HATE YOURSELF RIGHT NOW.
I'M JUST SAD FOR YOU. I CAN TELL YOU WERE PROBABLY ONCE A GREAT MAN, A WARRIOR AND A CREDIT TO YOUR HOMELAND. YOUR SKILLS ARE BEYOND IMPRESSIVE.
BUT NOW YOU'RE JUST A SAD MAN.
GHOST MAN.

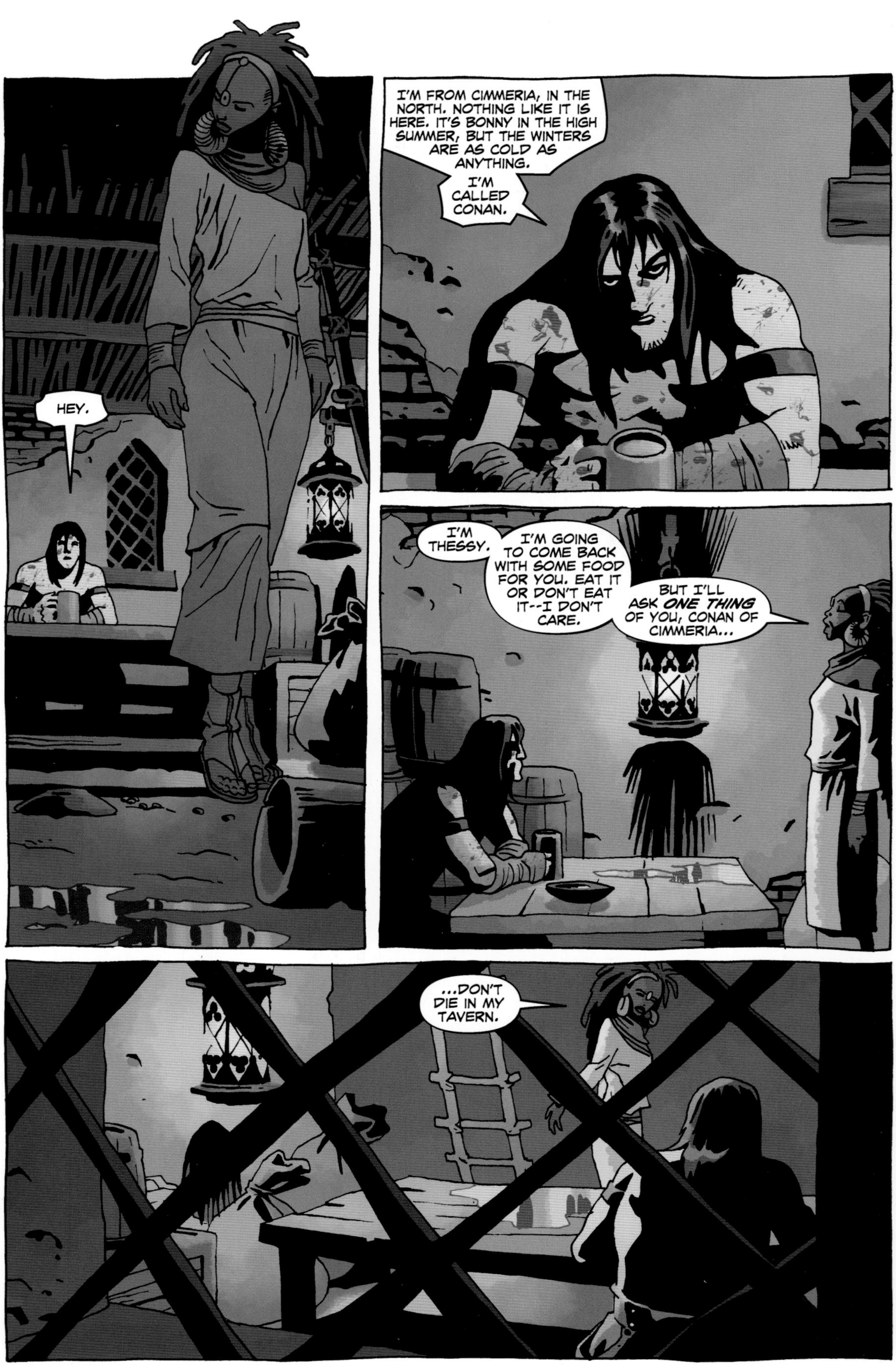
HEY.
I'M FROM CIMMERIA, IN THE NORTH. NOTHING LIKE IT IS HERE. IT'S BONNY IN THE HIGH SUMMER, BUT THE WINTERS ARE AS COLD AS ANYTHING.
I'M CALLED CONAN.
I'M THESSY.
I'M GOING TO COME BACK WITH SOME FOOD FOR YOU. EAT IT OR DON'T EAT IT--I DON'T CARE.
BUT I'LL ASK *ONE THING* OF YOU, CONAN OF CIMMERIA...
...DON'T DIE IN MY TAVERN.

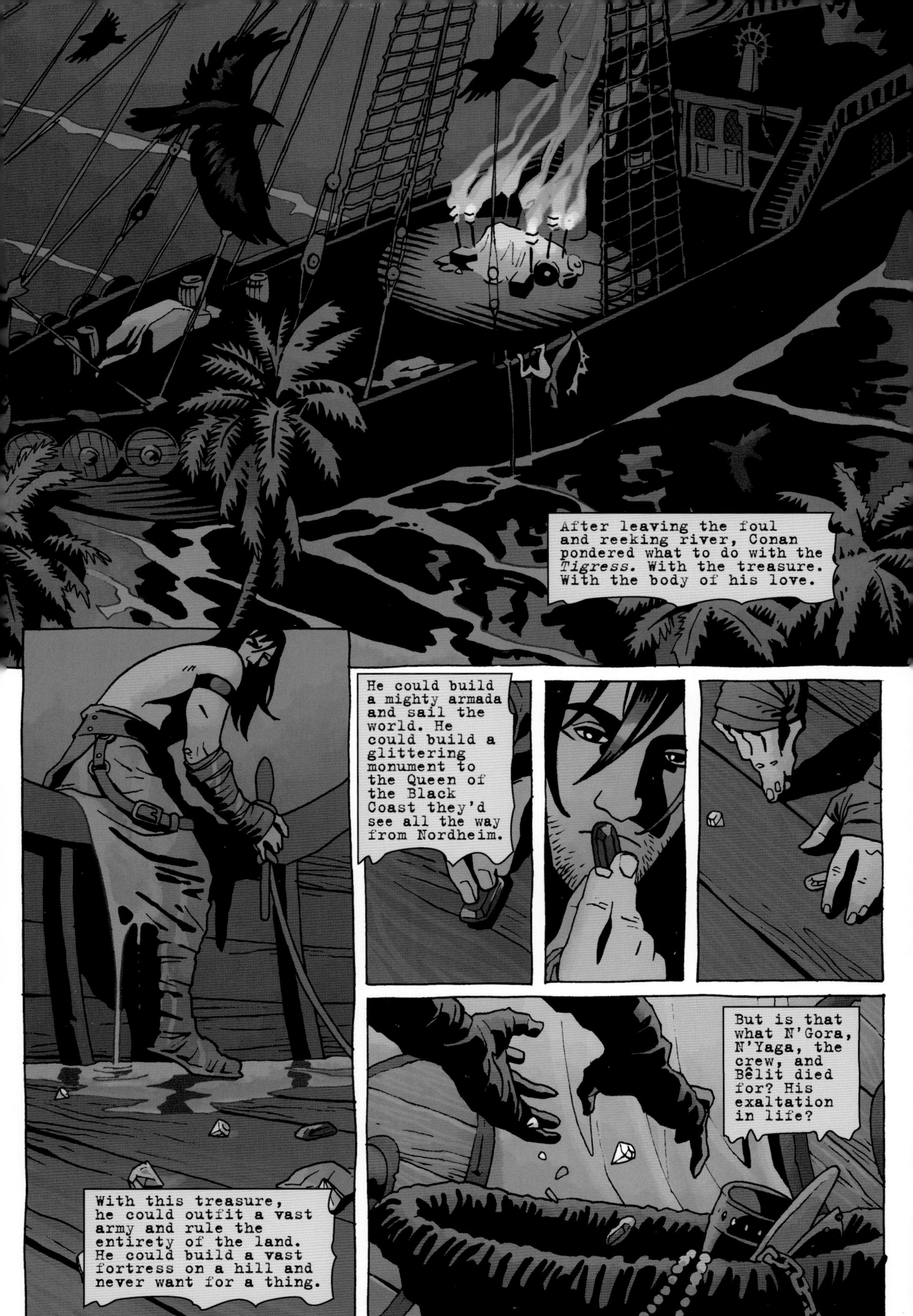
After leaving the foul and reeking river, Conan pondered what to do with the *Tigress.* With the treasure. With the body of his love.
With this treasure, he could outfit a vast army and rule the entirety of the land. He could build a vast fortress on a hill and never want for a thing.
He could build a mighty armada and sail the world. He could build a glittering monument to the Queen of the Black Coast they'd see all the way from Nordheim.
But is that what N'Gora, N'Yaga, the crew, and Bêlit died for? His exaltation in life?

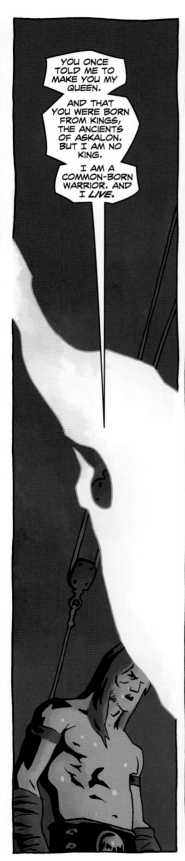

YOU ONCE TOLD ME TO MAKE YOU MY QUEEN.

AND THAT YOU WERE BORN FROM KINGS, THE ANCIENTS OF ASKALON. BUT I AM NO KING.

I AM A COMMON-BORN WARRIOR. AND I *LIVE*.

FORGIVE ME.

I NEVER DESERVED YOUR MERCY, OR YOUR LOVE.

YOU FOOL, CONAN.

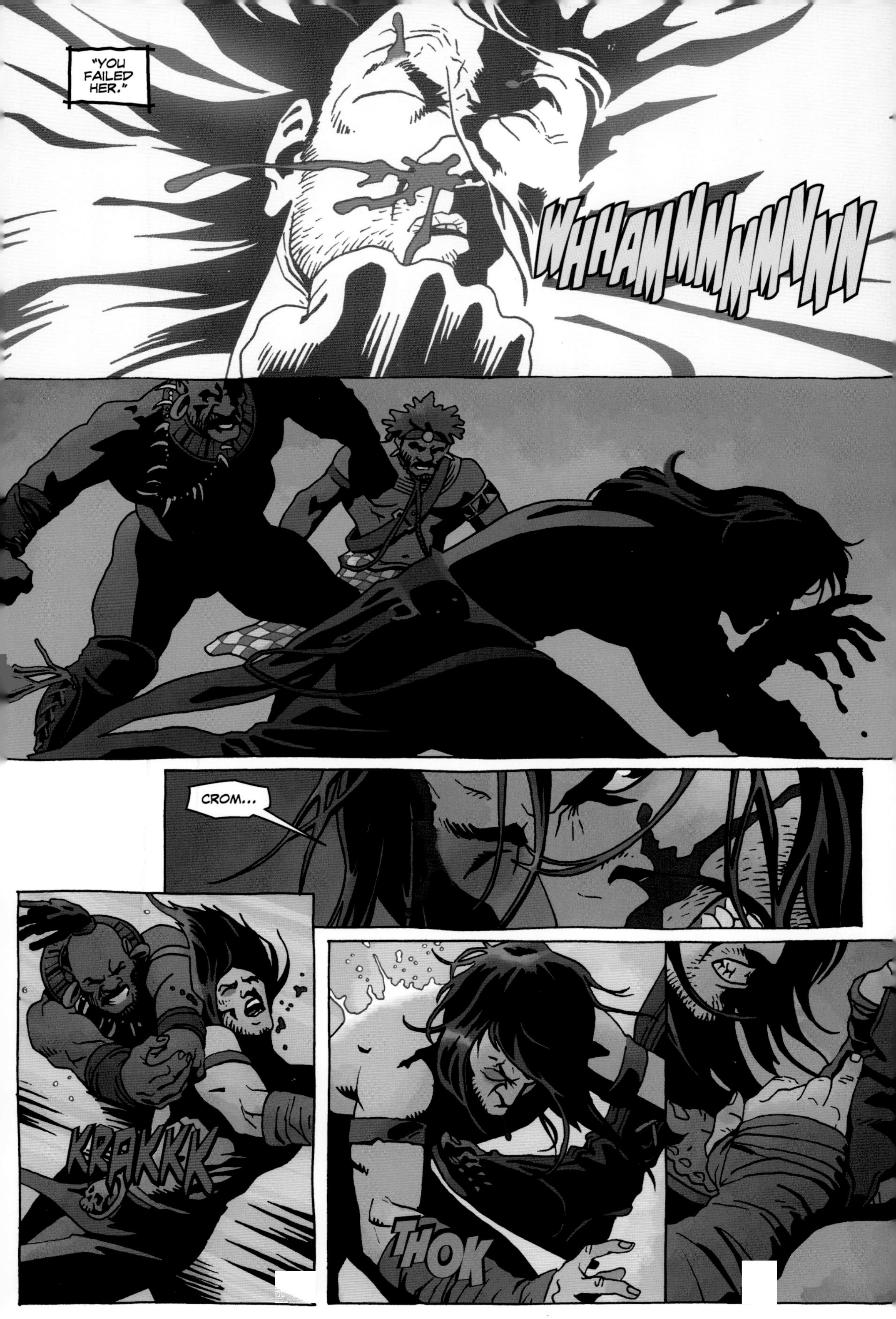
"YOU FAILED HER."
WHHAMMMMMNNN
CROM...
KRAKKK
THOK

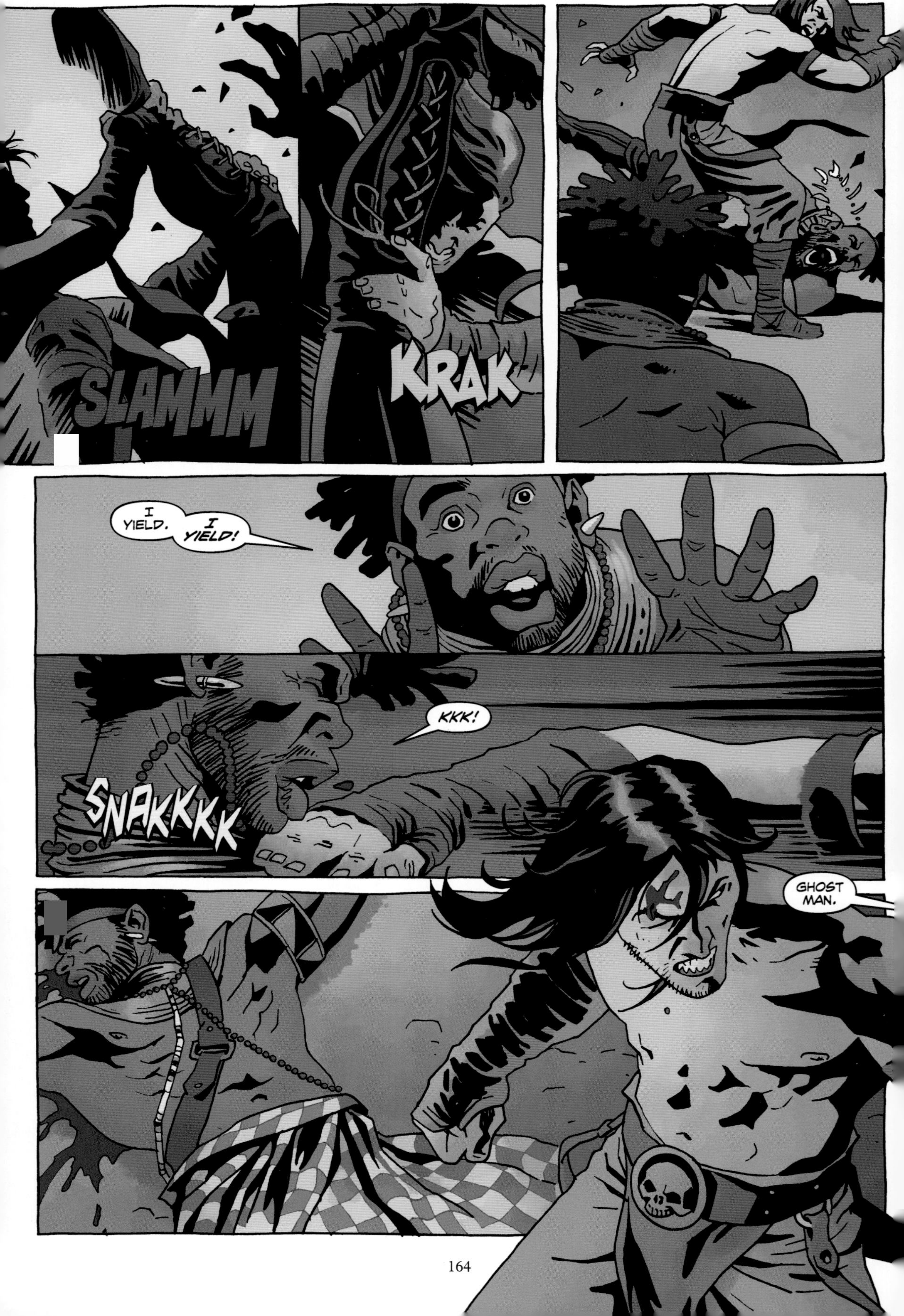
SLAMMM
KRAK
I YIELD.
I YIELD!
KKK!
SNAKKKK
GHOST MAN.

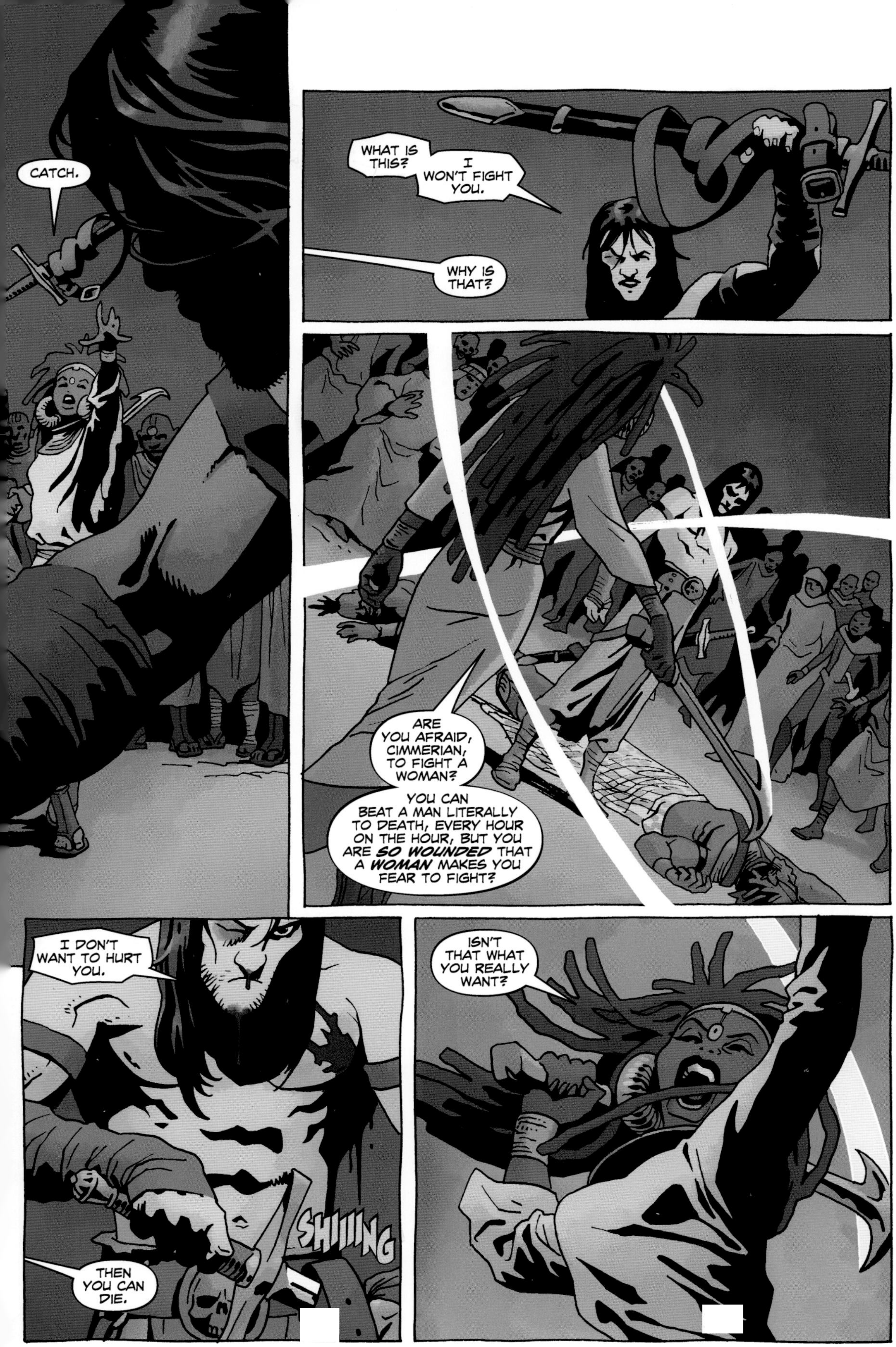
CATCH.
WHAT IS THIS?
I WON'T FIGHT YOU.
WHY IS THAT?
ARE YOU AFRAID, CIMMERIAN, TO FIGHT A WOMAN?
YOU CAN BEAT A MAN LITERALLY TO DEATH, EVERY HOUR ON THE HOUR, BUT YOU ARE SO WOUNDED THAT A WOMAN MAKES YOU FEAR TO FIGHT?
I DON'T WANT TO HURT YOU.
THEN YOU CAN DIE.
SHIIIING
ISN'T THAT WHAT YOU REALLY WANT?

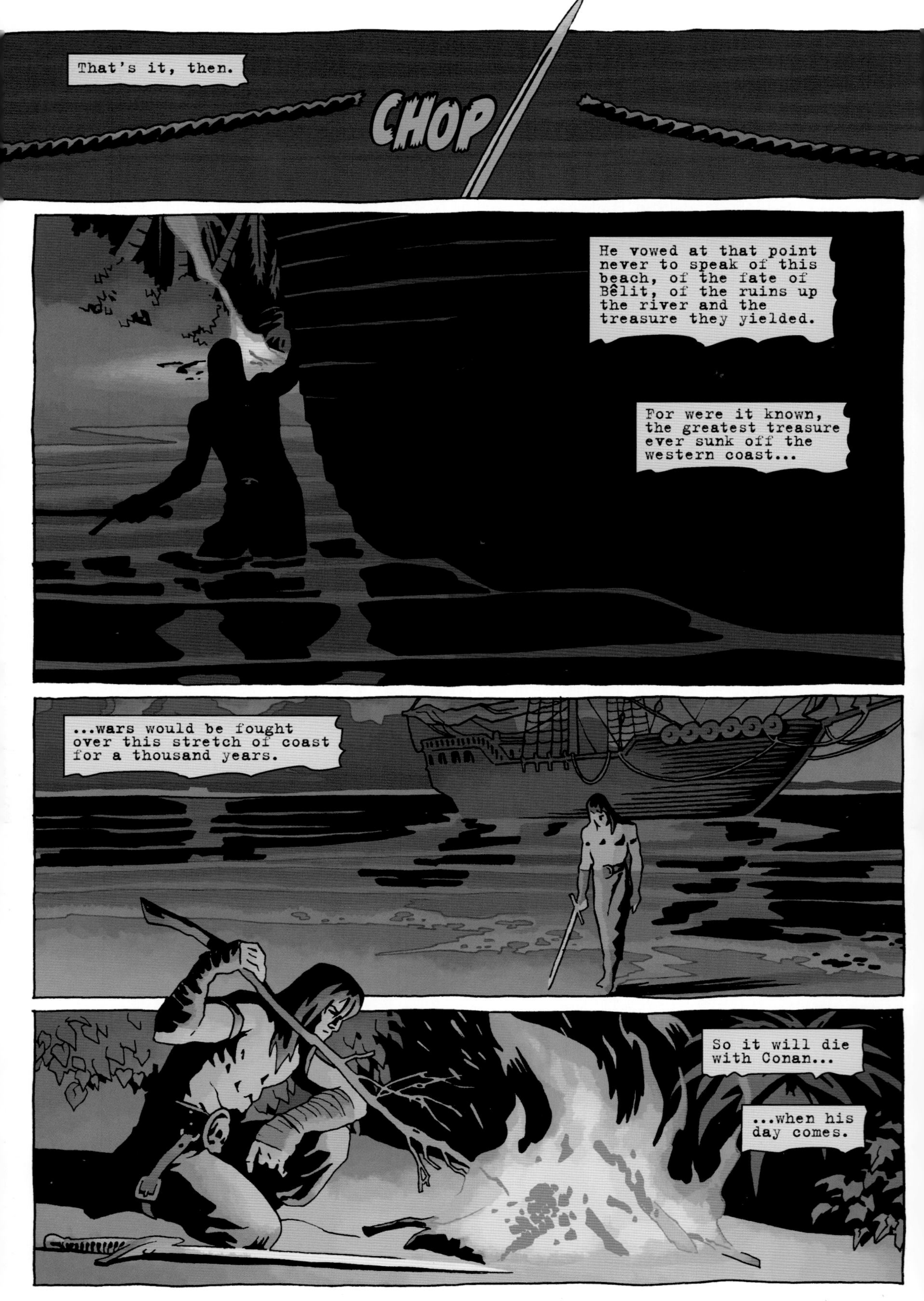

That's it, then.
CHOP
He vowed at that point never to speak of this beach, of the fate of Bêlit, of the ruins up the river and the treasure they yielded.
For were it known, the greatest treasure ever sunk off the western coast...
...wars would be fought over this stretch of coast for a thousand years.
So it will die with Conan...
...when his day comes.

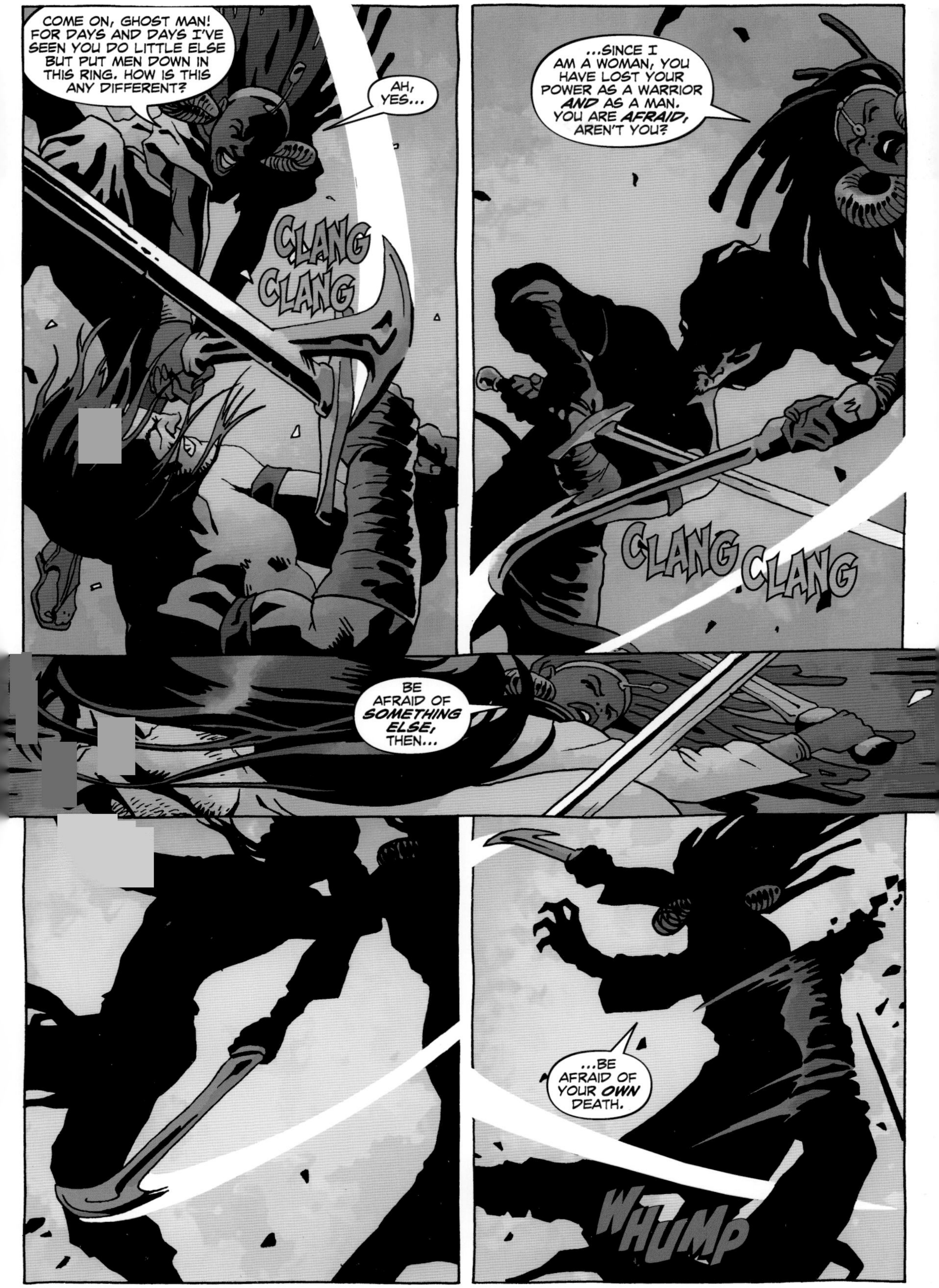
COME ON, GHOST MAN! FOR DAYS AND DAYS I'VE SEEN YOU DO LITTLE ELSE BUT PUT MEN DOWN IN THIS RING. HOW IS THIS ANY DIFFERENT?
AH, YES...
CLANG
CLANG
...SINCE I AM A WOMAN, YOU HAVE LOST YOUR POWER AS A WARRIOR AND AS A MAN. YOU ARE AFRAID, AREN'T YOU?
CLANG CLANG
BE AFRAID OF SOMETHING ELSE, THEN...
...BE AFRAID OF YOUR OWN DEATH.
WHUMP

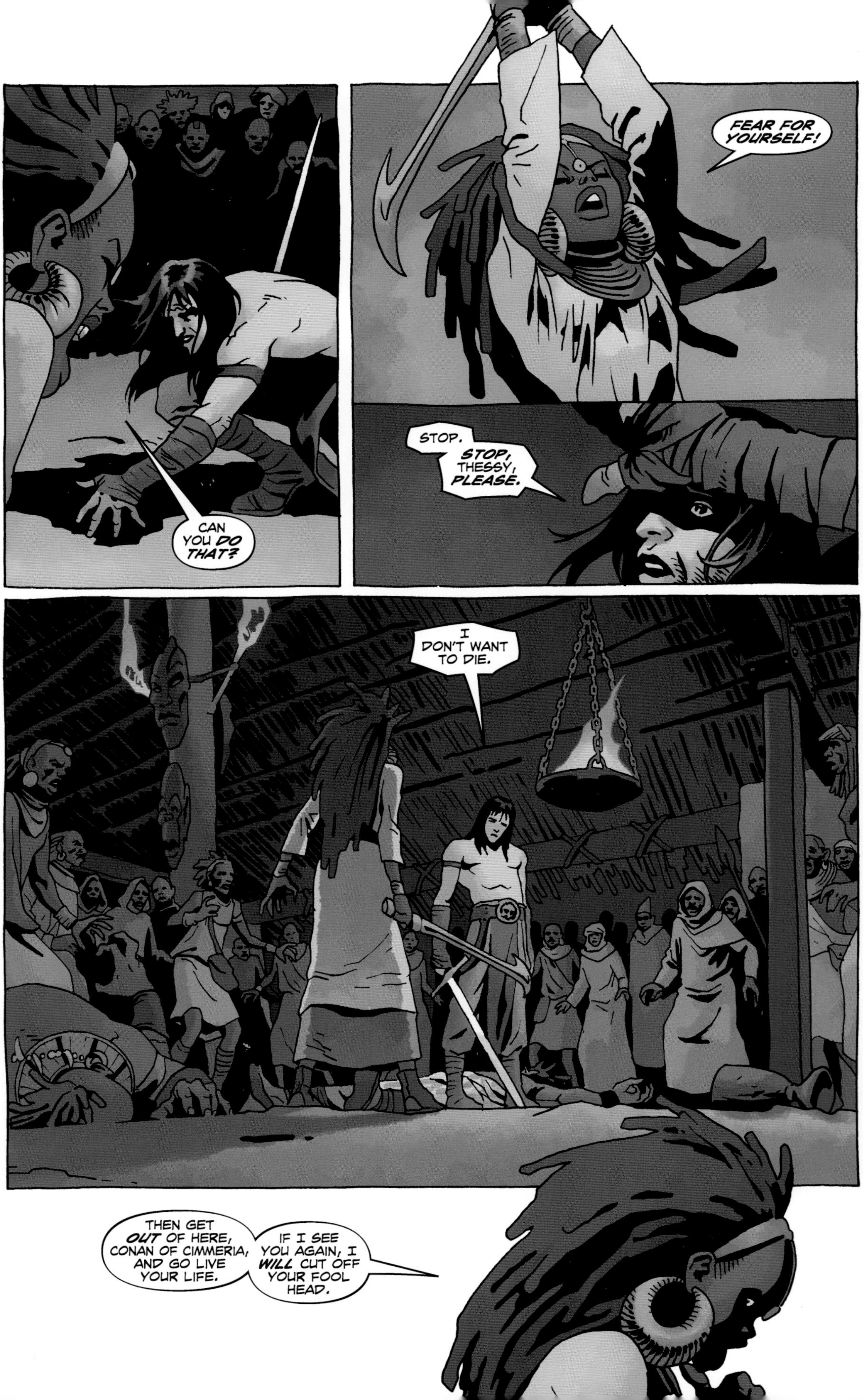
CAN YOU DO THAT?
FEAR FOR YOURSELF!
STOP. STOP, THESSY, PLEASE.
I DON'T WANT TO DIE.
THEN GET OUT OF HERE, CONAN OF CIMMERIA, AND GO LIVE YOUR LIFE.
IF I SEE YOU AGAIN, I WILL CUT OFF YOUR FOOL HEAD.

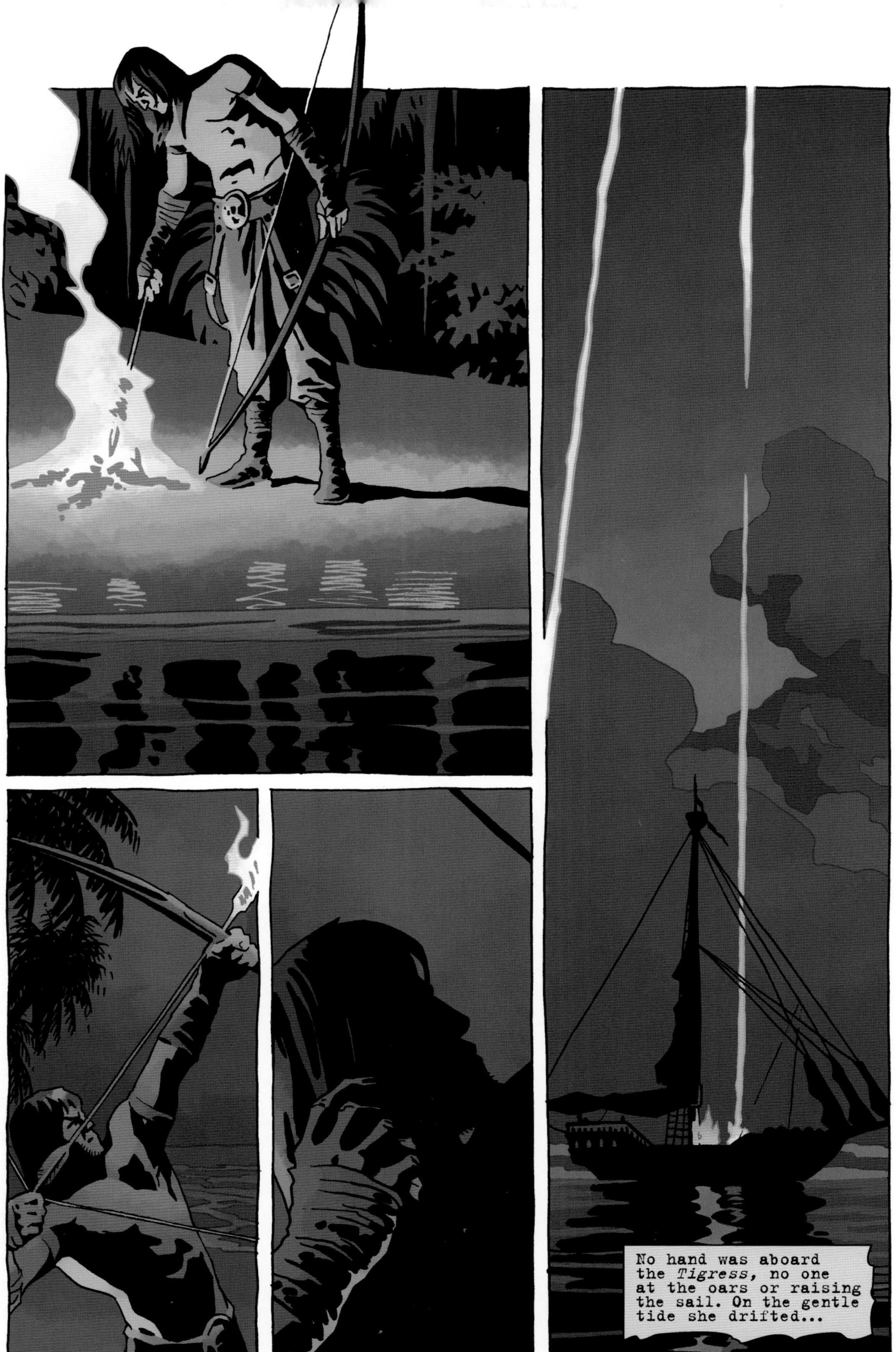
No hand was aboard the *Tigress,* no one at the oars or raising the sail. On the gentle tide she drifted...

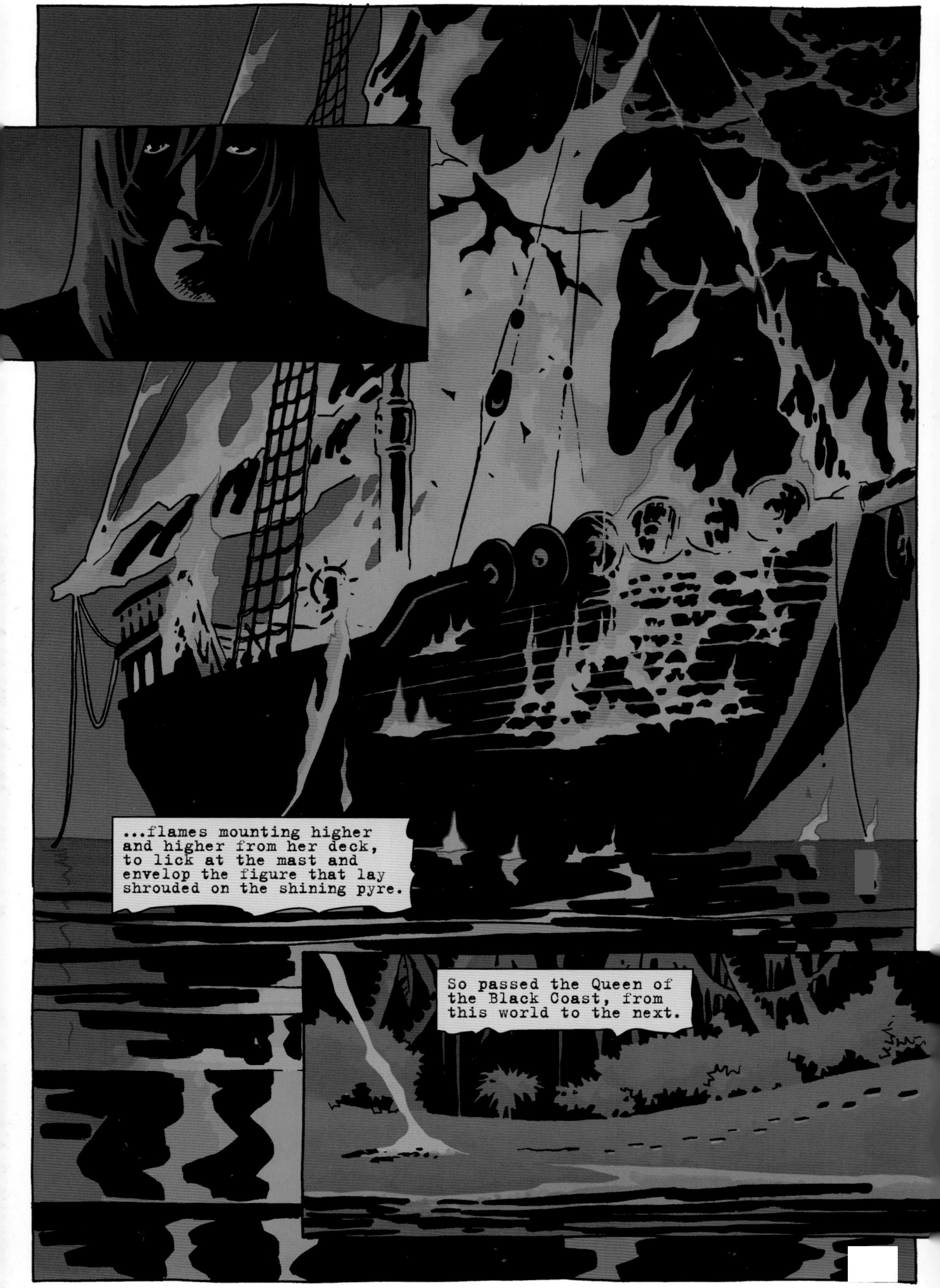
...flames mounting higher and higher from her deck, to lick at the mast and envelop the figure that lay shrouded on the shining pyre.
So passed the Queen of the Black Coast, from this world to the next.

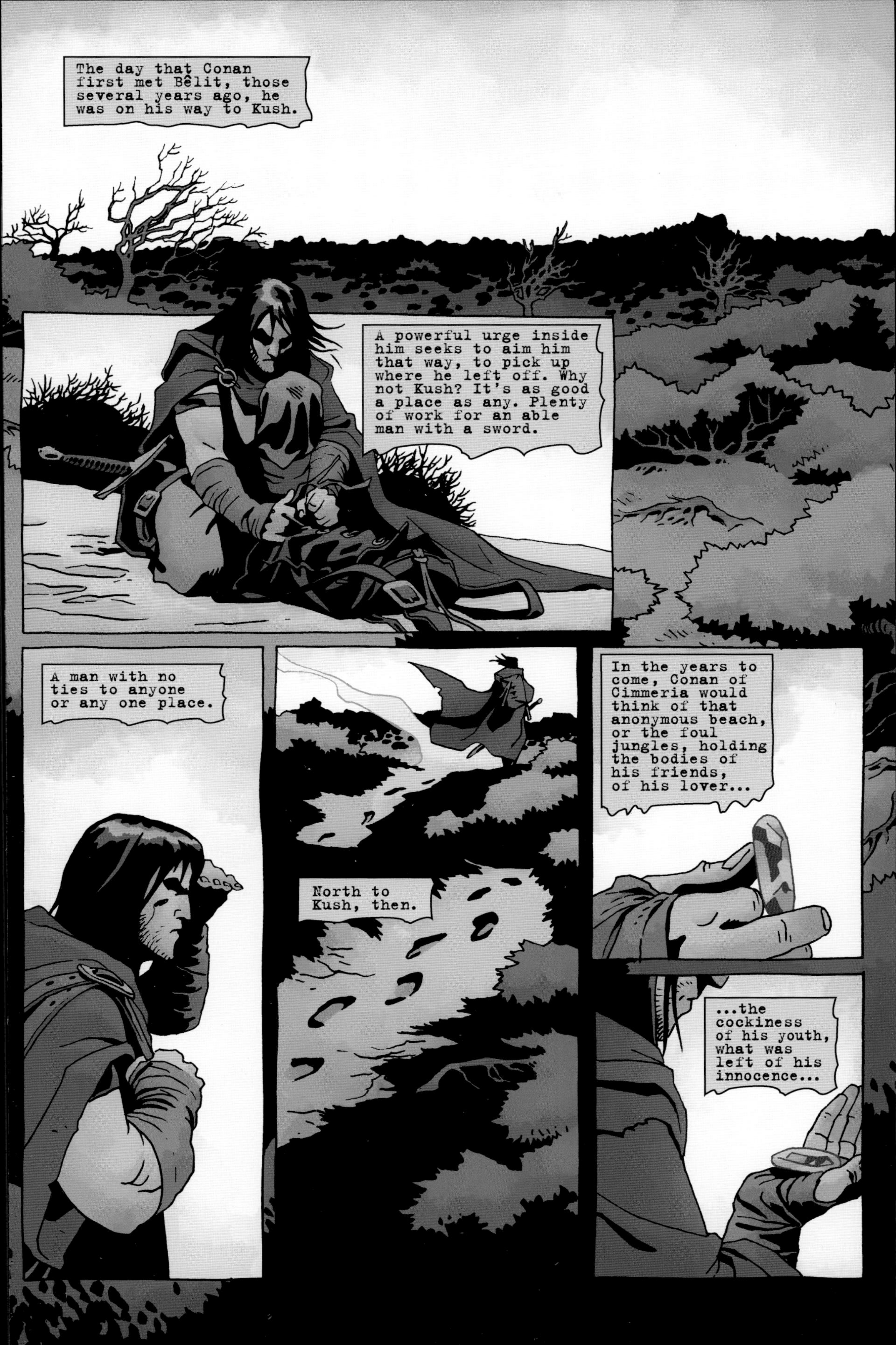

The day that Conan first met Bêlit, those several years ago, he was on his way to Kush.
A powerful urge inside him seeks to aim him that way, to pick up where he left off. Why not Kush? It's as good a place as any. Plenty of work for an able man with a sword.
A man with no ties to anyone or any one place.
North to Kush, then.
In the years to come, Conan of Cimmeria would think of that anonymous beach, or the foul jungles, holding the bodies of his friends, of his lover...
...the cockiness of his youth, what was left of his innocence...

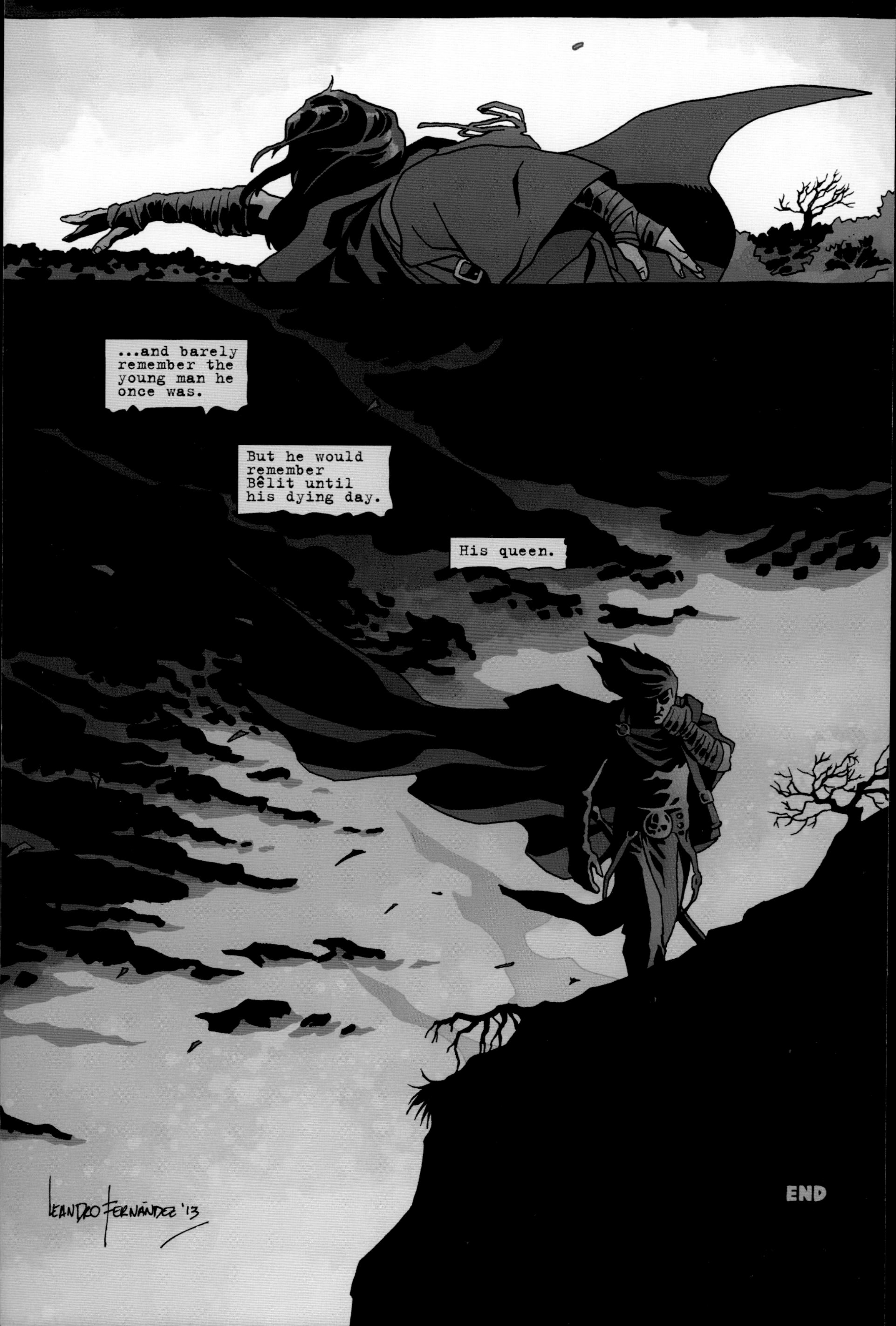
...and barely remember the young man he once was.
But he would remember Bêlit until his dying day.
His queen.
LEANDRO FERNÁNDEZ '13
END

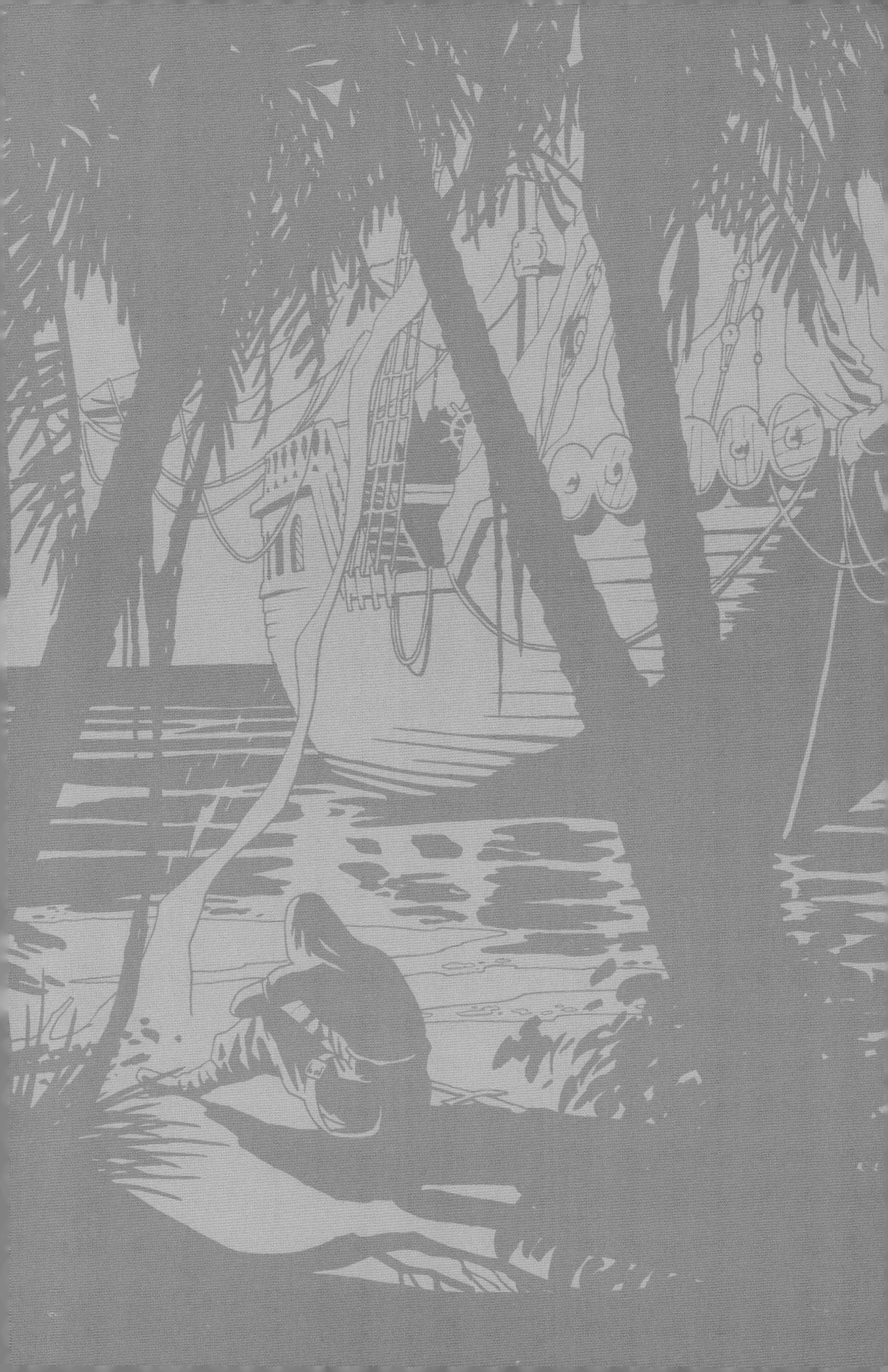

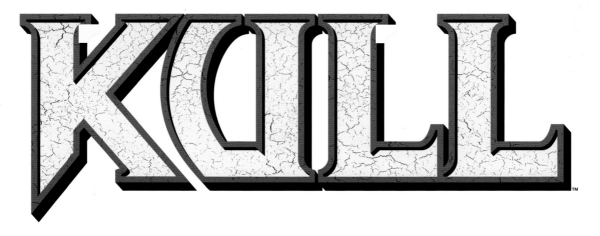

KULL

THE CHRONICLES OF KULL VOLUME 1: A KING COMES RIDING
Written by Roy Thomas, Gerry Conway, and Len Wein
Art by Wallace Wood, Bernie Wrightson, and others
ISBN 978-1-59582-413-4 | $18.99

THE CHRONICLES OF KULL VOLUME 2: THE HELL BENEATH ATLANTIS AND OTHER STORIES
Written by Roy Thomas, Gerry Conway, and Len Wein
Art by Wallace Wood, Bernie Wrightson, and others
ISBN 978-1-59582-413-4 | $18.99

THE CHRONICLES OF KULL VOLUME 3: SCREAMS IN THE DARK AND OTHER STORIES
Written by Roy Thomas, Don Glut, and Steve Englehart
Art by John Buscema, Ernie Chan, and Howard Chaykin
ISBN 978-1-59582-585-8 | $18.99

THE CHRONICLES OF KULL VOLUME 4: THE BLOOD OF KINGS AND OTHER STORIES
Written by Doug Moench and Bruce Jones
Art by John Buscema and John Bolton
ISBN 978-1-59582-684-8 | $18.99

THE CHRONICLES OF KULL VOLUME 5: DEAD MEN OF THE DEEP AND OTHER STORIES
Written by Alan Zelenetz
Art by John Buscema, Charles Vess, Klaus Janson, Bill Sienkiewicz, and others
ISBN 978-1-59582-906-1 | $18.99

KULL VOLUME 1: THE SHADOW KINGDOM
Written by Arvid Nelson
Art by Will Conrad and José Villarrubia
ISBN 978-1-59582-385-4 | $18.99

KULL VOLUME 2: THE HATE WITCH
Written by David Lapham
Art by Gabriel Guzman, Tom Fleming, and Mariano Taibo
ISBN 978-1-59582-730-2 | $15.99

KULL VOLUME 3: THE CAT AND THE SKULL
Written by David Lapham
Art by Gabriel Guzman
ISBN 978-1-59582-899-6 | $15.99

THE SAVAGE SWORD OF KULL VOLUME 1
ISBN 978-1-59582-593-3 | $19.99
VOLUME 2
ISBN 978-1-59582-788-3 | $19.99

DARK HORSE BOOKS
DarkHorse.com

AVAILABLE AT YOUR LOCAL COMICS SHOP OR BOOKSTORE
TO FIND A COMICS SHOP IN YOUR AREA, CALL 1-888-266-4226

For more information or to order direct:
• On the web: DarkHorse.com
• E-mail: mailorder@darkhorse.com
• Phone: 1-800-862-0052 Mon.–Fri. 9AM to 5PM Pacific Time.